FOURTH EDITION

POWER
& SOCIETY
An Introduction to the Social Sciences

US1

3071
SW27
APT 18

FOURTH EDITION

POWER & SOCIETY

An Introduction to the Social Sciences

THOMAS R. DYE
Florida State University
Foundation Professor
of Government

BROOKS/COLE PUBLISHING COMPANY
Monterey, California

Brooks/Cole Publishing Company
A Division of Wadsworth, Inc.

Printed in the United States of America

10 9 8 7 6 5 4 3 2 1

Library of Congress Cataloging-in-Publication Data

Dye, Thomas R.
    Power and society.

    Includes bibliographies and index.
        1. Social sciences.   2. Power (Social sciences)
I. Title.
H61.D95 1986   300   86-4250
ISBN 0-534-06564-3

Sponsoring Editor: Cynthia Stormer
Editorial Assistant: Maria Alsadi
Production Editor: Ellen Brownstein
Manuscript Editor: Meredy Amyx
Permissions Editor: Carline Haga
Interior and Cover Design: Victoria Van Deventer
Cover Photo: The Image Bank West/Mionel
Art Coordinator: Judith Macdonald
Interior Illustration: Ayxa
Photo Editor and Researcher: Judy Blamer
Typesetting: Allservice Phototypesetting Co.
Cover Printing: Phoenix Color Corporation
Printing and Binding: Malloy Lithographing

(Credits continue on p. 379.)

In memory of James C. "Jeff" Dye

PREFACE

Power and Society: An Introduction to the Social Sciences is designed as a basic text for an introductory, interdisciplinary social science course. It is written specifically for first- and second-year students at community colleges and at four-year colleges and universities that offer a basic studies program.

Power and Society introduces students to central concepts in

anthropology   psychology
sociology   political science
economics   history

But, more important, the text focuses these disciplinary perspectives on a central integrative theme—the nature and uses of power in society. In this way, students are made aware of the interdependence of the social sciences. Compartmentalization is avoided, and students are shown how each social science discipline contributes to an understanding of power.

Power and Society also introduces students to some of the central challenges facing American society:

ideological conflict   crime and violence
racism and sexism   urban affairs
poverty and powerlessness   defense and arms control

Each of these national challenges is approached from an interdisciplinary viewpoint, with *power* as the integrating concept.

Power has been defined as the capacity to modify the conduct of individuals through the real or threatened use of rewards and punishments. Doubtless there are other central concepts or ideas in the social sciences that might be employed to develop an integrated framework for an introduction to social science. But certainly *power* is a universal phenomenon that is reflected in virtually all forms of human interaction. Power is intimately related to many other key concepts and ideas in the social sciences—personality, behavior, aggression, role, class, mobility, wealth, income distribution, markets, culture, ideology, change, evolution, authority, oligarchy, elites. Power is also a universal instrument in approaching the various crises that afflict human beings and their societies—racism, sexism, poverty, violence, crime, urban decay, and ideological and international conflict.

Several special features are designed to help the student understand the meaning of various concepts. The first is the identification of specific masters of social thought and the clear, concise presentation of their central contributions to social science. Specific attention is given to the contributions of

Bertrand Russell	Charles Beard
Sigmund Freud	Frederick Jackson Turner
B. F. Skinner	John Locke
Adam Smith	Martin Luther King, Jr.
John M. Keynes	Ruth Benedict
C. Wright Mills	Karl Marx

The second special feature is the presentation of a timely, relevant case study at the end of each chapter to illustrate important concepts. Topics include

Social Science in Action—The Busing Controversy
Women in the Work Force—Changing American Culture
Sociobiology—It's All in Your Genes
The Power Elite
The Politics and Economics of Tax Reform
Authority and Obedience—The "Shocking" Experiments
Watergate and the Limits of Presidential Power
Political Power and the Mass Media
Reconstruction and Black History
Marxism-Leninism in the Soviet Union
The *Bakke* Case—Affirmative Action or Reverse Discrimination?
The Graying of America
The Death Penalty
Community Power Structures
"Star Wars" and the Superpowers

In addition, illustrative boxes throughout the text help to maintain student interest, with brief discussions on such topics as "Understanding the !Kung," "Conversational Power," "What Americans Think About Taxes," "The Telltale Behavior of Twins," "The Comparable Worth Controversy," "What Police Do," and "The Balance of Military Power."

A third and very important special feature is the running study guide provided in the wide page margins throughout the text. It defines key vocabulary items and outlines central arguments, keeping pace with the student's progress through the text.

I am particularly grateful for the many constructive comments and criticisms made at various stages of this work. Assistance in preparing the fourth edition was provided by reviewers Peder Hamm, University of Wisconsin, Stout, at Menomonie; Mark Stern, University of Central Florida, Orlando; and John F. Whitney, Lincoln Land Community College, Springfield, Illinois. I am also deeply indebted to Cindy Stormer and Ellen Brownstein at Brooks/Cole for their valuable editorial assistance.

Thomas R. Dye

CONTENTS

THE USES OF POWER   224   PART THREE

FOURTH EDITION

POWER
& SOCIETY
An Introduction to the Social Sciences

PART ONE

THE NATURE & STUDY OF POWER

The purpose of this book is to introduce you to the social sciences. Because power in society is a theme that pervades each of the social sciences, as well as the problems they study, we have chosen this theme as the focal point for our presentation. Part One is designed to familiarize you with the notion of power, with the nature of each of the social sciences, and with the scientific methods they employ. You will find that Chapter 1 reflects the structure of the entire text. Like the book as a whole, its first part focuses on the nature of power, its second part on the individual social sciences and the particular ways in which they contribute to our understanding of power, and its third and final part on the problems with which the social sciences are concerned. Chapter 2 is devoted to a discussion of the methods used in social science research.

CHAPTER 1

■ POWER, SOCIETY, & SOCIAL SCIENCE

Power in society is not just an abstract concept or a convenient focus for academic exercise. Nor is power something that is located exclusively in the nation's capitals. Power is *very* much a real factor that affects the lives of *every* one of us. We experience it in some form in our own families, in school, and at work; we feel its effects in the grocery store and on the highway. And we each react to it in characteristic ways. Our aim in this chapter is to understand just what power *is*. We will also see why it provides us with a useful perspective from which to gain a unified view of the social sciences and the social problems that concern us all.

After you have read this chapter, you should be able to

- define power in society and describe its characteristics,
- define the area of study of each of the social sciences, as well as their common focus, and discuss how each relates to power in society,
- identify the major social problems that the social sciences study and explain why they are interdisciplinary in nature and how they relate to power.

The nature of power

Ordinary men and women are driven by forces in society that they neither understand nor control. These forces are embodied in governmental authorities, economic organizations, social values and ideologies, accepted ways of life, and learned patterns of behavior. However diverse the nature of these forces, they have in common the ability to modify the conduct of individuals, to control their behavior, to shape their lives.

■ 5

power
the capacity to affect the conduct of others through the real or threatened use of rewards and punishments

power
based on control of valued resources unequally distributed exercised in interpersonal relations exercised through large institutions

elite and masses
the few who have power and the many who do not

Power is the capacity to affect the conduct of individuals through the real or threatened use of rewards and punishments. Power is exercised over individuals or groups by offering them some things they value or by threatening to deprive them of those things. These values are the *power base,* and they may include physical safety, health, and well-being; wealth and material possessions; jobs and means to a livelihood; knowledge and skills; social recognition, status, and prestige; love, affection, and acceptance by others; a satisfactory self-image and self-respect. To exercise power, then, control must be exercised over the things that are valued in society.

Power can rest on various power bases. The exercise of power assumes many different forms—the giving or withholding of many different values. Yet power bases are usually *interdependent*—individuals who control certain base values are likely to control other base values as well. Wealth, economic power, prestige, recognition, political influence, education, respect, and so on, all tend to "go together" in society.

Power is never equally distributed. "There is no power where power is equal." For power to be exercised, the "power holder" must control some base values. By *control* we mean that the power holder is in a position to offer these values as rewards to others, or to threaten to deprive others of these values.

Power is a relationship between individuals, groups, and institutions in society. Power is not really a "thing" that an individual possesses. Instead, power is a relationship in which some individuals or groups have control over certain base values.

The elite are the few who have power; the masses are the many who do not. The elite are the few who control what is valued in society and use that control to shape the lives of all of us. The masses are the many whose lives are shaped by institutions, events, and leaders over which they have little control. Political scientist Harold Lasswell writes, "The division of society into elites and masses is universal," and even in a democracy, "a few exercise a relatively great weight of power, and the many exercise comparatively little."[1]

Power is exercised in interpersonal relations. Psychologist Rollo May writes that "power means the ability to affect, to influence, and to change other persons." He argues that power is essential to one's "sense of significance"—one's conviction that one counts for something in the world, that one has an effect on others, and that one can get recognition of one's existence from others. Power is essential to the development of personality. An infant who is denied the experience of influencing others or of drawing their attention to its existence withdraws to a corner of its bed, does not talk or develop in any way, and withers away physiologically and psychologically. Thus power is essential to *being.* Political scientist Robert Dahl also defines power in terms of *individual interaction:* "A has power over B to the extent that he can get B to do something he would not otherwise do." He argues that every exercise of power depends upon interpersonal relations between the power holder and the responder. Since there are many different aspects of power in interpersonal situations, Dahl thinks it unlikely that there will ever be two cases in which power is exercised in precisely the same fashion.

Power is exercised in large institutions—governments, corporations, schools, the military, churches, newspapers, television networks, law firms, and so on. Power that stems from high positions in the social structures of society is stable and far-reaching. Sociologist C. Wright Mills observes: "No one can be truly powerful unless he has access to the command of major institutions, for it is over these institutional means of power that the truly powerful are, in the first instance, powerful."[2] Not all power, it is true, is anchored in or exercised through institutions. But institutional positions in society provide a continuous and important base of power. As Mills explains:

> If we took the one hundred most powerful men in America, the one hundred wealthiest, and the one hundred most celebrated away from the institutional positions they now occupy, away from their resources of men and women and money, away from the media of mass communication that are now focused upon them—then they would be powerless and poor and uncelebrated. For power is not of a man. Wealth does not center in the person of the wealthy. . . . To have power requires access to major institutions, for the institutional positions men occupy determine in large part their chances to have and to hold these valued experiences.[3]

Power and the social sciences

Social science is the study of human behavior. Actually, there are several social sciences, each specializing in a particular aspect of human behavior and each using different concepts, methods, and data in its studies. Anthropology, sociology, economics, psychology, political science, and history have developed into separate "disciplines," but all share an interest in human behavior.

social science
the study of human behavior

Power is *not* the central concern of the social sciences, yet all the social sciences deal with power in one form or another. Each of the social sciences contributes to an understanding of the forces that modify the conduct of individuals, control their behavior, and shape their lives. Thus, to fully understand power in society, we must approach this topic in an *interdisciplinary* fashion—using ideas, methods, data, and findings from all the social sciences.

Anthropology. Anthropology is the study of people and their ways of life. It is the most comprehensive of the social sciences. Some anthropologists are concerned primarily with people's biological and physical characteristics; this field is called *physical anthropology*. Other anthropologists are interested primarily in the ways of life of both ancient and modern peoples; this field is called *cultural anthropology*.

anthropology
the study of people and their ways of life

▪ Bertrand Russell: Power is to the social sciences what energy is to physics ▪

Bertrand Russell (1872–1970), English philosopher and mathematician, is regarded as one of the twentieth century's greatest thinkers, mainly because of his contributions to mathematics and symbolic logic. However, Russell possessed a great breadth of interest that included history, economics, and political science, as well as education, morals, and social problems. He received the Nobel Prize in literature "in recognition of his many-sided and significant authorship, in which he has constantly figured as a defender of humanity and freedom of thought." He summarized his views about the importance of power in society in a book significantly entitled *Power: A New Social Analysis.**

*Selection is reprinted from *Power: A New Social Analysis,* by Bertrand Russell, with the permission of W. W. Norton & Company, Inc. Copyright 1938 by Bertrand Russell. Copyright renewed 1966 by Bertrand Russell.

First of all, power is fundamental to the social sciences:

> The fundamental concept in the social sciences is power, in the same sense in which energy is the fundamental concept in physics.

Second, the desire for power as well as wealth motivates people:

> When a moderate degree of comfort is assured, both individuals and communities will pursue power rather than wealth: they may seek wealth as a means to power, or they may forgo an increase of wealth in order to secure an increase of power, but in the former case as in the latter their fundamental motive is not economic. . . .

Third, power takes many forms:

> Like energy, power has many forms, such as wealth, armaments, civil authority, influence on opinion. No one of these can be regarded as subordinate to any other, and there is no one form from which the others are derivative. The attempt to treat one form of power, say wealth, in isolation can only be partially successful. . . . To revert to the analogy of physics: power, like energy, must be regarded as continually passing from any one of its forms into any other, and it should be the business of social science to seek the laws of such transformations. The attempt to isolate any one form of power, more especially, in our day, the economic form, has been, and still is, a source of errors of great practical importance.

Finally, power produces social change:

> Those whose love of power is not strong are unlikely to have much influence on the course of events. The men who cause social changes are, as a rule, men who strongly desire to do so. Love of power, therefore, is a characteristic of the men who are causally important. We should, of course, be mistaken if we regarded it as the sole human motive, but this mistake

would not lead us so much astray as might be expected in the search for causal laws in social science, since love of power is the chief motive producing the changes which social science has to study.

Culture is all the common patterns and ways of living that characterize society. The anthropologist tries to describe and explain a great many things: child rearing and education; family arrangements; language and communication; technology; ways of making a living; the distribution of work; religious beliefs and values; social life; leadership patterns; and power structures.

Power is part of the culture or the way of life of a people. Power is exercised in all societies, because all societies have systems of sanctions designed to control the behavior of their members. Perhaps the most enduring structure of power in society is the family: power is exercised within the family when patterns of dominance and submission are established between male and female and parents and children. Societies also develop structures of power outside the family to maintain peace and order among their members; to organize individuals to accomplish large-scale tasks; to defend themselves against attack; and even to wage war and exploit other peoples.

In our study of power and culture we will examine how cultural patterns determine power relationships. We will examine patterns of authority in traditional and modern families and the changing power role

of women in society. We will examine the origins and development of power relationships, illustrating this development with examples of societies in which power is organized by family and kinship group (polar Eskimos), by tribe (Crow Indians), and by the state (the Aztec Empire). Finally, as a case study, we will look at the controversy over "sociobiology"—that is, the extent to which genetics or culture determines behaviors.

sociology
the study of relationships among individuals and groups

Sociology. Sociology is the study of relationships among individuals and groups. Sociologists describe the structure of formal and informal groups, their functions and purposes, and how they change over time. They study social institutions (such as families, schools, churches), social processes (for example, conflict, competition, assimilation, change), and social problems (crime, race relations, poverty, and so forth). They also study social classes.

social stratification
classifying and ranking members of society

All societies have some system of classifying and ranking their members—a system of *stratification*. In modern industrial societies, social status is associated with the various roles that individuals play in the economic system. Individuals are ranked according to how they make their living and the control they exercise over the living of others. Stratification into social classes is determined largely on the basis of occupation and control of economic resources.

Power derives from social status, prestige, and respect, as well as control of economic resources. Thus, the stratification system involves the unequal distribution of power.

In our study of power and social class, we will describe the stratification system in America and explore popular beliefs about "getting ahead." We will discuss the differential lifestyles of upper, middle, and lower classes in America and the extent of class conflict. We will examine the ideas of Karl Marx about the struggle for power among social classes. We will describe the differential in political power among social classes in America. Finally, we will explore the ideas of sociologist C. Wright Mills about a top "power elite" in America that occupies powerful positions in the governmental, corporate, and military bureaucracies of the nation.

economics
the study of the production and distribution of scarce goods and services

Economics. Economics is the study of the production and distribution of scarce goods and services. There are never enough goods and services to satisfy everyone's demands, and because of this, choices must be made. Economists study how individuals, firms, and nations make these choices about goods and services.

Economic power is the power to decide what will be produced, how much it will cost, how many people will be employed, what their wages will be, what the price of goods and services will be, what profits will be made, how these profits will be distributed, and how fast the economy will grow. Control over these decisions is a major source of power in society.

Capitalist societies rely heavily on the market mechanism to determine who gets what—what is to be produced, how much it will cost, and who will be able to buy it. In our study of economic power, we will explore both the strengths and weaknesses of this market system, as well as the ideas of economic philosophers Adam Smith and John M. Keynes. In addition, we will consider the role of government in the economy, which has increased over the years. We will examine "supply side" economics of the 1980s and describe the results of "Reaganomics." We will then turn to an examination of America's vast wealth—how it is measured, where it comes from, and where it goes. We will examine the relationship between wealth and the quality of life, which are not always equivalent things. We will also examine the concentration of private wealth and corporate power in America. Finally, in our case study, we will discuss the politics and economics of tax reform.

Psychology. Psychology may be defined as the study of the behavior of people and animals. Behavior, we know, is the product of both "nature and nurture"—that is, a product of both our biological makeup and our environmental conditioning. We will examine the continuing controversy over *how much* of our behavior is a product of our genes versus our environment. We will learn that there is great richness and diversity in psychological inquiry. For example, *behavioral psychologists* study the learning process—the way in which people and animals learn to respond to stimuli. They frequently study in experimental laboratory situations, with the hope that the knowledge gained can be useful in understanding more complex human behavior outside the laboratory. *Social psychologists,* on the other hand, study interpersonal behavior—the way in which social interactions shape an individual's beliefs, perceptions, motivations, attitudes, and behavior. They generally study the whole person in relation to the total environment. *Freudian psychologists* study the impact of unconscious feelings and emotions and of early childhood experiences on the behavior of adults. *Humanistic psychologists* are concerned with the human being's innate potential for growth and development. Many other psychologists combine theories and methods in different ways in their attempts to achieve a better understanding of behavior.

Personality is all the enduring, organized ways of behavior that characterize an individual. Psychologists differ over how personality characteristics are determined—whether they are learned habits acquired through the process of reinforcement and conditioning (behavioral psychology), or products of the individual's interaction with the significant people and groups in his or her life (social psychology), or manifestations of the continuous process of positive growth toward "self-actualization" (humanistic psychology), or the results of unconscious drives and long-

psychology
the study of the behavior of people and animals

personality
all the enduring, organized ways of behavior that characterize an individual

repressed emotions stemming from early childhood experiences (Freudian psychology), or some combination of all these.

The study of personality is essential in understanding how individuals react toward power and authority. Power is a personal experience. Everyone is subject to one form of power or another during all the waking hours of life. And everyone has exercised some power, if only in microscopic degree, at some time. Individuals react toward these experiences with power in different and characteristic ways. Some individuals seek power for personal fulfillment. Philosopher Bertrand Russell writes, "Of the infinite desires of man, the chief are the desires for power and glory."[4] Other individuals are submissive to authority, while still others are habitually rebellious. It is said that "power corrupts, and absolute power corrupts absolutely." However, there is ample psychological evidence that lack of power also corrupts. The feelings that one cannot influence anyone else, that one counts for little, and that one has no control over one's own life all contribute to a loss of personal identity.

In our study of power and personality, we will examine various theories of personality determination—specifically, those of behavioral psychology, social psychology, humanistic psychology, and Freudian psychology—in an effort to understand the forces shaping the individual's reaction to power. Using a Freudian perspective, we will study the "authoritarian personality"—the individual who is habitually dominant and aggressive toward others over whom he exercises power, yet submissive and weak toward others who have power over him; the individual who is extremely prejudiced, rigid, intolerant, cynical, and power-oriented. We will explore the power implications of B. F. Skinner's ideas of behavioral conditioning for the control of human behavior. To gain an understanding of humanistic psychology's approach to power relationships, we will examine Rollo May's formulation of the functions of power for the individual and Abraham Maslow's theory of a "hierarchy of needs." Finally, in our case study, we will describe the startling results of an experiment designed to test the relationship between authority and obedience.

political science
the study of government
and politics

authority
the legitimate use of
physical force

Political science. Political science is the study of government and politics. Governments possess authority, a particular form of power: the legitimate use of physical force. By *legitimate* we mean that people generally consent to the government's use of this power. Of course, other individuals and organizations in society—muggers, street gangs, the Mafia, violent revolutionaries—use force. But only government can legitimately threaten people with the loss of freedom and well-being to modify their behavior. Moreover, governments exercise power over all individuals and institutions in society—corporations, families, schools, and so forth. Obviously the power of government in modern society is very great, extending to nearly every aspect of modern life—"from womb to tomb."

Political scientists from Aristotle to the present have been concerned with the dangers of unlimited and unchecked governmental power. We will examine the American experience with limited, constitutional government; the philosophical legacy of English political thought; and the meaning of democracy in modern society. We will observe how the U.S. Constitution divides power, first between states and the national government, and second among the legislative, executive, and judicial branches of government. We will examine the growth of power in Washington, D.C., and the struggle for power among the different branches. We will also explore competition between political parties and interest groups and popular participation in decision making through elections. Finally, in our case study "Political Power and the Mass Media," we will examine the growing power of television in American politics.

History.   History is the recording, narrating, and interpreting of human experience. The historian recreates the past by collecting recorded facts, organizing them into a narrative, and interpreting their meaning. History is also concerned with change over time. It provides a perspective on the present by informing us of the way people lived in the past. It helps us to understand how society developed into what it is today.

history
the recording, narrating, and interpreting of human experience

The foundations of power vary from age to age. As power bases shift, new groups and individuals acquire control over them. Thus, power relationships are continuously developing and changing. An understanding of power in society requires an understanding of the historical development of power relationships.

In our consideration of the historical development of power relationships, we will look at the changing sources of power in American history and the characteristics of the individuals and groups who have acquired power. We will describe the men of power in the early days of the Republic and their shaping of the Constitution and the government that it established. We will discuss Charles Beard's interpretation of the Constitution as a document designed to protect the economic interests of those early power holders. We will also discuss historian Frederick Jackson Turner's ideas about how westward expansion and settlement created new bases of power and new power holders. We will explore the power struggle between northern commercial and industrial interests and southern planters and slaveowners for control of western land, and the Civil War that resulted from that struggle. In addition, we will explore the development of an industrial elite in America after the Civil War, the impact on that elite of the Depression, and the resulting growth of New Deal liberal reform. Finally, in our brief study "Reconstruction and Black History," we will examine how history occasionally overlooks the experiences of powerless minorities and later reinterprets their contributions to society.

Social sciences and social problems

Social problems—the major challenges confronting society—include ideological conflict, racism, sexism, poverty, crime, violence, pollution, urban decay, and international conflict. These problems do not confine themselves to one or another of the disciplines of social science. They spill over the boundaries of anthropology, economics, sociology, political science, psychology, and history—they are *interdisciplinary* in character. Each of these problems has its *historical* antecedents, its *social* and *psychological* roots, its *cultural* manifestations, its *economic* consequences, and its impact on *government* and public policy. The origins of these social problems, as well as the various solutions proposed, involve complex power relationships.

interdisciplinary study
the use of theory, methods, or findings from more than one social science

Ideological conflict. Ideas have power. Indeed, whole societies are shaped by systems of ideas that we call *ideologies*. The study of ideologies—liberalism, conservatism, socialism, communism, fascism, radicalism—is not a separate social science. Rather, the study of ideology spans all the social sciences, and it is closely related to philosophy. Ideologies are integrated systems of ideas that rationalize a way of life, establish standards of "rightness" and "wrongness," and provide emotional impulses to action. Ideologies usually include economic, political, social, psychological, and cultural ideas, as well as interpretations of history.

ideology
an integrated system of ideas that rationalize and justify the exercise of power in society

Ideologies rationalize and justify power in society. By providing a justification for the exercise of power, the ideology itself becomes a base of power in society. Ideology "legitimizes" power, making the exercise of power acceptable to the masses and thereby adding to the power of the elite. However, ideologies also affect the behavior of the elite, because once an ideology is deeply rooted in society, power holders themselves are bound by it.

In our study of power and ideology, we will first explore the ideology of *classical liberalism*—an ideology that attacked the established power of a hereditary aristocracy and asserted the dignity, worth, and freedom of the individual. Classical liberalism and capitalism justify the power of private enterprise and the market system. Whereas classical liberalism limits the powers of government, *modern liberalism* accepts governmental power as a positive force in freeing people from poverty, ignorance, discrimination, and ill health. It justifies the exercise of governmental power over private enterprise and the establishment of the welfare state. In contrast, *modern conservatism* doubts the ability of the governmental planners to solve society's problems; conservatism urges greater reliance on family, church, and individual initiative and effort.

We will then look at ideologies that have influenced other societies. *Fascism* is a power-oriented ideology that asserts the supremacy of a nation or race over the interests of individuals, groups, and other social institutions. *Marxism* attacks the market system, free enterprise, and individualism; it justifies revolutionary power in overthrowing liberal, capitalist systems and the establishment of a "dictatorship of the proletariat." *Socialism* calls for the evolutionary, democratic replacement of the private enterprise system with government ownership of industry.

In our case study of "Marxism-Leninism in the Soviet Union," we will see how an ideology justified the exercise of unlimited political and economic power by a totalitarian communist party.

Racial and sexual inequality.   Historically, no social problem has challenged the United States more than racial equality. It is the only issue over which Americans ever fought a civil war. We wish to describe briefly the American experience with racism and to describe the civil rights movement, which brought about significant changes in American life. We want to understand the philosophy of that movement, particularly the "nonviolent direct action" philosophy of Nobel Peace Prize winner Dr. Martin Luther King, Jr. We want to understand the social and psychological roots of the black power movement and to describe the more recent successes of blacks in acquiring political power. We are especially interested in the role played by Rev. Jesse Jackson in inspiring black political participation. We also want to confront sexism in American life, particularly in the economy. And we shall examine the arguments both for and against government efforts to assure "comparable worth" in the labor market. We will describe the successes and failures of the women's movement in recent years, and we shall examine the constitutional status of abortion laws. Finally, we will examine the controversy over "affirmative action" and "reverse discrimination" and its implication for how America is to achieve real equality.

Poverty and powerlessness.   The American economy has produced the highest standard of living in the world, and yet a significant number of Americans live in poverty. We will observe that poverty can be defined as *economic hardship* or as *economic inequality,* and that each definition implies a different governmental approach to this problem. Poverty can also be defined as *powerlessness*—a social-psychological condition of hopelessness, indifference, distrust, and cynicism. We will discuss whether or not there is a culture of poverty—a way of life of the poor that is passed on to future generations—and what its implications for government policy are. We will describe government efforts to cope with poverty, including recent changes in welfare policy by the Reagan administration. We will observe how the poor and powerless are represented in Washington. Finally, we will examine the future of the Social Security program in a look at "The Graying of America."

powerlessness
a psychological condition of hopelessness, indifference, distrust, and cynicism

*a problem of demo-
cratic government*
*to protect its citizens
without violating individual
liberty*

Crime and violence. Governmental power must be balanced against *individual freedom*. A democratic society must exercise police powers to protect its citizens, yet it must not unduly restrict individual liberty. We will explore the problem of crime in society, the constitutional rights of defendants, the role of the courts, and the relationship between drug use and crime. We will also describe briefly the history of violence in American society and the continuous role that violence has played in American struggles for power. We will summarize social-psychological explanations of violence; violence as a form of political activity; and violence as an aspect of lower-class culture. Finally, we will examine the arguments for and against the death penalty as society's ultimate sanction.

Urban life. There is a variety of social problems that affect the quality of life in the United States. The solution to these problems, if there is any solution, depends in great part on how government chooses to exercise its powers. We will explore the growth of urban and suburban populations in the United States. We will also explore the social patterns of urban life—the characteristic forms of social interaction and organization that typically emerge in a large metropolis—and the socioeconomic conflicts between cities and suburbs. We will observe how our nation's communities are governed. Finally, we will present a case study, "Community Power Structures," to compare power structures in different cities.

International conflict. The struggle for power is global—it involves all the nations and peoples of the world, whatever their goals or ideals. Nearly two hundred nations in the world claim *sovereignty:* authority over their internal affairs, freedom from outside intervention, and political and legal recognition by other nations. But sovereignty is a legal fiction; it requires power to make sovereignty a reality. Over the years nations have struggled for power through wars and diplomacy. The struggle has led to attempts at maintaining a fragile balance of power among large and small nations, as well as to attempts at achieving collective security through the United Nations and other alliances. Today the balance of power between the two "superpowers"—the United States and the U.S.S.R.—requires a delicate balance of strategic nuclear power. In our discussion of the international system, we will describe this "balance of terror," as well as the "triad" of weapons that maintain this balance. We will describe the history of the Strategic Arms Limitations Talks (SALT) between the United States and the Soviet Union and the current talks between the superpowers at Geneva. Finally, as our case study, we will explore the "Star Wars" controversy—the arguments over whether or not the United States should embark on the development of ground- and space-based missile defenses for the twenty-first century.

sovereignty
authority over internal affairs, freedom from outside intervention, and recognition by other nations

Notes

1. Harold Lasswell and Abraham Kaplan, *Power and Society* (New Haven, Conn.: Yale University Press, 1950), p. 219.
2. C. Wright Mills, *The Power Elite* (New York: Oxford University Press, 1956), p. 9
3. Ibid., p. 10.
4. Bertrand Russell, *Power: A New Social Analysis* (New York: W. W. Norton, 1938), p. 11.

Discussion questions

1. How would you define power? What characteristics of power deserve to be discussed in any definition of power?

2. Consider the power relationships that directly and indirectly affect your life. On the basis of your experiences and observations, assess the validity of these statements by Bertrand Russell: "The fundamental concept in the social sciences is power, in the same sense in which energy is the fundamental concept in physics. . . . When a moderate degree of comfort is assured, both individuals and communities will pursue power rather than wealth. . . . Love of power is the chief motive producing the changes which social science has to study."

3. Identify and briefly define the area of study of each of the social sciences. Discuss how you would study power from the perspective of each of these disciplines.

4. What is meant by the "interdisciplinary" study of social problems?

5. Choose two of the following social problems and briefly explain how they involve power: (a) racial and sexual inequality, (b) poverty, (c) crime and violence, (d) international conflict.

CHAPTER 2

■ HOW SCIENTIFIC ARE THE SOCIAL SCIENCES?

How can the subject matter of the social sciences actually be measured and identified? How, for example, can a psychologist accurately and objectively measure a person's reaction to authority, or a sociologist identify someone's social status? How can a political scientist be sure that a reduction in crime is the result of a governmental program and not the incidental effect of some other factor? Social scientists are often accused of not being truly scientific. Are they guilty as charged, and, if so, why? What are the problems, the promise, and the sometimes paradoxical effects of social science research?

These are the questions that Chapter 2 addresses. After you have read it, you should be able to

- define science and describe the scientific method,
- illustrate how social scientists develop and test hypotheses,
- describe the classic research design and discuss some of the problems that social scientists have in applying this design and the scientific method to their research.

Science and the scientific method

A *science* may be broadly defined as any organized *body of knowledge,* or it may be more narrowly defined as a discipline that employs the *scientific method.* If we use the broad definition, we can safely say that all the social sciences are indeed sciences. However, if we narrow our definition to only those disciplines that employ the scientific method, then some questions arise about whether the social sciences are really scientific. In other words, if science is defined as a *method of study,* rather than a *body of knowledge,* then not all studies in the social sciences are truly scientific.

scientific method
a method of explanation that develops and tests theories about how observable facts or events are related

The scientific method is a method of explanation that develops and tests theories about how observable facts or events are related. What does this definition really mean? How is this method of study actually applied in the social sciences? To answer these questions, let us examine each aspect of the scientific method separately.

Explaining relationships.   *The goal of the scientific method is explanation.* When using this method, we seek to answer the question "why." Any scientific inquiry must begin by observing and classifying things. Just as biology begins with the careful observation, description, and classification of thousands upon thousands of different forms of life, the social sciences also must begin with the careful observation, description, and classification of various forms of human behavior. But the goal is explanation, not just description. Just as biology seeks to develop theories of evolution and genetics to explain the various forms of life upon the earth, the social sciences seek to develop theories to explain why human beings behave as they do.

hypothesis
a tentative statement about a relationship between observable facts or events

To answer the question of "why," the scientific method searches for *relationships*. All scientific hypotheses assert some relationship between observable facts or events. The social sciences seek to find relationships that explain human behavior. The first question is whether two or more events or behaviors are related in any way—that is, do they occur together consistently? The second question is whether either event or behavior is the *cause* of the other. Social scientists first try to learn whether human events have occurred together merely by chance or accident, or whether they occur together so consistently that their relation-

ship cannot be a mere coincidence. A relationship that is not likely to have occurred by chance is said to be *significant*. After observing a significant relationship, social scientists next ask whether there is a *causal relationship* between the phenomena (that is, whether the facts or events occurred together because one is the cause of the other), or whether both phenomena are being caused by some third factor. Box 2-1 explains some of the terms used in scientific study of data.

significant
not likely to have
occurred by chance

Developing and testing hypotheses. *The scientific method seeks to develop statements ("hypotheses") about how events or behaviors might be related and then to determine the validity of these statements by careful, systematic, and logical tests.* Scientific tests are really exercises in logic. For example, if we wanted to find out something about the relationship between race and party voting, we might collect and record data from a national sample of black and white voters chosen at random.

BOX 2-1   The vocabulary of social science

▪ Social science researchers use many special terms in their work, some of which have already been defined. It helps in reading social science research reports to understand the specific meanings given to the following terms:

Theory: A causal explanation of relationship between observable facts or events. A good theory fits the facts, explains why they occur, and allows us to predict future events.

Hypothesis: A tentative statement about a relationship between facts or events. The hypothesis should be derived from the theory and should be testable.

Variable: A characteristic that varies among different individuals or groups.

Independent variable: Whatever is hypothesized to be the cause of something else.

Dependent variable: Whatever is hypothesized to be the effect of something.

Significant: Not likely to have occurred by chance.

Correlation: Significant relationships found in the data.

Spurious: Describing a relationship among facts or events that is *not* causal, but a product of the fact that both the independent and dependent variables are being caused by a third factor.

Case study: An in-depth investigation of a particular event. A good case study should suggest theories and hypotheses that can then be used later to study other cases.

random sampling
a method of selecting members to represent a group that gives each member an equal chance of being chosen

(*Random* means that the sample was chosen in such a fashion that every voter had an equal chance of getting into the sample, and therefore the sample should—if it is large enough—be an accurate reflection of all the voters.) If our data showed that *all* blacks voted Democratic and *all* whites Republican, it would be obvious that there was a perfect relationship between race and voting. In contrast, if both blacks and whites voted Republican and Democratic in the same proportions, then it would be obvious that there was *no* relationship. But in the social sciences we rarely have such obvious, clear-cut results. Generally our data will show a mixed pattern. For example, in the 1984 presidential election between Democrat Walter Mondale and Republican Ronald Reagan, 90 percent of blacks voted Democratic and only 9 percent voted Republican. In that same election, 66 percent of whites voted Republican and only 34 percent of whites voted Democratic. If there had been *no* relationship between race and voting, then blacks and whites would have voted Democratic and Republican in roughly the *same* proportions. But as we have just noted, blacks voted Democratic in far heavier proportions (90 percent) than whites (34 percent). This difference is not likely to have occurred by chance—thus we consider it "significant." The same pattern of heavy Democratic voting among blacks can be observed in other elections (see Table 2-1). So we can make the *inference* that race is related to voting.

inference
a causal statement based on data showing a significant relationship

However, the existence of a statistically significant relationship does not prove cause and effect. We must employ additional logic to find out which fact or event caused the other, or whether both were caused by a third fact or event. We can eliminate the possibility that voting Democratic causes one to become black as illogical; being black comes first in life and voting Democratic comes later. That leaves us with two possibilities: blackness may cause Democratic voting, or blackness and Democratic voting may both be caused by some third condition. For example,

TABLE 2-1 Voting by race in presidential elections 1968–1984
Testing the hypothesis: Blacks tend to vote Democratic

Election year	Candidates	All	Whites	Blacks
1984	Republican Reagan	59*	66	9
	Democrat Mondale	41	34	90
1980	Republican Reagan	51	56	10
	Democrat Carter	41	36	86
	Independent Anderson	7	7	2
1976	Republican Ford	48	52	15
	Democrat Carter	50	46	85
1972	Republican Nixon	62	68	13
	Democrat McGovern	38	32	87
1968	Republican Nixon	44	47	12
	Democrat Humphrey	43	38	85
	Independent Wallace	13	15	3

*Figures are percentages of the vote won by each candidate. Percentages in each election may not add up to 100 because of voting for minor-party candidates.
SOURCE: Data from the *Gallup Opinion Index*, December 1984.

the real causal relationship may be between low incomes and Democratic voting: low-income groups, which would include most blacks, tend to identify with the Democratic party. We can test this new hypothesis by looking at the voting behavior of other low-income groups to see if they voted Democratic in the same proportions as blacks. (It turns out that blacks vote more heavily Democratic than white low-income groups, so we can reject the low-income explanation. Race must therefore be independently related to voting behavior.) There are many other possible alternatives to our explanation of the relationship between race and voting behavior. Social scientists must test as many alternative explanations as possible before asserting a causal relationship.

Every time we can reject an alternative explanation for the relationship that we have observed, we increase our confidence that the relationship (as between race and voting behavior) is a causal one. Of course, in the areas of interest to social scientists someone can always think of new alternative explanations, so it is generally impossible to establish for certain that a causal relationship exists. Some social scientists react to the difficulties of proving "cause" by refusing to say that the relationships they find are anything more than *correlations,* or simply statistical relationships. The decision whether or not to call a relationship "causal" is a difficult one. Statistical techniques cannot guarantee that a relationship is causal. Social scientists must rely, finally, on the "feel" that comes from their familiarity with the details of the facts and events they are studying, and they must be prepared to deal with probabilities rather than absolutes.

correlations
significant relationships that may or may not be causal

Dealing with observable phenomena. *The scientific method deals only with observable—"empirical"—facts and events.* In other words, the scientific method deals with what *is,* rather than what *should be.* It cannot test the validity of values, norms, or feelings, except insofar as it can test for their existence in a society, group, or individual. For example, the scientific method can be employed to determine whether voting behavior *is* related to race, but it cannot determine whether voting behavior *should be* related to race. The latter question is a *normative* one (dealing with "oughts" and "shoulds"), rather than an empirical one (dealing with "is's"). The scientific method is *descriptive* and *explanatory,* but not *normative.* The social sciences can explain many aspects of human behavior but cannot tell human beings how they ought to behave. For guidance in values and norms—for prescriptions about how people should live—we must turn to ethics, religion, or philosophy.

empirical
referring to observable facts and events; what is

normative
referring to values or norms; what should be

Developing theory. *The scientific method strives to develop a systematic body of theory.* Science is more than crude empiricism—the listing of facts without any statement of relationships among them. Of course, especially in the early stages of a science, research may consist largely of collecting data; but the ultimate goal of the scientific method is the development of verifiable statements about relationships among facts and events. It is the task of social scientists to find patterns and regularities in human behavior, just as it is the task of physicists and chemists to find patterns and regularities in the behavior of matter and energy. The social scientist's use of the scientific method, then, assumes that human behavior is not random, but rather that it is regular and predictable.

theories
explanations of facts or events

Theories are developed at different *levels of generality*. Theories with low levels of generality explain only a small or narrow range of behaviors. For example, the statement that blacks tend to vote Democratic is a fairly low-level generality about political behavior. Theories with higher levels of generality explain a greater or wider range of behavior. For example, the statement that racial differences cause political conflict has a higher level of generality. Strictly speaking, *a theory is a set of interrelated concepts at a fairly high level of generality.* Some social scientists concentrate on theory building rather than empirical research; they try to develop sweeping social theories to explain all, or a large part of, human behavior. Still other social theorists provide merely insights, hunches, or vague notions that serve to suggest possible explanations of human behavior, thus developing new hypotheses for empirical research.

scientific attitude
doubt or skepticism about theories until they have been scientifically tested

Maintaining a scientific attitude. Perhaps more than anything else, *the scientific method is an attitude of doubt or skepticism.* It is an insistence upon careful collection of data and systematic testing of ideas, a commitment to keep bias out of one's work, to collect and record all relevant facts, and to interpret them rationally regardless of one's own feelings. For the social scientist, it is the determination to test explanations of human behavior by careful observations of real-world experiences. It is a recognition that any explanation is tentative and may be modified or disproved by careful investigation. Even the scientific theories that constitute the core knowledge in any discipline are not regarded as absolutes by the true social scientist; rather, they are regarded as probabilities or generalizations developed from what is known so far.

Why the social sciences aren't always "scientific"

Not all the knowledge in social science is derived scientifically. A great deal of knowledge about human behavior comes to us through insight, intuition, random observation, folklore, and common sense rather than by careful scientific investigation. The scientific method that we have just described was devised in the physical and biological sciences. There are many difficulties in applying this method to the study of individuals, groups, economies, classes, governments, nations, or whole societies. Let us examine some of the obstacles to the development of truly *scientific* social sciences.

Personal bias.   *Social science deals with very subjective topics and must rely on interpretation of results.* Social scientists are part of what they investigate—they belong to a family, class, political party, interest group, profession, nation; they earn money and consume goods like everybody else. If the topic is an emotional one, the social scientist may find it much harder to suppress personal bias than does the investigator in the physical sciences: it is easier to conduct an unbiased study of migratory birds than of migrant workers.

It is difficult to conduct "value-free" research. Even the selection of a topic reveals the values of the researcher. Researchers study what they think is important in society, and what they think is important is affected by their personal values. If it were only in the selection of the topic that researchers' values were reflected, there would be no great problem in social science research. But researchers' values are also frequently reflected in their perceptions of the data itself, in their statement of the hypotheses, in their design of the test for the hypotheses, and in their interpretation of the findings. "Value intrusion" can occur in many stages of the research process, which is why social scientists studying the same problems and using the same methods frequently end up with contradictory results.

Perhaps it is impossible to separate facts and values in social science research. As sociologist Louis Wirth explains:

> Since every assertion of a "fact" about the social world touches the interests of some individual or group, one cannot even call attention to the existence of certain "facts" without raising objections of those whose very raison d'etre in society rests upon a divergent interpretation of the "factual" situation.[1]

Public attitudes.   *Another problem in the scientific study of human behavior centers on public attitudes toward social science.* Few laypersons would consider arguing with atomic physicists or biochemists about their respective fields, but most people believe they know something about social problems. Many people think they know exactly what should be done about juvenile delinquency, expanding welfare rolls, and race relations. Very often their information is limited, and their view of the problem is a simplistic one. When a social scientist suggests that a problem is very complex, that it has many causes, and that information on the problem is incomplete, the layperson believes that the social scientist is simply obscuring matters that seem obvious.

Social science sometimes develops explanations of human behavior that contradict established ideas. Of course, the physical and biological

value-free research
scientific work unaffected by the values of society or the scientist

value intrusion
values may affect
selection of topic for
*   research*
perceptions of the data
formulation of hypotheses
construction of tests
interpretation of findings

sciences have long faced this same problem: Galileo faced the opposition of the established church when he suggested that the earth revolved around the sun, and Darwin's theory of evolution continues to be a public issue. But social science generates even more intense feelings when it deals with poverty, crime, sexual behavior, race relations, and other heated topics.

Limitations and design of social science research. *Another set of problems in social science centers on the limitations and design of social science research.* It is not really possible to conduct some forms of controlled experiments on human beings. For example, we cannot subject people to poverty and deprivation just to see if it makes them violent. Instead, social researchers must conduct their research in situations that have been produced naturally. They must, therefore, find situations of poverty and deprivation to make the necessary observations about causes of violence. In a laboratory we can control all or most of the factors that go into the experimental situation. But in real-world observations, we cannot control factors, which makes it difficult to pinpoint precisely what it is that causes the behavior we are studying. Moreover, even where some experimentation is permitted, human beings frequently modify their behavior simply because they know they are being observed in a social science experiment. This phenomenon, which is known as the *Hawthorne effect,* makes it difficult to determine whether the observed behavior is a product of the stimulus being introduced or merely a product of the experimental situation itself.

Complexity of human behavior. *Perhaps the most serious reservation about social science research is that human behavior is shaped by so many different forces that it resists scientific explanation.* A complete understanding of such a complex system as human society is beyond our current capabilities. At present, human behavior can be as well understood through art, literature, and music as through scientific research.

What is a "fact"?

In the social sciences very few statements can be made that apply to *every* circumstance. We cannot say, for example, that "all blacks vote Democratic." This is a *universal statement* covering every black person, and universal statements are seldom true in the social sciences. Moreover, it would be difficult to examine the voting behavior of every black person in the past and in the future to prove that our statement is true.

A more accurate statement might be: "Most blacks vote Democratic." This is a *probabilistic statement* covering "most" blacks, but it does not exclude the possibility that some blacks vote Republican. An even more accurate statement would be that "90 percent of blacks cast their ballots for Democratic candidate Walter Mondale in the 1984 presi-

---

Hawthorne effect
people modify their behavior simply because they know they are being observed by social scientists

---

universal statement
a statement that applies to every circumstance

---

probabilistic statement
a statement that applies to some proportion of circumstances

dential election." This means that there was a 90 percent *probability* of a black voter's casting his ballot for Democrat Walter Mondale.

A probabilistic statement is a fact, just like a universal statement. Students in the physical sciences deal with many universal statements— for example, "Water boils at 100° centigrade." Water always does this. But students of the social sciences must be prepared to deal with probabilistic statements—for example, "Blacks are three times more likely to experience poverty than whites." Social science students must learn to think in probabilities rather than in absolute terms.

Social scientists must also beware of substituting individual cases for statements of probability. They must be careful about reasoning from one or two observed cases. A statement such as "I know a black family that always votes Republican" may be true, but it would be very danger-ous to generalize about the voting habits of all black voters on the basis of this one case.

We always build up tentative generalizations from our own world of experiences. However, as social scientists, we must ensure that our own experiences are typical. To do so, we must study the behavior of *repre-sentative samples* of the groups we are investigating. This means using careful methods to ensure that the sample of cases observed is truly typical of the *universe* about which we wish to make some statements. It is impossible here to go into statistics and statistical inferences, with all their rules and methods for determining when a sample is likely to be representative of the universe. But we should keep in mind that the "facts" of the social sciences are seldom absolute—they rarely cover the complexity of any aspect of human behavior. So we must be prepared to study probabilities.

representative samples of the universe
cases selected in such a way as to ensure that they are typical of the behavior of a whole group

The classic scientific research design

An *experiment* is a scientific test that is controlled by the researcher and designed to observe the effect of a specific program or treatment. The *classic scientific research design* involves the comparison of specific changes in two or more carefully selected groups, both of which are identical in every way, except that one has been given the program or treatment under study while the other has not.

experiment
a scientific test controlled by the researcher to ob-serve effects of a specific program or treatment

This design involves the following:

1. Identification of the goals of the study and the selection of specific hypotheses to be tested.

2. Selection of the groups to be compared—the *experimental group,* which will participate in the program or undergo the treat-ment being studied, and the *control group,* which is similar to the experimental group in every way except that it will *not* participate in the program or undergo the treatment being studied.

3. Measurement of the characteristics of both the experimental and control groups *before* participation in the experiment.

control group
a group identical to the experimental group that does not undergo treatment; used for comparison

4. Application of the program or treatment to the experimental group, but not to the control group. (Members of the control group may be given a *placebo*—some activity or program known to have no effect—to make them believe they are participating in the experiment. Indeed, the scientific staff administering the experiment may not know which group is the real experimental group and which group is the control group. When neither the staff nor the groups themselves know who is really receiving the treatment, the experiment is called a *double-blind experiment.*)

5. Measurement of the condition of both the experimental and control groups *after* the program or treatment. If there are measurable differences between the experimental and control groups, the scientist can begin to infer that the program or treatment has a specific effect. If there are *no* measurable differences, then the scientist must accept the *null hypothesis*—the statement that the program or treatment has no effect.

null hypothesis
a statement that the program or treatment has no effect

6. Comparison of the preprogram/pretreatment status versus the postprogram/posttreatment status in both groups. This is a check to see if the difference between the experimental and control groups occurred during the experiment. This method, used alone, is sometimes called a "before–after" study.

7. A search for plausible explanations for differences after treatment between the control and experimental groups that might be due to factors other than the treatment itself.

Example. Let us consider a specific example of applying the classic scientific research design to social science research. A local government is considering the installation of street lighting in residential neighborhoods to combat neighborhood crime. The hypothesis is that increased lighting will reduce crime rates. Before spending large sums of money to light up the entire city without knowing whether the plan will work, the city council decides to put the program to a scientific test. The council selects several neighborhoods that have identical characteristics (same crime rates, land use, population density, unemployment, population ages, incomes, racial balances, and so forth). Some of the areas are randomly selected for the installation of new street lighting. Crime rates are carefully measured before and after the installation of street lights in those neighborhoods that received new lighting, as well as in those neighborhoods that did not (see Figure 2-1). After several months of new lighting, crime rates are again carefully measured in the experimental neighborhoods (which received lights) and the control neighborhoods (which did not). The results are compared. If a significant reduction in crime occurred in the neighborhoods with new lights, but did not occur in the neighborhoods without lights, and no other changes in the neighborhoods that might account for the differences can be identified, then the

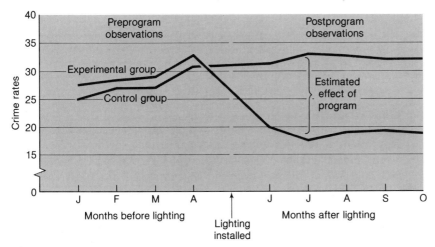

FIGURE 2-1   A scientific research design

city can have some confidence that lighting reduces crime. An expansion
of lighting to the rest of the city would then seem appropriate.

Special problems.   The classic research design is not without its
problems. Social scientists must be aware of the more difficult problems
in applying this research design to social science research and must be
prepared on occasion to change their procedures accordingly. These
problems include the following:

1. As noted earlier, members of the experimental group may
respond differently to a program if they know it is an experiment.
Because of this "Hawthorne effect," members of a control group are
often told they are participating in an experiment, even though
nothing is really being done to the control group.

2. If the experimental group is only one part of a larger city,
state, or nation, the response to the experiment may be different
from what it would have been had all parts of the city, state, or
nation been receiving the program. For example, if only one part of
a city receives street lights, criminals may simply operate as usual
(even with the lights), and total crime rates will be unaffected.

3. If persons are allowed to *volunteer* for the experiment, then
experimental and control groups may not be representative of the
population as a whole.

4. In some situations, political pressures may make it impossible to provide one neighborhood or group with certain services,
while denying these same services to the rest of the city, state, or
nation. If everyone *thinks* the program is beneficial before the experiment begins, no one will want to be in the control group.

5. It may also be considered morally wrong to provide some groups or persons with services, benefits, or treatment while denying the same to other groups or persons (control groups) who are identical in their needs or problems.

6. Careful research is costly and time-consuming. Public officials often need to make immediate decisions. They cannot spend time or money on research even if they understand the long-term benefits of careful investigation. Too often politicians must operate on "short-run" rather than "long-run" considerations.

■ Social science in action—The busing controversy   ■

One of the most interesting and controversial uses of social science in recent years has centered on equal educational opportunity and how to achieve it. Social science has played an important role in the development of governmental policy in this area. Indeed, in the historic decision of *Brown* v. *Board of Education of Topeka, Kansas* (1954), which first declared racial segregation unconstitutional, the U.S. Supreme Court referred to social science studies showing that segregation had "a detrimental effect" on black children. Over the years, public policies, including busing to achieve racial balance in public schools, have been affected by social science research.

An early influential report on equal opportunity in American education was sociologist James S. Coleman's *Equality of Educational Opportunity,* published in 1966, frequently referred to as the "Coleman report."[2] Although Coleman's study is not without its critics, it remains today one of the most comprehensive analyses of the American public school system ever made.[3] The Coleman report included data on 600,000 children in 4,000 schools. This report, and the reaction to it, can help us to understand the problems, as well as the possibilities, of social science research.

Coleman began his study with the conventional hypothesis that factors such as the number of pupils in the classroom, the amount of money spent on each pupil, library and laboratory facilities, teachers' salaries, the quality of the curriculum, and other characteristics of the school affected student achievement levels. However, scientific testing revealed that these factors had *no* significant effect on student learning or achievement. Moreover, Coleman found that student achievement was *not* affected by the presence or absence of a "track system," grouping by ability, guidance counseling, or other standard educational programs. Even the size of the class was found to be unrelated to learning, although educators had asserted the importance of this factor for decades. In short, the things that "everybody knew" about education turned out not to be so.

The only factors that were found to affect a student's learning to any significant degree were the student's family class background and the family class background of the student's classmates. Family class background affected the child's verbal abilities and attitudes toward education, and those factors correlated very closely with scholastic achievement. Of some significance, though secondary, were the verbal abilities and attitudes toward education of the child's classmates.

Coleman made no recommendations about what should be done in American education. However, his research was quickly taken up by the U.S. Commission on Civil

Rights, which was concerned with equality of education for black students throughout the country. The commission asked another sociologist, Thomas F. Pettigrew, to reanalyze Coleman's data to focus on *racial* inequalities rather than *class* inequalities.

Pettigrew found that black students attending predominantly black schools had lower achievement scores than black students *with comparable family backgrounds* who attended predominantly white schools.[4] When black students attending predominantly white schools were compared with black students attending predominantly black schools, the average difference in levels of achievement amounted to more than *two grade levels.* Moreover, special programs to raise achievement levels in predominantly black schools were found to have no lasting effect.

The U.S. Commission on Civil Rights used the Coleman report to buttress its policy proposals to end racial imbalance in public schools in both the North and the South.

Inasmuch as money, facilities, and compensatory programs have little effect on student learning, and inasmuch as the class background of the student's classmates does affect the student's learning, it seemed reasonable to argue that the assignment of lower-class black students to predominantly middle-class white schools would be the only way to improve educational opportunities for ghetto children. Hence, the commission called for an end to neighborhood schools and for the *busing* of black and white children to racially balanced schools.

The Coleman report and the report of the U.S. Commission on Civil Rights were often cited by proponents of busing—those urging deliberate governmental action to achieve racial balance in public schools. Courts and school officials in northern and southern cities used the Coleman report as evidence that racial imbalance denies equality of educational opportunity to black children, and as evidence that deliberate racial balancing in the schools, or busing, was required to achieve "the equal protection of the laws" that is guaranteed by the Fourteenth Amendment.

However, James S. Coleman conducted a second study, published in 1975, which analyzed the success of busing in achieving racial integration in the schools of large cities. This new report, *Trends in School Desegregation,* appeared to counter earlier implications about busing as a means to achieving equality of educational opportunity.[5] In examining changes in segregation over time in twenty-two large cities and forty-six medium-sized cities, Coleman found that an increase in desegregation was associated with a loss of white pupils — "white flight." This response to desegregation was greatest in large cities with large proportions of black pupils, and with surrounding, predominantly white, independent, suburban school districts. The long-run effect of white pupil loss in these cities was predicted to offset governmental efforts to desegregate public schools and to contribute to *greater,* rather than less, racial imbalance.

In short, governmental effort to guarantee equality of educational opportunity by busing large numbers of students within school systems in large cities was not working out.

According to Coleman's second study, busing was creating "white flight" and causing racial segregation in big cities to increase.

What are the effects of busing on black pupils? Social science research has produced contradictory findings. Some studies concluded that busing did not improve the achievement levels of black pupils.[6] (The black pupils in integrated schools studied in the original Coleman report were not bused to integrated schools.) Indeed, these studies suggest that busing only increases racial hostility between the races. Other studies, however, continue to maintain that over time busing improves academic performance of black pupils.[7] Today federal courts appear to use busing as a "last resort" when other means of school integration have failed.

The point of this brief case study is that social science research sometimes produces unexpected and even embarrassing findings, that public policies do not always "work" as intended, and that different political interests will interpret the findings of social science research differently — accepting, rejecting, or using the findings as they fit their own purposes.

Notes

1. Louis Wirth, preface to *Ideology and Utopia: An Introduction to the Sociology of Knowledge,* by Karl Mannheim (New York: Harcourt Brace Jovanovich, 1936).
2. James S. Coleman, *Equality of Educational Opportunity* (Washington, D.C.: U.S. Government Printing Office, 1966).
3. For reviews of the Coleman report, see Robert A. Dentler, "Equality of Educational Opportunity: A Special Review," *The Urban Review,* December 1966; Christopher Jencks, "Education: The Racial Gap," *The New Republic* 1 October 1966; James K. Kent, "The Coleman Report: Opening Pandora's Box," *Phi Delta Kappan,* January 1968; James S. Coleman, "Educational Dilemmas: Equal Schools or Equal Students," *The Public Interest,* Summer 1966; James S. Coleman, "Toward Open Schools," *The Public Interest,* Fall 1967; and a special

issue, devoted to educational opportunity, of *Harvard Educational Review* 38, Winter 1968.

4. U.S. Commission on Civil Rights, *Racial Isolation in the Public Schools,* 2 vols. (Washington, D.C.: U.S. Government Printing Office, 1967).
5. James S. Coleman et al., *Trends in School Desegregation 1968–1973* (Washington, D.C.: Urban Institute, 1975).
6. David J. Armor, "The Evidence on Busing," *The Public Interest* (Summer 1972), 90–120.
7. Martin Patchen, *Black-White Contact in Schools: Its Social and Academic Effects* (West Lafayette: Purdue University Press, 1982).

Discussion questions

1. You are about to begin a social science research project, and you want it to be "scientific" rather than normative. Describe the method you would choose, explaining how it works and what its goals are. Using this method, will you be able to prove cause and effect? Why or why not?
2. Discuss some of the difficulties the social scientist has in applying the scientific method to the study of social problems.
3. Suppose you are a school psychologist who wishes to determine if students learn more when television is used in the classroom than when only conventional teaching methods are used. Construct a classical research design for this purpose. Describe some of the problems you might encounter in applying the design.
4. Referring to the Coleman report as an illustration, explain how social science research sometimes produces unexpected results and how different political interests may use those results.

PART TWO

POWER & THE SOCIAL SCIENCES

■ In Part Two we will take a close look at the ways in which each of the social sciences contributes to our understanding of power in society. In so doing, we hope to gain some feel not only for the different topics, theories, methods, and data of each of the social sciences but also for the goal that they share in common—that is, an improved understanding of human behavior.

In Chapter 3 we will focus on what *anthropology*, with its concern for culture, has to tell us about the growth of power relationships in societies. In Chapter 4 we will examine the *sociology* of relationships between power and social class, particularly as evidenced by stratification in American society. Control of economic resources is an important base of power in any society, and in Chapter 5 we will turn our attention to *economics*. In Chapter 6 we will attempt to determine how and why it is that individuals react in characteristic and different ways to power and authority. Here we will turn to the theories of personality determination offered by various schools of *psychology*. In Chapter 7 we will examine government and power from the point of view of *political science*. Finally in Chapter 8 we will look at how the perspective of *history* can increase our understanding of power in society.

CHAPTER 3

■ POWER & CULTURE

"No-no" is one of the first phrases that most of us have ever spoken. This mimicking of a parental reprimand is evidence that by age two most of us have had our first encounter with power and authority. Even earlier, as helpless infants, we have, with our insistent cries, had the power to control the behavior of our parents. When we are older and our parents assign us household chores, we experience yet another instance of the exercise of power within the family.

Anthropologists, in their study of human culture, have been able to document that the exercise of power and the division of labor within the family constitute the most basic power relationship, the one from which true political power structures develop. What causes these structures to develop? Why should we need to control each other's behavior and how do we manage to do it? How do anthropologists document the growth of power relationships? How, in fact, do they approach the study of something as diverse as human culture?

These questions are the focus of Chapter 3. After you have read it, you should be able to

- describe how power in society is exercised and for what purposes,
- discuss how and why it is that the family is the fundamental social unit in which power relationships originate,
- discuss the changing roles of women in American society,
- discuss the stages of development of power relationships and the factors that influence this development,
- discuss anthropological approaches to the study of culture.

The origins of power

Power is exercised in all societies. Every society has a system of *sanctions,* whether formal or informal, designed to control the behavior

sanctions
formal and informal ways
of censuring behavior

of its members. Informal sanctions may include expressions of disapproval, ridicule, or fear of supernatural punishments. Formal sanctions involve recognized ways of censuring behavior—for example, ostracism or exile from the group, loss of freedom, physical punishment, mutilation or death, or retribution visited upon the offender by a member of the family or group that has been wronged.

functions of power in society
maintain internal peace
organize and direct community enterprise
conduct war
rule and exploit

Power in society is exercised for four broad purposes:

1. to maintain peace within the society,
2. to organize and direct community enterprises,
3. to conduct warfare, both defensive and aggressive, against other societies,
4. to rule and exploit subject peoples.

Even in the most primitive societies, power relationships emerge for the purposes of maintaining order, organizing economic enterprise, conducting offensive and defensive warfare, and ruling subject peoples.

At the base of power relationships in society is the family or kinship group. Power is exercised, first of all, within the family, when work is divided between male and female and parents and children, and when patterns of dominance and submission are established between male and female parents and children. In the simplest societies, power relationships are found partially or wholly *within* family and kinship groups. True political (power) organizations begin with the *development* of power relationships *among* family and kinship groups. As long as kinship units are relatively self-sufficient economically and require no aid in defending themselves against hostile outsiders, political organization has little opportunity to develop. But the habitual association of human beings in communities or local groups generally leads to the introduction of some form of political (power) organization. The basic power structures are voluntary alliances of families and clans who acknowledge the same leaders, habitually work together in economic enterprises, agree to certain ways of conduct for the maintenance of peace among themselves, and cooperate in the conduct of offensive and defensive warfare. Thus, power structures begin with the development of cooperation among families and kinship groups.

Warfare frequently leads to another purpose for power structures—ruling and exploiting peoples who have been conquered in war. Frequently primitive societies that have been successful in war learn that they can do more than simply kill or drive off enemy groups. Well-organized and militarily successful tribes learn to subjugate other peoples for purposes of political and economic exploitation, retaining them as subjects. The power structure of the conquering tribe takes on another function—that of maintaining control over and exploiting conquered peoples.

Culture: Ways of life

The ways of life that are common to a society make up its *culture*. The culture of any society represents *generalizations* about the behavior of many members of that society; culture does not describe the personal habits of any one individual. Common ways of behaving in different societies vary enormously. For example, some societies view dogmeat as a delicacy, whereas others find the idea of dogmeat nauseating. Some people paint their entire bodies with intricate designs, while others paint only the faces of the females. In some cultures a man is required to support, educate, and discipline his children, and in others these functions belong to the children's uncle.

The concept of culture is basic to what *anthropology* is all about. One could say that anthropology is the study of culture. Anthropologist Clyde Kluckhohn has defined culture as all the "historically created designs for living, explicit and implicit, rational, irrational, and nonrational which may exist at any given time as potential guides for the behavior of man."[1] In contrast with psychologists, who are interested primarily in describing and explaining individual behavior, anthropologists tend to make *generalizations about behavior in a whole society.* Of course, generalizations about behavior in a whole society do not describe the personal habits of any one individual. Some of them apply only to a portion of that society's membership. In other words, there may be *variations* in ways of life among different groups within one society, variations frequently referred to as *subcultures.*

Actually the term *culture* encompasses two major types of behavioral patterns: the ideal and the real. *Ideal cultural patterns* are what the people of a society would do or say if they conformed completely to the standards of their culture. *Real behavioral patterns,* on the other hand, are derived from observations of how people actually behave. For example, anthropologist Morris Opler reports that when an Apache husband discovers that his wife has been unfaithful he is supposed to mutilate or kill her and then find and kill her lover. However, affronted husbands do not always take such extreme steps. In one account, the husband simply "didn't care. He married right away to a Comanche."[2] Thus, the ideal patterns of a culture represent the "musts" and "shoulds," but these patterns may differ to a greater or lesser extent from actual behavior patterns.

Most anthropologists believe that various aspects of cultures are interrelated—that the religious rituals, the work habits, the beliefs and ideologies, the marriage relationships, and so forth, form a whole system whose parts are related to and affect one another. Anthropologists frequently attempt to analyze each aspect of culture in terms of its relationship to other aspects and to the functioning of the total system. Thus, for example, religious rituals will be associated with agricultural activities in

culture
ways of life common to a society

anthropology
the study of cultures

subcultures
variations in ways of life within a society

a society that relies upon farming for its food; but religious activities will center about hunting in a society that hunts for its food. Anthropologists frequently search for underlying themes that give unity to a culture. Only recently has anthropology departed from this *holistic* approach. Some anthropologists now believe that many cultures, perhaps even a majority, are not dominated by a single unifying idea, but instead encompass a number of general themes, which may not be interrelated at all. Nevertheless, most anthropologists still hold that culture is systematically related, its parts influencing one another.

Anthropologists believe that culture is learned. They believe that culture is transferred from one generation to another, but that it is *not* genetically transmitted. Culture is passed down through the generations because people are brought up differently. Individuals learn from other people how to speak, think, and act in certain ways.

symbolism
*creation and use
of symbols*

Symbolism plays a key role in culture, for it is the creation and use of symbols—including words, pictures, and writing—that distinguishes human beings from other animals. A symbol is anything that has meaning bestowed upon it by those who use it. Words are symbols, and language is symbolic communication. Objects or artifacts can also be used as symbols: A cross may be a symbol of Christianity. The color red may stand for danger or it may be a symbol of revolution. Mathematics is symbolic. It is the creation and use of such symbols that enable human beings to transmit their learned ways of behaving to each new generation. Children are not limited to knowledge acquired through their own experiences and observations; they can learn about the ways of behaving in society through symbolic communication, receiving, in a relatively short time, the result of centuries of experience and observation. Human beings therefore can learn more rapidly than other animals, and they can employ symbols to solve increasingly complex problems. Because of symbolic communication, human beings can transmit a body of learned ways of life accumulated by many people over many generations.

cultural categories
*technology
economics
social organization
religion
symbolism*

It is possible to divide culture into several categories. Anthropologists commonly use the following divisions:

1. *Technology:* the ways in which people create and use tools and other material artifacts.
2. *Economics:* the patterns of behaving relative to the production, distribution, and consumption of goods and services.
3. *Social organization:* characteristic relations among individuals within a society, including the division of labor and the social and political organization; and the relationships between a society and other societies.
4. *Religion:* ways of life relative to the human concern for the unknown.
5. *Symbolism:* systems of symbols (such as language, art, music, literature) used to acquire, order, and transfer knowledge.

The functions of culture

Culture assists people in adapting to the conditions in which they live. Even ways of life that at first glance appear to be quaint or curious may play an important role in helping individuals or societies cope with problems (see Box 3-1). Many anthropologists approach the study of culture by asking what function a particular institution or practice performs for a society. How does the institution or practice serve individual or societal needs? Does it work? How does it work? Why does it work? This approach is known as *functionalism*.[3]

Functionalism assumes that there are certain minimum *biological needs* that must be satisfied if individuals and society are to survive, as well as *social and psychological needs*. The biological needs are fairly well defined: food, shelter, bodily comfort, reproduction, health maintenance, physical movement, and defense. Despite great variety in the way these needs are met in different cultures, we can still ask how a culture goes about fulfilling them and how well it does so. Social and psychological needs are less well defined, but they probably include affection, commu-

functionalism
the assumption that cultural institutions and practices serve individual or societal needs

---

BOX 3-1   Understanding the !Kung

■ Someone not very knowledgeable about the !Kung* of the Kalahari Desert of South Africa might decide that those people are inferior savages. The !Kung wear little clothing, have few possessions, live in meager shelters, and enjoy none of our technological niceties. But let us reflect on how a typical American community might react if it awoke to find itself in an environment similar to that in which the !Kung live. The Americans would find that the absence of arable and pasture land makes both agriculture and animal husbandry impossible, and they might have to think about adopting a nomadic existence. They might then discard many of their material possessions so that they could travel easily, in order to take advantage of changing water and wild food supplies. Because of the extreme heat and the lack of extra water for doing laundry, they might find it more practical to be almost naked than to wear clothes. They would undoubtedly find it impossible to build elaborate homes. For social security, they might start to share the food brought into the group. Thus, if they survived at all, they might end up looking and acting far more like the !Kung than like typical Americans.

*The exclamation point in the name !Kung signifies a clicking sound made with the tongue.
SOURCE: Carol R. Ember and Melvin Ember, *Cultural Anthropology* (4th ed.) (New York: Prentice-Hall, 1985), p. 11. Reprinted with permission.

▪ Ruth Benedict: Patterns of culture ▪

The concept of culture helps us to understand ourselves by allowing us to see ourselves in relation to individuals in other societies and other cultures. Not only does culture explain many of the regularized behaviors of people—for example, eating, sleeping, dress, or sexual habits—but, perhaps more important, it helps us to gain a wider perspective on our own behavior. Through the study of diverse cultures we realize that there are many different ways of living—many different ways in which people can satisfy their social and psychological needs as well as their biological requirements; that our own culture is not the only possible way of life. Awareness of other cultures provides us with some perspective on the conscious and unconscious values and assumptions of our own culture. The realization that there are other ways of life besides our own may make us more tolerant, even appreciative, of alien cultures. Thus, we not only learn more of the variety of human experience but also become more sensitive to the values and lifestyles of others.

Perhaps this perception of the diversity of human existence was the really important contribution of cultural anthropologist Ruth Benedict in her widely read *Patterns of Culture.* As professor of anthropology at Columbia University, Ruth Benedict (1887–1947) popularized the notion that different cultures can be organized around characteristic purposes or themes. "A culture, like an individual, is a more or less consistent pattern of thought and action. Within each culture there come into being characteristic purposes not necessarily shared by other types of societies."[4] According to Benedict, each culture has its own patterns of thought, action, and expression dominated by a certain theme that is expressed in social relations, art, and religion.

For example, Benedict identified the characteristic theme of life among Zuñi Pueblo

Indians as moderation, sobriety, and cooperation. There was little competition, contention, or violence among tribal members. In contrast, the Kwakiutls of the northwestern United States engaged in fierce and violent competition for prestige and self-glorification. Kwakiutls were distrustful of one another, emotionally volatile, and paranoid. Members of the Dobu tribe of New Guinea, too, were suspicious, aggressive, and paranoid:

> Life in Dobu fosters extreme forms of animosity and malignancy which most societies have minimized by their institutions. Dobuan institutions, on the other hand, exalt them to the highest degree. The Dobuan lives out without repression man's worst nightmares of the ill-will of the universe, and according to his view of life virtue consists in selecting a victim upon whom he can vent the malignancy he attributes alike to human society and to the powers of nature. All existence appears to him as a cut-throat struggle in which deadly antagonists are pitted against one another in a contest for each one of the goods of life. Suspicion and cruelty are his trusted weapons in the strife and he gives no mercy, as he asks for none.[5]

Yet Benedict was convinced that *abnormality* and *normality* were relative terms. What is "normal" in Dobuan society would be regarded as "abnormal" in Zuñi society, and vice versa. She believed that there is hardly a form of abnormal behavior in any society that would not be regarded as normal in some other society. Hence, Benedict helped social scientists realize the great variability in the patterns of human existence. People can live in competitive as well as cooperative societies, in peaceful as well as aggressive societies, in trusting as well as suspicious societies.

Today many anthropologists have reservations about Benedict's idea that the culture of a society reflects a single dominant theme. This idea is now known as *configurationism,* and it includes the notion that societies, like individuals, have characteristic personalities. However, it is doubtful that societies can really be as well integrated as individuals. There is probably a multiplicity of themes in any society, and some societies may be poorly

integrated indeed. Moreover, Benedict may have underestimated the fact that regardless of the importance of culture in shaping individual behavior, even within a single culture wide variations of individual behavior exist.

nication, education in the ways of the culture, material satisfaction, leadership, social control, security, and a sense of unity and belongingness. Functionalists tend to examine every custom, material object, idea, belief, and institution in terms of the task or function it performs.

To understand a culture functionally, we have to find out how a particular institution or practice relates to biological, social, or psychological needs and how it relates to other cultural institutions and practices. For example, a society that fulfills its biological needs by hunting may fulfill its psychological needs by worshiping animals. Similarly, we find an agricultural society worshiping a sun-god or a rain-god. The function of magic is to give human beings courage to face the unknown; myth preserves social traditions; religion fosters individual security and social solidarity; and so forth.

Technology, with its tools, weapons, and artifacts, underlies nearly all these human activities. Variations in ways of life reflect different attempts by human beings to adjust or adapt to their environment. Technology can be viewed as a cultural screen that people set up between themselves and their environment. While most animals simply use the environment for food and shelter, changing it very little in the process, human beings alter or transform their environment. As a result human beings, who probably originated as tropical animals, can live almost anywhere on the earth's surface. Of course, peoples differ widely in the degree to which they exploit environmental resources. A society without means of transportation is restricted to a single area and depends on that area's resources. The technologies of "primitive" societies are not necessarily simple; the products of Eskimo technology, for example, are often ingenious and complex and require great skill to manufacture.

Anthropology helps us to appreciate other cultures. It requires impartial observation and testing of explanations of customs, practices, and institutions. Anthropologists cannot judge other cultures by the same standards that we use to judge our own. Ethnocentrism, or judging other cultures solely in terms of one's own culture, is an obstacle to good anthropological work.

ethnocentrism
judging other cultures solely in terms of one's own culture

Authority in the family

The family is the principal agent of socialization into society. It is the most intimate and most important of all social groups. Of course, the family can assume different shapes in different cultures, and it can perform a variety of functions and meet a variety of needs. But in *all* societies the family relationship centers on sexual and child-rearing functions. A cross-cultural comparison reveals that in all societies the family possesses these common characteristics:[6]

characteristics of the family

1. sexual mating,
2. childbearing and child rearing,
3. a system of names and a method of determining kinship,
4. a common habitation,
5. socialization and education of the young,
6. a system of roles and expectations based on family membership.

These common characteristics indicate why the family is so important in human societies. It replenishes the population and rears each new generation. It is within the family that the individual personality is formed. The family transmits and carries forward the culture of the society. It establishes the primary system of roles with differential rights, duties, and behaviors. And it is within the family that the child first encounters *authority*.

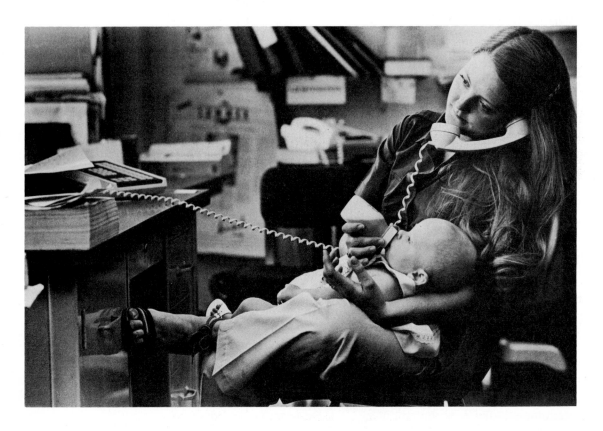

Family arrangements vary. First of all, the marriage relationship may take on such institutional forms as monogamy, polygyny, and polyandry. *Monogamy* is the union of one husband and one wife; *polygyny,* the union of one husband and two or more wives; *polyandry,* the union of one wife and two or more husbands. (Throughout the world, monogamy is the most widespread marriage form, probably because the *sex ratio* [number of males per 100 females] is near 100 in all societies, meaning there is about an equal number of men and women.)

Second, marriage mates may be selected by *parents,* by the *elders* of the community, or by the *individuals concerned.*

Third, the reckoning of descent may be through the male line (*patrilineal*), through the female line (*matrilineal*), or through both (*bilineal*).

Fourth, the newlyweds may reside with the family of the husband (*patrilocal* residence), with the family of the wife (*matrilocal*), or in a new residence of their own (*neolocal*).

Fifth, the family may be dominated by the husband-father (*patriarchal*) or the wife-mother (*matriarchal*), or the dominance pattern may be diffused so that both parents (and in some instances even the children) have considerable authority (*democratic or equalitarian*).

As we have noted, the child's first experience with authority in all societies is within the family. Indeed, the entire culture first appears to children as something their fathers or mothers want them to do. Differences in the type of authority exercised, and whether or not the authority is exercised primarily by the mother or father, can shape the character and personality of the growing individual.

The family in agricultural societies. In most agricultural societies the family is *patriarchal* and *patrilineal:* the male is the dominant authority and kinship is determined through the male line. The family is an economic institution, as well as a sexual and child-rearing one; it owns land, produces many artifacts, and cares for its old as well as its young. Male family heads exercise power in the wider community; patriarchs may govern the village or tribe. Male authority frequently means the subjugation of both women and children. This family arrangement is buttressed by traditional moral values and religious teachings that emphasize discipline, self-sacrifice, and the sanctity of the family unit.

Women face a lifetime of childbearing, child rearing, and household work. Families of ten or fifteen children are not uncommon. The property rights of a woman are vested in her husband. Women are taught to serve and obey their husbands. Women are not considered as mentally competent as men. The husband owns and manages the family's economic enterprise. Tasks are divided: men raise crops, tend animals, and perform heavy work; women make clothes, prepare food, tend the sick, and perform endless household services.

---

monogamy
marriage union of one husband and one wife

the patriarchal family
the male is the dominant authority and kinship is determined through the male line

*effects of industrial-
ization on the family*

The family in industrialized societies. Industrialization alters the economic functions of the family and brings about changes in the traditional patterns of authority. In industrialized societies the household is no longer an important unit of production, even though it retains an economic role as a consumer unit. Work is to be found outside the home, and industrial technology provides gainful employment for women as well as for men. This means an increase in opportunities for women outside the family unit and the possibility of economic independence. The number of women in the labor force increases; today in the United States more than 60 percent of adult women are employed outside the home.

role of women

The patriarchal authority structure that typifies the family in an agricultural economy is altered by the new opportunities for women in an advanced industrial nation. Not only do women acquire employment alternatives but their opportunities for education also expand. Independence permits them to modify many of the more oppressive features of patriarchy. Women in an advanced industrialized society have fewer children. Divorce becomes a realistic alternative to an unhappy marriage. The trend in divorce rates in industrialized societies is upward.

role of government

At the same time, governments in industrialized societies assume many of the traditional functions of the family, further increasing opportunities for women. The government steps into the field of formal education—not just in the instruction of reading, writing, and arithmetic, but in support of home economics, driver training, health care, and perhaps even sex education, all areas that were once the province of the family. Governmental welfare programs provide assistance to mothers of dependent children when a family breadwinner is absent or unable to provide for the children. The government undertakes to care for the aged, the sick, and others incapable of supporting themselves, thus relieving families of still another traditional function.

Despite these characteristics of industrial society, however, the family remains the fundamental social unit. The family is not disappearing; marriage and family life are as popular as ever. But the father-dominated authority structure, with its traditional duties and rigid sex roles, is changing. The family is becoming an institution in which both husband and wife seek individual happiness, rather than the perpetuation of the species and economic efficiency. Many women still choose to seek fulfillment in marriage and child rearing, rather than in outside employment. The important point is that now this is a *choice* and not a cultural requirement.

family as fundamental social unit

The American family. The American family endures. Its nature may change, but the family unit nonetheless continues to be the fundamental unit of society.

Today there are more than 61 million families in America, and 200 million of the nation's 235 million people live in these family units.[7] Only about 13 percent of the population lives outside family units. The U.S. Bureau of the Census calls these people "unrelated individuals."

However, the nature of the family unit has indeed been changing. Husband–wife families compose 83 percent of all families, while 17 percent of all families have only a single adult. Of all husband–wife families, 47 percent have no children. The birth rate has declined from 3.7 births per woman of childbearing age in the 1950s to 2.6 in the 1960s, and to only 1.8 in the 1980s. This last figure is *below* the projected zero population growth rate (2.1 children per female of childbearing age). In addition, there are about four abortions for every ten live births in the United States.

It is not really clear what factors are contributing to these changes in the American family. Certainly new opportunities for women in the occupational world have increased the number of women in the work force and altered the "traditional" patterns of family life. Only about half of today's mothers stay at home and devote full time to child rearing. The availability of preschools and public child-care centers has also helped to increase the number of mothers in the work force. Inflation may be an even more important factor: as inflation spreads, a middle-class family must increasingly depend on the incomes of both husband and wife to support itself.

Power and sex

Although some societies have reduced sexual inequalities, no society has entirely eliminated male dominance.[8] Sex role differentiation in work differs among cultures (see Table 3-1), but the most common pattern is for women to work close to home. Moreover, comparisons of numbers of different cultures studied by anthropologists reveal that men rather than women are usually dominant in *political leadership and warfare*. A recent cross-cultural survey reports that in 85 percent of the societies studied, *only* men were political leaders.[9] In the other 15 percent of societies studied, female leaders were either outnumbered by male leaders or less powerful than the men. In 88 percent of the world's societies women never participate in war.

Why have men dominated in politics and war in most cultures? There are many theories on this topic.

A theory of *physical strength* suggests that men prevail in warfare, particularly in primitive warfare, which relies mainly on physical strength of the combatants. Because men did the fighting, they also had to make the decisions about whether or not to engage in war. Decisions about whether to fight or not were vital to the survival of the culture; therefore, decisions about war were the most important political decisions in a society. Dominance in those decisions assisted men in other aspects of societal decision making and led to their general political dominance.

A related *hunting* theory suggests that in most societies men do the hunting, wandering far from home and using great strength and endurance. The skills of hunting are closely related to the skills of war; people can be hunted and killed in the same fashion as animals. Because men dominated in hunting, they also dominated in war.

A *child care* theory argues that women's biological function of bearing and nursing children prevents women from going far from home. Infants cannot be taken into potential danger. (In most cultures women

TABLE 3-1 Division of labor by sex: A cross-cultural comparison

	Numbers of cultures dominated by				
	Men always	*Men usually*	*Either sex equally*	*Women usually*	*Women always*
Hunting	166	13	0	0	0
Herding	38	4	4	0	5
Fishing	98	34	19	3	4
Planting	31	23	33	20	37
Harvesting	10	15	35	39	44
Cooking	5	1	9	28	158
Carrying water	7	0	5	7	119

Adapted from George P. Murdock, "Comparative Data on the Division of Labor by Sex," *Social Forces*, Vol. 15 (May 1935), 551–553.

breast feed their children for up to two years.) This circumstance explains why women in most cultures perform functions that allow them to remain at home—for example, cooking, harvesting, and planting—and why men in most cultures undertake tasks requiring them to leave home—hunting, herding, fishing. Warfare, of course, requires long stays away from home.

BOX 3-2 Conversational power

■ Recent sociological research suggests that power is exercised in ordinary conversation. In conversations between the sexes, men frequently exercise power over women through blunt, forceful, and dominating speech and behavior. Men tend to control the topic of conversation. Men do not try as hard as women to keep conversations going but instead lapse into long silences. Women use more tag questions such as "You know?" at the end of statements in an attempt to elicit responses from men. Men interrupt women more often than women interrupt men.

Here is an example of power in a conversation taken from a tape made by sociologists. The brackets indicate when both the man and the woman are speaking at the same time.

Woman: How's your paper coming?

Man: All right, I guess. (*Pause*) I haven't done much in the past two weeks. (*Pause*)

Woman: Yeah, I know how that can . . .

Man: Hey, ya got an extra cigarette? (*Pause*)

Woman: Oh, uh, sure. (*Hands him the pack*)
Like my [pa—]

Man: [How] 'bout a match?

Woman: Here you go. Uh, like my [pa—   ]

Man: [Thanks]

Woman: Sure. (*Pause*) I was
gonna tell [my]

Man: [Hey] I'd really like to talk but I gotta run.
(*Long pause*)

Woman: Yeah.

SOURCES: Sample conversation from Mary Brown Parlee, "Conversational Politics," reprinted with permission from *Psychology Today Magazine*. Copyright © 1979 American Psychological Association, p. 52; see also Cheris Kramarae, *Women and Men Speaking* (New York: Newberry House, 1981).

▪ Women in the work force—Changing American culture ▪

The number of American women who work has been rising steadily since 1947. Responding both to changing views of their role in society and to economic pressures on family budgets, women are entering the U.S. labor force at an unprecedented rate (see Table 3-2). Not even in World War II, in the days of Rosie the Riveter, did so many women work outside the home. More than 60 percent of American women aged 16 to 64 held jobs or were actively looking for work in 1984. It is estimated that by 1995 more than 80 percent of adult women will work outside the home.

Like all complex social changes, the back-to-work movement has been shaped by many economic and cultural forces. A number of factors other than economic need coupled with the rising divorce rate have contributed to the increased number of working women. These factors include (1) more effective

TABLE 3-2 Women in the work force

Year	Number (add 000)	Percent of adult female population*	Percent of married female population**
1940	13,840	27.4	16.7
1950	17,795	31.4	24.8
1960	22,516	34.8	31.7
1970	31,233	42.6	41.4
1980	44,934	51.1	50.7
1984	49,210	53.3	52.2

*Age 16 and over
**Includes married with spouse absent
SOURCE: *Statistical Abstract of the United States 1985*, p. 398.

means of birth control and the trend toward fewer children; (2) the increased life expectancy of women; (3) the greater number of college-educated women; and (4) the widespread use of labor-saving devices in the home. Other factors are (5) the expansion of the white-collar job market in which most

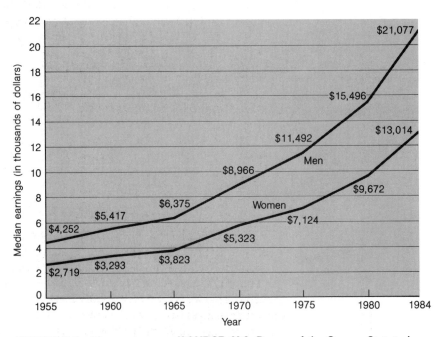

FIGURE 3-1 The earnings gap (SOURCE: U.S. Bureau of the Census, *Statistical Abstract of the United States, 1985*. Washington, D.C.: U.S. Government Printing Office, 1985.)

women are employed; (6) the increase in opportunities for part-time employment, and (7) legal action prohibiting job discrimination based on sex.

Women's pay has increased significantly in recent years, but it is still well below the pay of men (see Figure 3-1). Currently for all year-round full-time workers, the median earnings of women is 62 percent of men.[10]

The wage gap between the sexes reflects the continued concentration of women in relatively low-skilled, low-paying jobs. More than two-fifths of all female workers were employed in just ten job categories: secretary, retail sales worker, bookkeeper, private household worker, elementary school teacher, waitress, typist, cashier, sewer and stitcher, and registered nurse.

Occupational segregation stems from many sources—discrimination, cultural conditioning, and the personal desires of women themselves. The jobs women have traditionally held are frequently related to the work they perform in the home—teaching children and young adults, nursing the sick, preparing food, and assisting their husbands and other men.

Despite statistics indicating that the majority of women work because of economic need, many employers still hold to the traditional view that men ought to be paid more than women. Because they see women as temporary entries in the labor force, many employers tend to shuttle women into jobs in which the skills can be quickly learned and which hold little opportunity for advancement.

Growing numbers of women are gaining access to such traditionally male-dominated professions as law, medicine, architecture, business, and engineering. Consider, for example, the changes over twenty years in various traditionally male occupations (see Table 3-3).

However, the trend toward work and careers outside the home has placed a double burden on many married women. Sociological

TABLE 3-3 Women in traditionally male occupations

	Percentage of women	
	1960	1982
Physicians	10	15
Lawyers	4	15
Engineers	1	6
College professors	28	35
Chemists	10	20
Architects	3	9
Computer analysts	11	26

SOURCE: U.S. Department of Labor, *Employment in Perspective: Working Women* (Washington, D.C.: U.S. Government Printing Office, 1983).

studies consistently show that women in the United States perform many more hours of housework than men even when both hold full-time paid jobs. Moreover, families with small children require much more housework than families without children, yet men typically do not assume much of the additional work themselves. The same findings have been reported for the U.S.S.R., China, and many other nations.[11]

Still another theory, an *aggression* theory, proposes that males on the average possess more aggressive personalities than females. Some anthropologists contend that male aggression is biologically determined and occurs in all societies. Even at very young ages, boys try to hurt others and establish dominance more frequently than girls; these behaviors seem to occur without being taught and even when efforts are made to teach boys just the opposite.[12]

All these theories are arguable, of course. Some theories may be thinly disguised attempts to justify an inferior status for women—for keeping women at home and allowing them less power than men. Moreover, these theories do not go very far in explaining why the status of women varies so much from one society to another.

Stages of development of power relationships

As a general guide to the study of the development of power relationships in society, we can identify the following stages:

family and kinship

1. Societies in which there is no separate power organization outside the family or kinship group. In these societies there is no continuous or well-defined system of leaders over or above those who head the individual families. These societies do not have any clear-cut division of labor or economic organization outside the family, and there is no structured method for resolving differences and maintaining peace among members of the group. These societies do not engage in organized offensive or defensive warfare. They tend to be small and widely dispersed, to have economies that yield only a bare subsistence, and to lack any form of organized defense. Power relationships are present, but they are closely tied to family and kinship.

bands and tribes

2. Societies in which families are organized in larger bands, tribes, or confederacies that have organized sets of power arrange-

ments extending beyond family ties. In these societies population tends to be somewhat more concentrated; the economy yields a richer subsistence but no real surplus; and warfare, although frequent and often of great importance, is usually a matter of raiding between neighboring societies. When wars are decisive, they result in the killing or driving off of enemy tribes, rather than their conquest for exploitation.

3. Societies that are organized as permanent states and that have a more or less well-defined territory and a recognized organization to make and enforce rules of conduct. In these societies populations are large and highly concentrated; the economy produces a surplus; and there are recognized rules of conduct for the members of the society, with positive and negative sanctions. These societies have an organized military establishment for offensive and defensive wars. In war, conquered people are not usually destroyed, but instead held as tributaries or incorporated as inferior classes into the state. In the vast majority of these societies, power is centered in a small, hereditary elite.

state
a defined territory and a recognized organization to make and enforce rules of conduct

These stages of development of power relationships in societies certainly do not exhaust the variety of current and past power arrangements. They represent only broad divisions, each of which can be subdivided. (For example, a state can be classified in Aristotelian fashion as a *monarchy, aristocracy,* or *democracy*—rule by the one, the few, or the many.) Sharp lines cannot be drawn among these three stages; each stage shades into the next, and there are many transitional forms.

Let us consider three examples of societies in which power is organized by these broad divisions: (1) family and kinship group (polar Eskimos); (2) tribe (Crow Indians); and (3) state (the Aztec Empire).

Power among the polar Eskimos

Societies lacking formal power organizations are found today only in the very marginal areas of the world. These societies, with no formal power structures beyond *family and kinship groups,* exist only in the most difficult environments, where physical hardship and a lack of adequate food resources keep the human population small and thinly scattered. Among the polar Eskimos of northern Greenland, for example, a harsh environment and a limited food supply, together with a limited technology, force families to wander great distances to maintain themselves. Inadequate food resources make it physically impossible for these Eskimos to maintain, except temporarily, any groupings larger than one or two families. As a result, there is little in the way of power organization outside the family.

environment

Anthropologists who have observed Eskimo culture note that it has just two social units: the primary family, a small but autonomous kinship *economy*

leadership

organization

group; and the winter village, an unstable association of primary families who are not necessarily linked by kinship ties. The winter village is only partially a power grouping. Its member families do not stay together long enough or undertake the common enterprises necessary for the development of a stable leadership system. Ordinarily the families in a winter village, though temporarily united by common residence, act independently of each other. Their technology, whether in food gathering or house building, requires no high degree of cooperative labor. In times of stress, when a storm or lack of game reduces food stores to the danger point, a *shaman,* respected for his supernatural powers, may call the families together to participate in a ceremony intended to restore the food supply. But the shaman's authority is limited to such occasions; at other times he has no right to direct or command.

A strong and aggressive hunter may gain the esteem and respect of his fellows, but there are few occasions when he may capitalize on this prestige to assume a position of leadership. In short, the winter village has little need for leadership outside the family. There is not even the occasion of warfare to call for the organization of families for offensive or defensive action. Leadership resides only within the primary family, where it is shared by husband and wife, each in his or her sphere of activity. The family maintains itself largely through its own efforts. It is linked to other families through intermarriage, remote kinship, or ties of mutual affection and regard. Conflicts are often resolved by song sessions in which the disputants lampoon each other in songs that they sing before an audience of their neighbors. More aggressive behavior is inhibited by fear of retaliation by kinsmen of the victims. Protracted disputes may be resolved among some Eskimos by one party's moving to another winter village, although an overbearing and abusive individual may be speared while on a hunt.

Among these Eskimos, then, there is no structure of power outside the family group. Cooperation among families in joint enterprises is rare. Leadership outside the family is seldom evidenced, usually only during a crisis, when some particularly able member of the community takes charge. Ecological circumstances prohibit large permanent groupings of people, and the technology of the society is so simple that it utilizes individual rather than group effort. Variations on this fundamental type of power system that exists solely within the family group are also found among other primitive peoples living in harsh environments.

Power among the Crow Indians

Perhaps the simplest form of power arrangement outside the family is a *band, clan,* or *tribe.* Although its members may be linked by kinship, such a group is generally made up of many family units, not all of which need to be related by marriage. These groups form the next stage of

development in power relationships above that of the family or kinship groups. The band, clan, or tribe consists of numbers of individuals and families who (1) live and travel together; (2) regularly engage in one or more large community enterprises—for example, an organized hunt; (3) regulate conflict and maintain order among themselves; and (4) organize to protect themselves from their enemies and wage war against them.

Within the band there is as a rule an acknowledged leader—a chief—together with other respected individuals who assist in implementing authority. This authority may be backed by force, but more often it rests on the ability of the leadership to *persuade* and *influence* its followers. The leaders generally owe their status to their personal achievements as hunters or warriors.

leadership

Anthropological research on the American Crow Indians in the early nineteenth century provides an example of the development of power relationships at the tribal level. The Crows were more or less continually hostile to their neighbors. Any non-Crow was automatically an enemy. Warfare, however, was largely a matter of small-scale raiding, either to steal horses or to avenge the death of a tribesman. Horse-stealing parties tried to take as many horses as they could without disturbing the enemy camp; they fought only when necessary to defend themselves. When revenge was the object of a war party, however, they tried to surprise the enemy and to kill as many as possible without losing any of their own men. A war leader, whether he set out to capture horses or to get revenge, was not considered successful unless he brought his own party home intact.

warfare

Success in warfare was very important. Crow men achieved reputation and prestige through the slow accumulation of war honors. War honors were clearly defined. They were awarded for (1) leading a successful war party, (2) capturing an enemy's weapon in actual combat, (3) being first to strike an enemy in the course of a fight, and (4) driving off a horse tethered in an enemy encampment. A man who performed all these deeds became, in Crow terms, a "good and valiant man," and his status increased as the number of his earned war honors increased. A Crow who had not yet attained the minimum four honors was regarded as not yet a man, but only an untried youth.

economy

The warriors formed a kind of military aristocracy that made up the band council. One of their number, usually an older man with many war honors, was recognized as chief. He decided when the band was to move or settle down in its yearly wanderings in search of food and when war parties were to be sent out. He directed the annual buffalo hunt, a cooperative endeavor in which the whole band united to secure a store of winter food.

authority

However, the chief's authority was by no means absolute; he was "neither a ruler nor a judge." In effect, the chief was a leader rather than a ruler; it was his function to persuade and influence rather than to command. This point is illustrated by the procedure employed among the Crows to settle disputes. When quarrels and violence occurred among members of the same clan, they were resolved by the older kin, acting as clan heads. But when a feud threatened between clans, the chief, his council, and influential warriors belonging to neutral clans exerted their powers to prevent further hostilities and restore peace. Their efforts were often successful, because the Crows, continually at war with their neighbors, fully realized the values of solidarity among bands.

discipline

On some occasions, mainly the annual buffalo hunts, the chief and other council warriors had the authority to resort to force rather than persuasion to maintain order. In such instances the senior warriors "severely whipped anyone who prematurely attacked the herd, broke his weapons, and confiscated the game he had illegally killed."[13] The need for a winter's supply of food, and the fact that this need could not be adequately served without the closest coordination of effort, clearly justified, in Crow eyes, the chief's authority over his tribesmen. However, apart from such special occasions as the community buffalo hunt, members of the band were allowed to act pretty much as they pleased, subject only to the discipline of public opinion. The threat of ridicule and the obligations imposed by kinship were normally sufficient deterrents to antisocial behavior.

Band or tribal organizations similar to that of the Crow are widespread among nonliterate peoples. As environment and technology permit higher concentrations of population, bands form into larger tribes. From this stage there emerge even larger political units with recognized power structures.

Power and the Aztec Empire

The most fully developed system of power relationships is the state—the last of our major categories. Power in the state is employed to maintain order among peoples and to carry on large-scale community enterprises, just as in the band or tribe. But power in the state is also closely linked to defense, aggression, and the exploitation of conquered peoples. Frequently states emerge in response to attacks by others. Where there is a fairly high density of population, frequent and continuing contact among bands, and some commonality of language and culture, there is the potential for "national" unity in the form of a state. But a state may not emerge if there is no compelling motivation for large-scale cooperation. Motivation is very often provided initially by the need for defense against outside invasion.

States differ from bands or tribes to the extent that there is a *centralized authority* with recognized power, backed by force, to carry out its decrees. This *legitimate use of force* distinguishes the state as a form of power structure from the band or tribe, in which power depends largely on persuasion or the personal achievements of individuals. Power in the state is a more impersonal kind of authority.

authority
the legitimate use of force

The Aztec Empire, which was conquered by the Spaniards under Cortez in 1521, is an excellent example of an early state. Anthropologists have been able to trace its beginnings to an earlier tribal order

economy
*specialization of labor
and trade*

*warfare and
exploitation*

Aztec aristocracy

state council

confined to the valley of Mexico. The rich agricultural economy developed by the Aztecs produced far in excess of their immediate needs. With the exchangeable surplus there soon evolved a complex specialization of labor and an extensive trade that brought the Aztecs into frequent and profitable contact with neighboring groups.

Early in the fifteenth century the Aztecs embarked on a series of military conquests that led ultimately to their economic and political control over most of central and southern Mexico. The Aztecs did not destroy the cities and states that they had conquered. On the contrary, the commercially minded Aztecs permitted those cities and states to retain local autonomy, demanding only political allegiance and a yearly tribute in goods and services to the Aztec emperor. It was this economic empire, politically a loose aggregate of city-states controlled from the Aztec capital city of Tenochtitlán, that Cortez took over in 1521.

At the time of the conquest, the Aztec aristocracy was divided into twenty *calpulli,* small groups composed of nuclear families organized in ranked lineages. Each calpulli owned a tract of arable land, a council house, and a temple. The land was allotted in small farms to each family within the calpulli, to hold as long as the family continued its cultivation. Families could cultivate their own land, retaining the proceeds for their own support, or rent it to others, but it could not be sold or otherwise alienated from the calpulli. Should the family line die out or a family fail to cultivate its land for two successive years, the land reverted to the calpulli for reallotment. Some lands within the territory of a calpulli belonged to the chief and some were cultivated by subordinates. Others, set aside for the support of religious establishments and for the payment of tributes to the central government, were cultivated communally.

Calpulli were governed by a council of family heads. The council was under the leadership of a chief, who was in charge of land distribution and who kept a record of landholdings. Together with the council, the chief adjudicated property disputes and other conflicts between calpulli members, administered the public stores, and carried on various other administrative and judicial duties. The chief was selected by the council, but the successor to the position was customarily chosen among the sons or other near relatives of the chief.

The state council consisted of twenty speakers, who met at frequent intervals to administer affairs of state, declare war, make peace, and judge disputes among the calpulli. A speaker or delegate represented the calpulli in the state council. In addition, there was a great council, which included the twenty chiefs (one from each calpulli), the speakers, the warlords, the ranking priests, and a number of other state officials. The council judged exceptional legal cases submitted to it by the state council and, at the death of the king, selected a successor. The king was always chosen from a single royal family and was usually a younger son or nephew of the deceased king. The king was the supreme military commander and collector and distributor of tribute from conquered peoples.

The early Aztec power structure, although more complicated than that of primitive tribes, still retained a measure of democratic procedure. The core of the Aztec Empire was ruled by its citizens, the members of the calpulli. While the positions of chief and king were in part hereditary (they were customarily chosen from particular families), the choice of a leader also depended on reputation and ability. Although the king had great power as a military leader in a state more or less continuously at war, his power was modified by the councils.

However, as the Aztecs grew wealthier by their numerous conquests and ever-widening control of trade, the power structure underwent a gradual change. Most important, there developed a class division in Aztec society along socioeconomic lines. An upper class appeared, composed of honorary lords known as *tecutin*. These were men, calpulli members, who were given titles for outstanding services to the state as warriors, merchants, public officials, or priests. They were universally esteemed, had many privileges, including certain exemptions from taxation, were preferred for high governmental and military positions, and were given large estates and shares of tribute by the king, to be held as private property during their lifetime. These rewards clearly made the tecutin economically independent of their calpulli and, moreover, allied them with the king, who, while he gave the tecutin their honors, also had the power to withdraw them. *upper class*

A middle class also emerged, made up of calpulli members who were not tecutin. These formed the bulk of the population of the capital city. They were self-supporting through their membership in the calpulli and had a voice in the government through their representatives in the state and great councils. Often they rented their calpulli lands, and some acquired great wealth. *middle class*

Finally, a lower class was divided into propertyless freemen and serfs. The latter were attached to the lands of the nobility as slaves. The former were men exiled from the calpulli for various crimes and who were thus without any way of making a living except by hiring themselves out as agricultural laborers or as porters in the caravans of the merchants. Slaves were similarly dependent for a living on their own labor. Neither slaves nor propertyless freemen had a voice in the government. Though initially small, the lower class grew as conquests increased. *slaves*

As class lines become more sharply drawn, Aztec government moved inevitably in the direction of an *absolute, hereditary monarchy.* Tecutin clearly supported this tendency to their advantage and increasingly, by various devices, managed to pass on their titles and private property to their heirs. Slowly a *hereditary nobility* arose. At the time of the conquest, the Aztec Empire was essentially an emerging feudal or- *hereditary monarchy and nobility* der, with political power centered more and more in the king and his tecutin, rather than in the elected representatives of the calpulli.

Power and society: Some anthropological observations

Let us summarize the contributions that anthropological studies can make to our understanding of the growth of power relationships in societies. First, it is clear that the *physical environment* plays an important role in the development of power systems. Where the physical environment is harsh and the human population must of necessity be spread thinly, power relationships are restricted to the family and kinship groupings. Larger political groupings are essentially impossible. Elites emerge only after there is some concentration of population, where food resources permit groupings of people larger than one or two families.

power and the physical environment

Second, power relationships are linked to the *economic patterns* of a culture. In subsistence economies, power relationships are limited to the band or tribal level. Only in surplus-producing economies do we find states or statelike power systems. Developed power systems are associated with *patterns of settled life,* a certain degree of *technological advance,* and *economic surplus.*

power and the economy

Third, *patterns of warfare* are linked to the development of power relationships. Warfare is rare or lacking among people such as the Eskimos who have no real power system outside the family. Where power relationships emerge at the band or tribal level, as in the culture of the Crows, warfare appears to be continuous, in the form of periodic raiding for small economic gains or the achievement of personal glory and status; victory assumes the form of killing or driving off enemy groups. Only at the state level is warfare well organized and pursued for the purpose of conquest and economic exploitation. This does not mean necessarily that statelike power systems *cause* war, but rather, that some common factor underlies both the rise of state power systems and organized warfare. Warfare and conquest are not essential to the maintenance of the state; in fact, in the modern world, warfare between major states may slowly give way to other forms of competition, if only because of the increasing threat of total destruction.

power and warfare

Fourth, anthropological research makes it clear that power relationships exist in simple forms in primitive societies and that *no society is void of a power structure.* Power structures become more complex and hierarchical, and more impersonal and based on physical force, as societies move from the subsistence level with simple technology to a surplus-producing level with advanced technology and large cooperative enterprises. The simpler power systems are frequently headed by chiefs and councils selected for their age, wisdom, or demonstrated capacity as hunters or warriors. These leaders tend to rule more by example and

power in advanced societies

■ Sociobiology—It's all in your genes ■

A highly controversial topic in the social sciences is that of *sociobiology*. Sociobiology may be defined as the branch of biology that deals with the biological basis of social behavior in all kinds of organisms, including human beings. In general, sociobiologists argue that at least some aspects of human behavior are based on *genetics*—that is, that these behaviors are the result of millions of years of heredity and evolution. Some sociobiologists, whose ranks include biologists and zoologists as well as social scientists, believe that genetics largely determines culture—from educational and child-rearing practices to sexual behavior.

In 1975 Harvard zoologist Edward Wilson's book *Sociobiology: The New Synthesis* brought many of the insights of the rapidly advancing field of genetics to the study of human social behavior. The book, and the field of sociobiology itself, are highly controversial. Some people claim that the field is reactionary and denies the possibility of improving social conditions because of the pull of the genes. Others fear that genetic explanations of human behavior may be used to justify racism or sexual discrimination.

Sociobiologists, however, claim that their research builds on our scientific knowledge of genetic evolution and applies this knowledge to animal and human behavior. They maintain that many of the behavioral patterns of humans, as well as of other animals, are not "learned" but are instead the results of genetic coding. Songbirds that have been raised in complete isolation from any other members of their own species can sing the exact melody that their species sings, even though the isolated birds never had any opportunity to "learn" the melody. The melody is built into the DNA sequences in their genes. Many similar animal experiments reveal that behaviors occur in a species even though the animal has never had the opportunity to "learn" the behaviors.

Sociobiology, natural selection, and the selfish gene. Sociobiology is related to Darwin's theory of evolution, which holds that all animals (including humans) evolve by *natural selection*—that those that are better adapted to their environment survive and reproduce; the rest tend to become extinct. Darwin, however, in attempting to explain natural selection, focused on the animal itself, rather than its particular genetic code. Sociobiologists, on the other hand, focus on the genetic coding, for they believe that it is within this coding that natural selection takes place. The genes struggle *within* the animal to protect themselves. Darwin was never really able to explain why some animals (including humans) acted altruistically—giving up their own lives to save others. Such behavior—birds risking their own lives to cry out to warn the flock of danger; dolphins swimming beside an injured companion to keep it from drowning; ants giving up their lives fighting for the colony—seems to contradict the theory of natural selection.

Sociobiologists explain this altruism by claiming that the genetic coding of each animal in these particular species includes directions to save the others in order to protect the same genes. In other words, altruism is really *genetic selfishness.* Moreover, most sociobiologists argue that animals will act more altruistically to save relatives (who share more of their own genes) than nonrelatives. Altruism extended to general charitable acts (even by human beings) may simply be a genetic code that urges individuals to risk their lives to save their genes. Many true heroes who feel they acted on impulse in risking their lives to save others may really have been obeying genetically coded directions.

Sociobiological explanations of various behavior. Sociobiologists do *not* necessarily agree that humans are always instinctively aggressive (as suggested by Konrad Lorenz in his popular book *On Aggression*). The optimal genetic coding for survival will include just enough aggression not to be beaten out by others, but not too much to waste energy and risk death by pointless fighting. In other words, genetic coding includes a rough cost-benefit analysis for aggression.

Is it possible that upper social classes acquire power because they have acquired superior genes? Responsible sociobiologists reject this notion. It requires millions of years for any significant change to occur in the genetic coding of a group. Culture moves too fast for genes to be able to create any permanent class system. Even the two-thousand-year-old castes of India are not genetically different, despite their prohibitions on intermarriage and rigid separation between castes (restrictions that have been lifted since India's independence). On the other hand, sociobiologists may attribute an individual's success in such areas as sports, business, war, or science to the individual's genetic makeup.

Sociobiologists also offer genetic explanations for sexual behavior. They contend that the object of sexual behavior in animals and humans is to pass on as many of their own genes to succeeding generations as possible, at the lowest possible cost in energy and time. Because a male can start thousands of pregnancies, thus ensuring that some of his offspring will survive, he can ignore the nurturing of his offspring. But a female can give birth only a limited number of times during her lifetime and therefore must invest more time in nurturing her young in order to ensure their survival. Thus, promiscuity among males of many species is common, as is the nesting urge of females. Females of many species stay near to the nest, while males roam far in search of opportunities to breed. Moreover, males often engage in openly aggressive behavior against other males, not only to beat out the competition for available females but also to impress females with the strength of their genes. Over millions of years of evolution, the result, say the sociobiologists, is a different and stronger male physique. Of course, these views have irritated many women, who fear that sociobiologists are telling them to stay home and mind the babies.

It is difficult to estimate how much human behavior is genetically directed (as the sociobiologists contend) and how much is learned from parents and others (as cultural anthropologists contend). It is impossible to say, for example, that 20 or 30 percent of human behavior is genetically based and the rest is culturally based. All we know now is that both genetics and culture affect human behavior.

persuasion than by formal decree or force. As more complex state systems emerge, leaders are endowed with the exclusive right to coerce. Characteristically, political and economic power in the state is concentrated in a small hereditary elite. Modern representative government, in the form of European and American democracies, is relatively rare in the history of human societies.

Notes

1. Clyde Kluckhohn and William Kelly, "The Concept of Culture," in Ralph Linton, ed., *The Science of Man in the World Crisis* (New York: Columbia University Press, 1945), p. 97.

2. Morris E. Opler, *An Apache Life Way* (Chicago: University of Chicago Press, 1941), pp. 409–410.

3. This approach was developed by Bronislaw Malinowski. *A Scientific Theory of Culture and Other Essays* (Chapel Hill: University of North Carolina Press, 1944).

4. Ruth Benedict, *Patterns of Culture* (Boston: Houghton Mifflin, 1934), p. 46.

5. Ibid., p. 172.

6. William W. Stephens, *The Family in Cross-Cultural Perspective* (New York: Holt, Rinehart & Winston, 1963).

7. U.S. Bureau of the Census, *Statistical Abstract of the United States, 1985* (Washington, D.C.: U.S. Government Printing Office, 1985), p. 45.

8. Carol R. Ember and Melvin Ember, *Cultural Anthropology* (4th ed.) (Englewood Cliffs, N.J.: Prentice-Hall, 1985), ch. 9; George P. Murdock and Caterina Post, "Factors in the Division of Labor by Sex: A Cross-Cultural Analysis," *Ethnology,* Vol. 12 (1973), 203–225.

9. Martin K. Whyte, "Cross-Cultural Codes Dealing with the Relative Status of Women," *Ethnology,* Vol. 17 (1978), 217.

10. U.S. Bureau of the Census, *Statistical Abstract of the United States, 1985* (Washington, D.C.: U.S. Government Printing Office, 1985), p. 419.

11. Jean Stockard and Miriam M. Johnson, *Sex Roles, Sex Inequality, and Sex Role Development* (Englewood Cliffs, N.J.: Prentice-Hall, 1980).

12. Beatrice B. Whiting and Carolyn P. Edwards, "A Cross-Cultural Analysis of Sex Differences in the Behavior of Children Aged Three through Eleven," *Journal of Social Psychology,* Vol. 91 (1973), 171–188; Eleanor E. MacCoby and Carol N. Jacklin, *The Psychology of Sex Differences* (Stanford, Calif.: Stanford University Press, 1974).

13. Robert H. Lowie, *The Crow Indians* (New York: Rinehart, 1935), p. 5.

Discussion questions

1. Describe how societies attempt to control the behavior of their members. Discuss the four broad purposes for which societies exercise power.

2. Describe how power and relationships begin within the family and how they develop into political organizations. What effect can warfare have on the power structure?

3. Choose a "subculture" that is familiar to you. If you were asked to explain in anthropological terms what sets this subculture apart

from the society at large, what cultural categories would you examine? Identify the variations in lifestyle that make this a subculture.

4. Describe how an anthropologist of the functionalist school would approach the study of culture.

5. Discuss Ruth Benedict's contributions to anthropology. In your discussion, describe how an anthropologist of the configurationist school would approach the study of culture.

6. Identify the characteristics of the family that are found in all societies. Explain why these characteristics account for the family's being the most important social group. Describe the variations in family arrangements that are found in different societies.

7. "In all societies the child's first experience with authority is within the family. . . . Differences in the type of authority exercised, and whether or not the authority is exercised primarily by the mother or father, can shape the character and personality of the growing individual." Describe the type of adult woman you might expect to have grown up within a family in an agricultural society and contrast with an adult woman who has grown up within a family in an industrialized society. Describe the influences contributing to the development of both women.

8. Discuss changes in the American family. Comment on the continuing strength of family life; the number of families with a single adult; and the declining birth rate.

9. Discuss the changing roles of women in American society, particularly their changing role in the work force.

10. Describe the broad stages of development of power relationships and the power groups associated with them. Compare these groups in terms of leadership, economic systems, patterns of warfare, population density, and patterns of settlement. How have anthropological studies contributed to our understanding of these power relationships?

11. "Culture is learned. . . . Culture is transferred from one generation to another, but . . . it is *not* genetically transmitted." What arguments do sociobiologists advance against this contention? Why does sociobiology arouse so much controversy? Identify the areas of human social behavior that sociobiologists believe may be genetically directed. Discuss your opinions about the relative effects of genetics and culture on human behavior.

CHAPTER 4

■ POWER & SOCIAL CLASS

"In worn out, king-ridden Europe, men must stay where they are born. But in America a man is accounted a failure, and certainly ought to be, who has not risen above his father's station in life." These are the words of Charles O'Conor, the self-made son of an Irish immigrant, who himself rose "above his father's station" to acquire the symbols of social status— power and authority as the recognized leader of the New York bar, wealth as the owner of a stately Nantucket mansion, and prestige as the holder of five honorary degrees from universities.[1] Although O'Conor made his statement more than a century ago, his words are still an accurate reflection of the ideology on which the American class system is based.

In this chapter we will look at how Americans "stratify" themselves into social classes; at how sociologists measure this stratification; at the functions that ideology serves; and at the relationship between social class and power. After you have read Chapter 4, you should be able to

- describe the stratification system and the methods that sociologists use to identify and measure stratification,
- describe functional and conflict explanations of social classes,
- discuss the functions of ideology and describe how the American ideology influences social stratification,
- define class consciousness and identify the factors that help to stabilize the existing class system in America,
- discuss the basic notions set forth by Karl Marx about social classes and describe what some of the problems are in Marxist analysis,
- discuss the relationships between social class and lifestyle and between social class and political power.

Power pyramids and pecking orders

All known societies have some system of ranking their members along a superiority-inferiority scale. Although some societies claim to grant "equality" to their members, in no society have people in fact been considered equal. The *stratification* of society involves the *classification* of individuals and the *ranking* of classifications on a superiority-inferiority scale. This system of classification and ranking is itself a source of prestige, wealth, income, authority, and power.

Individuals can be classified on a wide variety of characteristics— physical strength, fighting prowess, family lineage, ethnic or racial category, age, sex, religion, birth order, and so on. But *the most important bases of stratification in a modern industrial society are the various roles that individuals play in the economic system.* Individuals are ranked according to how they make their living and how much control they exercise over the livelihood of others. Ranking by occupation and control of economic resources occurs not only in the United States but in most other modern nations as well; both communist and noncommunist nations have stratification systems based on these same factors.[2]

The evaluation of individuals along a superiority-inferiority scale means, of course, a differential distribution of prestige. Thus, the elite strata will receive the *deference* of individuals who are ranked below them. Deference may take many forms: acquiescence in the material advantages or privileges of the elite (the use of titles and symbols of rank, distinctive clothing, housing, and automobiles); accordance of influence and respect; acceptance of leadership in decision making; and so on. The stratification system also involves *different styles of life:* foods eaten, magazines and books read, places of residence, favorite sports, schools attended, pronunciation and accent, recreational activities, and so forth. In addition, of course, the stratification system is associated with the *uneven distribution of wealth and income:* in every society higher-ranking persons enjoy better housing, clothing, food, automobiles, and other material goods and services than persons ranked lower on the scale.

Finally, the stratification system involves the *unequal distribution of power*—the ability to control the acts of others. Sociologists agree that power and stratification are closely related, but they disagree on the specific value of this relationship. Some theorize that power is a *product* of economic well-being, prestige, or status. Others believe that power *determines* the distribution of wealth, prestige, and status.[3]

It is the stratification system that creates social classes. The term *social class* simply refers to all individuals who occupy a broadly similar category and ranking in the stratification system. Members of the same social class may or may not interact or even realize that they have much in common. Since all societies have stratification systems, all societies have social classes.

---

stratification
classifying people and ranking the classifications on a superiority–inferiority scale

---

stratification results in unequal
deference
styles of life
wealth and income
power

---

social class
a category and ranking in the stratification system

Why do we have social classes?

Sociologists disagree on why societies distribute wealth, power, and prestige unequally. On one side are the *functional theorists,* who argue that stratification is necessary and perhaps inevitable for maintaining society. On the other side are the *conflict theorists,* who argue that stratification results from the selfish interests of groups trying to preserve their advantages over others.

The functional argument might be summarized as follows:

functional theory
inequality is necessary to get people to work harder in more demanding jobs that require longer training and greater skills

1. Certain positions are more important to a society's survival than other positions and require special skills. For example, in most societies, occupations such as governor, physician, teacher, and priest are considered vital.
2. Only a few persons in society have the ability (intelligence, energy, personality) to perform well in these positions.
3. These positions require that persons who do have ability undergo extensive training and education before they occupy these positions.
4. In order to motivate able people to endure the training and sacrifice their time and energy for education, society must provide them with additional rewards.
5. The result is social inequality, with some classes of people receiving more rewards than others. Inequality is inevitable and essential in order to "insure that the most important positions are conscientiously filled by the most qualified persons."[4]

In other words, an expectation of inequality is essential in getting people to work harder in more difficult jobs requiring longer training and greater skill.

In contrast, conflict theory focuses on the struggle among competing groups in society over scarce resources. Conflict theorists have argued:

conflict theory
inequality is imposed on society by those who want to retain their wealth and power

1. People who possess property, income, power, or prestige—the upper classes—simply wish to protect their position in society. Thus, the stratification system is perpetuated.
2. There are many "functionally important" positions in society that are *not* highly rewarded. It might be argued that an electrician, an auto mechanic, or a plumber is just as important to the survival of society as is a doctor or a lawyer.
3. Many persons in the lower classes have the ability to perform in high-status occupations, but because of unequal educational opportunities they never get the chance to do so.
4. Wealth is not the only way of motivating people. Conceivably, societies might reward people merely by recognizing their services. Cooperation could then replace competition as a motivating force.

5. Stratification negatively affects the thinking of members of the lower class. Stratification may even be "dysfunctional" to society if it fosters feelings of suspicion, hostility, and disloyalty to society among those in the lower classes.

In short, the stratification system is imposed on society by those at the top. It allows them to use their power and prestige to keep what they have. Later in this chapter we will examine the ideas of Karl Marx, who argued that the struggle between classes was the driving force in history and politics.

Stratification in American society

methods of identifying and measuring stratification

Social classes are of interest to sociologists, with their concern for the relationships among individuals and groups. Sociologists have devised several methods of identifying and measuring social stratification. These include: (1) the *subjective method,* in which individuals are asked how they see themselves in the class system; (2) the *reputational method,* in which individuals are asked to rank positions in the class system; and (3) the *objective method,* in which social scientists observe characteristics that discriminate among patterns of life associated by them with social class.

equality of opportunity versus absolute equality, or "leveling"

The American ideology encompasses the notion that position should be based on personal qualities and achievements. Individuals in a free society should have the opportunity to achieve the social rankings that they can earn by ability, effort, and moral worth. They are supposed to rise or fall according to their merits. The American ideology does not deny the existence of a superiority–inferiority scale for evaluating people in society; nor does it call for absolute equality, or "leveling," with all people given equal income, wealth, position, and prestige regardless of their individual merit. But it does call for *equality of opportunity;* that is, all should have an equal opportunity to achieve high position in accordance with their individual merits and endeavors. In the American ideal, "anyone who has it in him can get ahead." The logical sequel to this is that those who are at the top are worthy of being there because of their talents and efforts.

subjective identification
individuals identify their own social class

In view of this ideology, it is not surprising that most Americans think of themselves as middle class. Nearly nine out of ten will describe themselves as middle class when they are forced to choose between this term and either upper or lower class. It is apparent that to characterize oneself as upper class is regarded as "snobbish" and to view oneself as lower class is to admit that one is a loser in the great game of life. Even people who admit to being poor consider it an insult to be called lower class.[5]

However, the fact that most Americans label themselves as middle class does not mean that American society is one big middle-class society. In fact, when *working class* is added to the list of choices, and individuals are asked for subjective evaluations of their own class membership, a different picture emerges. Table 4-1 shows the distribution of responses when people are asked to rank themselves on more precise scales. Obviously the inclusion of "working class" reveals that Americans by no means see themselves as members of a single class; more than one-third of a national sample placed themselves in this category.[6]

How well does *subjective* evaluation of class conform to the ideas of social scientists about the *objective* meaning of class? As we have already noted, social scientists view occupation and control of economic resources as the principal determinants of social class in the United States. Sociologist Richard Centers writes, "A man's way of getting his livelihood dominates much of his waking life, and it is out of the forces acting upon him in this economic sphere that class consciousness has been seen to emerge."[7] In an interesting test of this idea, sociologists Hodge and Treiman examined the way that individuals' subjective identification of their own class correlated with their actual income, occupation, education, and ownership of real estate, savings bonds, and corporate stocks and bonds. It turned out that occupation, income, and education were all associated with subjective class identification (occupation was more intimately connected with class identification than anything else), but that ownership of real estate, savings bonds, or corporate stocks and bonds had almost nothing to do with this identification process. Persons who did not own these resources were just as likely to rank themselves as middle or upper-middle class as those who did. Moreover, the authors found that the other objective criteria of class—occupation, income, and education—were not as closely related to subjective evaluations as had been expected. They found it difficult to predict what class people would put themselves in on the basis of occupation, income, or education. In addition, Hodge and Treiman reported that the social class of friends and neighbors affected a person's self-identification. Those whose friends were in the upper occupation and income categories tended to rank themselves as middle class, whereas those whose friends

objective identification
ranking by occupation or income or education

TABLE 4-1 Subjective class identifications of Americans

Upper class	2.2%
Upper-middle class	16.6
Middle class	44.0
Working class	34.3
Lower class	2.3
Deny idea of class	1.0

SOURCE: Adapted from Robert W. Hodge and Donald J. Treiman, "Class Identification in the United States," *American Journal of Sociology,* 73 (March 1968): 535-47.

and neighbors were blue-collar workers tended to rank themselves as working class. In short, there is some relationship between subjective and objective measures of social class, but subjective evaluation of one's own social class can be affected by factors other than objective circumstances.

reputational method
individuals ranking the prestige of occupations

Social scientists have spent a great deal of time studying the prestige ranking of occupations as another aspect of the stratification system of modern society. Individuals are asked in national surveys to make a superiority–inferiority ranking of specific occupations—for example, "For each job mentioned, please pick out the statement that best gives *your own personal opinion of the general standing* that such a job has." Respondents are then asked to choose *excellent, good, somewhat below average,* or *poor* as their answer. The resulting prestige scores for ninety separate occupations are shown in Table 4-2. It is interesting to note that these rankings remained stable for several decades. U.S. Supreme Court justice and physician held first and second places, respectively, from the end of World War II at least through 1964. Sharecropper, garbage collector, street sweeper, and shoe shiner occupied the last four rankings

TABLE 4-2 Prestige ratings of occupations

Occupation	Prestige rank	Occupation	Prestige rank
U.S. Supreme Court justice	1	Sociologist	26
Physician	2	Instructor in public schools	27.5
Nuclear physicist	3.5	Captain in the regular army	27.5
Scientist	3.5	Accountant for a large business	29.5
Government scientist	5.5	Public school teacher	29.5
State governor	5.5	Owner of a factory that employs about 100 people	31.5
Cabinet member in the federal government	8	Building contractor	31.5
College professor	8	Artist who paints pictures that are exhibited in galleries	34.5
U.S. representative in Congress	8	Musician in a symphony orchestra	34.5
Chemist	11	Author of novels	34.5
Lawyer	11	Economist	34.5
Diplomat in the U.S. foreign service	11	Official of an international labor union	37
Dentist	14	Railroad engineer	39
Architect	14	Electrician	39
County judge	14	County agricultural agent	39
Psychologist	17.5	Owner-operator of a printing shop	41.5
Minister	17.5	Trained machinist	41.5
Member of the board of directors of a large corporation	17.5	Farm owner and operator	44
Mayor of a large city	17.5	Undertaker	44
Priest	21.5	Welfare worker for a city government	44
Head of a department in a state government	21.5	Newspaper columnist	46
Civil engineer	21.5	Policeman	47
Airline pilot	21.5	Reporter on a daily newspaper	48
Banker	24.5		
Biologist	24.5		

over those years. It should be noted that knowledge about occupational prestige and relatively strong consensus on relative ratings of occupations are widespread throughout the American population. Even more noteworthy is the fact that occupational-prestige rankings are similar from nation to nation among modern societies, both socialist and capitalist, developed and underdeveloped.

The *principal objective criteria* of social class are income, occupation, and education. If sociologists are correct in the assumption that occupation and control of economic resources are the source of stratification in society, then these indexes are the best available measures of class. Certainly income, jobs, and education are unequally distributed in American society, as they are in all other societies. Table 4-3 reveals the distribution of income in the United States, as well as the distribution of income by education. Generally individuals with prestigious occupations and good educations enjoy high incomes. Table 4-3 shows that individuals who have acquired higher educations tend to enjoy higher annual incomes. However, Table 4-3 also shows that there are two separate scales by which income is distributed—one white and one black. Blacks

TABLE 4-2   Continued

Occupation	Prestige rank	Occupation	Prestige rank
Radio announcer	49.5	Milk route man	70
Bookkeeper	49.5	Streetcar motorman	70
Tenant farmer—one who owns		Lumberjack	72.5
livestock and machinery		Restaurant cook	72.5
and manages the farm	51.5	Singer in a nightclub	74
Insurance agent	51.5	Filling station attendant	75
Carpenter	53	Dockworker	77.5
Manager of a small store in		Railroad section hand	77.5
a city	54.5	Night watchman	77.5
Local official of a labor union	54.5	Coal miner	77.5
Mail carrier	57	Restaurant waiter	80.5
Railroad conductor	57	Taxi driver	80.5
Traveling salesman for a		Farmhand	83
wholesale concern	57	Janitor	83
Plumber	59	Bartender	83
Automobile repairman	60	Clothes presser in a laundry	85
Playground director	62.5	Soda fountain clerk	86
Barber	62.5	Sharecropper—one who	
Machine operator in a		owns no livestock or	
factory	62.5	equipment and does not	
Owner-operator of a lunch		manage farm	87
stand	62.5	Garbage collector	88
Corporal in the regular army	65.5	Street sweeper	89
Garage mechanic	65.5	Shoe shiner	90
Truck driver	67		
Fisherman who owns his own			
boat	68		
Clerk in a store	70		

SOURCE: From "Occupation Prestige in the United States," by Robert W. Hodge, Paul M. Siegel, and Peter H. Rossi. In *American Journal of Sociology*, 69 (November 1964): 286–302. By permission of the University of Chicago Press.

TABLE 4-3   Distribution of family income in the United States

Family income	Percentage of families
Less than $5000	5.7
$5000–9,999	10.2
10,000–14,999	11.6
15,000–19,999	11.8
20,000–24,999	11.5
25,000–34,999	19.5
35,000–49,999	17.0
Over 50,000	12.6

Median family income in 1983 = $24,580

Education	Median family income	
	White	Black
Less than eight years	$12,708	$ 9,796
Eight years school	15,783	11,390
One to three years high school	18,779	11,358
Four years high school	24,617	16,425
One to three years college	28,330	18,705
Four years college or more	38,980	30,412

SOURCE: U.S. Bureau of the Census, *Statistical Abstract of the United States, 1985* (Washington, D.C.: U.S. Government Printing Office, 1985), p. 446.

with equivalent educations tend to earn less than whites. These disparities between blacks and whites are changing slowly over time. But there is still considerable racial inequality in the distribution of income in America.

Ideology and stratification: Dreams about getting ahead

The ideology of a stratification system *explains and justifies the distribution of power and rewards* in society. The ideology *helps to reduce tensions between classes* by explaining and justifying differences in their well-being. At the same time, it *helps to consolidate the power of the elite* by giving legitimacy to their superior standing in society. Thus, ideology itself is a source of power (see Chapter 9).

In the American ideal, one who works hard ought to get ahead, does get ahead, and in getting ahead proves that hard work is justified. The

the American ideology

American ideology is one of equality of opportunity. Its major points are

1. the belief in an open opportunity structure in the United States, with equality of chances for upward and downward mobility,
2. personal responsibility for movement upward or downward in the class system, with movement based largely on personal effort, ambition, hard work, skill, and education,
3. relative accessibility of education to everyone who has the ability,
4. the impartial functioning of the political and legal systems.

Do Americans believe in this ideology? A majority of them endorse it when it is presented to them in very general statements. However, when general statements are translated into specific questions, there is much less agreement. Moreover, acceptance of both general and specific statements about opportunity in the United States varies widely from one social class to another. Wealthy white Americans believe more strongly in the American ideal of equality of opportunity than do black Americans.

To test beliefs about the opportunity structure, sociologists asked a sample of Americans a series of questions relating to the American ideology. First was a general question about the existence of "plenty of opportunity" to get ahead. *Some people say there's not much opportunity in America today—that the average man doesn't have much chance to really get ahead. Others say there's plenty of opportunity and anyone who works hard can go as far as he wants. How do you feel?* Then came a more specific question about opportunities to get ahead. *Do you think that a boy whose father is poor and a boy whose father is rich have the same opportunity to make the same amount of money if they work equally hard, or do you think that the boy whose father is rich has a better chance of earning a lot more money?*

The responses to these questions clearly indicate that Americans believe in the ideology of opportunity only when it is stated in the most general and vague terms (see Table 4-4). There is far less belief in the existence of equal opportunity when the ideology is presented in concrete, specific situations. White Americans, who feel there is "plenty of opportunity" in general terms, divide over the question of whether or not a boy whose father is poor can achieve as much by working hard as a boy whose father is rich. Moreover, support for the specific statement about equality of opportunity in the United States declines with income: lower-income groups have less faith in equality of opportunity than upper-income groups. Finally, it is significant that black Americans are far less likely than white Americans to believe in the existence of equal opportunity.

American attitudes

testing for belief in opportunity

principles versus applications

TABLE 4-4   Beliefs about getting ahead in America

	Percentage in agreement					
	Low income		*Middle income*		*Upper income*	
Belief	*Black*	*White*	*Black*	*White*	*White*	*Total*
Rich and poor have plenty of opportunity (general)	56	90	58	80	93	78
Rich and poor have equal opportunity (specific)	11	47	21	49	57	42

SOURCE: Data from Joan H. Rytina, William H. Form, and John Pease, "Income and Stratification Ideology: Beliefs about the American Opportunity Structure," *American Journal of Sociology,* 75 (January 1970): 703–716; from a sample of residents in Muskegon, Michigan.

Social mobility: The ups and downs

Although all societies are stratified, societies differ greatly in social mobility—that is, in the opportunity people have to move from one class to another. The social mobility of individuals may be "upward," when they achieve a status higher than that of their parents, or "downward," when their status is lower. In the United States, there is a great deal of social mobility, both upward and downward.

The results of one study of social mobility in America are presented in Table 4-5. This study compared the occupational status of sons and fathers, and it did so in two different years, 1962 and 1973. A majority of the sons of upper-white-collar fathers (53.8 percent in 1962 and 52 percent in 1973) were themselves in upper-white-collar occupations. But the rest of those sons descended to less prestigious occupations than their fathers' (downward mobility). At the other end of the scale, only about 40 percent of the sons of lower-manual workers (43.8 percent in 1962 and 40.8 percent in 1973) ended up in the same occupational category as their fathers. This means that nearly 60 percent of those sons rose to more prestigious occupations than their fathers' (upward mobility).

Overall there appears to be more *upward* social mobility in the United States than *downward* social mobility. This finding is usually attributed to economic growth, industrialization, and technological development—changes that create more jobs at the upper end of the occupational ladder.

TABLE 4-5   Social mobility in America*

Year and father's occupation	Son's current occupation						Father's percentage totals
	Upper white collar	Lower white collar	Upper manual	Lower manual	Farm	Total	
1962							
Upper white collar	53.8	17.6	12.5	14.8	1.3	100.0	16.5
Lower white collar	45.6	20.0	14.4	18.3	1.7	100.0	7.6
Upper manual	28.1	13.4	27.8	29.5	1.2	100.0	19.0
Lower manual	20.3	12.3	21.6	43.8	2.0	100.0	27.5
Farm	15.6	7.0	19.2	36.1	22.2	100.0	29.4
Son's percentage totals	27.8	12.4	20.0	32.1	7.7	100.0	100.0
1973							
Upper white collar	52.0	16.0	13.8	17.1	1.1	100.0	18.2
Lower white collar	42.3	19.7	15.3	21.9	0.8	100.0	9.0
Upper manual	29.4	13.0	27.4	29.0	1.1	100.0	20.5
Lower manual	22.5	12.0	23.7	40.8	1.0	100.0	29.7
Farm	17.5	7.8	22.7	37.2	14.8	100.0	22.6
Son's percentage totals	29.9	12.7	21.7	31.5	4.1	100.0	100.0

*Mobility from father's (or other family head's) occupation to current occupation: U.S. men in the experienced civilian labor force aged 20 to 64 in 1962 and 1973. Figures in percentages.
The basic source of information is David Featherman and Robert Hauser, *Opportunity and Change* (New York: Academic Press, 1978). Data are from March 1962 and March 1973 Current Population Surveys and Occupational Changes in a Generation Survey. Occupation groups are upper white collar: professional and kindred workers and managers, officials and proprietors, except farm; lower white collar: sales, clerical and kindred workers; upper manual: craftspeople, forepersons and kindred workers; lower manual: operatives and kindred workers, service workers, and laborers, except farm; farm: farmers and farm managers, farm laborers and forepersons.

However, the rate of upward social mobility appears to be slowing down. This trend may reflect slower rates of economic growth in the 1970s and jobs in industry and technology lost to foreign competition.

Class as a determinant of style of life

Life in each social class is different. Differences in ways of life mean differences in culture, or rather (since the style of life in each class is really a variant of one common culture in American society) a division of the culture into *subcultures*. Class subcultures have been described by many sociologists. There are class differences in almost *every* aspect of life: health, hygiene, vocabulary, table manners, standards of right and wrong, recreation and entertainment, religion, sexual activity, family and child-rearing practices, political beliefs and attitudes, club memberships, dress, birth rates, attitudes toward education, toilet training, reading habits, and so on. It is impossible to provide a complete description of all the class differences that have been reported by sociologists. Moreover, class lifestyles overlap, and there are no rigid boundaries in America between classes. Class subcultures should be thought of as a *continuous scale* with styles of life that blend; hence there are many "in-between" positions. And finally, it should be remembered that any generalizations about broad classes in the United States do not necessarily describe the style of life of any particular individuals. So the following paragraphs are merely a general summary of the subcultures.

The upper class. The typical upper-class individual is future-oriented and cosmopolitan. Persons of this class expect a long life, look forward to their future and the future of their children and grandchildren, and are concerned about what lies ahead for the community, the nation, and mankind. They are self-confident, believing that within limits they can shape their own destiny and that of the community. They are willing to invest in the future—that is, to sacrifice some present satisfaction in the expectation of enjoying greater satisfaction in time to come. They are self-respecting; they place great value on independence, creativity, and developing potential to the fullest. In rearing their children, they teach them to be guided by abstract standards of social justice rather than by conformity to a given code ("Do things not because you're told to but because you take the other person into consideration"). Child rearing is permissive, and the only coercive measures taken against the child are verbal and emotional. Instructions to the child are always rationalized. Upper-class parents are not alarmed if their children remain in school or travel until the age of thirty. Sex life in upper classes is innovative and expressive, with great variety in sexual practices. Women enjoy nearly equal status with men in family relationships. The goals of life include individuality, self-expression, and personal happiness. Wealth permits a

wide variety of entertainment and recreation: theater, concerts, and art; yachting, tennis, skiing; travel abroad; and so on.

Upper-class individuals take a tolerant attitude toward unconventional behavior in sex, the arts, fashions, lifestyles, and so forth. They deplore bigotry and abhor violence. They feel they have a responsibility to "serve" the community and to "do good." They are active in "public service" and contribute time, money, and effort to worthy causes. They have an attachment to the community, the nation, and the world, and they believe they can help shape the future. This "public-regardingness" inclines them toward "liberal" politics; the upper classes provide the leadership for the liberal wings of both Republican and Democratic parties.

The middle class. Middle-class individuals are also future-oriented; they plan ahead for themselves and their children. But they are not likely to be so cosmopolitan as the upper-class person, being more concerned with their immediate families than about "humanity" in the abstract. They are confident about their ability to influence their own futures and that of their children, but they do not really expect to have an effect on community, state, or national events. They show some independence and creativity, but their taste for self-expression is modified by their concern for "getting ahead."

The middle-class individual is perhaps even more self-disciplined and willing to sacrifice present gratification for the future advantage than the upper-class individual. In the lower-middle class, investing time, energy, and effort in self-improvement and getting ahead is a principal

theme of life. Middle-class people strongly want their children to go to college and acquire the kind of formal training that will help them get ahead. Child rearing in the middle class is slightly less permissive than in the upper class; it is still based largely upon verbal and emotional punishment. This can be quite severe, however, and the middle-class child may be more closely supervised and disciplined than either upper- or lower-class children. Authority is rationalized for the child, but values and standards of behavior are drawn from surrounding middle-class society rather than from abstract concepts of social justice. In matters of sex the middle-class individual is outwardly conventional. The middle-class adolescent experiences first intercourse at a later age than the lower-class youth. However, in adult life, vis-à-vis lower-class individuals, the middle-class person enjoys greater variety in sexual activity, women have greater equality in the family, and the family has fewer children (though home activities are frequently child-centered). Recreation and entertainment include golf, swimming, movies, sports events, and travel in the United States. In general, the middle-class person is less able than the upper-class one to afford an interest in theater, art, symphonies, or travel abroad.

As a rule, middle-class individuals deal with others according to established codes of conduct and behavior. They are likely to be middle-of-the-road or conservative in politics; they tend to vote Republican. They have regard for the rights of others and generally oppose bigotry and violence. However, they do not hold those attitudes as strongly as do members of the upper class, nor do they feel as much responsibility to the community as the upper-class individual does. Though they join voluntary organizations, many of which are formally committed to community service, they are less willing to give their time, money, and effort to public causes.

The working class. Working-class individuals do not invest heavily in the future; they are much more oriented toward the present. They expect their children to make their own way in life. They have less confidence than the middle class in their ability to shape the future, and a stronger sense of being at the mercy of fate and other uncontrollable forces. They attach more importance to "luck" in getting ahead than to education, hard work, or self-sacrifice. They are self-respecting and self-confident, but these feelings extend over a narrower range of matters than they do in middle-class individuals. The horizon of the working class is limited by job, family, immediate friends, and neighborhood. Self-improvement or getting ahead is not a major concern of life; there is more interest in having a "good time" with family and companions. The working-class family has more children than do middle-class or upper-class families.

Working-class individuals work to maintain themselves and their families; they do not look upon their jobs as a means of getting ahead and certainly not as a means of self-expression. In rearing their children, they emphasize the virtues of neatness, cleanliness, honesty, obedience, and respect for authority. They seldom rationalize authority over their children ("Because I said so, that's why") and sometimes use physical punishment. They are not interested in stimulating their children to self-expression, but rather in controlling them—teaching them traditional family values. They would like their children to go to college, but if they do not, it is no great matter. The working-class youth experiences first sexual intercourse at an earlier age than do middle- and upper-class young people; young working-class men are more likely to categorize women as "good" or "bad" depending on their sexual activity. There is very little variety in the adult sexual behavior of the working class, and the woman is relegated to a subordinate role in sexual and family affairs. Frequently a double standard allows promiscuity in the man, whereas extramarital sex by the woman can be the cause of family disruption.

In relationships with others the working-class individual is often intolerant and sometimes aggressive. Open bigotry is more likely to be encountered in the working class than in the middle or upper classes. Violence is less shocking to the working class than to middle-class persons; indeed, sometimes it is regarded as a normal expression of a masculine style. To the working class, the upper class appears somewhat lacking in masculinity. The working-class individual's deepest attachment is to family. Most visiting is done with relatives rather than friends. Working-class persons do not belong to many organizations other than union and church. Whether Protestant or Catholic, their religious beliefs are fundamentalist in character; they believe in the literal meaning of the scriptures and respect the authority of the church. In their views towards others in the community, they are very "private-regarding"; they believe they work hard for a living and feel others should do the same. They are not interested in public service or "do-goodism"; they look down on people who accept welfare or charity unless those people are forced to do so by circumstances over which they have no control. When they vote, they generally vote Democratic, but they are often apathetic about politics. Their opinions on public matters are more likely to be clichés or slogans than anything else. They are liberal on economic issues (job security, fair labor standards, government guarantees of full employment, and so on), but conservative on social issues (civil rights, welfare, youth, and so forth). The working-class position in politics is motivated not by political ideology but by ethnic and party loyalties, by the appeal of personalities, or by the hope for occasional favors. For recreation the working-class individual turns to bowling, stock-car racing, circuses, fairs, carnivals, drive-in restaurants, and drive-in movies.

The lower class. Lower-class individuals live from day to day, with little interest in the future. They have no confidence in their ability to influence what happens to them. Things happen *to* them; they do not *make* them happen. They do not discipline themselves to sacrifice for the future because they have no sense of future. They look for immediate gratification, and their behavior is governed largely by impulse. When they work, it is often from payday to payday, and they frequently drift from one unskilled job to another, taking scant interest in the work. Their self-confidence is low, and occasionally they even suffer from feelings of self-contempt. In relations with others, they are suspicious, hostile, and aggressive. They feel little attachment to community, neighbors, and friends and resent all authority (for example, that of policemen, social workers, teachers, landlords, and employers). Lower-class individuals are nonparticipants—they belong to no voluntary organizations, attend church infrequently, have no political interests, and seldom vote.

The lower-class family is frequently headed by a woman. Lower-class women not only have more children than middle- or upper-class women but also have them earlier in life. A woman may have a succession of mates who contribute intermittently to the support of the family but who take almost no part in rearing children. In child rearing, the mother (or the grandmother) is impulsive; children may be alternately loved, disciplined, and neglected, and often do not know what to expect next. The mother may receive welfare or work at a low-paying job, but in either case children are generally unsupervised once they have passed babyhood. Physical punishment is frequent. When these children enter school, they are already behind other children in verbal abilities and abstract reasoning. For the male offspring of a lower-class matriarchal family, the future is often depressing, with defeat and frustration repeating themselves throughout his life. He may drop out of school in the eighth or ninth grade because of lack of success. Without parental supervision, and having little to do, he may get into trouble with the police. The police record will further hurt his chances of getting a job. With limited job skills, little self-discipline, and low aspiration levels, the lower-class male is not likely to find a steady job that will pay enough to support a family. Yet he yearns for the material standard of living of higher classes—a car, a television set, and other conveniences. He may tie up much of his income in installment debts; because of his low credit rating he will be forced to pay excessive interest rates, and sooner or later his creditors will garnish his salary. If he marries, he and his family will have overcrowded substandard housing. As pressures mount, he may decide to leave his family, either because his inability to support a wife and children is humiliating, or because he is psychologically unprepared for a stable family relationship, or because only in this way will his wife and children be eligible for welfare payments.

Frequently, to compensate for defeat and frustration, the lower-class male will resort to risk taking, conquest, and fighting to assert his masculinity. Lower-class life is violent. The incidence of mental illness is greater in the lower class than in any other class. The lower-class youth may have engaged in sexual activities from a very early age, but they are stereotyped in a male-dominant–female-subordinate fashion. Entertainment may be limited to drinking and gambling. Many aspects of lower-class culture are unattractive to women. Sociologist Herbert Gans writes:

> The woman tries to develop a stable routine in the midst of poverty and deprivation; the action-seeking man upsets it. In order to have any male relationships, however, the woman must participate to some extent in his episodic lifestyle. On rare occasions, she may even pursue it herself. Even then, however, she will try to encourage her children to seek a routine way of life. Thus the woman is much closer to working class culture, at least in her aspirations, although she is not often successful in achieving them.[8]

Social classes: Conflict and conciliation

class consciousness
believing that all members of one's class have similar political and economic interests, adverse to those of other classes

An awareness of class membership is not the same as class consciousness. *Class consciousness* is the belief that all members of one's social class have similar economic and political interests that are adverse to the interests of other classes and ought to be promoted through common action. As we have already seen, Americans are *aware* of class membership, but members of the same class do not always share political interests, feel that collective class action is necessary, or see themselves as locked in a struggle against opposing classes. Few Americans believe in the militant ideology of class struggle. Americans do not have a strong sense of class consciousness.

Nonetheless, there is some evidence of awareness of class interest in voting behavior. Although Democratic and Republican candidates draw their support from all social classes in America, social class bases of the Democratic and Republican parties are slightly different (see Chapter 7). Professional and managerial groups and other white-collar employees give greater support to the Republican party than skilled, semiskilled, and unskilled workers. Likewise, people with some college education tend to vote Republican more often than persons with a high school or grade school education do. Of course, not all of the upper-class vote goes to the Republican party, and not all of the lower-class vote goes to the Democratic party. In fact, the differences in voter support are not very great. But there is some indication that class has an impact on voting behavior.

Why is there no militant class consciousness in America? This is a difficult question to answer precisely, but we can summarize some of the factors that appear to help *stabilize the existing class system* in America and *reduce class conflict:*

factors in American life reducing class conflict
high standard of living
upward mobility
large middle class
widespread belief in the
  system
many cross-cutting
  allegiances

1. the high level of real income of Americans of all social classes and the relatively wide distribution of a very comfortable standard of living;
2. a great deal of upward mobility in the American system, which diverts lower-class attention away from collective class action and focuses it toward individual efforts at "getting ahead";
3. the existence of a large middle-income, middle-prestige class;
4. widespread belief in the legitimacy of the class structure and the resulting acceptance of it;
5. many cross-cutting allegiances of individuals to churches, communities, races, unions, professional associations, voluntary organizations, and so forth, which interfere with class solidarity.

In stabilizing the class system, these factors also stabilize the *existing distribution of power* in America.

The American system has produced a high level of material comfort for the great majority of the population. The real possibilities of acquiring greater income and prestige have reinforced efforts to strive within the system rather than to challenge it. Even individuals who realize that their own social mobility is limited can transfer their hope and ambition to their children. A large middle class, diverse in occupation and ambiguous in political orientation, helps to blur potential lines of class identification and conflict. This class stands as a symbol and an embodiment of the reality of opportunity. A widely accepted set of ideologies, beliefs, and attitudes supports the existing system. Finally, cleavages caused by religious affiliations, ethnic backgrounds, and racial categories, as well as other types of diversity (region, skill level, occupational group), have all worked against the development of a unified class movement.

▪ Karl Marx: The class struggle ▪

Conflict between social classes is a central feature of communist ideology. In the opening of his famous *Communist Manifesto,* Karl Marx wrote:

> The history of all hitherto existing society is the history of class struggles. Freeman and slave, patrician and plebeian, lord and serf, guild-master and journeyman, in a word, oppressor and oppressed, stood in constant opposition to one another, carried on uninterrupted, now hidden, now open fight, a fight that each time ended, either in a revolutionary reconstitution of society at large, or in the common ruin of the contending classes. . . . Our epoch, the epoch of the bourgeoisie, possesses, however, this distinctive feature: it has simplified the class antagonisms. Society as a whole is more and more splitting up into two great hostile camps, into two great classes directly facing each other: Bourgeoisie and Proletariat.

Karl Marx was born in Prussia in 1818. His parents were Jews who converted to Christianity when Marx was a child. He studied history, law, and philosophy at Bonn, Berlin, and Jena and received his doctor of philosophy degree in 1841. Soon after, he entered revolutionary socialist politics as a journalist and pamphleteer; he was expelled from Prussia and engaged in conspiratorial activities in France and Belgium from 1843 to 1849. *The Communist Manifesto,* written with Friedrich Engels, appeared in 1848 as a revolutionary pamphlet. In 1849 Marx fled to London, where he spent the remainder of his life writing occasional pamphlets on socialism, advising socialist leaders, and setting forth his views in a lengthy work, *Das Kapital.* He lived largely on the money given him by Friedrich Engels, who was the son of a wealthy textile manufacturer.

According to Marx, social classes develop on the basis of the different positions that individuals fulfill in the prevailing "mode of production"—that is, the economy. In an agricultural economy, the principal classes are landowner and tenant, serf, or slave; in a handicraft economy, guild-master and apprentice; and in an industrial economy, the capitalist (owner of the factory) and the nonproperty-owning worker. Marx believed that one's position in the economy determines one's interests, beliefs, and actions. The bourgeoisie who own the factories have an interest in maximizing profit and seek to keep for themselves the surplus of profit that has been created by the worker. Workers are exploited in that they produce more than they receive in wages; this "surplus value" is stolen from the workers by the capitalists. In the long run bourgeois society is doomed to destruction because gradually the workers will realize they are being exploited, will become aware of their historic role and act collectively to improve their situation, and ultimately will take over the ownership of the instruments of production in violent revolution. In Marx's opinion it was inevitable that the development of capitalism would lead eventually to the proletarian revolution. He believed that as the capitalist became richer the workers would become poorer:

> Accumulation of wealth at one pole is, therefore, at the same time accumulation of misery, agony of toil, slavery, ignorance, brutality, mental degradation, at the opposite pole.[9]

Class consciousness was viewed by Marx as an important prerequisite to successful proletarian revolution. Class consciousness would increase as the proletariat grew in numbers, as factories concentrated the proletariat in greater masses, as workers communicated among themselves and achieved solidarity in unions and political organizations, and as conflict between workers and owners intensified. The bourgeoisie would not relinquish their control over the means of production without a fight, and therefore violent revolution was necessary and inevitable. Marx said little about the details of revolution; this aspect of communist ideology was developed later by Lenin (see Chapter 9). But after the successful proletarian revolution, Marx envisioned a society without social classes. This *classless society* would be a "dictatorship of the proletariat" with all other social classes eliminated. The state would control the means of production, and everyone would be in the same relationship to the state as everyone else. Only when all were employees of the state would true equality exist. Class distinctions and class antagonisms would then be abolished. Social relations would be based upon the rule: "From each according to his ability; to each according to his needs." The state, which functions in bourgeois society to help the bourgeoisie oppress the masses, would gradually wither away in a communist society. As soon as there was no longer any social class to be held in subjection, the special repressive force, the state, would no longer be necessary.

The truth of the matter is, of course, that in the end neither capitalist societies nor communist societies conformed to Marx's analysis. There are several reasons why the capitalist society of the United States failed to meet Marx's expectations. First, Americans do not define their interests strictly on the basis of their class membership. Allegiances to church, ethnic group, racial category, voluntary organizations, union, occupational group, and so forth prevent the emergence of a militant class consciousness. Second, and perhaps more important, the workers in the United States did not become poorer over time but improved their standard of living. It turned out that capitalism provided workers with considerable material comfort. Third, American society provided a great deal of social mobility that enabled many individuals in the working class to move into the middle class. Marx did not foresee this growth of the middle class. Moreover, the social mobility of American society encouraged people in the working class to work within the system to improve their lives and the lives of their children, rather than to organize to destroy the system.

With regard to the failure of communist societies to conform to Marx's analysis, even though the bourgeois class was eliminated at great cost in human lives, new social groups emerged that were just as oppressive as the former bourgeoisie, if not more so. Communist party officials, government bureaucrats, and military officers monopolized power, prestige, and wealth. The state did not wither away at all, but instead became all-encompassing and all-powerful.

nities to make contacts with potential clients are two important benefits. Yet another answer is that lawyers naturally have a monopoly on public offices in the legal and judicial system, and the office of judge or prosecuting attorney often provides a stepping stone to higher public office, including Congress.

Members of Congress are among the most educated occupational groups in the United States. They are much better educated than most members of the populations they represent. Of course, their education reflects their occupational background and their middle- and upper-class origins.

To sum up, information on the occupational background of legislators indicates that more than high social status is necessary for election to Congress. It is also helpful to have experience in interpersonal relations and public contacts, easy access to politics, and a great deal of free time to devote to political activity.[10]

social class and executive and judicial power

Power in the *executive branch,* which most analysts now see as more important than Congress in policy formulation, is also exercised by individuals from the upper and upper-middle classes. Cabinet secretaries, undersecretaries, and top civil servants tend to come from eastern Ivy League schools; most are lawyers or business people at the time of their appointment; many accept lower salaries out of a sense of obligation to perform "public service."[11] The same class origins are found among judges in federal courts, particularly the Supreme Court.[12]

We know that political power is largely in the hands of individuals from upper social classes, but what does this really mean for the great majority of Americans? We might *infer* that people drawn from upper social classes share values and interests that are different from those of

elitist view of society

the majority of people. We might also infer that this elite will use their power to implement the values of the upper social classes and that, consequently, public policy will reflect upper-class values more than mass values.

On the other hand, several factors may modify the impact of upper social classes in politics. First, there may be considerable conflict among members of upper social classes about the basic directions of public policy—that is, despite similarity in social backgrounds, individuals may *not* share a consensus about public affairs. Competition rather than consensus may characterize their relationships.

Second, the elite may be very "public-regarding" in their exercise of power; they may take the welfare of the masses into account as an aspect of their own sense of well-being. Indeed, there is a great deal of evidence that America's upper classes are liberal and reformist and that "do-goodism" is a widespread impulse. Many public leaders from very wealthy families of the highest social status (for instance, Franklin D. Roosevelt, Adlai Stevenson, John F. Kennedy) have championed the interests of the poor and the downtrodden. Thus, upper-class values may foster public service rather than political exploitation.

Third, upper-class leaders, whatever their values, can be held accountable for their exercise of power by the majority in elections. Our system of parties and elections forces public officials to compete for mass support to acquire public office and the political power that goes with it. This competition requires them to modify their public statements and actions to fit popular preferences. Hence, in a democracy the fact that the upper social classes tend to hold public office does not necessarily mean that the masses are oppressed or exploited or powerless.

■ The power elite ■

The most popular and controversial analysis of power in the United States is *The Power Elite,* by sociologist C. Wright Mills.[13] Since its appearance in 1956, most writers have been unable to discuss national power without reference to this important study.

According to Mills, power in the United States is concentrated at the top of the nation's corporate, governmental, and military organizations, which closely interlock to form a single structure of power—*a power elite.* Power rests in these three domains: "the corporation chieftains, the political directorate, and the warlords." Occasionally there is tension among them, but they share a broad consensus about the general direction of public policy and the main course of society. Other institutions (the family, churches, schools, and so forth) are subordinate to the three major institutions of power:

> Families and churches and schools adapt to modern life; governments and armies and corporations shape it; and, as they do, they turn these lesser institutions into means for their ends.

The *emergence* of the power elite is a product of *technology, bureaucratization, and centralization.* The economy—once a scatter of many small competing units—is now dominated by a few hundred giant corporate and financial institutions. The political system—once a decentralized structure of states and communities with a small central government—has become a giant centralized bureaucracy in Washington that has assumed power over nearly every aspect of American life. The military—once a slim establishment depending largely on citizen-soldiers to meet specific crises—has become the largest and most expensive function of government and a sprawling bureaucratic domain.

> The history of modern society may readily be understood as the story of the enlargement and the centralization of the means of power—in economic, in political, and in military institutions.[14]

As each of these sectors of society enlarged and centralized, they increasingly came together to coordinate decision making.

> At the pinnacle of each of the three enlarged and centralized domains, there have arisen those higher circles which make up the economic, the political, and the military elites. At the top of the economy, among the corporate rich, there are the chief executives; at the top of the political order, the members of the political directorate; at the top of the military establishment, the elite of soldier-statesmen clustered in and around the Joint Chiefs of Staff and the upper echelon. As each of these domains has coincided with the others, as decisions tend to become total in their consequences, the leading men in each of the three domains of power—the warlords, the corporation chieftains, the political directorate—tend to come together, to form the power elite of America.[15]

The power elite holds power because of its position at the top of the institutional structures of society. These people are powerful *not* because of any individual qualities—wealth, prestige, skill, or cunning—but because of the *institutional positions* they occupy. As society has concentrated more and more power in a few giant institutions, the people in command of these institutions have acquired enormous power over all of us.

> If we took the one hundred most powerful men in America, the one hundred wealthiest, and the one hundred most celebrated away from the institutional positions they now occupy, away from their resources of men and women and money, away from the media of mass communication that are now focused upon them—then they would be powerless and poor and uncelebrated. For power is not of a man. Wealth does not center in the person of the wealthy. Celebrity is not inherent in any personality. To be celebrated, to be wealthy, to have power requires access to major institutions, for the institutional positions men occupy determine in large part their chances to have and to hold these valued experiences.[16]

Mills is aware that his description of power in the United States conflicts with the "pluralist" interpretation. But he believes that notions of power holders who balance and compromise interests or who engage in competition between parties and groups apply to middle-level power holders in America and not to the top power elite. Political journalists and scholars write about middle levels because this is all they know about or understand; these levels provide the noisy content of most "political" news and gossip. The major directions of national and international policy are determined by persons beyond the "clang and clash of American politics." Political campaigns actually distract attention from the really important national and international decisions.

The *unity* of the top elite rests on several factors. First of all, these people are recruited from the same upper social classes; they have similar education, wealth, and upbringing. Moreover, they continue to associate with each other, reinforcing their common feelings. They belong to the same clubs, attend the same parties, meet at the same resorts, and serve on the same civic, cultural, and philanthropic committees. Members of the elite incorporate into their own viewpoints the viewpoints, expectations, and values of those who "count." Factions exist and individual ambitions clash, but their community of interest is far greater than any divisions among them. Perhaps what accounts for their consensus more than anything else is their experience in command positions in giant institutions. "As the requirements of the top places in each of the major hierarchies become similar, the types of men occupying these roles at the top—by selection and by training in the jobs—become similar."

Mills finds American democracy severely deficient, and his work is frequently cited by radical critics of American society. According to Mills, the power elite is guilty of "a higher immorality," which is not necessarily personal corruption or even mistaken policies and deeds, but rather the moral insensitivity of institutional bureaucracy. More important, it is the failure of the power elite to be responsive and responsible to "Knowledgeable publics." Mills implies that true democracy is possible only where persons in power are truly responsible to "men of Knowledge." He is not very specific about who the "men of Knowledge" are, but the reader is left with the impression that he means intellectuals like himself.

Notes

1. Eric I. Goldman, *Rendezvous with Destiny* (New York: Vintage Books, 1956), pp. 7–8.

2. Alex Inkeles and Peter H. Rossi, "National Comparisons of Occupational Prestige," *American Journal of Sociology* 61, January 1956; R. Murray Thomas, "Reinspecting a Structural Position on Occupational Prestige," *American Journal of Sociology,* 67, March 1962.

3. Gerhard Lenski, *Power and Privilege* (New York: McGraw-Hill, 1966); Jack Roach, Llewellyn Gross, and Orville R. Gursslin, *Social Stratification in the United States* (Englewood Cliffs, N.J.: Prentice-Hall, 1969).

4. Kingsley Davis and Wilbert Moore, "Some Principles of Stratification," *American Sociological Review,* 10, April 1945, p. 243.

5. Richard Centers, *The Psychology of Social Classes* (Princeton, N.J.: Princeton University Press, 1949).

6. Robert W. Hodge and Donald J. Treiman, "Class Identification in the United States," *American Journal of Sociology,* 73, March 1968.

7. Centers, *Psychology of Social Classes,* p. 218.

8. Herbert Gans, *The Urban Villagers* (New York: Free Press, 1962), p. 246. See also Edward C. Banfield, *The Unheavenly City* (Boston: Little, Brown, 1968), ch. 3.

9. Karl Marx, *Capital* (New York: Modern Library, 1936), p. 709.

10. See Joseph A. Schlesinger, *Ambition and Politics* (Chicago: Rand McNally, 1968).

11. David T. Stanley, Dean E. Mann, and Jameson W. Doig, *Men Who Govern* (Washington, D.C.: Brookings, 1966).

12. John Schmidhauser, "The Justices of the Supreme Court: A Collective Portrait," *Midwest Journal of Political Science,* 3, 1959.

13. C. Wright Mills, *The Power Elite* (New York: Oxford University Press, 1956).

14. C. Wright Mills, "The Structure of Power in American Society," in Irving L. Horowitz, ed., *Power, Politics and People: The Collected Writings of C. Wright Mills* (New York: Oxford University Press, 1963), p. 24.

15. Mills, *The Power Elite,* pp. 8-9.

16. Ibid., p. 10.

Discussion questions

1. Discuss the social stratification system. Include in your discussion a description of the bases used for stratification, as well as the characteristics associated with the stratification system.

2. Describe the functional and conflict theories of social class.

3. If you were studying social class, what methods might you use to identify and measure social stratification? If in the course of your study you were to ask average Americans how they see themselves in the class system, what class would they choose, and why? How might the respondents' subjective evaluations differ from the results

you as a social scientist obtained? What are the objective criteria you would use to identify social class?

4. Discuss the functions of the ideology of a stratification system. Describe the American ideology and the attitudes of Americans toward that ideology.

5. Choose two of the American social classes and contrast them according to orientation toward life; individual self-confidence; child-rearing practices; sexual attitudes; women's roles; activities and interests; and political participation and party identification.

6. Contrast class consciousness with class awareness. Discuss the factors that appear to stabilize the existing class system in the United States and to reduce class conflict.

7. Discuss Karl Marx's views of economic roles and class consciousness in the struggle for power among social classes. What sort of society did Marx envision and what are the reasons for the failure of capitalist and communist societies to conform to his vision?

8. Political power in the United States is largely in the hands of individuals from upper social classes. Discuss the factors that account for this, what impact it might have on the "masses," and what factors may modify the impact. In your discussion distinguish between the "elitist" view of society and the "pluralist" view of society.

9. Define the *power elite* that was identified by C. Wright Mills and describe the factors that contribute to the emergence of such an elite. What is its actual base of power and on what factors does its unity rest? How does Mills's interpretation of power in the United States conflict with the "pluralist" interpretation?

CHAPTER 5

■ POWER & THE ECONOMIC ORDER

In 1985 there were more than 125 million automobiles registered in the United States, or one for every two people. We produced about 7 million new cars and imported another 3 million foreign cars. The average full-size new car cost $11,554 and the average compact $8,799. But the average car in use was seven years old. How were the decisions about production, distribution, pricing, and purchasing of cars made?

In this chapter we will examine the content of economic decisions and observe how individuals, government, and corporations make them. After you have read it, you should be able to

- describe the operation of the market in a private enterprise economy,
- define the various cycles that an economy experiences,
- discuss the reasons why government intervenes in the economy, thus creating a "mixed" economic system, and some of the means by which government does this,
- define "supply-side" economics and discuss its policy implications,
- discuss the growth of multinational corporations,
- describe how the wealth of the United States is measured and discuss some of the shortcomings of this system of measurement,
- discuss personal wealth in the United States and the increasing concentration of corporate power,
- discuss the causes of inflation and various proposals to deal with it.

Power and economic organization

A great deal of power in the United States is centered in large economic organizations—corporations, banks, utilities, investment firms,

economic resources and power

■ 91

and government agencies charged with the responsibility of overseeing the economy. Not all power, it is true, is anchored in or exercised through these institutions; power is also embodied in class, cultural, political, and ideological institutions and processes, as discussed elsewhere in this volume. *But control of economic resources provides a continuous and important base of power in any society.*

Economics is the study of the production and distribution of scarce goods and services. Economics decides the following questions:

economics
the study of the production and distribution of scarce resources

1. *What should be produced?* What goods and services should be produced and in what quantities? Should we produce more automobiles or more trains and subways, more food and fertilizer or more clean air and water, more B-1 bombers or higher social security benefits? Should we produce more for immediate consumption, or should we save and invest more now in order to be able to enjoy even more later? Every economic system must answer questions like these.

economic decisions
*what to produce
how to produce it
for whom it will be
    produced*

2. *How will goods and services be produced?* The decision to produce particular goods and services does not accomplish the task. Resources must be organized and allocated and people must be motivated to work. Various combinations of resources—land, labor, capital (factories, machinery, supplies), and technology—might be used to produce a particular item. Wheat might be grown with less land and labor if more fertilizer and machinery and better technology are employed. And all these resources must be organized for production, either by providing economic incentives (wages and profits) or by threats of force.

3. *For whom will goods and services be produced?* Who will consume these products and services? Economists refer to this question as the question of *distribution*. Should people be paid according to their skills, or knowledge, or contribution to the production of goods and services? Or should everyone be paid equally regardless of their skills, knowledge, or contribution to production? Should people be allowed to bid for goods and services, with the most going to the highest bidders? Or should goods and services be distributed by government, with the most going to those who are best able to influence government decisions?

**economic decisions
can be made**
*individually, through a
market system, or collectively, through
government*

In general, there are two ways of making these economic decisions: (1) individually, through the market system, or (2) collectively, through governments.

The *market* system allows individuals and firms to make their own decisions about who gets what and how. It works through unregulated prices and decentralized decisions of many separate individuals and businesses.

Governments also decide who gets what and how by *collective decision making.* In democracies, collective decisions are influenced by individual voters, interest groups, and parties; in nondemocratic governments the decisions are influenced primarily by ideology and the interests of government leaders themselves.

In most economies, including that of the United States, economic decisions are made by *both* the market system and the government.

The market system, hard-boiled and impersonal

The *economic system* consists of the *institutions and processes by which a society produces and distributes scarce resources.* There is not enough of everything for all of us to have all we want. If nature provided everything that everyone wanted without work, there would be no need for an economic system. But resources are "scarce," and some scheme must be created to decide who gets what. Scarcity, together with the problem of choice that it raises, is the fundamental question of economics.

The American economic system is a capitalist, free enterprise system. It is largely "unplanned"; no government bureau tells all 115 million workers in the United States where to work, what to do, or how to do it. On the whole, the *private enterprise economy* organizes itself, with a minimum of central planning or direction. The American system relies chiefly on private individuals in search of wages and profits in order to get the job done. No government agency directs that shirts be produced: if people want shirts, then there is profit to be made in producing them, and business people who recognize the potential profit will begin turning them out. No government agency directs how many shirts shall be produced: as shirt output increases, a point is reached at which there are so many shirts that the price that people are willing to pay falls below the cost of producing them, and business people then begin curtailing their production of shirts. This same production-in-search-of-profits goes on for thousands of other products simultaneously.

A private enterprise economy decides what is to be produced, how it is to be produced, and how it is to be distributed, all in a fashion that is for the most part automatic and impersonal. Everyone, by following self-interest, decides who gets what. The absence of planning and control does not mean chaos. Rather, it means a complex system of production and distribution that no single mind, and probably no government planning agency, could organize or control in all its infinite detail.

A *market* is any place or arrangement that enables people to exchange money for goods, services, or labor. The exchange rate is called the *price*. Under the private enterprise system, the *market determines what is to be produced, how much it will cost, and who will be able to buy it.* Consumers decide what shall be produced by expressing their preferences in terms of the amount of money they spend on various goods and services (*consumer demand*). When consumers *are willing and able to pay* for something, they will bid up the *price* of that item. The price is an

economic system
institutions and processes by which society produces and distributes scarce resources

private enterprise economy
private individuals in search of wages and profit, acting on their own, without government direction

the market
arrangement that enables people to exchange goods, services, and labor

consumer demand
preferences for goods and services, expressed by willingness to pay

indication of how much of the item consumers want produced. Businesses are out to make *profits*. Profits motivate producers to satisfy consumer demands. Profits drive the free enterprise system. Profits occur when selling prices are higher than the costs of production. Business people move into industries in which consumers bid prices up and the business people can bring costs down. Where consumer demand bids prices up, business people can afford to pay higher wages; and workers tend to move toward those industries with higher pay and better working conditions. Thus consumer demand shifts both business and labor into industries in which prices are high. Business people play a key role in a private enterprise system because they channel production toward industries having the strongest consumer demand and organize productive activity in the most efficient (lowest-cost) way possible. Profits are the mainspring of the market system. In seeking profits, business people perform a vital economic function.

Who gets the goods that are produced? The price system allocates them to those who have both the *willingness to pay* and the *ability to pay*. The willingness to pay determines the desirability of producing a certain item. No government agency determines whether we "need" goods and services; the market reveals whether individuals are willing to pay for them. Consumers, however, must also have the ability to pay: they must earn incomes by working to produce goods and services that consumers want. The *labor market* largely determines where people will work and how much they will be paid. The income received for their labor depends primarily on their worth to the businesses that employ them. They are worth more when they contribute more to production and profit.

Where production and profits are low, wages will be low and individuals will be frequently unemployed.

The market is hard-boiled and impersonal. If a business produces too much of a particular item—more than consumers are willing to buy at a particular price—the price will have to be lowered or production (supply) will have to be cut back. Competition among businesses also checks prices, for a business that sets a price higher than that set by competitors will lose sales. Thus *consumer demand, product supply, and competition determine prices.* In the absence of interfering factors, the price depends upon a relationship of supply and demand at any given time. If demand increases, prices tend to rise; if demand decreases, prices tend to fall. If supply increases, prices tend to fall; if supply decreases, prices tend to rise.

The market reconciles the interests of buyers and sellers, labor and business, in the process of getting people to agree on prices. The market in a free enterprise system undertakes this reconciliation automatically, without assistance from outside individuals or forces. The ideal conditions for a market operation are these:

1. The existence of a perfect competition, in which the market has so many buyers and sellers that no single trader has any control over the price of the good or service being exchanged, and the price is made by the market through the impersonal forces of supply and demand. (If one or a few sellers have control over supply, the market is said to be *monopolistic;* if one or a few buyers have control over demand, the market is said to be *monopsonistic.*)

prices
allocate goods and services by willingness and ability to pay
determined by consumer demand, product supply, and competition

ideal conditions for a market operation
competition among many buyers and sellers
ability of buyer to exclude others from benefits of purchase
mobility of resources and labor

2. The ability of a buyer of the good to exclude others from the satisfactions that it provides so that no one can enjoy the benefits of someone else's purchase. (When people benefit from the purchases of others, there are said to be *spillover effects,* as, for example, in the case of national defense products, which cannot be sold on the open market.)

3. The complete mobility of resources and labor so that they can move in response to changes in prices. (In a completely mobile economy, each individual [or business] is prepared to alter the pattern of spending and working in response to changes in prices of goods and labor.)

In other words, in an ideal market there is a great deal of competition, and prices are determined solely by supply and demand. All must pay for the goods and benefits they receive, and resources and labor shift easily in response to changes in prices and wages.

Supply, demand, and the market price

Let us try to illustrate what happens in a true market economy, where price is governed by supply and demand.

an example of market pricing

Along with many other commodities, millions of bushels of wheat are bought and sold every day at the Chicago Board of Trade. Let us suppose that the first buyer of the day offers $2 per bushel for wheat (see Table 5-1). Let us also suppose that there are buyers for 20 million bushels of wheat at this low price (demand). However, few owners are willing to sell at this price, and therefore there are only 10 million bushels of wheat offered at $2 per bushel (supply). The result is an imbalance in supply and demand—a 10 million bushel shortfall in supply at the low $2 price. Those still wishing to buy must therefore raise their price to attract more wheat to the market. Let us suppose that the price then shoots up to $4 per bushel. At this price there are fewer buyers (let us say only an 8 million bushel demand) and many more sellers (let us say an 18 million bushel supply). The result is an excess supply of 10 million bushels at the high price; this excess will eventually push prices back down.

TABLE 5-1 An example of supply and demand

Supply: bushels of wheat offered for sale (millions)	*Price*	*Demand: bushels of wheat demanded (millions)*
18	$4.00	8
16	3.50	11
14	3.00	14
12	2.50	17
10	2.00	20

Thus, the price tends to stabilize at a point low enough to attract sufficient demand for wheat but high enough to attract an equivalent supply of wheat. In our example (Table 5-1) this price is $3 per bushel, where 14 million bushels are demanded and 14 million bushels are offered.

Figure 5-1 shows our example of supply and demand in graphic form. The supply curve is low at a low price, but increases as the price increases. Demand is high at a low price, but it declines as the price increases. The two lines for supply and demand intersect at a price where the amount demanded just matches the amount supplied. This will tend to be the market price. In our example, it is set at $3 per bushel. Any other price will produce either an excess supply (at a higher price) or an excess demand (at a lower price).

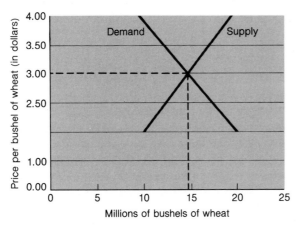

FIGURE 5-1   An example of supply and demand

Government and the economy

The free enterprise system that we have just described is subject to major modifications by the activities of government. In fact, government is now so involved in the economy that we might call the American economic system a *mixed* economy rather than a *private enterprise* economy. Government intervenes in the free market for many reasons:

1. to assure competition among businesses by breaking up monopolies and prohibiting unfair competitive practices;
2. to set minimum standards for wages and working conditions;
3. to regulate industries (like communications, broadcasting, and transportation) in which there is a strong public interest and in which unbridled competition may hurt more than it helps;
4. to protect the consumer from phony goods and services and false or misleading advertising;

*reasons for govern-
ment intervention*
assure fair competition
set minimum wages
regulate public industries
protect consumers
provide public services
*care for persons not in
    the marketplace*
stabilize the market

■ Adam Smith: Laissez-faire economics   ■

In the same year the Declaration of Independence was signed, Adam Smith, a Scots professor of philosophy, published his *Wealth of Nations* and thereby secured recognition as the founder of free enterprise economics. Today the economic model set forth by Adam Smith is frequently referred to as *classical economics* or *laissez-faire economics* (from the French phrase meaning "allow to do as one pleases"). Smith wrote *The Wealth of Nations* as an attack on the *mercantilism* of nations in his day—that is, the attempt of governments to intervene in the economy with special tariffs, regulations, subsidies, and exclusive charters to businesses, all designed to maximize the acquisition of gold and silver in government treasuries. Smith argued against mercantilism and in favor of *free competition* in the marketplace. He believed that a worldwide market, *unfettered by government restrictions or subsidies,* would result in lower prices and high standards of living for all. A free market would allow the businesses and nations most capable of producing particular goods cheaply and efficiently to do so. There would be greater specialization as each business and nation concentrated on what it did best. The outcome of the specialization and efficiency created by free competition would be a high standard of living for everyone. Thus, pursuit of private profit was actually in the public interest.

> Every individual endeavors to employ his capital so that its produce may be of greater value. He generally neither intends to promote the public interest, nor knows how much he is promoting it. He intends only his . . . own gain. He is in this led by an invisible hand to promote an end which was no part of his intention. By pursuing his own interest he frequently promotes that of society more effectively than if he really intended to promote it.[1]

Laissez-faire economics is based on the idea that people are rational, that they will pursue their own economic self-interest, that they are mobile and able to shift their resources and labor as the market demands. According to this economic system, there should be no artificial blocks to the most efficient use of people and materials. The market has a large number of competitors buying and selling products, services, and labor; and no one alone has control over supply or demand or price. Buyers buy from producers who make the best goods at the lowest price. Thus efficiency is rewarded and inefficiency driven out of the economy. Guided by demand and high prices, producers again constantly shift to new lines of production. As competition increases supply and lowers prices, some producers shift to more lucrative lines. The market continuously corrects unproductive use of resources. The system is *self-adjusting* and *self-regulating.*

Smith objected to government interference in the natural operations of the marketplace. Government should do only two things: (1) create an environment for an orderly marketplace—that is, maintain law and order, protect private property, enforce contracts, and provide a monetary system; and (2) supply those services that the marketplace cannot provide, such as defense, public works, and care of widows, orphans, and other helpless people.

Laissez-faire economics has much in common with *traditional democracy.* It is important to realize that at the same time that Adam Smith was setting forth a model economic system that stressed individual rationality, freedom of choice, and limited government intervention, democrats in America were developing a model political system emphasizing individual responsibility, freedom of expression, rational voter choice, and limitations on governmental power over individual liberty. The free enterprise economic system *paralleled* the democratic political system. In politics, every man was to be free to speak out, to form a political party, and to vote as he pleased—to pursue his political interests as he thought best. In economic life every man was to be free to find work, start a business, and spend money as he pleased—to pursue his economic self-interest as he thought best. The ballot box in politics and the market in economics were the impartial arbiters of conflict in society. Government was to be restricted in both its power over individual liberty and its power over economic life.

Today many "classical" economists echo Adam Smith's ideas. Although it is now widely recognized that government must play an important role in stabilizing the economy (avoiding both inflation and depression), protecting consumers, regulating business and labor practices, and assisting individuals who cannot care for themselves, classical economists nonetheless argue that economic planning by government is incompatible with *personal freedom*. They contend that bureaucratic intervention in the economy not only is inefficient and wasteful but also gradually erodes individual freedom and initiative.

This fear is not unfounded; political scientist Roland Pennock warns of the political consequences of the government-controlled economy:

> The existing freedom to choose one's vocation, one's employer, and the way one would manage his savings or spend his income would give way in greater and lesser degree to regimentation in all these areas by governmental fiat. It might provide greater security or more equality, but it could hardly fail to reduce liberty.[2]

And conservative economist Friedrich Hayek writes:

> We have progressively abandoned the freedom in economic affairs without which personal and political freedom have never existed in the past. . . .
>
> What our planners demand is central direction of all economic activity according to a single plan, saying how the resources of the society should be "consciously directed" to serve particular ends in a definite way.[3]

Thus the appeal of laissez-faire economics is based not only upon the efficiency of the marketplace in channeling labor and resources into their most productive uses but also upon the personal freedom in economic affairs that this system guarantees.

■ John M. Keynes: The mixed economy ■

The Great Depression of the 1930s significantly altered American thinking about laissez-faire economics. It is difficult to realize today what a tremendous economic disaster befell the nation in those days. Following the stock market crash of October 1929 and in spite of President Herbert Hoover's assurances that prosperity lay "just around the corner," the American economy virtually collapsed. Businesses failed, factories shut down, new construction practically ceased, banks closed, and millions in savings were wiped out. One out of four American workers was unemployed, and one out of six was receiving welfare relief. Persons who had never before known unemployment lost their jobs, used up their savings or lost them when the banks folded, cashed in their life insurance, and gave up their homes or farms because they could not continue the mortgage payments. Economic catastrophe struck far into the ranks of the middle classes. Fear was widespread that violent revolution would soon sweep the country. Many lost faith in the free enterprise system and urged the abandonment of the market economy. The "solutions" of fascism in Italy and Germany and communism in the Soviet Union were looked to as alternatives to a "doomed" capitalist system.

Laissez-faire economics recognizes the possibilities of economic cycles. A *recession* occurs when consumer demand declines for any reason, and businesses cut back on production. Cutbacks involve laying off workers and postponing plans for capital investment in new plants or facilities. The resulting increase in unemployment means fewer dollars in the hands of consumers and thus a *further* cutback in consumer demands, leading to *further* cutbacks in production.

But classical economics believed that the system would eventually adjust itself, reverse its downward cycle, and resume a forward movement. The turnabout would happen largely because of the effect of lower prices. To stimulate demand for their products, businesses were expected to lower their prices. Workers would be willing to work for lower wages. Moreover, interest rates—the price charged for borrowing money—would decline, and businesses would be encouraged to borrow money again, to invest in new plants and facilities, and thereby to stimulate employment. As employment rose, consumer demand would increase, and the economy would revive. President Hoover, a believer in laissez-faire economics, waited three years for the economy to adjust itself according to the classical model. But the economy continued its downward spiral, and Hoover was overwhelmingly defeated in the 1932 presidential election by Franklin D. Roosevelt.

In 1936 John M. Keynes, a British economist, wrote a landmark book called *The General Theory of Employment, Interest and Money.* Keynes attacked the basic notion of classical economics—that the free enterprise system was a self-adapting mechanism that tended to produce full employment and maximum use of resources. He believed that not all savings went into investment. When there was little prospect of profit, savings were likely

to be hoarded and unused. This removal of money from the economy brought depression. Moreover, he argued, low interest rates would not necessarily stir businesses to reinvest; it was the expectation of *profit,* not the availability of money, that motivated investment. Keynes believed that as confidence in the future is diminished, investment will decline, regardless of interest rates.

In Keynes's view only *government* can reverse a downward economic cycle. Private businesses cannot be expected to invest when consumer demand is low and there is no prospect of profit. And consumers cannot be expected to increase their purchases when their incomes are falling. So the responsibility rests on the government to take *countercyclical* action to increase income and consumption.

Governments can act, first of all, by means of *fiscal policy*—that is, by making decisions regarding government expenditures, taxes, and debt. In recessions government can *increase its own expenditures or lower taxes or do both* in order to raise total demand and private income. Government purchases add directly to total demand and stimulate production and employment. Government payments to individuals in the form of social security, unemployment compensation, or welfare make more money available to individuals for consumption. Reducing taxes also makes more money available to individuals for purchasing. Of course, increasing expenditures or lowering taxes or both means an *increase in government debt,* but only in this fashion can government pump money into the economy.

At the same time, government can act in a countercyclical way by means of *monetary policy*—that is, by making decisions regarding the availability of money and credit and rates of interest. To encourage investment, government can expand the money supply by *lowering interest rates and increasing the amount of money available for circulation.* However, monetary policy may not have a really direct or immediate impact on the economy if businesses do not take advantage of the availability of cheaper money. Thus *Keynes relied more heavily on fiscal policy than monetary policy to bring about economic recovery during recessions.*

Keynes also argued that governments should pursue countercyclical fiscal and monetary policies to offset inflation as well as depression. *Inflation* means a general rise in the price level of goods and services. Inflation occurs when total demand exceeds or nears the productive capacity of the economy. An excess of demand over supply forces prices up.

Keynes believed that when inflation threatens, government should gear its *fiscal policy* toward *reducing its own expenditures or increasing taxes or both.* Reducing government purchases would reduce total demand and bring it back into equilibrium with supply. Raising taxes would reduce the money available for consumption and therefore also help bring demand back into equilibrium with supply. These fiscal policies (to be pursued during inflationary times) would enable the government to reduce its debt (which is incurred during depressions).

At the same time, governments would pursue *monetary policies* to fight inflation. Government could *reduce the total amount of money in circulation and increase interest rates.* These policies are fairly certain to reduce total demand. In fact, *monetary policy is more effective in fighting inflation than it is in fighting recession.*

Keynes was no revolutionary. On the contrary, he wished to preserve the private enterprise system by developing effective governmental measures to overcome disastrous economic cycles. In December 1933 he wrote an open letter to Roosevelt emphasizing the importance of saving the capitalist system:

> You have made yourself the trustee for those in every country who seek to mend the evils of our condition by reasoned experiment within the framework of the existing social system. If you fail, rational change will be gravely prejudiced throughout the world, leaving orthodoxy and revolution to fight it out.[4]

---

5. to provide a wide range of public services (defense, education, highways, police protection) that cannot be reasonably provided on a private-profit basis;
6. to provide support and care (welfare, social security, unemployment compensation, medicare, health care, and so forth) to individuals who cannot supply these things for themselves through the market system;
7. to ensure that the economic system functions properly and avoids depression, inflation, or unemployment.

marginal tax rates
tax rate applied to additional income

results of high marginal tax rates
less work
less investment risk
more unproductive "tax shelters"
a large "underground economy" hiding income

Inflation will be brought under control by producing more goods, not by limiting demand. Americans will be encouraged to save a greater proportion of their income, and businesses will be encouraged to build new plants and provide more jobs.

Central to supply-side economics is the idea of reducing *marginal* rates of taxation. (The *marginal* rate of taxation is the rate at which *additional* income is taxed.) Prior to the Reagan-supported Economic Recovery Tax Cut Act of 1981, the marginal rates of the federal personal income tax ranged from 14 to 70 percent. Persons with taxable incomes under $5,000 paid about 14 percent (or $140) in taxes on each $1,000 of income. But persons with over $100,000 in taxable income paid 70 percent (or $700) in taxes for each additional $1,000 of income.

Supply-side economists argue that these high marginal rates of taxation (especially the 50 to 70 percent brackets) reduce economic output and productivity. People will prefer leisure time over extra work if, for example, 50 percent of the additional money they make from the extra work is "snatched away" by income taxes. Individuals will not risk their money in new business investments if, for example, 70 percent of the income from the investment will be taken away by the income tax. High marginal tax rates also encourage people to seek out "tax shelters"— special provisions in the tax laws that reduce personal income taxes. Tax shelters direct money to special investments (municipal bonds, commercial property, movies, horse farms, and so on) that are not really important for the nation's economic health. In addition, a large "underground economy" flourishes when tax rates are high; in the "underground economy" people hide their real incomes and/or trade goods and services rather than conducting transactions out in the open where they will be subject to taxation.

Taxes discourage work, productivity, investment, and economic growth. If tax rates are reduced, the paradoxical result may be to *increase* government revenue because more people will work harder and start new businesses knowing they can keep a larger share of their earnings. Tax cuts will stimulate increased economic activity, and this increased activity will produce more government revenue even though tax rates are lower.

Economist Arthur Laffer developed the diagram shown in Figure 5-2. If the government imposed a zero tax rate, of course, the government would receive no revenue (point A). Initially government revenues rise with increases in the tax rate. However, when tax rates become too high (beyond point B), they discourage workers and businesses from producing and investing. When discouragement occurs, the economy declines, and government revenues fall. Indeed, if the government imposed a 100 percent tax rate (if the government confiscated everything anyone produced), then everyone would quit working and government revenues would fall to zero (point C).

According to the "Laffer curve," modest increases in tax rates will result in increased government revenues, up to an optimal point (point B), after which further tax increases discourage work and investment. Laffer does not claim to know exactly what the optimal rate of taxation should be. But Laffer (and the Reagan administration) clearly believe that the United States has been in the "prohibitive range" throughout the last decade.

the "Laffer curve"
high marginal tax rates actually reduce government revenue by discouraging production and investment

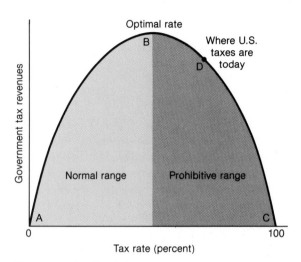

FIGURE 5-2 The Laffer curve

"Bracket creep" occurs when individuals receive higher wages due to inflation, but because of that inflation the higher wages do not add to their buying power. However, higher wages cause higher tax rates. In this way inflation gradually pushes all wage earners into higher tax brackets and increases everyone's tax burden. These tax increases occur "automatically," without a need for Congress to enact higher taxes. According to supply-side economists, bracket creep, by increasing tax burdens, further erodes incentives to work, save, invest, and produce.

bracket creep
individuals are forced by inflation to pay higher tax rates

The Economic Recovery Tax Cut Act of 1981, pushed through Congress by President Reagan, provided a 25 percent reduction in personal income taxes over a three-year period. Marginal tax rates were reduced to a range of 12 to 50 percent; this was only a minor reduction at the bottom end of the income brackets but a very significant reduction (from 70 to 50 percent) in the highest income brackets. In addition, the Act granted many new investment incentives for business. Finally, the Act "indexes" taxes against inflation in future years in order to prevent bracket creep. Tax brackets are automatically lowered as inflation increases.

BOX 5-1 "Reaganomics" in perspective

■ Accurate evaluation of supply-side economic policies—or any government policies, for that matter—is very difficult. Our problem is that the economy is constantly changing, independently of government policies. For example, as more women enter the labor force, the economy must create many new jobs just to absorb the larger percentage of the population who are seeking work. The unemployment rate may increase even though many more people are working, simply because jobs cannot be created as fast as new workers enter the job market.

Another problem: the economy often requires one or two years to respond to government policies. The first two years of the Reagan administration, 1981 to 1983, saw the deepest recession in the United States since the 1930s. Did this recession occur because of Reagan policies, or did it occur as a product of high inflation and high interest rates in the preceding Carter administration? Finally, government policies can have different effects, some good and some bad. Political opponents of the administration in power will emphasize the bad effects, while the administration itself emphasizes the good.

Let us try to compare the economy of 1980 with that of 1985 (see Table 5-2). On the positive side we should note that the annual *inflation rate* declined from 14.5 percent to 4.5 percent, a truly impressive performance. Unemployment remained stubbornly high, even though the economy absorbed about six million new workers during the five-year period. The rate of participation in the labor force (the percentage of the population who are working) has increased slightly. Real growth in the GNP (growth measured in constant dollars) has rebounded from the sluggishness of the late 1970s to about 4 percent per year, a very healthy growth rate if it can be sustained.

TABLE 5-2 A comparison of the 1980 and 1985 economies

	1980	*1985*
Inflation rate	14.5%	4.5%
Unemployment	7.4%	7.5%
Participation in labor force	63.7 million	64.0 million
Growth in real GNP	−0.3%	4.0%
Federal government increase in spending	17.4%	7.3%
Federal deficit	$59.6 billion	$183.7 billion
Poverty	13.0%	14.4%
Personal income after taxes in real dollars	$8,032	$8,820

The Reagan administration succeeded in cutting *the rate of growth* of government spending, even though government spending continued to increase during the Reagan years. Both domestic and defense spending under Reagan continued to rise, although defense spending increased faster than domestic spending. The result was that defense took a larger share of the federal budget (29%) in 1985 than in 1980 (24%).

The Reagan tax cuts in 1981 averaging 25 percent did *not* result in greatly increased revenues as predicted by the Laffer Curve. Instead the tax cuts slowed the rate of growth of government revenue. Domestic spending was not slowed sufficiently to offset those lost revenues, and defense spending was increased. Reagan had promised a balanced budget, but it was impossible to cut taxes, increase defense spending, and maintain Social Security and other popular domestic spending programs without increasing the federal deficit. Indeed, in recent years the federal government has run *the largest peacetime deficits in history.*

These deficits threaten the future of the economy. As the federal government borrows high amounts of capital to fund its debts, less capital is available to the private market for economic growth. Interest rates are kept high by the government's own demand for loans.

Real disposable personal income (income after taxes adjusted for inflation) rose for the average American by almost 10 percent. But many Americans were left out of this generally rosy picture. The poverty rate (the percentage of the people living below the government's official poverty line) rose from 13.0 to 15.2 percent in 1983 and then fell back to 14.4. The new poor were mostly children in female-headed families. The poverty rate among blacks rose from 32.5 percent to 35.7 percent in 1983. Whatever positive

effects "Reaganomics" had on the economy in general, these benefits were not widely shared among the poor.

The Reagan record follows:

- lower inflation
- unemployment unchanged
- more people working
- recession followed by growth
- government growth slowed
- very large government deficits
- poverty remains

SOURCES: John L. Palmer and Isabel V. Sawhill, eds., *The Reagan Record* (Washington,
D.C.: Urban Institute, 1984); and *Economic Report of the President, 1985, Statistical Abstract
of the United States, 1985, Budget of the United States Government, 1986* (Washington,
D.C.: U.S. Government Printing Office, 1985).

Measuring America's wealth: National income accounting

Underlying the power of nations is the strength of their economy—
their total productive capacity. The United States can produce nearly
$4 trillion worth of goods and services in a single year for its 235 million
people. This is more than $17,000 worth of output per person. To
understand America's vast wealth, we must learn how to measure it. We
need to know where the wealth comes from and where it goes. The
system of *national income accounts* provides these measures.

GNP (gross national product)
total value of nation's production of goods and services for a year

Let us begin with the gross national product. *The gross national
product (GNP) is the nation's total production of goods and services for a
single year valued in terms of market prices.* It is the sum of all the goods
and services that people have been willing to pay for, from wheat production to bake sales, from machine tools to maid service, from aircraft
manufacturing to bus service, from automobiles to chewing gum, from
wages and salaries to interest on bank deposits.

*The gross national product is also the total income received by all
sellers of goods and services.* It really does not matter whether we view
the GNP as the *value* of all goods and services *produced,* or the sum of
all *expenditures* on these goods and services, for they are the same thing.

computing the GNP

To compute the GNP, economists sum up all the expenditures on
goods and services, plus government purchases. Care is taken to count
only the final product sold to consumers, so that raw materials will not be
counted twice—that is, both in original sale to a manufacturer and in the
final price of the product. Business investment includes *only new investment goods* (buildings, machinery, and so on) and does not include financial transfers such as the purchase of stocks and bonds. Government
purchases for goods and services include the money spent on *goods*

(weapons, roads, buildings, parks, and so on), as well as the *wages* paid for the *services* of government employees. "Transfer payments" such as welfare payments, unemployment insurance, and social security payments are *not* part of the gross national product because they are not payments for currently produced goods or services. Thus the gross national product becomes a measure of the nation's production of goods and services. It can be thought of as the total national pie for a given year, and it is the most widely used measure of total national production.

National income accounting helps us to understand the circular flow that makes up both the *income* and *expenditure* sides of the gross national product. Figure 5-3 shows the circular flow of goods and services. Note that the GNP is composed of consumer outlays, plus business investment, plus government purchases of goods and services. Table 5-3 shows national income accounting figures for 1983. The *net national product* is the sum of all goods and services produced (GNP) less "depreciation"—that is, the wearing out of producer goods that must be replaced to maintain the nation's productive capacities. The *national income* is the total of all income earned by the basic factors of production—land, labor, capital, and management—less indirect business taxes. The national income is always less than the net national product

GNP − depreciation = net national product

net national product − indirect business taxes = national income

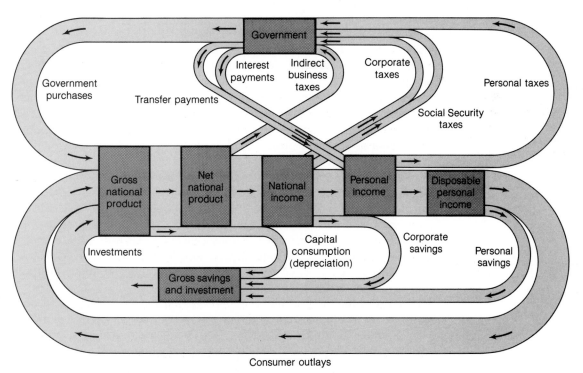

FIGURE 5-3 Circular flow of goods and services

**TABLE 5-3   National income accounting
and the GNP, 1983**

	Billions
Gross national product	$3,305
Less capital consumption (depreciation of capital goods that must be replaced)	−377
Net national product	$2,928
Less indirect business taxes (sales, excise, property taxes that must be paid to government)	−280
National income	$2,648
Less corporate profit taxes	−225
Net interest	−257
Social security taxes	−273
Plus government transfer payments (social security, welfare)	389
Personal interest income	376
Dividends	70
Business transfer payments	16
Personal income	$2,744
Less personal taxes	−404
Disposable personal income	$2,340
Personal savings	−118
Consumer outlays	$2,222

SOURCE: *Statistical Abstract of the United States 1985*, p. 433.

because the factors of production do not actually receive the full value of their output; businesses must pay many indirect taxes to government, which cut down on the income left to pay for the factors of production. *Personal income* is the total received by all individuals in the country— what people actually have to spend or to save to pay their taxes. Personal income includes government transfer payments to individuals— mainly social security and welfare payments. Personal income is what remains of national income after corporations have paid their income taxes, made their social security contributions, and decided upon their corporate savings—that is, how much they want to plow back into the business rather than pay out to stockholders. *Disposable personal income* is what people have left after they pay their taxes. Disposable personal income goes either to *personal savings* or to *consumer outlays*.

Since prices have increased over time through inflation, to get a meaningful measure of actual growth and output we must view the gross national product in *constant* dollars. Doubling the GNP merely by doubling prices signifies no real gain in production, so in order to separate actual increases in the GNP from mere "dollar" increases we must adjust for changes in the value of the dollar over the years. Economists account for changes in the value of a dollar by establishing the value of a dollar in a particular time base (for example, 1972) and then using "constant"

personal income − personal taxes = disposable personal income

disposable personal income − personal savings = consumer outlays

actual and "dollar" increases

dollars to measure the value of goods over time. Figure 5-4 shows that the GNP has grown both in "current" dollars *and* in "constant" dollars. Thus, America's economic growth is not just a product of inflation. Between 1970 and 1985 the gross national product in current dollars rose from $1 billion to $3.9 trillion. Even with inflation taken into account, the growth is still real—in "constant" dollars, from about $1.1 trillion to $1.7 trillion. Real GNP has grown about 4.6 percent on the average each year since 1970.

The gross national product and the quality of life

Although the gross national product is our best measure of economic well-being, it does not necessarily measure the quality of life in American society. First of all, it measures the size of the pie and not how the pie is cut up. Extremes of wealth and poverty can exist in the nation at any level of GNP. We will return to a discussion of the distribution of wealth, but for the moment it is important to realize that the GNP is *not* necessarily a measure of the extent of *poverty*.

weaknesses of the GNP

The GNP does not identify *what goods and services get produced*. The GNP includes expenditures for tobacco as well as for medical care. Not all these expenditures contribute equally to improving the quality of life.

Some expenditures that are reflected in the GNP represent *costs of life* in a modern industrial society, rather than *benefits*. For example, we must build elaborate subways and mass highway transport systems in our cities to move millions of people to and from work each day. The billions of dollars spent contribute to the annual GNP. But do they mean increased well-being for city dwellers and workers? Or do they simply

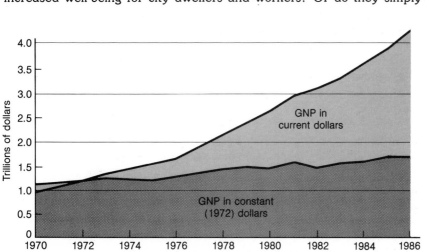

FIGURE 5-4 Gross national product (GNP): 1970 to 1985

mean that money is being spent on a painful necessity of life in crowded cities?

Moreover, the GNP does not give any negative weight to the *adverse side effects of economic development*. For example, until recently producers could pollute the air and water freely, and the cost of their products did not reflect the costs of pollution. Increasingly, efforts to control pollution will add to the cost of goods. But to the extent that the cost of goods does not include the damage done to the environment in the process of production, the GNP is misleading.

Nor does the GNP include the *costs of goods and services that are not reflected in money transactions*. The services of women who work in their own home and care for their own children are not included in the GNP; yet if women hire housekeepers and child-care personnel, their wages become part of the GNP.

The GNP places no value on *leisure*. Over the past fifty years, the average work week has been cut from six long days (over sixty hours) to five short days (less than forty hours), and vacations have greatly lengthened. In consequence, the quality of life has certainly improved. Yet the GNP does not reflect this increase in leisure. The fact that the GNP has continued to rise *despite* the growth in leisure is further evidence of the success of our system in producing goods and services. Thus, national income accounting focuses largely on the quantity of production rather than on the quality of life.

Public sector economics

Governments in the United States—the federal government, together with 50 state governments, and eighty thousand local governments—account for about 35 percent of the gross national product. The goods and services produced by these governments include social security and welfare, health and hospitals, education, highways, police and fire protection, and national defense (see Figure 5-5).

Government employment—federal, state, and local—comprises more than 15 percent of the total civilian labor force (see Figure 5-6). About one out of every six workers is employed by government.

Obviously government plays a very important role in our economy. Nonetheless, the United States remains primarily a private free enterprise economy. In Great Britain and France the governmental proportion of the GNP is 40 to 45 percent; in Sweden and Israel it is 55 to 60 percent; and in socialist bloc nations, Cuba and the Soviet Union, the governmental percentage of the GNP is 85 to 90 percent.

The federal government itself accounts for nearly two-thirds of all government spending in the United States. Washington's *trillion*-dollar budgets of recent years have funded national defense (29%), Social Security and Medicare (28%), welfare (12%), and interest on the national debt (15%).

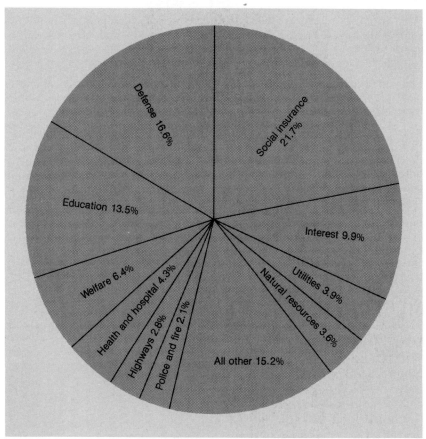

FIGURE 5-5 Total government spending—federal, state, and local—by function

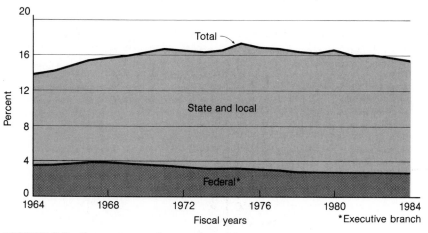

FIGURE 5-6 Government civilian employment as a percentage of total civilian employment (SOURCE: U.S. Bureau of the Census, *Statistical Abstract of the United States, 1985*. Washington, D.C.: U.S. Government Printing Office.)

Federal spending far outstrips federal taxing each year. The federal government must borrow new money each year to make up the difference. This borrowing expands the national debt and forces the federal government to pay more money in interest to lenders (see Figure 5-7). The lenders include banks, insurance companies, trust funds, and private individuals—anyone who buys government bonds.

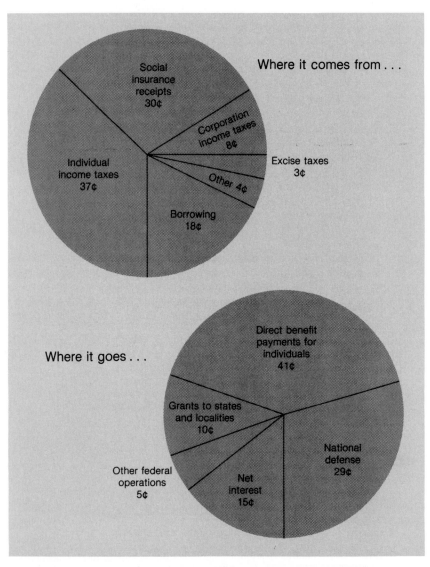

FIGURE 5-7 The federal budget dollar (SOURCE: *Budget of the United States Government, 1986.*)

Taxes, loopholes, and reforms

Federal, state, and local government revenues now amount to about one-third of the gross national product. Americans may consider their tax burden a heavy one, but taxes range between 35 and 51 percent of the GNP in Western European nations.

The federal government relies primarily on the individual income tax and the social security payroll tax for its income. State governments rely primarily on sales taxes, although 45 states also tax personal income. Local governments rely primarily on property taxes.

BOX 5-2   What Americans think about taxes

■ It comes as no surprise that most Americans believe the federal tax system is unfair. Interestingly, this evaluation does *not* differ much by income class; people at all income levels believe federal taxes are unfair. Respondents to a national poll showed high rates of concurrence with the following statements.

	Percent agreeing
The federal tax system is unfair.	59%
The present income tax system benefits the rich and is unfair to the ordinary working man or woman.	75%
Corporations are undertaxed.	52%
The rich tend to get out of paying taxes by using accountants and lawyers.	92%
Cheating on taxes is becoming more common these days.	54%

Despite these generally negative views of the federal tax system, Americans consider most of the major personal deductions to be a "perfectly reasonable deduction" and not a tax loophole.

	Percent saying "perfectly reasonable"
Property taxes paid by homeowners	93%
Interest on home mortgages	92%
State and local income taxes	88%
Interest paid on loans	87%
Child care for working parents	84%
Contributions to charity	71%
Social security income as nontaxable	92%
Municipal bond income as nontaxable	53%

Obviously, the popularity of these deductions and exemptions makes it difficult for the president and Congress to fashion true tax reform.

Public opinion generally supports a shift from individual income taxes to corporate taxes and "sin" taxes on liquor and cigarettes. Other types of federal revenue raising are generally unpopular, even "to reduce the deficit."

	Percent agreeing that the step should be considered very seriously to reduce the deficit
An increase in corporate income taxes	78%
Raising taxes on liquor and cigarettes	76%
A national lottery	66%
Raising user taxes—gasoline taxes for drivers, airport taxes for passengers, etc.	38%
A value-added or national sales tax	34%
An increase in personal income taxes	24%

SOURCE: Opinion research data from *Public Opinion*, February/March 1985; used with permission of the American Enterprise Institute. (Several categories of the original data were omitted from this box: "State and local sales tax," "Gasoline tax," "Fees for having income tax done by someone else," and "Capital gains." Also, under the category of "Municipal bond income as nontaxable," 17% responded "Don't know.")

The federal income tax was adopted in 1913 following the passage of the 16th Amendment to the U.S. Constitution authorizing taxes on income. For many years the income tax was very modest and applied only to very high incomes. But during World War II, rates were increased dramatically, and a "withholding" system was begun that automatically deducts federal income taxes from paychecks.

Marginal federal income tax rates are *progressive*. (*Marginal* is a term used by economists to mean *additional*.) A progressive income tax means that additional income of each taxpayer is taxed at higher rates. For example, in 1985 the first $3,400 of taxable income for all families was taxed at a rate of zero (see Table 5-4). The next $2100 they earn (from $3400 to $5500) is taxed at 11 percent; the next $2000 (from $5,500 to $7600) is taxed at 12 percent; and so on up the income scale to the maximum 50 percent rate on income over $162,400.

Note that the marginal tax rate is *not* the average or *effective* tax rate. The effective tax rate is proportion of total income paid in taxes. For example, a single person making $81,800 does not pay half of *all* of his income to the federal government, but only half of the *additional* income he earns over this top bracket amount. Since his earlier income was taxed at lower amounts, his tax liability is $28,455 or 35 percent of his total income.

Note also that federal tax rates apply to *taxable* income. Federal tax laws in 1985 allowed many reductions in adjusted gross income (the total income, less business expenses, that an individual actually receives

TABLE 5-4   Federal individual income tax rates, 1985

Single persons		Married persons filing joint returns	
Taxable income	Rate (percent)	Taxable income	Rate (percent)
0–2,300	0	0–3,400	0
2,300–3,400	11	3,400–5,500	11
3,400–4,400	12	5,500–7,600	12
4,400–6,500	14	7,600–11,900	14
6,500–8,500	15	11,900–16,000	16
8,500–10,800	16	16,000–20,200	18
10,800–12,900	18	20,200–24,600	22
12,900–15,000	20	24,600–29,900	25
15,000–18,200	23	29,900–35,200	28
18,200–23,500	26	35,200–45,800	33
23,500–28,800	30	45,800–60,000	38
28,800–34,100	34	60,000–85,600	42
34,100–41,500	38	85,600–109,400	45
41,500–55,300	42	109,400–162,400	49
55,300–81,800	48	162,400 and over	50
81,800 and over	50		

SOURCE: Internal Revenue Service

in a year) in the calculation of taxable income. For example, tax laws allowed deductions from gross personal income for such items as

charitable contributions
home mortgage and other interest paid
state and local taxes
medical and dental costs in excess of 5% of income
social security benefits
welfare and unemployment benefits
child care costs for workers
personal exemptions of $1,000 for each dependent; double exemptions for the aged and blind
interest received from state and local bonds
contributions to individual retirement accounts (IRAs)

In calculating income from business ventures, the tax laws allowed individuals to subtract such items as

10% "investment tax credit" deducted from the cost of new equipment
estimates of depreciation of buildings and equipment
business entertainment and travel
estimates of the depletion of oil and gas reserves
all expenses associated with the business itself

Income derived from profit on the sale of any asset that was originally purchased at a lower cost is called a "capital gain." Capital gains are commonly made on the sale of stocks, bonds, and real estate. Cap-

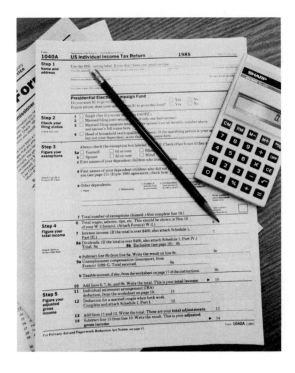

ital gains are given special treatment in tax laws: they are taxed at about half the rate of earned income.

All these exemptions, deductions, and special treatments add up to more than half of the nation's personal income![5] In other words, about 52 percent of total personal income in the nation escapes taxation. Most Americans, particularly those with lower incomes, do *not* itemize their deductions; they frequently do not or cannot take advantage of these many exemptions, deductions, and special treatments.

The problem in trying to close all the tax loopholes and achieve fairness and simplicity in the tax laws is that no one really agrees on what is a "loophole" and what is a socially useful tax provision. For example, the deduction for charitable contributions is often defended as important assistance for the nation's charities. The deduction for home mortgage interest is said to encourage home ownership. IRAs encourage people to save for their retirement. The taxation of capital gains at lower rates is believed to stimulate investment, as does the investment tax credit. The oil and gas depletion allowance is said to be a necessary incentive in the search for new sources of energy. And so on.

If total income of taxpayers was taxable at the nominal rates, the effective tax would begin at 11 percent and rise to 50 percent at the highest income levels. But no taxpayer pays the full nominal rate, because of the many deductions, exemptions, and special treatments in the tax laws. The effective tax rate is near zero through $5,000 and does not rise to 10% until $50,000. The maximum effective tax rate never rises above 26 percent.

Who pays the taxes? The American middle class pays the bulk of federal income taxes. About 100 million tax returns are received by the Internal Revenue Service (IRS) each year. About 35 percent of those returns are sent by people with adjusted gross incomes under $10,000; but these low-income taxpayers account for less than 3 percent of all income taxes paid. At the other end of the scale, about 8,000 people—less than 1 percent—make more than $1 million *per year;* they account for about 2.5 percent of all income taxes paid. The taxpayers with adjusted gross incomes of $20,000 to $75,000 a year pay 62 percent of all the dollars collected by the federal individual income tax.

For fifty years, politicians in Washington have promised to make tax laws simple and fair. Almost every year Congress has tinkered with the laws, but the results of these changes have only made matters worse. Or as President Reagan observed, "They made it more like Washington itself: complicated, unfair, cluttered with gobbledygook and loopholes designed for those with the power and influence to hire high-priced legal and tax advisers."[6]

These are among the many objections to the nation's tax laws:

- Tax returns are costly and complicated to prepare. A majority of Americans must hire professional tax preparers to assist them.
- Top marginal tax rates for individuals are too high. Rates up to 50 percent discourage work, savings, and risk, and slow economic growth.
- Tax laws are unfair in treating various sources of income differently. People with the same incomes should pay the same taxes.
- Tax laws encourage cheating and reduce trust in government. Too many exemptions, deductions, and special treatments are perceived as "loopholes" that allow the rich to escape fair taxation. Tax laws encourage the growth of an "underground economy," transactions that are never reported on tax forms.
- Tax laws encourage individuals and businesses to seek "tax shelters," directing investment away from its most efficient uses. When people make decisions about savings and investments on the basis of tax laws instead of most productive use, the whole economy suffers.

The concentration of corporate power

Control over the economic resources of the nation is becoming increasingly concentrated in the hands of a very few people, largely because of the *consolidation of economic enterprise* into a small number of giant corporations. The following statistics can only suggest the scale and concentration of modern corporate enterprise in the United States.

corporate power
concentration of assets in small number of large corporations

There are nearly 200,000 corporations in the United States, but the 100 largest corporations hold over half of the nation's industrial assets. Indeed, just ten industrial corporations hold more than 20 percent of the nation's industrial assets (see Box 5-3). Concentration in banking is even greater: there are nearly 15,000 banks in the United States, but the ten largest banks hold 36 percent of all banking assets. The rate of corporate mergers in recent years suggests that this concentration of economic resources is increasing.

The modern corporation is governed by its board of directors. The directors include the chairman of the board, the president, selected senior vice-presidents, and some "outside" members who are not manag-

governing the corporation
"inside" and "outside" directors

BOX 5-3 The concentration of economic power

The ten largest industrial corporations in the United States (ranked by assets)

	Assets ($ billion)	Cumulative percentage of all U.S. industrial assets*
1. Exxon	62.9	3.9
2. General Motors	45.7	6.7
3. IBM	37.2	9.0
4. Mobil	35.1	11.2
5. Texaco	27.2	12.9
6. Standard Oil (Indiana)	25.8	14.5
7. DuPont	24.4	16.0
8. Standard Oil (California)	24.0	17.5
9. Ford Motor	23.9	19.0
10. General Electric	23.3	20.4

The ten largest commercial banks in the United States (ranked by assets)

	Assets ($ billion)	Cumulative percentage of all U.S. industrial assets*
1. Citicorp (New York)	134.7	7.2
2. BankAmerica (San Francisco)	121.2	13.6
3. Chase Manhattan (New York)	81.9	18.0
4. Manufacturers Hanover (New York)	64.3	21.4
5. J.P. Morgan & Co. (New York)	56.0	24.5
6. Chemical New York & Co.	51.2	27.2
7. First Interstate Bancorp (Los Angeles)	44.4	29.6
8. Continental Illinois (Chicago)	42.1	31.8
9. Security Pacific (Los Angeles)	40.4	34.0
10. Bankers Trust of New York	40.0	36.1

*Cumulative percentage refers to the total percentage of the nation's assets in industry or banking at a specific ranking. Thus, ten banks (through Bankers Trust) hold 36.1 percent of all banking assets in the United States.
SOURCE: Fortune, June 11, 1984.

ers of the corporation. The "inside" directors, who are also full-time presidents or vice-presidents of the corporation, tend to dominate board proceedings because they know more about the day-to-day operations of the corporation than the outside directors. Outside directors may sit on the corporate board as representatives of families who still own large blocks of stock or of banks who have loaned money to the corporation. Occasionally outside directors are prominent citizens, women, members of minorities, or representatives of civic associations. Outside directors are usually chosen by inside directors. All directors are officially elected by the corporation's stockholders. However, the inside directors draw up the "management slate," which almost always wins, because top management (the presidents and vice-presidents) cast many "proxy" votes, which they solicit in advance from stockholders.

A. A. Berle, Jr., a corporate lawyer and director himself, referred to the corporate directors as "a self-perpetuating oligarchy."[7] Corporate power does *not* rest in the hands of masses of corporate employees or even in the hands of millions of middle- and upper-middle-class Americans who own corporate stock.

Corporate power is further concentrated by a system of *interlocking directorates,* in which a director of one corporation also sits on the boards of other corporations, and by a *corporate ownership* system in which control blocks of stock are owned by financial institutions rather than by private individuals. Interlocking directorates enable key corporate elites to wield influence over a large number of corporations. It is not uncommon for members of the top elite to hold six, eight, or ten directorships.

Berle has also suggested that *managers,* rather than major stockholders, have come to exercise dominant influence in American corporations:

> Management control is a phrase meaning merely that no large concentrated stockholding exists which maintains a close working relationship with the management or is capable of challenging it, so that the board of directors may regularly expect a majority, composed of small and scattered holdings, to follow their lead. Thus, they need not consult with anyone when making up their slate of directors, and may simply request their stockholders to sign and send in a ceremonial proxy. They select their own successors. . . . Nominal power still resides in the stockholders; actual power in the board of directors.[8]

Economist Gabriel Kolko summarizes the impact of the concentration of corporate power:

> The concentration of economic power in a very small elite is an indisputable fact. . . . A social theory assuming a democratized economic system— or even a trend in this direction—is quite obviously not in accord with social reality. Whether the men who control industry are socially responsive or trustees of the social welfare is quite another matter: it is one thing to speculate about their motivations, another to generalize about economic

interlocking directorates
a director of one corporation is also a director of other corporations

management control
stock ownership is scattered among many small investors and management controls the corporation itself

facts. And even if we assume that these men act benevolently toward their workers and the larger community, their actions still would not be the result of social control through a formal democratic structure and group participation, which are the essentials for democracy; they would be an arbitrary noblesse oblige by the economic elite. When discussing the existing corporate system, it would be more realistic to drop all references to democracy.[9]

The management technostructure

Today the requirements of technology and planning have greatly increased industry's need for specialized talent and skill in organization. Capital is something that a corporation can now supply to itself. Thus there is a shift in power in the American economy from capital to organized intelligence, and we can reasonably expect that this shift will be reflected in the deployment of power in society at large.

decline of the individual investor

Individual capitalists are no longer essential to the accumulation of capital for investment. Approximately three-fifths of industrial capital now come from retained earnings of corporations rather than from the investments of individual capitalists. Another one-fifth of industrial capital is borrowed, chiefly from banks. Even though the remaining one-fifth of the capital funds of industry comes from "outside" investments, the bulk of these funds is from large insurance companies, mutual funds, and pension trusts rather than from individual investors. Thus *the individual capitalist investor is no longer in a position of dominance in American capital formation.*

nonaction by investors

American capital is administered and expended primarily by managers of large corporations and financial institutions. Stockholders are supposed to have ultimate power over management, but individual stockholders seldom have any control over the activities of the corporations they own. Usually "management slates" for the board of directors are selected by management and automatically approved by stockholders. Banks and financial institutions and pension trust or mutual fund managers occasionally get together to replace a management-selected board of directors. But, more often than not, banks and trust funds sell their stock in corporations whose management they distrust, rather than using the voting power of their stock to replace management. Generally, banks and trust funds vote their stock for the management slate. This *policy of nonaction* by investors means that the directors and managements of corporations become increasingly self-appointed and unchallengeable; and this policy freezes absolute power in the corporate managements.

profit motive

Of course, the *profit motive* is still important to the corporate managers, since profits are the basis of capital formation within the corporation. Increased capital at the disposal of corporate managers means increased power; losses mean a decrease in the capital available to the managers, a decrease in their power, and perhaps eventual extinction for the organization. There is also some evidence that management today has more concern for the interests of the public than did the individual industrial capitalists of a few decades ago. The management class is more sympathetic to the philosophy of the liberal establishment to which it belongs; it is concerned with the public interest and expresses a devotion to the *corporate conscience.* As Berle explains:

> This is the existence of a set of ideas, widely held by the community and often by the organization itself and the men who direct it, that certain uses of power are "wrong," that is, contrary to the established interest and value system of the community. Indulgence of these ideas as a limitation on economic power, and regard for them by the managers of great corporations, is sometimes called—and ridiculed as—the "corporate conscience." The ridicule is pragmatically unjustified. The first sanction enforcing limitations imposed by the public consensus is a lively appreciation of that consensus by corporate managements. This is the reality of the "corporate conscience."[10]

corporate conscience

Management fears loss of prestige and popular esteem. Although the public has no direct economic control over management, and government control is more symbolic than real, the deprivation of prestige is one of the oldest methods by which any society enforces its values upon individuals and groups. Moreover, most of the values of the prevailing liberal consensus have been internalized by corporate managers themselves; that is, they have come to believe in a public-regarding philosophy.

▪ The politics and economics of tax reform ▪

Tax reform as a general theme is politically popular. Most Americans believe federal tax laws are complicated and unfair (see Box 5-2). But most Americans want to keep their own favorite deductions, and a host of interest groups want to keep special provisions in the tax laws that benefit their own members. These interest groups, representing manufacturers, oil and gas companies, farmers, accountants, real estate developers, bankers, charities and foundations, and even state and local government officials, all combine to place in Washington major obstacles to comprehensive tax reform.

In 1985, President Reagan launched a campaign for the most sweeping tax reform in many years:

For the sake of fairness, simplicity, and growth, we must radically change the structure of a tax system that still treats our earnings as the personal property of the Internal Revenue Service, radically change a system that still treats similar incomes much differently. And yes, radically change a system that still causes some to invest their money, not to make a better mousetrap, but simply to avoid a tax trap.[11]

The major features of the Reagan tax reform package were

- Reducing marginal tax rates to three brackets: 15, 25, and 35 percent (from fourteen brackets, 11 to 50 percent).
- Indexing these bracket amounts to protect taxpayers from inflation.

- Increasing the personal exemption to $2000 (from $1000) and indexing it in later years for inflation.
- Raising the zero bracket amount so that most families of four with income under $12,000 would pay no federal income tax.
- Eliminating interest deductions except for home mortgage interest plus $5,000 additional interest payments.
- Eliminating deductions for state and local taxes paid.
- Ending investment tax credits for business.
- Tightening rules for estimating depreciation of buildings and machinery.
- Reducing the number and size of many business deductions, including entertainment.
- Retaining deductions for charitable contributions, as well as medical expenses exceeding 5% of income, and retaining special lower rates for capital gains.

The Reagan plan was supposed to be "revenue neutral"; that is, overall federal tax revenues would not be increased or reduced by the changes. However, the plan would shift part of the federal tax burden away from individuals and onto corporations. Despite a reduction in the maximum corporate tax rate from 46 to 33 percent, business was expected to pay more taxes because of the elimination of investment tax credits, liberal depreciation rules, and restrictions on business deductions.

Leading Democrats in the Congress joined in the fight for tax reform. Representative Dan Rostenkowski of Chicago, Chairman of the House Ways and Means Committee, urged support for the president's program:

> We gave oil companies breaks to fuel our industry. We gave real estate incentives to build more housing. We sharpened our technology with research and development credits. We gave tax breaks to encourage people to save. We pile one tax benefit on top of another—each one backed with good intention.
>
> Unfortunately it didn't take too long before those with the best accountants and lawyers figured out how to beat the system . . . and the cost of government was shifted to families like those in my neighborhood who don't have the guile to play the game of hide and seek with the IRS. . . .
>
> In the end tax reform comes down to a struggle between the narrow interests of the few—and the broad interests of working American families.[12]

Despite tax-reform pronouncements made by the president and congressional leaders, special-interest groups clearly dominate the writing of tax legislation. When the president's bill emerged from the House Ways and Means Committee, most of the deductions, exemptions, and special treatments had been put back into the tax bill as a result of heavy lobbying pressure. For example, consider the fate of the modest reform proposal to limit deductions of *more than* $50 for each "business lunch": the restaurant industry complained that it would hurt business and the Committee voted to retain unlimited business lunch deductions. When the Committee considered eliminating "entertainment" deductions from business expense accounts, the owners of professional sports teams in the NFL, NBA, and NHA complained that this reform would hurt their block-ticket sales and the deduction was retained. More important, tax "breaks" were retained for the oil and gas industry, the real estate industry, and high-income taxpayers in high-tax states who deduct their state and local taxes from their federal taxable income.

True tax reform is economically desirable but politically difficult.

Notes

1. Adam Smith, *The Wealth of Nations* (New York: Modern Library), p. 423.
2. J. Roland Pennock, *Liberal Democracy: Its Merits and Prospects* (New York: Holt, 1950), p. 333.
3. Friedrich Hayek, *The Road to Serfdom* (Chicago: Phoenix Books, 1957), p. 35.
4. Richard Hofstadter, *American Political Tradition* (New York: Knopf, 1948), p. 332.
5. Joseph A. Pechman, *Federal Tax Policy* (4th ed.) (Washington, D.C.: The Brookings Institution, 1983).
6. Text of Presidential Address on Tax Reform, May 28, 1985. Congressional Quarterly, *Weekly Report,* June 1, 1985, p. 1074.
7. A. A. Berle, Jr., *Economic Power and the Free Society* (New York: Fund for the Republic, 1958), p. 14.
8. A. A. Berle, Jr., *Power without Property* (New York: Harcourt Brace Jovanovich, 1959), p. 73. See also Ferdinand Lundberg, *The Rich and the Super Rich* (New York: Lyle Stuart, 1968).
9. Gabriel Kolko, *Wealth and Power in America* (New York: Praeger, 1962), pp. 68–69.
10. Berle, *Power without Property,* pp. 90–91.
11. Text of Presidential Address on Tax Reform, p. 1074.
12. Text of address by U.S. Representative Dan Rostenkowski, May 28, 1985. Congressional Quarterly, *Weekly Report,* June 1, 1985, p. 1077.

Discussion questions

1. Identify the components of an economic system. Discuss how the market in a private enterprise economy determines what is to be produced, how much it will cost, and who will be able to buy it. Comment on the roles that the following factors play in a market operation: consumer demands, profits, prices, willingness to pay and ability to pay, labor market, competition, product supply.
2. Describe the ideal conditions for a market operation in a free enterprise system. What are the reasons for government interference in such a system?
3. Discuss the similarities between laissez-faire (classical) economics and a traditional democratic political system. Describe the conflict between laissez-faire economics and Keynesian economics over the self-adaptability of the free enterprise system.
4. Describe the kinds of fiscal and monetary policies that a Keynesian economist would recommend during a recessionary period and an inflationary period. How do the automatic stabilizers work during each of these periods?

5. Discuss some of the problems that government has in using fiscal and monetary policies.

6. Define "supply-side" economics. What government policies are proposed by supply-side economists?

7. Describe some of the means by which government has attempted to regulate business.

8. Explain how economists compute the gross national product (GNP). Differentiate between actual increases in the GNP and "dollar" increases in GNP. Describe some of the weaknesses of the GNP measure and some of the alternative measures that social scientists have suggested. What are the difficulties with *these* measures?

9. Describe the trend of income concentration in the United States. Discuss some of the "loopholes" of the American taxation system, the reasons for the "loophole" provisions, and the overall effect of taxation on the distribution of income.

10. Discuss the reasons for the increasing concentration of corporate power in the United States. Describe the factors contributing to the absolute power of corporate management and the factors that work against such absolute power.

11. Describe the "multinationals." Are the multinationals primarily American corporations?

12. Describe some of the factors that contribute to inflation. Identify the various counterinflationary measures that might be employed and the problems that would be encountered in employing them. Which measures do you think might be most feasible?

CHAPTER 6

■ POWER & PERSONALITY

You are alone in a corridor of an airport in a foreign city. You are tired after an all-night plane trip and in a hurry to catch a connecting flight. You are suddenly stopped by a uniformed policeman and, without explanation, "frisked." How do you react? If you were not tired and in a hurry, would you have reacted any differently? Is there any similarity between the way you react here and the way you reacted when your fourth grade teacher accused you of passing notes? In other words, is this way of responding to this sort of authority characteristic of you? Is it part of your *personality?* If it is, how do you think you came to develop your particular way of responding?

An understanding of personality, of individual behavioral responses and their determinants, is essential to a full understanding of power in society. In this chapter we will explore the meaning of personality and various psychological theories regarding the determinants of personality. We will also see what various schools of psychology have to say about the relationship between personality and power. After you have read Chapter 6, you should be able to

- describe the "nature versus nurture" controversy in the shaping of personality,
- discuss how psychoanalytic (Freudian) theory views personality and its development and how it interprets individual responses to power and authority,
- discuss behavioral psychology's use of learning theory in its approach to the study of personality, and B. F. Skinner's ideas for the control of human behavior,
- describe humanistic psychology's view of the "self," Rollo May's concept of powerlessness, and Abraham Maslow's construction of a "hierarchy of needs,"

▪ discuss how power in the form of authority and legitimacy can command obedience, and the implications of such obedience.

Personality and individual responses to power

Individuals react toward power and authority in characteristic ways. In many different situations and over a relatively prolonged period of time, their responses to power and authority are fairly predictable. Some individuals regularly seek power and authority, while others avoid it. Some individuals are submissive to authority, whereas others are habitually rebellious. Some individuals try to conform to the expectations of other people, and others are guided by internalized standards. Some individuals feel powerless, helpless, and isolated; they believe they have little control over their own lives. Other individuals are self-assured and aggressive; they speak out at meetings, organize groups, and take over leadership positions. Some individuals are habitually suspicious of others, unwilling to compromise; they prefer simple, final, and forceful solutions to complex problems. Some individuals are assertive, self-confident, and strong-willed, while others are timid, submissive, and self-conscious. There are as many different ways of responding to power as there are types of personalities.

Personality is all the characteristic ways of behaving that an individual exhibits; it is the enduring and organized sets of responses that an individual habitually makes when subjected to particular stimuli. By *characteristic* and *habitual* we mean that individuals tend to respond in a similar fashion to many separate situations. For example, their attitudes toward authority in general may affect their response to any number of different leaders, supervisors, directors, or other authority figures, in different situations. By *enduring* we mean that these characteristic ways of behaving may operate over a long time, perhaps through youth, young adulthood, and maturity. Attitudes toward authority in the home may carry over to school, university, job, church, government, and so forth. By *organized* we mean that there are relationships between various elements of an individual's personality. A change in one element (let us say, a growing need for social approval) would bring about a change in another element (let us say, an increased willingness to conform to group norms). Thus, personality is not just a bundle of traits but an *integrated pattern of responses.*

personality
characteristic way of behaving; enduring and organized responses that individuals habitually make to particular stimuli

Nature versus nurture

Children often have the same personality characteristics as their parents. Is the similarity a result of what they learned in the home? Or do children inherit personality characteristics from their parents? Actually, this is not an "either-or" question: psychologists generally acknowledge that personality is shaped by *both* heredity and environment. The

only question is what is the relative influence of these factors on personality.

The question of the relative influence of heredity versus environment on personality is part of a larger controversy about the influence of genetics on behavior. (We encountered this same controversy in our discussion of sociobiology in Chapter 3.) Some psychologists attribute greater influence to heredity in determining many personality characteristics by chemical and hormonal balances, the functioning of the senses (sight, hearing, smell, taste, touch), and one's physique. Other psychologists attribute greater influence to environment. The influence of the environment may begin even before birth, depending, for example, on whether the mother has a good diet, avoids smoking, alcohol, and drugs, is active or inactive, and is in good emotional health. Infants respond to their earliest environment and acquire characteristic ways of responding—that is, personality—very early in life.

It is very difficult to determine whether a specific personality characteristic shared by a parent and child has been genetically inherited or transferred through social interaction in the home. However, some studies of twins have suggested that heredity plays an important role in personality. Identical twins (who have the same genetic composition) score more alike on standard personality tests than fraternal twins (whose genetic composition is different).[1] Identical twins reared in separate families tend to share more personality and behavior characteristics than fraternal twins raised in the same household (see Box 6-1). According to one study, separated identical twins shared the same smoking and eating habits and scored similarly on tests of intelligence, extroversion, and neuroticism.[2]

BOX 6-1   Telltale behavior of twins

■ There is a mystique about twins, especially about identical twins reared apart. Stories of twins meeting for the first time capture the imagination. . . .

Over the years, scientists have reported provocative similarities in identical twins brought up separately. In 1962, for instance, the British investigator James Shields described the case of Herta and Berta, who were reared on different continents without even a first language in common. Nevertheless, both reported a tendency toward the dramatic, enjoyed artistic pursuits, and were prone to excitability and depression. They had been given the same nickname, "Pussy"—in different languages—because each purred like a cat when she was contented. . . .

Alfred and Harry . . . both nodded their heads in the same way as they spoke, and each closed his eyes as he turned his head. Jacqueline and Beryl had the same firm handshakes and made the same half-thoughtful, half-humorous face before answering a question. James and Robert both tapped on the table to make points; both flicked their fingers when unable to think of an answer immediately. Kathleen and Jenny laughed, giggled, and wept over the same things and reported that they often found themselves sitting in the same positions. Olwen and Gwaldys had the same wild look about them, their eyes darting from place to place. Their expressions and gestures mirrored each other, and their hands frequently went to their mouths in a tense finger-biting gesture. Both held their fingers stiffly for fingerprinting. One of the more interesting mannerisms was reported for Madeline and Lilian, whose husbands were impressed with the similarities in their movements; particularly, each twin had a habit of rubbing her nose and rocking when tired. They had developed the habit with no knowledge of each other. . . .

My speculation is that when families have identical twins, they treat them in subtly different ways probably without consciously intending to do so, in an attempt to differentiate them. For instance, if one twin is quicker to walk in infancy and is generally more active physically, parents may assign that twin the role of "athlete," while the quiet child becomes the "intellectual." The twins themselves, as we know from observation and from their own reports, seesaw between close identification with each other and exaggerated independence. If one does well in math, the other maps out territory elsewhere, simply out of a need for individuality. . . .

Overall, the findings underscore the significance of individuality. If twins reared in even moderately different homes remain markedly alike, what more do we need in order to acknowledge the genetic uniqueness of each individual? Similarly, if twins make themselves "artificially" different as a result of contact with each other, what more do we need to indicate the need of each individual to be an individual, separate unto himself and clearly bounded?

Excerpted from Susan Farber, "Telltale Behavior of Twins," *Psychology Today* (January 1981), pp. 59–80.

Reprinted with permission from *Psychology Today* Magazine. Copyright © 1981 American Psychological Association.

The mother is probably the single most important influence in anyone's early environment. We cannot deprive human babies of contact with their mothers for the sake of experimentation, but psychologists have placed newborn monkeys in isolation and observed their development. The results showed abnormal and irreversible behavior—extreme fear, anxiety, avoidance of all social contact with other monkeys, and emotional and intellectual retardation.[3]

Some psychologists argue that early mother-child relationships are instinctual. Newborn babies possess five instinctual responses—sucking, crying, smiling, clinging, and following. Together these responses bind the child to the mother and the mother to the child. Some psychologists contend that these inherited responses were acquired over millions of years by natural selection.[4] There is also evidence that clinging and following are inherited responses. Infant monkeys reared in isolation from their mothers were supplied with two surrogate mother figures. One was made of wire mesh, while the other was made of soft "cuddly" cloth. The baby monkeys chose to be near the soft surrogate, even when the wire mesh surrogate had a bottle attached to it for feeding.[5]

As we examine personality in this chapter, we should remember that both heredity and environment play important roles in shaping human beings. We will examine some theories of personality that emphasize instincts and heredity, others that emphasize early childhood experiences, and still others that emphasize continuing growth and development over a lifetime. There is no single "right" theory of personality.

Approaches to psychology and personality

Psychologists differ over the precise meaning of personality. Definitions tend to be linked to major theories or approaches to individual behavior and to the major approaches within psychology itself.[6]

clinical psychology
treatment of psychological disorder

Clinical psychology has to do with the treatment of psychological disorder. It is closely related to *psychiatry* in that both clinical psychologists and psychiatrists deal with the diagnosis and treatment of psychological disorders. The psychiatrist, however, is also a medical doctor. Clinicians deal with real persons with real psychological problems. They enter the patient's world and concern themselves with the subjective human experience, including wishes, fears, anxieties, ambitions. Clinical psychology stresses therapy, ranging from chemical therapy and shock treatment to various behavior therapies and insight therapies.

psychoanalysis
insight-oriented therapy

Psychoanalysis is a type of insight-oriented therapy that encourages patients to think about themselves—their problems, dreams, memories—so that they can gain insight into the causes of their own difficulties. Psychoanalysis enables patients to talk about early childhood experiences and thus to reveal unconscious motivations, emotions, and conflicts. The psychoanalytic approach to personality emphasizes *childhood experiences* and *unconscious feelings* as determining factors in personality development. Although the practice of psychoanalysis has always been the domain of the Freudian-trained psychiatrist, many clinical psychologists do use *psychoanalytic theory* in their approach to therapy.

experimental psychology
scientific study of behavioral responses to stimuli

Experimental psychology, another major division of psychology, is concerned with the scientific study of the behavioral responses of human beings and animals to various stimuli. Experimental psychology focuses on observed behavior—it is frequently termed *behavioral psychology*. Its setting is the academic laboratory, and rats and pigeons are frequent subjects of experimentation. There is an emphasis on careful observation, quantitative data, and statistical methods. Behavioral psychology relies heavily on *learning theory* (stimulus-response theory), which views all behavior as a product of learning or conditioning. Behavioral patterns are learned through a process whereby a stimulus evokes a response that is either rewarded or punished, and habits are formed. The behavioral approach to personality views personality as a *pattern of learned, reinforced responses.*

Social psychology is concerned with the individual's relationship with other individuals and groups. The social psychologist studies the whole person and the impact of the social world on the person—the world of social interaction and group life, which constantly shapes and modifies the individual's goals, perceptions, attitudes, and behavior. The social-psychological approach to personality emphasizes the individual's *socialization*—the development of individual identity through *interpersonal experiences,* and the *internalizing of the expectations of significant others.*

social psychology
the study of the individual's relationships with other individuals and groups

Humanistic psychology focuses on human experience and human fulfillment; it emphasizes the individual's innate potential to grow and develop. According to the humanists, human beings are unique among animals because they alone have psychological as well as biological needs. The individual is internally motivated to fulfill those needs, to grow and develop and expand the capacity for creativity. Humanistic psychology views personality development as a *continuous process of positive growth* in which the individual, having fulfilled a lower need, pursues the fulfillment of a higher one.

humanistic psychology
the study of human experience and human fulfillment

In the following pages we will see how each of these approaches can contribute to our understanding of personality and individual reactions to power and authority. We will begin with an exploration of psychoanalytic (Freudian) theory and a consideration of the Freudian approach to power relationships, as exemplified by the study *The Authoritarian Personality.* We will then examine behavioral psychology's reliance on learning (stimulus-response) theory and the ideas of behavioral psychologist B. F. Skinner about the need to control human behavior. Next we will consider how social psychology uses interpersonal-interaction theory to explain personality. To illustrate the general approach of this school of psychology to power relationships, we will explore David Riesman's concept of the "other-directed" person. We will then briefly describe humanistic psychology's theory of personality, Rollo May's views of powerlessness, and Abraham Maslow's construction of a "hierachy of needs." The chapter concludes with a case study of authority and obedience, which describes the startling results of one of the most interesting social science experiments of recent times.

▪ Sigmund Freud: Psychoanalytic theory ▪

Perhaps no other scholar has had a greater impact on the social sciences than the Viennese psychiatrist Sigmund Freud (1856-1939). Freud completed medical school at the Uni-

versity of Vienna in 1881. He would have preferred an academic position at a university, but discrimination against Jews forced him to enter private practice. Freud's interest in neurology led him to specialize in the treatment of nervous disorders; he studied hypnosis because a French neurologist, Jean Charcot, had learned that neurotic symptoms could be removed during hypnotic trance. He also collaborated with another Viennese physician, Joseph Breuer, who learned that some worries could be alleviated by having the patient talk about them.

In his initial treatment of neurotic patients, Freud used hypnosis. He soon found that patients did not really need to be in a full hypnotic trance so long as they felt relaxed and uninhibited. He encouraged them to engage in *free association*—that is, to say anything that came into their minds without regard to organization, logic, or embarrassment over socially unacceptable ideas. He wanted to make the patient's *unconscious* motives,

drives, feelings, and anxieties *conscious ones.* The goal of psychoanalysis, as it was called, was to help patients attain *insight,* or self-knowledge. Once that was achieved, the neurotic symptoms tended to disappear.

According to Freud, the personality is composed of three major systems: the *id,* the *ego,* and the *superego.* The interaction of these components determines an individual's behavior. The *id* is the basic system of life instincts, or drives—hunger, thirst, sex, rest, pain avoidance, and so on. The id is in close touch with the body's needs; these needs produce psychic energy, which is experienced as uncomfortable states of tension. The id endeavors to reduce the tensions—it operates on the *pleasure* principle—but the id has no knowledge of objective reality. A newborn baby's personality is almost pure id. It seeks immediate gratification of bodily urges and has no knowledge of reality or morals.

The *ego* is the part of the personality that is in contact with objective reality. It directs the energies of the id toward real-world objects that are appropriate for the satisfaction of the urge and the reduction of tension. The ego operates on the *reality* principle, formulating plans for the satisfaction of needs, testing the plans, and deciding what needs will be satisfied first and in what manner. The ego exercises important executive functions, coordinating the sometimes conflicting desires of the id with the conditions of the external world.

The *superego,* the last part of the personality to develop, is the internal representative of the values, standards, and morals that the child is taught. The superego is the *moral* arm of the personality and develops through rewards and punishments that the parents impose upon the child and through the child's identification with the parents' standards. The superego decides what is right and wrong, rewarding the individual with feelings of pride or punishing with feelings of guilt. It inhibits the impulses of the id, persuades the ego to direct energies toward moralistic goals rather than realistic ones, and strives for moral perfection.

Anxiety is a state of tension that results from an apprehension of impending pain or danger, whether physical or psychological. Anxiety reduction is a drive like hunger or thirst, the difference being that it results from psychological, rather than bodily, discomfort. Anxiety is an important force in structuring early personality development. If it becomes too intense at too early an age, when the ego is unprepared to deal with it, it can produce serious personality disorders. However, anxiety should not be construed as being necessarily pathological. It serves the important function of warning us of impending danger, making us more alert, perceptive, and better prepared to deal with the situation. When its intensity and nature are appropriate to the real situation, the anxiety is *normal*. When there does not seem to be adequate cause for it in the real world, when it is caused by unconscious or irrational fears, and when it interferes with the person's functioning, the anxiety is *neurotic*.

Identification is important as a process in early personality development and as a way of reducing anxiety. The infant imitates the characteristics of the persons in its environment who satisfy its needs. These characteristics—for example, a parent's way of walking or talking—are incorporated into the child's developing personality. As we have noted, identification is also important in the development of the superego, as the child identifies with and incorporates the parents' moral values.

Children (or adults) may also identify with persons whom they perceive as aggressive, threatening, or all-powerful, and it is in this sense that identification is used to reduce anxiety. By becoming like the feared person who causes the anxiety, one is able to perceive the aggression as if it were one's own and were under one's own control. This type of identification is known as *identification with the aggressor*, and it constitutes one type of defense against anxiety. Hostages sometimes identify with their terrorist kidnappers in order to reduce anxiety.

There are many other *defense mechanisms* that the personality may use, often unconsciously, to reduce anxiety and tension. When it is dangerous to express an instinctual drive, be it in the form of love or hate, the individual may use *displacement* to defend against the anxiety—that is, shift the impulse from the original object to a less dangerous one. For example, a man who is angry at his employer, on whom he is dependent for his livelihood, may become furious with his wife over a petty matter, without realizing why he is acting as he is.

The most important of the defense mechanisms is *repression:* the ego protects the individual from unbearable impulses by forcing them out of consciousness. This defensive maneuver may occur when an impulse would endanger life, risk punishment, or risk feelings of guilt. But there are costs to repression. A severely repressed individual who has denied many strong impulses may suffer fatigue, nervousness, or depression. Repression can even interfere with the functioning of the body; in a male, sexual impotence can result from severely repressed sexual impulses.

Freud never drew up a comprehensive list of instincts or needs. However, he was convinced that of all of our many instincts, those of sex and aggression were the most seriously repressed by society. This repression begins with the newborn infant and extends through adulthood. If we feel hunger, we can immediately go out and buy a hamburger; but if we feel a sexual urge, it usually must be denied until an appropriate outlet is found. Aggressive impulses are also severely restricted. Thus Freud's seeming emphasis on sex was a product not of his belief that this drive was any more powerful than others but of his view that it was the most repressed and therefore the source of many personality disorders.

Freud believed that an individual passes through a series of *stages of personality development*. The first stages are decisive. The newborn infant at the *oral stage* derives pleasure from sucking and eating. It is a passive and receptive stage that centers on oral gratification. In adulthood oral characteristics include smoking, overeating, and extreme dependence on others. Sarcasm and argumentativeness may be a displaced form of oral aggression or biting.

The *anal stage* centers about control of the sphincter and the tension reduction involved in the release of feces. When toilet training is introduced, the infant experiences its first external regulation of an instinctual pleasure. Overreaction to demands that relief be postponed may lead to *anal-retentive* personality characteristics. The individual becomes possessive, stingy, excessively orderly, interested in collections of various sorts, and frequently constipated. Excessive praise for producing feces on demand may lead to *anal-expulsive* characteristics—an excessive concern with creativity and productivity.

In the *phallic stage* the infant becomes aware of the pleasure to be derived from the genital organs. Autoerotic activity (masturbation) is often quickly repressed by parents. Later the child (three to five years old) feels sexual attraction toward the parent of the opposite sex and hostile feelings toward the parent who appears as a love rival. According to Freud, every small boy goes through a period when he lusts after his mother and wishes his father were out of the way. (The term *Oedipus complex* comes from an ancient Greek play, *Oedipus Rex,* in which Oedipus unknowingly kills his own father and marries a woman who he later finds out is his mother.) These feelings produce various anxieties but usually the male child resolves his problems by eventually *identifying* with his father and replacing his dangerous sexual attraction to his mother with harmless tender affection.

After age five or six the child enters a *latency* period, in which many of the early oral, anal, and phallic problems are repressed. Indeed, the repression of these early feelings is responsible for our loss of memory of early childhood and infancy. It is not until puberty that latent feelings are reawakened by physical maturation, and repression is again attempted.

The *genital stage* represents maturity in personality development. The gratification an individual received from his own bodily pleasure as a child is redirected toward external love objects. The person approaching adulthood begins to love others not simply for selfish or narcissistic reasons. Earlier oral, anal, and phallic stages are fused into genital impulses; the personality gradually stabilizes with habitual displacements, sublimations, and identifications. The final organization of personality represents contributions from all four stages.

Perhaps no other social science theory has been subjected to such searching and bitter criticism as Freudian theory. The criticism ranges from charges that Freud was a "sex maniac" (Freud was a dedicated father and husband whose marriage lasted a lifetime; Freud's daughter, Anna, became a distinguished psychoanalyst herself) to more serious scientific reservations. One criticism centers on psychoanalytic therapy: it can be long and costly, and it is not always successful. Drugs, shock treatment, and behavioral therapy frequently produce more complete results in less time and at less expense. Another criticism is that Freud's observations were based on abnormal, clinical cases rather than normal adults; most of his patients were middle-class Europeans; and he worked in a cultural period when sexual repression in society was much greater than it is today. All these factors may have produced distortions in his theory.

Another problem with Freudian theory is that it is difficult to test scientifically. Freudian explanations proceed from observed behavior *back* to unconscious feelings and childhood experiences; but they do not permit exact predictions of future behavior from these factors. For example, Freudian theory might hypothesize that a boy who has a severe Oedipus complex and cannot "cut the apron strings" and identify with his father may cope with this problem by becoming a homosexual. But Freudian theory might also hypothesize that the same Oedipus complex could lead the boy to become a Don Juan, with a string of sexual conquests to prove his masculinity to himself.

A scientist may object that Freudian theory provides two completely different behaviors with the same explanation. It does not predict which of the two behaviors may result from an Oedipus complex; hence it is "bad" scientific theory. Nevertheless, psychologist William McDougall concluded, "In my opinion Freud has, quite unquestionably, done more for the advancement of our understanding of human nature than any other man since Aristotle."[7]

Box 6-2 offers a glossary of selected Freudian terminology.

BOX 6-2	Developing your psychoanalytic vocabulary
id	The component of the personality that is completely unconscious and contains all the instincts. It is the animalistic portion of the personality and is governed by the pleasure principle.
ego	The executive of the personality, whose job it is to satisfy the needs of both the id and the superego by engaging in appropriate environmental activities. The ego is governed by the reality principle.
superego	The moral component of the personality.
anxiety	The general feeling of uneasiness that one experiences when one engages in, or thinks of engaging in, activities that violate the internalized values of the superego.
ego defense mechanisms	Unconscious processes that falsify or distort reality in order to reduce or prevent anxiety.
displacement	The substitution of an anxiety-free emotional outlet for one that is anxiety-provoking. For example, substituting dancing for sexual intercourse in expressing sexual drive.
identification	The incorporation of another person's values and/or characteristics either to enhance one's self-esteem or to minimize that person as a threat.

repression	The ego defense mechanism by which anxiety-provoking thoughts are held in the unconscious mind, thereby preventing a conscious awareness of them.
oral stage of development	The first stage of psychological development, when pleasure comes mainly from the mouth.
anal stage of development	The second stage of psychological development, when the child must first learn to control bodily functions.
phallic stage of development	The stage when the child first becomes aware of pleasure to be derived from the genitals.
latency stage	The psychosexual stage that lasts from about the sixth year to about the twelfth year of life. It is a time when sexual activity is repressed and an abundance of substitute activities are engaged in, such as learning and athletics.
genital stage	The final psychosexual stage, and the one that follows puberty. It is a time when the full adult personality emerges and when the experiences that occurred during the other psychosexual stages manifest themselves.
Oedipus complex	The situation that arises during the phallic stage, in which a male child is attracted to his mother and hostile toward his father.
free association	Called by Freud "The Fundamental Rule of Psychoanalysis," it entails instructing the patient to say whatever comes to his or her mind, no matter how irrelevant, unimportant, or nonsensical it seems to be.
Freudian slip	A verbal "accident" that is thought to reveal the speaker's true feelings, such as occurred when Dr. Freud was introduced as Dr. Fraud.

The authoritarian personality

the Freudian approach to power relationships

The Freudian approach to power relationships focuses upon the channeling and blocking of drives; the conflicts among the id, ego, and superego; unconscious processes; and early childhood determinations of habitual responses to power and authority. Power motives—for example, a need to dominate others or, the opposite, pleasure in leaving decision making to others and accepting direction—are organized into the personality early in life. They are later *displaced* onto general power structures in society—for example, a desire to acquire powerful office or position, or a willingness to accept directions and orders of superiors. The real motives for people's public behavior are largely unconscious, so they *rationalize* their behavior in terms of the public interest.

Perhaps the most influential study of power, authority, and personality, one that was conducted mainly within the framework of Freudian theory, is the landmark volume entitled *The Authoritarian Personality.*[8] This study was undertaken after World War II by a group of psychologists who sought to identify potentially antidemocratic individuals—those whose personality structures render them particularly susceptible to authoritarian appeals. The research was supported by the American Jewish Committee because of its interest in finding the causes of antisemitism and social prejudice. The study ended with an identification of an entire "syndrome" of authoritarianism—an organized set of related attitudes.

The *Authoritarian Personality* study employed a variety of methodological tools to identify and explain authoritarianism: questionnaires, in-depth interviews, responses to pictures and inkblots, and psychiatric clinical observations. One of the tools developed in the course of the study was the F (fascism) Scale, now widely used by social scientists to identify authoritarianism. Part of the original F Scale is reproduced in Table 6-1. Persons who agree with all or most of the items in the F Scale are said to be authoritarian.

The central attitudes of authoritarianism are *dominance* and *submission*—dominance over subordinates in any power hierarchy and submissiveness toward superiors. Authoritarians are highly ambivalent in their attitudes toward authority. They are outwardly servile toward those they perceive as their superiors, but in fact they also harbor strong negative feelings toward them. They conceal this hate with the ego defense of *reaction formation*—bending over backward in excessive praise of authority and admiration for the strong. Their repressed rage toward their superiors is redirected into hostility toward the weak and inferior.

Authoritarians are *oriented toward power.* They tend to think in power terms, to be acutely sensitive in any situation to questions of who dominates whom. They are very uncomfortable when they do not know what the chain of command is. They need to know whom they should obey and who should obey them.

Authoritarians are *rigid.* They are "intolerant of ambiguity." They like order and are uncomfortable in the presence of disorder. When matters are complex, they impose their own rigid categories on them. Their thinking, therefore, is largely in *stereotypes.*

Authoritarians show *exaggerated concern with virility and strength.* Feelings of personal weakness are covered with a facade of toughness.

characteristics of the authoritarian personality
dominance and submission
orientation toward power
rigidity
exaggerated concern with strength
anti-introception
cynicism
ethnocentrism

TABLE 6-1 Items from the F (fascism) scale

Conventionalism Rigid adherence to conventional middle-class values.
  Obedience and respect for authority are the most important virtues children should learn.
  A person who has bad manners, habits, and breeding can hardly expect to get along with decent people.

Authoritarian submission Submissive, uncritical attitude toward idealized moral authorities of the ingroup.
  Obedience and respect for authority are the most important virtues children should learn.
  What this country needs most, more than laws and political programs, is a few courageous, tireless, devoted leaders in whom the people can put their faith.

Authoritarian aggression Tendency to be on the lookout for and to condemn, reject, and punish people who violate conventional values.
  What the youth needs most is strict discipline, rugged determination, and the will to work and fight for family and country.
  An insult to our honor should always be punished.

Anti-introception Opposition to the subjective, the imaginative, the tender-minded.
  When people have problems or worries, it is best for them not to think about it, but to keep busy with more cheerful things.
  Nowadays more and more people are prying into matters that should remain personal and private.
  If people would talk less and work more, everybody would be better off.

Power and "toughness" Preoccupation with the dominance-submission, strong-weak, leader-follower dimension; identification with power figures; overemphasis upon the conventionalized attributes of the ego; exaggerated assertion of strength and toughness.
  No weakness or difficulty can hold us back if we have enough will power.
  What the youth needs most is strict discipline, rugged determination, and the will to work and fight for family and country.
  People can be divided into two distinct classes: the weak and the strong.

Destructiveness and cynicism Generalized hostility, vilification of the human.
  Human nature being what it is, there will always be war and conflict.
  Familiarity breeds contempt.

SOURCE: Abridgement of table 7 (pp. 255–57), "The F (Fascism) Scale," from T. Adorno et al., *The Authoritarian Personality.* Copyright 1950 by The American Jewish Committee. Reprinted by permission of Harper & Row, Publishers, Inc.

They are unusually preoccupied with masculine virtues, and they also stereotype women as feminine and soft.

Authoritarians are *anti-introceptive.* They are impatient with, and opposed to, the subjective and tender-minded. They are unimaginative and reluctant to acknowledge their own feelings and fantasies.

Authoritarians are *cynical.* They distrust the motives of others and are generally pessimistic about human nature. They are disposed to believe that the world is a jungle and that various conspiracies exist to threaten them and their ways of life.

Authoritarians are *ethnocentric.* They view members of social groups other than their own as outsiders who are different, strange, unwholesome, and threatening. They hold an exalted opinion of their own groups. They reject outsiders and *project* many of their own aggressive impulses on them. They place stereotyped labels on outsiders.

The *Authoritarian Personality* study cites early childhood experiences with authority as one probable cause of authoritarianism:

> When we consider the childhood situation . . . we find reports of a tendency toward rigid discipline on the part of the parents, with affection which is conditional rather than unconditional, i.e., dependent upon approved behavior on the part of the child. Related to this is a tendency apparent in families of prejudiced subjects to base interrelationships on rather clearly defined roles of dominance and submission. . . . Forced into a surface submission to parental authority, the child develops hostility and aggression which are poorly channelized. The displacement of a repressed antagonism toward authority may be one of the sources, and perhaps the principal source, of his antagonism toward outgroups.[9]

Children who have been socialized in warm, close, affectionate interpersonal relationships are less likely to have authoritarian attitudes than children who have been socialized in strict, rigid, punitive situations. (This explanation is also consistent with interpersonal-interaction theory.)

Another psychoanalytic explanation of the authoritarian syndrome is the male child's *sadomasochistic resolution of the Oedipus complex.* According to this theory, love for the mother is severely repressed, and hatred for the father is transformed through reaction formation into a strong identification with authority, masculinity, and toughness. The transformation is a difficult task that never succeeds completely. While part of the original hostility toward the father is transformed into pleasure in obedience and subordination, some of the hostility is left over as sadism, which seeks an outlet in aggressive behavior toward outgroups and subordinates. Authoritarians never perceive the ambivalence of their view: blind submission to authority, yet a readiness to attack those who are deemed weak.

A great deal of research followed the *Authoritarian Personality* study, much of it using the F Scale to identify authoritarians and then observing related attitudes, environments, and behaviors. Some of the subsequent research on authoritarianism raised serious criticisms and reservations about the original work. First, it was observed that poorly educated persons tend to agree with F Scale statements more frequently than do well-educated persons. This finding does not necessarily mean that a lack of education *causes* authoritarianism, but it does suggest that differences in F Scale scores may be a product of education and *not* of personality development. Well-educated persons, whether they are authoritarian or not, simply know enough not to agree with the obviously biased statements on the F Scale.

Another problem is that the F Scale tests only for *right-wing* (fascist) authoritarianism and fails to identify *left-wing* authoritarianism. Yet there is ample evidence of exaggerated submission to authority in revolutionary and communist movements; aggression and sadism practiced by left-wing authoritarians against the hated outgroup—the "bourgeoisie";

---

sources of
authoritarianism
childhood experiences
with authority
resolution of the Oedipus
complex

---

criticisms of **The**
Authoritarian
Personality
educated persons recognize bias in F Scale
fails to identify left-wing authoritarians
not really a complete and separate syndrome

rigidity, toughness, and an orientation toward power among revolutionaries; extreme cynicism toward society among leftists, as well as conspiratorial views about politics; and rigid conformity to stereotyped Marxist ideas. Unfortunately, the F Scale equates authoritarianism with only fascist ideas.

Another criticism is that authoritarianism is *not* really a *complete* and *separate syndrome;* some of the attitudes of authoritarianism are found in individuals who do not exhibit other attitudes of the supposed syndrome. For example, ethnocentricity is frequently encountered in individuals who are not dominant-submissive. Ethnocentric attitudes may be acquired in a family or subculture that is otherwise warm and affectionate. Thus stable and loving individuals may have ethnocentric, stereotyped views of outgroups, and even harbor suspicion toward them, simply because their culture or subculture has taught them to do so. In other words, ethnocentricity may be part of a culture or subculture, rather than a component of a personality syndrome. The same may be true of superstition, rigidity, and conventionalism.

Despite these reservations, *The Authoritarian Personality* remains one of the most important studies of the relationship between power and personality. It provides us with invaluable insight into the psychological mechanisms by which some individuals adjust themselves to power and authority.

Behaviorism and learning theory

behaviorism
an approach to psychology that asserts that only observable behavior can be studied

Behavioral psychology is heavily indebted to learning theory or, more precisely, stimulus-response (SR) theory. It is not an overstatement to say that rats have had more to do with shaping this theory than human beings; SR theory grew out of experimental laboratory studies with animals. Academic psychology is based largely on SR theory; most college courses in psychology are oriented toward this approach. Behavioral psychology asserts that the goal of psychologists should be to study *behavior* by employing the same *scientific* tests as the natural sciences. Behavioral psychologists discount Freudian notions about the mind or the personality, which cannot be directly observed. For the behaviorists, one is what one does; personality *is* behavior, a pattern of learned, reinforced responses.

Pavlov's dogs

conditioned response
a behavior that is elicited by a previously neutral stimulus

The founder of modern stimulus-response theory was the famous Russian physiologist Ivan Petrovich Pavlov (1849–1936), who had already won a Nobel Prize for his studies of digestive glands before he undertook his landmark experiments with salivating dogs. Pavlov's early experiments established the notion of *conditioning*. Saliva flows when meat is placed in a dog's mouth. If a bell is consistently sounded just a moment before the meat is placed in its mouth, the dog will soon begin to salivate merely upon hearing a bell even if the meat is not given. Dogs do not normally salivate at the sound of a bell, so such a response is a *conditioned response*. The bell and the meat have become associated in the dog's mind by their occurring together.

The learning process is a bit more complex than it first appears. To establish a linkage between a conditioned stimulus and response, there must be a *drive,* a *cue,* a *response,* and *reinforcement*. Learning depends on the establishment of this SR linkage. In simple terms, in order to learn, one must want something as a result of one's action (*drive*). For example, for a rat that is placed in a box and given electric shocks through a wire grid floor, reinforcement is the relief of pain. Pain provides the *drive,* which is the first factor that must be present if learning is to occur. Hunger, thirst, or curiosity may also provide the drive to learn. In our example the electric shocks that the rat receives are accompanied by a buzzer. The buzzer provides the *cue,* the stimulus that is associated with the response. The stimulus may be visual (objects, colors, lights, designs, printed words), auditory (bells, whistles, spoken words), or related to any of the other senses. Of course, for a response to be linked to a cue, a response must first occur. A critical stage in the learning process is the production of the *appropriate response*. The rat experiencing an electric shock and hearing the buzzer will make a variety of responses; eventually it may pull on the lever that turns off the current. The particular response that satisfies the drive is likely to recur the next time the same situation is encountered. Learning takes place gradually, not so much through "trial and error" as through "trial and success." The rat's first success in pulling the lever will be an accident. After several shocking experiences, however, the rat will learn to pull the lever immediately to stop the current.

The key to the learning process is the *reinforcement* of the appropriate behavior. Reinforcement occurs each time the behavior is accompanied by reduction in the drive. The cue itself will eventually elicit the same response as the original drive. Thus the rat will pull the lever when it hears the sound of the buzzer whether it is shocked or not. In this way a previously neutral stimulus (the buzzer) becomes a *conditioned stimulus,* the rat having learned to respond to it in a particular way.

The strength of the SR linkage depends on (1) the strength of the original drive, (2) the closeness of the drive reduction to the response, and (3) the number of consistently reinforced trials. Thus the combination of a strong shock, the quick elimination of the shock after the rat pulls the lever, and a large number of trials makes a well-trained rat.

Higher-order learning takes place when an organism establishes complex and abstract linkages between stimulus and response. Higher-order conditioning occurs, for example, when a child learns to associate the written word *bell* spelled on a card with the sound of a bell. Cues become stimuli that provoke a response, which in turn becomes a cue to still another response. Certainly *language* can be viewed as an abstract

conditioned SR linkage requires
drive
cue
response
reinforcement

reinforcement
repeating conditioned stimulus and response

strength of SR linkage depends on
strength of drive
immediate drive reduction
number of trials

higher-order learning
complex and abstract linkages between stimulus and response

set of cues. By labeling and naming events, things, and experiences, people can increase their powers of stimulus generalization and discrimination.

Thinking itself may be the tracing out of elaborate and abstract series of linkages between cues and responses. We substitute mental cue-producing responses (thoughts) for overt behavior. It is possible through a series of thoughts to begin at a goal situation and work backward to identify the correct instrumental response. This higher-order learning substitutes for the direct response. Indeed, to think, we must first learn to inhibit or delay direct responses. Without such inhibition or delay, higher-order learning would not have an opportunity to function.

behavioral therapy
treatment based on learning or unlearning behavior

In recent years behavioral psychologists have come out of the laboratory to engage in some types of treatment for mental disorders. Behaviorists define disorders in terms of the undesirable behaviors that are exhibited. Behavioral psychologists seldom talk about oral or anal personalities or Oedipus complexes; they talk in terms of *functional* (desirable) and *dysfunctional* (undesirable) behaviors. They believe that neurotic behavior has been learned—generally by inconsistent use of rewards and punishment. (Hungry rats that are shocked when they pull a lever that previously produced food develop symptoms similar to "nervous breakdowns"!) Undesirable behaviors can be extinguished by withholding rewards or by administering punishment. Neurotic behavior can be unlearned by the same combination of principles by which it was taught. Behavioral psychotherapy establishes a set of conditions by which neurotic habits are unlearned and nonneurotic habits learned. The behavioral therapist is regarded as a kind of teacher and the patient as a learner. Thus the behavioral therapist may reward patients in mental hospitals for good behavior with tokens to be used to buy small luxuries. A therapist of this school believes that smokers can learn avoidance reaction by having thick, obnoxious cigarette smoke blown in their faces; or that bed wetters can unlearn their habit by sleeping on a wired blanket that produces a mild shock when it becomes wet. Even repression (viewed by the behaviorists as "learned nonthinking") can be overcome by forcing individuals to confront situations, events, or experiences they have repressed.

Social psychology—The self in relation to others

Social psychology is concerned primarily with interpersonal interactions—how the individual interacts with others. The social psychologist studies the individual as a whole person, interacting with the environment, rather than studying particular responses, behaviors, or reflexes. Many social psychologists are critical of the "reductionism" of behavioral psychology—the tendency to reduce individual behavior to a series of stimulus–response linkages. Social psychology is strongly influenced by

■ B. F. Skinner: The control of human behavior ■

Power is the capacity to control human behavior. What if behavioral science learns to control human behavior and develops a "behavioral technology" to do so? Who will apply this technology and for what purposes? Will the behavioral scientist acquire the ultimate power in society?

Behavioral psychologist B. F. Skinner believes that society can no longer afford individual freedom and self-determination. He argues that human behavior must be controlled to insure the survival of humanity and that *behavioral conditioning* must be employed on a massive scale to remold human beings and human culture. In the Skinnerian world people will be conditioned to be humanitarian rather than selfish, to refrain from polluting, from overpopulating, from rioting, and from making war. Behavioral conditioning will create a utopian society of communal ownership, egalitarian relationships, and devotion to art, music, and literature. Outmoded ideas of individual freedom and self-determination will be discarded in favor of a scientifically designed culture that will condition people to be "good."

Skinner believes that the freedom and dignity of an autonomous human being are "illusions" anyhow. All behavior is determined by prior conditioning. The apparent freedom of human beings is merely inconspicuous control: a permissive government is simply relying on other sources of control—family, church, schools, values, ideologies. If people behave well without government control, it is because they are being controlled by these other agencies. There is, however, ample evidence— war, crime, poverty, racism—that existing control mechanisms are inadequate for survival. Behavioral conditioning replaces imperfect and haphazard control methods with a more effective technology of behavioral control. *Brainwashing* is attacked by scholars who otherwise support changing people's minds by

less obvious control mechanisms. Yet, according to Skinner, brainwashing is an effective means of accomplishing *behavioral modification.*

> A common technique is to build up a strong aversive condition, such as hunger or lack of sleep, and, by alleviating it, to reinforce any behavior which "shows a positive attitude" toward a political or religious system. A favorable "opinion" is built up simply by reinforcing favorable statements.[10]

Skinner believes that all attitudes are developed in this way; the only difference is that formal behavioral conditioning appears obvious and conspicuous.

Skinner developed his ideas through a lifetime of laboratory research on behavioral conditioning. He is the inventor of the famous "Skinner box," a soundproof enclosure with a food dispenser that can be operated by a rat pressing a lever or a pigeon pecking at a bar. Skinner has long been preoccupied with the ideas of conditioning and control:

> I've had only one idea in my life—a true idée fixe. To put it as bluntly as possible—the idea of having my own way. "Control" expresses it. The control of human behavior. In my early experimental days it was a frenzied, selfish desire to dominate. I remember the rage I used to feel when a prediction went awry. I could have shouted at the subjects of my experiments, "Behave, damn you! Behave as you ought!"[11]

Skinner pioneered in the development of teaching machines and programmed instruction, which employ conditioning principles by reinforcing correct answers with a printed statement that the student's response is correct.

Can behavioral conditioning be used on a massive scale? Skinner believes it can. Social science has been slowed, he thinks, because of its concentration on states of mind, feelings, and traits. "Unable to understand how or why the person we see behaves as he does, we attribute his behavior to the person inside." Mistakenly we believe that the individual "initiates, originates, and creates" and that the individual is autonomous. But in fact human behavior is a product of conditioning. "Behavior is shaped and maintained by its consequences. Once this fact is recognized, we can formulate the interaction between the organism and environment in a much more comprehensive way." Behavior that operates on the environment to produce consequences (operant behavior) can be modified by arranging environments in which specific consequences are contingent upon it. In short, according to Skinner, the environment can be designed so that "good" behavior is reinforced and "bad" behavior extinguished.

Although arranging effective reinforcements in a laboratory setting is sometimes very complicated, it is far more complex in the real world. Skinner does not provide much specific information on how behavioral technology is to be employed. So the first problem with Skinner's world is that it may be unworkable.

Still more serious dilemmas of power are raised by Skinner's proposals. Who is to determine what is "good" and "bad" behavior? What standards will be used? Who decides what constitutes pleasure and pain and reward and punishment? In Skinner's utopia immense power would be placed in the hands of the behavioral scientist who designs the culture. Skinner's utopia, although benevolent, is totalitarian. Can the behavioral scientist always be trusted to be "good"? How can the power entrusted in the scientist be checked if the scientist has full capacity to manipulate human behavior? Moreover, what kind of human beings would be produced under a system that manipulates behavior, choices, tastes, and desires? If we believe that individual freedom and dignity are essential components of humanity, then behavioral conditioning on a massive scale is dehumanizing. Giving up freedom and dignity to achieve a secure, comfortable, unpolluted, egalitarian world may be too high a price to pay.

Gestalt psychology
the study of the whole individual

early Gestalt psychologists, who argued that the whole person is an entity that cannot be understood by breaking it into sensory elements. (The German word *Gestalt* means "whole," "pattern," or "configuration.")

Social psychologists view *interpersonal interaction* as the critical determinant of personality development. Indeed, an individual develops an

awareness of *self* only by interaction with the environment. The newborn infant cannot distinguish its own body from the outer world. It acquires an identity—a sense of self—only by moving out into the world and relating to other people. As the infant observes and responds to its mother, she becomes a meaningful object, bringing pleasure, frustration, pain, and so on. The infant becomes aware of itself only in relation to others. An infant who is totally ignored withdraws to a corner of its crib, does not talk or develop in any way, and withers away physiologically and psychologically. The emergence of self-identity requires interpersonal interaction; without others there is no self.

    The process by which an individual internalizes the values, attitudes, and judgments of others is called *socialization*. By *interacting* with others, people come to understand what is expected of them and *internalize* these expectations as part of their personalities. George Herbert Mead conceived the notion of *roles* to explain how the individual internalizes the expectations of others and acquires the values of society. The essential process in the development of self is the individual's taking on the roles of others.

    Years ago Charles H. Cooley described the self as a *system of ideas drawn from the social world*. The "looking-glass" self is a product of

self
the individual's awareness of himself or herself derived from interpersonal interaction

socialization
assuming the roles expected of us by others

1. our image of how we appear to others. We all try to see how we are regarded by others—how our actions are viewed and interpreted.
2. our image of the judgment of others. We each imagine how others are evaluating us.
3. our self-feeling. We all react to our perceptions of others' judgments with feelings of pride, shame, guilt, self-esteem, self-hate, and so forth.

In short, our self-conception derives from *interaction* with others from infancy through adulthood.

Through interaction with its parents, the child learns that certain sounds—such as "Mama" and "Daddy"—gain favorable attention. The child begins to repeat these sounds because of the response they evoke in others, and in this way begins to learn language. Children also learn that the things they do are meaningful to those around them, and thus they develop a sense of *self*. Infants who are ignored fail to develop either language or self-identity. Later the small child at play tries on a variety of *roles*—"mother," "father," "fireman," "soldier"—and increases self-realization in the process. Even such basic social roles as male and female may be viewed as a product of socialization rather than biology. Masculine and feminine traits develop through the child's internalization of the expectations of others and through role playing. Schools, games, and group activities provide more and more role-playing opportunities. Of course, not all of the "others" in one's life are equally influential in shaping self-identity; each person has some *significant others* whose judgments carry more weight than the judgments of others. As socialization continues, knowledge of roles and attitudes of others becomes more generalized. We gradually unify and consolidate the many roles we have played into a generalized self-conception. At this point the mature personality emerges.

Over time an individual acquires a *distinctive pattern of interpersonal response traits*—relatively consistent and stable dispositions to respond in a distinctive way toward others. These interpersonal response traits constitute the *personality*. They represent the sum of one's socialization, one's role experiences, one's history of successes and failures with various interpersonal responses. Table 6-2 presents twelve interpersonal response traits.

Many social psychologists believe that interpersonal-interaction theory provides a basis for the treatment of personality disorders. They define an *integrated personality* as one in which the individual plays fairly well-defined and stable roles that are not incompatible or conflicting and that are consistent with the values of the groups and culture in which the individual lives. *Personality disorganization* occurs when people find themselves in conflicting roles. Most people can handle mildly conflicting roles, such as being mother and office worker simultaneously; but serious

role playing
developing a sense of self by trying on a variety of roles

interpersonal response traits
the sum of all of an individual's socializing experience, or personality

causes of personality disorder
conflicting role expectations
abrupt changes in roles
inadequate socialization
desocialization: consistent defeat, frustration, and withdrawal

TABLE 6-2 Some interpersonal response traits

Role dispositions

Ascendance (*social timidity*)[a]: defends one's rights; does not mind being conspicuous; is not self-reticent; is self-assured; forcefully puts self forward.

Dominance (*submissiveness*): assertive; self-confident; power-oriented; tough; strong-willed; order-giving or directive leader.

Social initiative (*social passivity*): organizes groups; does not stay in background; makes suggestions at meetings; takes over leadership.

Independence (*dependence*): prefers to do own planning, to work things out in own way; does not seek support or advice; emotionally self-sufficient.

Sociometric dispositions

Acceptance of others (*rejection of others*): nonjudgmental in attitude toward others; permissive; believing and trustful; overlooks weaknesses and sees best in others.

Sociability (*unsociability*): participates in social affairs; likes to be with people; outgoing.

Friendliness (*unfriendliness*): genial, warm; open and approachable; approaches other persons easily; forms many social relationships.

Sympathy (*lack of sympathy*): concerned with the feelings and wants of others; displays kindly, generous behavior; defends underdog.

Expressive dispositions

Competitiveness (*noncompetitiveness*): sees every relationship as a contest—other people are rivals to be defeated; self-aggrandizing; noncooperative.

Aggressiveness (*nonaggressiveness*): attacks others directly or indirectly; shows defiant resentment of authority; quarrelsome; negativistic.

Self-consciousness (*social poise*): embarrassed when entering a room after others are seated; suffers excessively from stage fright; hesitates to volunteer in group discussions; bothered at work when people watch; feels uncomfortable if different from others.

Exhibitionism (*self-effacement*): is given to excess and ostentation in behavior and dress; seeks recognition and applause; shows off and behaves in odd ways to attract attention.

[a]Opposite trait appears in parentheses.

role conflicts, such as an inability to fully assume either a male or a female identification, create deeper problems. Another source of personality disorganization may be an abrupt change in roles—caused, for example, by the loss of a job by a breadwinner, the loss of a wife or husband by a devoted spouse, a change from rural to urban living, even war and natural disaster. Failure to be adequately "socialized" in the first place is another recognized source of personality disorder—for example, the adult who exhibits childlike behavior, or adolescents who cannot "find themselves," that is, find mature responsible roles for themselves in society. *Desocialization* occurs when an individual, encountering consistent defeat and frustration in interpersonal situations, withdraws from contacts with others. Thus social psychologists tend to view mental disorders in terms of people's relationships to their social environment—whether they are well adjusted and capable of functioning in a socially acceptable fashion.

Humanistic psychology—The innate human potential

Humanistic psychology, like social psychology, focuses on the *whole* person, rather than on particular defensive structures or behavioral responses. However, while social psychology focuses on the process of

humanistic psychology
a focus on individual development and self-fulfillment

socialization as the key factor in determining personality, humanistic psychology emphasizes the individual's innate potential for development, the human need for self-fulfillment. According to the humanists, the goal of psychology should be to understand human beings and human experience rather than to predict or control human behavior.

Humanistic psychology, which has been called the "third force" in psychology, came into its own around 1960. It represented a reaction against behaviorism and psychoanalytic theory, the two forces that dominated psychology at that time. Humanistic psychology rejects behaviorism's insistence on using the strictly scientific, objective, value-free methods of the natural sciences. It views behaviorism as lacking in concern for the meaningfulness of human experience; behaviorism, with its narrow focus on behavior itself and its disregard of the subjective human experience, is unable to explain the totality of the person. Humanistic psychology also rejects the Freudian emphasis on the biological needs, or drives, of the body and the defensive structure of the personality. For the humanists the basic "self" is not a negative force that must be repressed or controlled; the self is good and has the innate and unique capacity to grow and develop and expand its creativity.

According to the humanists, we are unique among animals because we alone have psychological as well as biological needs. Psychological needs include the need for safety and security, for friendships and intimacies, for self-esteem and self-expression. The highest psychological need is the need for "self-actualization." Human beings are internally motivated to fulfill these needs, to realize their potential; they have an innate propensity toward self-actualization. Personality development is the continuous process of positive growth in search of fulfilling ever higher needs, the ultimate goal being self-actualization.

Self-actualization requires first of all that individuals be aware of their own feelings; without such self-awareness, they can never know themselves, let alone realize their innate potential. In addition, self-actualization is affected by social, or environmental, factors. Like the social psychologists, humanistic psychologists believe that an individual's concept of "self" is in large measure socially determined, that others in one's world have an important impact on the way one feels about oneself. Although all people have the innate need to realize their potential, certain types of "socialization" experiences may prevent the individual from achieving self-actualization. If one is fully and unconditionally accepted as a person, then one develops positive feelings about oneself; if, on the other hand, acceptance is contingent on certain types of behavior, then one may experience anxiety and the need to function defensively, to close oneself off from feelings and a subjective experience of the world. This type of functioning interferes with the process of self-actualization.

Because of its orientation toward a "good" human nature and its emphasis on the need for openness and self-awareness, humanistic psychology does not talk in terms of "personality disorder" or "mental ill-

Margin notes

"third force" psychology
humanistic psychology seen as an alternative to psychoanalysis and behaviorism

the need to "self-actualize"

factors in personality development

humanistic therapies

ness." Nor does it concern itself with past experiences; the primary focus is on "the here and now." People are not "sick" but simply in need of ridding themselves of anxiety and the defensive functioning that closes them off from subjective experience. The various forms of therapy that fall under the umbrella of humanistic psychology range from individual psychotherapy to consciousness-raising and encounter groups, sensitivity training, biofeedback, and meditation. What these therapies have in common is a focus on promoting self-acceptance and an openness in experiencing the world. Positive personality change is accomplished by bringing people into touch with their feelings, by helping them to become accepting of themselves and others, and by showing them how to assume full responsibility for the direction of their lives. This, in turn, opens the way to self-actualization.

Power and the hierarchy of human needs

From the point of view of humanistic psychology, the ultimate power of the individual might be regarded as the ability to achieve self-actualization. Abraham Maslow, one of the foremost spokespersons of the humanistic movement, devised a "hierarchy of needs" that distinguishes between the "higher" and "lower" needs that are inherent in each individual. The highest need is, of course, self-actualization. However, before one can fulfill the higher needs, one must first satisfy the lower needs. Individual behavior at any point in time is determined by the individual's strongest need at that time. The higher needs are reflective of later stages of personality development. Figure 6-1 shows Maslow's formulation of the hierarchy of needs. (Note that the peak of an earlier main class of needs must be passed before the next "higher" need can begin to assume a dominant role. Note also that as psychological development takes place, the number and variety of needs increase.)

hierarchy of needs
the arrangement of needs from lowest to highest in potency

At the base of Maslow's hierarchy are *physiological needs* (food, clothing, shelter). These basic needs must be satisfied first. Once they have been, other levels of needs become important and begin to motivate individual behavior. Above physiological needs are the needs for *safety* and *security*. These needs may not always be apparent to the individual; they may be subconscious and not easily identified. A need for safety or security may become highly motivating, depending on early childhood experiences. The insecure child may later prefer occupations that offer insurance, retirement, protection from layoffs, and a predictable life. In contrast, the adult who had a secure childhood may prefer occupations that offer continuing challenges to imagination and ingenuity and that penalize failure.

physiological needs
the most basic cluster of needs, include water, food, oxygen, sleep, elimination, and sex

safety needs
include order, security, and predictability

Once physiological and safety needs are fairly well-satisfied, *social needs* become dominant. The individual, according to Maslow, now seeks group acceptance, friendships, and intimacies. Indeed, studies of group dynamics suggest that group approval may occasionally become

belongingness and love needs
include affiliation with others and the feeling of being loved

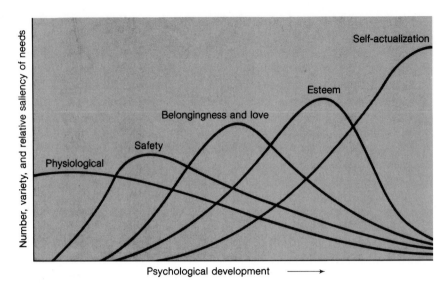

FIGURE 6-1 Maslow's hierarchy of needs, showing progressive changes in number, variety, and relative importance of needs

so important that it tends to override realistic appraisal of other sources of action. The individual may actually become a victim of group pressures in his or her search to satisfy social needs and find acceptance in life.

Assuming that an individual's social needs are reasonably well satisfied, a fourth need comes into prominence—*esteem*. Failure to understand this need may lead parents to complain: "We've given our child everything—a good home, stable family, all the things he ever asked for, even our own time and assistance—yet he is still dissatisfied." However, it may be that it is precisely because children have had the three basic needs sufficiently satisfied that a fourth need emerges—recognition of worth as an individual. Like security or social needs, the need for personal esteem appears in a variety of forms; a search for *recognition* is one manifestation of the need for personal esteem.

Evidence from studies of large corporate and governmental organizations suggests that recognition or symbols of prestige may be more important in motivating management employees than money. Most of the employees make enough money to satisfy their physiological and security needs, and their social needs may be satisfied in relationships with family, work group, neighborhood, church, and so on. But their job performance suffers when they feel they do not receive personal recognition for their work by their supervisors. Their salary carries some prestige value, but often an impressive sounding title (for example, "vice-president for operations," "director of planning," or "deputy secretary") is even more important. In business organizations it is frequently remarked that "a name on the door and a rug on the floor" are the key to

esteem needs
include status, prestige, competence, and confidence

recognition. Many individuals will sacrifice salary to achieve these symbols of esteem.

When these four needs are more or less satisfied, we can expect to witness the emergence of Maslow's fifth and final need—the need for *self-actualization*. It is not always clear what self-actualization really is. According to Maslow, "Self-actualizing people are, without one single exception, involved in a cause outside of their own skin, in something outside of themselves."[12]

Despite problems in defining self-actualization, it does seem true that at some point in life—frequently in the late thirties or early forties—many individuals feel a vague sense of dissatisfaction. This "midlife crisis" may be related to the need for self-actualization. Individuals who have provided well for themselves and their families, who face no serious threats to their security, who are well accepted by their family, friends, and neighbors, and who have won recognition in their field of work may nonetheless feel that something is "missing." These individuals may have been content while striving to achieve their positions in life, but once they have achieved them, they ask, "Is that all there is?" According to Maslow, these individuals have reached a point at which they must turn to their fifth and final need, self-actualization.

Powerlessness and mental health

There is a common adage that "power corrupts, and absolute power corrupts absolutely." It reflects our negative view of power and our association of power with abuse. But the distinguished psychologist Rollo May, whose contributions to the humanistic movement are highly significant, contends that power is a fundamental aspect of the life process. Indeed, he believes that *powerlessness* corrupts the human personality by robbing the individual of a sense of meaning and significance.

Rollo May's argument[13] is that power occurs in an individual's life in five functional forms. The first is the *power to be*. The word *power* comes from the Latin root meaning "to be able." The newborn infant must have the power to make others respond to its needs—it cries and waves its arms violently as signs of its discomfort. An infant who cannot get a response from others fails to develop as a separate personality. *Power as self-affirmation* is the recognition of one's own worth and significance in life. Some power is essential for self-esteem and self-belief. *Power as self-assertion* makes it clear who we are and what we believe. It gives us the potential to react to attack and protect ourselves from becoming victims. Power also occurs in everyone's life as *aggression*—thrusting out against a person or thing seen as an adversary. The constructive aspects of aggression include cutting through barriers to initiate relationships; confronting another person not with the intent to hurt but in order to penetrate that individual's consciousness; and actualizing one's own self in a hostile environment. The destructive side of aggres-

self-actualization
the highest level in the hierarchy, reached only if the preceding need levels have been adequately satisfied; the self-actualizing individual operates at full capacity

power is functional
*power to be
power as self-affirmation
power as self-assertion
power as violence*

sion, of course, includes thrusting out to inflict injury and the taking of power simply to increase one's own range of control. Finally, power occurs as *violence.* May believes that violence is an attempt to exercise power. Violence may result from a failure at self-affirmation or self-assertion, or it may accompany aggression. Nonetheless, it can be regarded as functional to the individual if there is no other way for that person to gain significance in life.

It is May's belief that modern mass society impairs the individual's self-esteem and self-worth. The feeling of personal powerlessness is widespread.

> To admit our own individual feelings of powerlessness—that we cannot influence many people; that we count for little; that the values to which our parents devoted their lives are to us insubstantial and worthless; that we feel ourselves to be "faceless others," insignificant to other people and therefore not worth much to ourselves—that is, indeed, difficult to admit.[14]

He believes that much irrational violence—riots, assassinations, senseless murders—is a product of feelings of powerlessness.

■ Authority and obedience—The "shocking" experiments ■

A significant theme in the study of human behavior has been the reaction of individuals who were commanded to inflict pain, injury, or death upon others. An estimated six million Jews were murdered in Nazi death camps in World War II—men, women, and children—by individuals who frequently claimed they were "only carrying out orders."

"Authority," as we have noted, is a form of power that is perceived as legitimate by society. Doubtless throughout the ages more pain, injury, and death have been inflicted on humanity by "authorities" than by recognized "criminals." The criminal's claim to power is sanctioned only by a gun, knife, fist, or fraud—not by "legitimacy." But what are the psychological mechanisms that provide legitimacy to the exercise of power, and how far will ordinary Americans go in inflicting pain, injury, or even death if they believe they are acting legitimately?

These are some of the questions explored by psychologist Stanley Milgram in a series of experiments at Yale University in which experimenters told subjects to administer electric shocks to other people.[15] The subjects in these experiments were all adult males of various ages and representing a cross section of occupations. Each subject was told that he was participating in a "learning experiment"; the "learner" (actually an associate of the experimenter) was strapped into an "electric chair" and given a list of questions and answers to memorize. The subject was told by the experimenter to administer an ever-increasing electric shock every time the "learner" made a mistake. Thirty separate voltage levers were used, with signs reading from 15 to 450 volts. Signs also announced that the shocks ranged from "Slight Shock" to "Danger: Severe Shock." Actually the "learner" did not receive any shocks at all, but the subject did not know this. Moreover, the subject could watch the "learner" through a window and hear any sounds the "learner" made. Starting with 75 volts the "learner" begins to twitch, grunt, and groan with each shock. At 150 volts the "learner" demands that he be let out of the experiment. At 180 volts the "learner" screams that he can no longer stand the pain. At 300 volts the "learner" slumps over, refuses to provide any more answers to questions, and appears in dire distress. In response to each of the acts by the "learner," the experimenter tells the subject who is administering the shocks: "You have no choice, you must go on!"

Before the experiments began, Professor Milgram asked forty psychiatrists at a leading medical school to predict the behavior of most subjects; specifically these psychiatrists were asked to predict when the subject would break off the experiment and refuse to administer any more pain to the "learner." These psychiatrists predicted that *most* subjects would refuse to continue beyond the 150-volt level, and that only one-tenth would continue to the full 450-volt level. However, the shocking results of the "shocking" experiments were that 62 percent of the subjects obeyed the experimenter's commands completely and proceeded to administer the highest shock level on the board (450 volts). Only 38 percent of the subjects broke off the experiment when the "learner" groaned, screamed, demanded to be released, and finally pretended to be near death.

Many subjects expressed concern about their "learner" victims but continued the experiment anyway:

150 volts.	"You want me to keep going?"
165 volts.	"That guy is hollering in there. He's liable to have a heart attack. You want me to go on?"
180 volts.	"He can't stand it. I'm not going to kill that man in there! You hear him hollering. He's hollering. He can't stand it. What if something happens to him? . . . I mean who is going to take the responsibility if something happens to that gentleman?"

	(The experimenter says he will accept responsibility.)
195 volts.	"You see he's hollering. Hear that? Gee, I don't know."
	(The experimenter says, "The experiment requires that you go on.")
210 volts.	
225 volts.	
240 volts.	"Aw, no. You mean I've got to keep going up the scale? No, sir. I'm not going to kill that man! I'm not going to give him 450 volts!"
	(The experimenter repeats, "The experiment requires that you go on.")
	The subject proceeds to the highest shock level, 450 volts.*

One point made in these experiments is that the subjects were not simply sadistic. They were average men selected from all walks of life. Most objected verbally to what they were doing at some point in the experiment. But in the context of *authority* (an experimenter who told them to continue no matter what happened) and *legitimacy* (the idea that they were participating in a scientific experiment at a prestigious university), these individuals performed acts of brutality that they would not otherwise consider doing.

Psychologist Milgram concluded:

> With numbing regularity good people were seen to knuckle under to the demands of authority and perform actions that were callous and severe. Men who are in everyday life responsible and decent were seduced by trappings of authority, by the control of their perceptions, and by uncritical acceptance of the experimenter's definition of the situation, into performing harsh acts.
> What is the limit of obedience?[16]

It is not clear how far we can generalize from these experiments. But it is certainly not far-fetched to suspect that under the right conditions otherwise normal people can become un-usually cruel. If those who are invested with authority and legitimacy encourage sadistic behavior toward others, we can reasonably expect that a substantial proportion of the population will engage in such behavior. Another holocaust is not impossible.

*Reprinted with permission of the author from S. Milgram, *Obedience to Authority, An Experimental View* (New York: Harper & Row, 1974).

Notes

1. I. J. Gottesman, "Heritability of Personality," *Psychological Monographs* 77 (1963): 1–21.
2. J. Shields, *Monozygotic Twins Brought up Apart and Brought up Together* (London: Oxford University Press, 1962).
3. Harry F. Harlow, "Learning to Love," *American Scientist* 54 (1966): 244–272.
4. John Bowlby, "The Nature of the Child's Tie to His Mother," *International Journal of Psychoanalysis* 39 (1958): 350–373.
5. Harry F. Harlow and R. R. Zimmerman, "Affectionate Responses in the Infant Monkey," *Science* 130 (1959): 421–432.
6. Gordon Allport, *Personality* (New York: Holt, 1937), pp. 24–54.
7. William McDougall, quoted in Gardner Lindzey, ed., *Handbook of Social Psychology,* 5 vols. (Reading, Mass.: Addison-Wesley, 1954), vol. I, p. 144.
8. T. W. Adorno et al., *The Authoritarian Personality* (New York: Harper, 1950).
9. Ibid., p. 482.
10. B. F. Skinner, *Beyond Freedom and Dignity* (New York: Knopf, 1971).
11. Ibid., p. 96.
12. A. H. Maslow, *The Farther Reaches of Human Nature* (New York: Viking Press, 1971), p. 43.
13. Rollo May, *Power and Innocence* (New York: W. W. Norton, 1972).
14. Ibid., p. 21.
15. Stanley Milgram, "Some Conditions of Obedience and Disobedience to Authority," *Human Relations* 18 (1965).
16. Ibid., p. 74.

Discussion questions

1. Describe the "nature versus nurture" controversy over the determination of personality. How does research on the personality characteristics of identical twins help us learn more about the relative effects of heredity versus environment on human behavior?
2. Discuss the psychoanalytic (Freudian) view of the determinants of behavior. Identify the three major systems that Freudians believe compose the personality and describe the roles played by each of

these systems. Differentiate between normal and neurotic anxiety and describe the functions of identification. Briefly outline Freud's stages of personality development.

3. Describe the authoritarian personality. What are some psychoanalytic explanations of the authoritarian personality? Discuss the criticisms of the *Authoritarian Personality* study.

4. How would a behavioral psychologist define personality and the goal of psychology? Describe how a linkage between a conditioned stimulus and response is established.

5. Describe how a social psychologist would approach the study of personality. Identify the processes that social psychologists believe are critical determinants of personality development. Discuss the meaning of the *looking-glass self* and *interpersonal response traits*.

6. Discuss humanistic psychology's view of the individual, Rollo May's formulation of the functions of power, and Abraham Maslow's "hierarchy of needs."

7. Discuss the results of the experiments that psychologist Stanley Milgram carried out at Yale University. What do these results tell us about the power of authority and legitimacy to command obedience? What are the implications of such obedience?

8. If you were interested in becoming a clinical psychologist, which type of therapy do you think you would want to practice—psychoanalytic therapy, behavioral therapy, a therapy based on the principles of interpersonal-interaction theory, or one that uses the approach of humanistic psychology? Describe how the theory you would choose views "personality disorder."

9. Which of the theories studied do you think provides the most cogent view of personality and the relationship between personality and power? Discuss your reasoning, including any criticisms you may have about any of these theories.

CHAPTER 7

■ POWER & GOVERNMENT

The power of government is truly awesome. In the nuclear age, the government controls the button that can virtually destroy humanity. Government power influences every facet of our lives "from the cradle to the grave." We eat government-inspected foods, which have been transported on government-regulated railroads and highways and grown on government-subsidized farms. We live in government-inspected homes, paid for by government-subsidized mortgages from government-regulated banks. We attend government-subsidized schools, or work in government-inspected shops, or manage government-regulated businesses. The awesome powers of government have worried people for centuries. How can governmental power be limited? How can we enjoy the benefits and protections of government yet not become slaves to it? How can government leaders be restrained? How can we guarantee that our personal liberties will not be threatened by governments?

These questions are the province of political science, and in this chapter we will see what answers political science can provide. After you have read Chapter 7, you should be able to

- discuss the political philosophy that is embodied in the U.S. Constitution,
- discuss the separation of powers around which our government is structured and the reasons why the Founding Fathers designed it this way,
- understand the limits of presidential power, especially in relation to the forced resignation of Richard Nixon,
- describe changes in the structure of governmental power,
- discuss actual political behaviors and processes in America and describe their effect on the exercise of power,
- discuss the increasing power of the mass media in American politics.

Politics, political science, and governmental power

A distinguished American political scientist, Harold Lasswell, defined *politics* as "who gets what, when, and how." "The study of politics," he said, "is the study of influence and the influential. The influential are those who get the most of what there is to get. . . . Those who get the most are the *elite;* the rest are *mass.*" He went on to define *political science* as the study of "the shaping and sharing of power."

Admittedly, Lasswell's definition of political science is very broad. Indeed, if we accept Lasswell's definition of political science as *the study of power,* then political science includes cultural, economic, social, and personal power relationships—topics we have already discussed in anthropology, economics, sociology, and psychology.

Although some political scientists have accepted Lasswell's challenge to study power in all its forms in society, most limit the definition of political science to *the study of government and politics.*

What distinguishes *governmental power* from the power of other institutions, groups, and individuals? The power of government, unlike that of other institutions in society, is distinguished by (1) *the legitimate use of physical force* and (2) *coverage of the whole society* rather than only segments of it. Because governmental decisions extend to the whole of society, and because only government can legitimately use physical force, government has the primary responsibility for maintaining order and for resolving differences that arise *between* segments of society. Thus government must regulate conflict by establishing and enforcing general rules by which conflict is to be carried on in society, by arranging compromises and balancing interests, and by imposing settlements that the parties in the dispute must accept. In other words, government lays down the "rules of the game" in conflict and competition between individuals, organizations, and institutions within society.

The concerns of political science

Political scientists ever since Plato have constructed ideal political systems—notions of what a *good* "polity" should be like. Today we refer to efforts to devise *good* political systems as *political philosophy.* Political philosophy concerns itself with political norms and values—criteria for judging the "rightness" or "wrongness" of governmental structures and actions. In Chapter 9 we discuss political ideologies—liberalism, conservatism, communism, socialism, and fascism—and examine these political philosophies more closely.

Political science also concerns itself with describing *the structure of political systems.* Schemes for classifying political systems are as old as the study of politics itself. Aristotle, for example, produced a classification based on two criteria: (1) the number of citizens who could participate in making rules—one, few, or many; and (2) whether the rulers

politics
the study of power

distinguishing governmental power
the legitimate use of force; coverage of the whole society

political philosophy
the study of political norms and values

Aristotle's classification of governments

governed in "the common interest" or in their own selfish interest. Aristotle's classification system (Table 7-1) included six types of government. Note that Aristotle believed that "democracy" was a corrupt form of government in which the masses pursued their selfish interests at the expense of the common good. Not until the nineteenth century did the word *democracy* come to have positive connotation.

The German social and political scientist Max Weber also classified political systems, but he focused on their *sources of legitimacy.* He suggested that the authority of governmental leaders can be based on

Weber's classification of the sources of legitimacy

1. *tradition:* legitimacy rests on established beliefs in the sanctity of authority and the moral need to obey leaders;
2. *charisma:* legitimacy rests on the personal heroic qualities of a particular leader;
3. *legality:* legitimacy is based on a commitment to constitutional rules that bind both leaders and the people.

political processes and behaviors

Political scientists are also concerned with *the political processes and behaviors among individuals and groups.* The study of political processes and behaviors goes beyond the study of political philosophy and the study of political structures. It asks how voters, interest groups, parties, legislators, executives, bureaucrats, judges, and other political actors behave and why. Social scientists who explore these questions are known as *behavioral* political scientists. Behavioral political scientists study the way individuals acquire political values and attitudes and how those values and attitudes shape their political activity; why people vote as they do or choose not to vote at all; how and why interest groups are formed and what influence they have on governments; how and why city councilmen and state and national legislators vote as they do on pieces of legislation; what motivates the actions of mayors, governors, and presidents, and what influences the decisions of judges; what the attitudes and functions of political parties are before and after elections; and so on.

But political philosophy and ideology, the structure of governments, and the behavior of political figures can seldom be studied separately. Discovering how these important areas of study interact is essential for a better understanding of power in society. In our examination of power and government in this chapter, we will first take up the political philos-

TABLE 7-1 Aristotle's classification of governments

Number of persons who rule	Interests served	
	Common	*Selfish*
One	Monarchy	Tyranny
Few	Aristocracy	Oligarchy
Many	Polity	Democracy

■ John Locke: Constitutionalism

The potential power of governments has worried people for a long time. Indeed, since the earliest recorded history, people have attempted to limit the powers of government, to set standards of legitimate authority, and to prevent the arbitrary use of governmental power. Of course, not all people or societies share the belief that governmental power should be limited. *Totalitarianism* is a belief that the state should be orderly, harmonious, and unified in purpose and values and that the power of government should be unlimited and all-embracing. In a totalitarian state, government exercises unlimited authority in all segments of life—the economy, education, the church, the family, and so on.

Constitutionalism is the belief that governmental power should be *limited*. A fundamental ideal of constitutionalism—"a government of laws and not of men"—suggests that those who exercise governmental authority are restricted in their use of it by a higher law. A *constitution* governs government. A constitution describes the offices and agencies of government, defines their prerogatives, prescribes how they should function, sets limits on the authority of government, and protects the freedoms of individual citizens. In other words, a constitution defines what governmental authority can and cannot do. A constitution should not be subject to change by the ordinary acts of government officials; change should come only through a process of general public consent. Most important, a constitution must truly limit and control the exercise of authority by government; the so-called constitutions of totalitarian states, which merely describe government offices and agencies but do not actually limit their powers, are not genuine constitutions.

In the eighteenth century the notion of constitutionalism was associated with the idea of a higher natural law. *Natural law* is based on human nature and the nature of society: it is immutable and it provides the standards and guidelines for governmental institutions and human law. Natural law binds both rulers and the ruled. The natural law includes natural rights possessed by all people; these rights are not derived from, or subject to, government but derive from human nature itself and have an independent and unchanging existence. The natural law *limits governments;* more important, it limits the power of majorities over individuals. Thus, natural law deprives even *majorities* of the power to violate the *inalienable rights of individuals to life, liberty, and property.*

A famous exponent of the idea of natural law and constitutional government was the English political philosopher John Locke (1632–1704). Perhaps more than anyone else, Locke inspired the political thought of our nation's Founding Fathers in that critical period of American history in which the new nation won its independence and established its constitution. Locke's ideas are written into both the Declaration of Independence and the Constitution of the United States. His writings, particularly his *Essay Concerning Human Understanding* and his *Two Treatises on Civil Government,* were widely read in early America and even plagiarized in part by Thomas Jefferson in the Declaration of Independence.

According to Locke, people are essentially rational beings, capable of self-government and able to participate in political decision making. Locke believed that human beings formed a contract among themselves to establish a government in order to better protect their natural rights, maintain peace, and protect themselves from foreign invasion. The *social contract* that established government made for safe and peaceful living and for the secure enjoyment of one's life, liberty, and property. Thus the ultimate *legitimacy* of government derived from a contract among the people themselves and not from gods or kings.

It was based on the *consent* of the governed. To safeguard their individual rights, the people agreed to be governed.

Since government was instituted as a contract to secure the rights of citizens, government itself could not violate individual rights. If government did so, it would dissolve the contract establishing it. Revolution, then, was justified if government was not serving the purpose for which it had been set up. However, according to Locke, revolution was justified only after a long period of abuses by government, not over any minor mismanagement.

Locke expounded upon six primary features of constitutional government: (1) the authority of government must be limited by the purposes and ends for which government is instituted—that is, preservation and protection of the natural rights of the individual; (2) government must conform to the law of nature and cannot violate the inalienable rights to life, liberty, and property; (3) laws must have the expressed or implied consent of the governed; (4) laws must apply equally to all; (5) laws must not be arbitrary or oppressive; and (6) taxes must not be levied without the consent of the people or their representatives.

Thomas Jefferson eloquently expressed Lockean ideals in the Declaration of Independence:

> We hold these truths to be self-evident, that all men are created equal, that they are endowed by their Creator with certain inalienable rights, that among these are life, liberty, and the pursuit of happiness. That to secure these rights, governments are instituted among men, deriving their just powers from the consent of the governed. That whenever any form of government becomes destructive of these ends, it is the right of the people to alter or to abolish it, and to institute new government, laying its foundation on such principles and organizing its powers in such form, as to them shall seem most likely to effect their safety and happiness.

Notice that Jefferson varied slightly from Locke in his description of inalienable rights. While Locke had affirmed the right of the individual to "life, liberty, and *property*," Jefferson substituted the more general idea in his famous formulation of the right to "life, liberty, and the *pursuit of happiness*."

ophies that are influential in shaping American government and politics; then consider how power is structured in American government; and finally describe political processes and behaviors in the presidency, Congress, the courts, voters, and political parties. We will conclude with a case study illustrating the growing involvement of the mass media, particularly television, in American politics.

The meaning of democracy

1. popular participation in government

Ideally, *democracy* means *individual participation* in the decisions that affect one's life. In traditional democratic theory, popular participation has been valued as an opportunity for *individual self-development*. Responsibility for the governing of one's own conduct develops one's character, self-reliance, intelligence, and moral judgment—in short, one's dignity. Even if a benevolent king could govern in the public interest, the classic democrat would reject him. The argument for citizen participation in public affairs is based not upon the policy outcomes it would produce but on the belief that such involvement is essential to the full development of human capacities.

Procedurally, popular participation was to be achieved through *majority rule* and *respect for the rights of minorities.* Self-development means *self-government,* and self-government can be accomplished only by encouraging each individual to contribute to the creation of public policy and by resolving conflicts over public policy through majority rule. Minorities who had had the opportunity to influence policy but whose views had not succeeded in winning majority support would accept the decisions of majorities. In return, majorities would permit minorities to attempt openly to win majority support for their views. Freedom of speech and press, freedom to dissent, and freedom to form opposition parties and organizations are essential to ensure meaningful individual participation. This *freedom of expression* is also necessary for ascertaining what the majority views really are.

2. majority rule, with minority rights

The underlying value of democracy is *individual dignity.* Human beings, by virtue of their existence, are entitled to life, liberty, and the pursuit of happiness. Implicit in the democratic notion of *freedom* is the commitment that governmental activity and social control over the individual be kept to a minimum; hence the removal of as many external restrictions, controls, and regulations on the individual as possible without infringing on the freedom of other citizens.

3. the value of individual dignity

Another vital aspect of classic democracy is a belief in the *equality* of all people. The Declaration of Independence expresses the conviction that "all men are created equal." The Founding Fathers believed in equality *before the law,* notwithstanding the circumstances of the accused. A person was not to be judged by social position, economic class, creed, or race. Many early democrats also believed in *political equality*— that is, equal opportunity to influence public policy. Political equality is expressed in the concept of "one person, one vote."

4. equality of opportunity

Over time, the notion of equality has also come to include *equality of opportunity* in all aspects of American life—social, educational, and economic, as well as political—and to encompass employment, housing, recreation, and public accommodations. All people are to have equal opportunity to develop their individual capacities to their natural limits.

In summary, democratic thinking involves the following ideas:

1. popular participation in the decisions that shape the lives of individuals in a society;
2. government by majority rule, with recognition of the rights of minorities to try to become majorities; these rights include the freedoms of speech, press, assembly, and petition and the freedom to dissent, to form opposition parties, and to run for public office;
3. a commitment to individual dignity and the preservation of the liberal values of liberty and property;

4. a commitment to equal opportunity for all to develop their individual capacities.

The political philosophy of the Founding Fathers

The Founding Fathers—those fifty-five men who met in the summer of 1787 in Philadelphia to establish a new national government—shared a political philosophy. They agreed with Locke that the fundamental purpose of government was the *protection of liberty and property*. They believed in government by the *consent* of the governed. They believed that the origin of government is an implied *contract* among citizens: people pledged allegiance and obedience to government in return for the protection of their natural rights, the maintenance of peace, and protection from foreign invasion. They believed that the ultimate legitimacy of government (that is, "sovereignty") rested with the people themselves and not with kings. But they also feared the *tyranny of the majority*—the tendency of the masses to use their majority position to capture powers of government and use those powers to attack individual rights, particularly rights of *property*. Their greatest fear was not that a *minority* would seize control of government and trample property rights but that a *majority* would do so.

The Founding Fathers believed in *republican government,* by which they meant representative, responsible, and nonhereditary government. They did not, however, mean mass democracy with direct participation by people in decision making. Rather, they expected the masses to consent to be governed by men of principle and property out of recognition of their abilities, talents, and education. Many of the Founding Fathers felt that men of wealth and property had a greater "stake in society" than the masses and were therefore more entitled to govern. In their opinion the masses should have only a limited part in the selection of government leaders.

The Founding Fathers believed in *limited government.* Government should be designed so it would not become a threat to liberty or property. Not only should the Constitution limit the government in its exercise of power but the structure of government itself should prevent the concentration of power. Power should be divided among separate bodies of the government, capable of checking each other in the event that any one branch should pose a threat to liberty or property.

Finally, the Founding Fathers regarded a *strong national government* as a safer repository of power than state and local governments. State and local governments, they thought, were more vulnerable to takeover by propertyless masses than a national government. Thus, at that period in history, American men of property supported a strong national government, while elsewhere most champions of the common people supported strong state and local governments.

The compromises that took place in the Constitutional Convention in 1787 were relatively unimportant in comparison to the consensus among the Founding Fathers on fundamentals. Consensus in this elite group in 1787 was profoundly conservative in that it wished to preserve the status quo in the distribution of power and property in America. At the same time, that consensus was radical in comparison with the beliefs of other elites in the world. Most governments adhered to the principle of hereditary monarchy—and a privileged nobility—while American elites were committed to republicanism. Other elites asserted the divine right of kings, while American elites talked about government by the consent of the governed. American elites believed in the equality of human beings with respect to inalienable human rights, while the elites of Europe rationalized and defended a hereditary aristocracy.

The structure of governmental power: The United States Constitution

The Constitution grants authority to the national government. The Founding Fathers tried to implement Locke's idea of limiting government by granting to the national government *only* certain expressed powers (sometimes called *enumerated powers*), together with powers

enumerated (delegated) powers
powers expressly granted to the national government in the Constitution

BOX 7-1 Power in the American Constitution

■ The design of American federalism is found in the Constitution's division of governmental authority between the national and state governments. The Constitution sets out several types of powers: (1) the delegated powers of the national government, both expressed and implied; (2) the reserved powers of the states; (3) concurrent powers, exercised by both national and state governments; and (4) powers denied to the national and state governments.

POWERS GRANTED BY THE CONSTITUTION

To the national government	To the national and state governments	To state governments
Delegated • to coin money • to conduct foreign relations • to regulate interstate commerce • to levy and collect taxes • to declare war • to raise and support military forces • to establish post offices • to establish courts inferior to the Supreme Court • to admit new states	• to levy and collect taxes • to borrow money • to make and enforce laws • to establish courts • to provide for the general welfare • to charter banks and corporations	• to regulate intrastate commerce • to conduct elections • to provide for public health, safety, and morals • to establish local governments • to ratify amendments to the federal constitution

Implied
"To make all laws which shall be necessary and proper for carrying into execution the foregoing powers, and all other powers vested by this Constitution in the Government of the United States, or in any Department or Officer thereof." (Article 1, Section 8:18)

POWERS DENIED BY THE CONSTITUTION

To the national government	To the national and state governments	To state governments
■ to tax articles exported from one state to another ■ to change state boundaries	■ to grant titles of nobility ■ to permit slavery ■ to deny citizens the right to vote ■ to deprive a person of life, liberty, or property without due process of law ■ to deny any person equal protection of the law	■ to tax imports or exports ■ to coin money ■ to enter into treaties ■ to impair obligations of contracts ■ to abridge the privileges or immunities of citizens

The Constitution also contains many specific restrictions on governmental power. The original text of the Constitution that emerged from the Philadelphia convention in 1787 did *not* contain a "Bill of Rights"—a listing of individual freedoms and restrictions on governmental power. The Founding Fathers argued that a specific listing of individual freedoms was unnecessary because the national government possessed only enumerated powers; since the power to restrict free speech or press or religion was not an enumerated power, the national government could not do these things. But Anti-Federalists in the state ratifying conventions were suspicious of the power of the new national government. They were not satisfied with the mere inference that the national government could not interfere with personal liberty; they wanted specific written guarantees of fundamental freedoms. The Federalist supporters of the new Constitution agreed to add a "Bill of Rights" as the first ten amendments to the Constitution in order to win ratification in the state conventions. This is why our fundamental freedoms—speech, press, religion, assembly, petition, due process of law—appear in the Constitution as *amendments*.

States may not enter into relations with foreign states. They cannot make treaties or agreements (unless Congress consents) with other countries. In short, they have no foreign policy. Similarly, although the states have never completely given up their armies (they retain the state militia and the National Guard, with congressional consent), the national government can control these armies; and they have certainly become less significant than they once were. In the economic sphere, the states cannot coin money or create any new legal tender for payment of debts. In addition, the states cannot impair the obligation of contracts and hence cannot pass laws that invalidate private agreements. In effect, a limit is placed on changing the rules of the economic game. Finally, states may not levy import and export duties.

that might reasonably be *implied* by the expressed powers. Article I, Section 8, of the Constitution provides a fairly lengthy list of specific powers given to Congress. They are the foundation stones of the national power.

The national government is given the power to *declare war and make peace.* Congress is authorized to raise and support armies and to provide a navy. It can define and punish piracy and other international offenses. Article II of the Constitution specifies that the president shall be commander in chief of the armed forces and have power to make treaties with the consent of the Senate and to give or withhold diplomatic recognition (to appoint and receive ambassadors). These significant foreign and military powers recognize the urgent need for a strong national government to provide defense against common enemies.

A second group of powers expressly given to Congress prepared the way for the economic and commercial unity and stability of the nation. Congress is authorized to *regulate commerce* among the states, with foreign nations, and with the Indian tribes. It is authorized to coin money, to make uniform rules for bankruptcy, and to borrow money. By way of aiding economic and social development, Congress is authorized to establish post offices and post roads, to provide for patents and copyrights, and to fix standards of weights and measures. (For a listing of the national powers, see Box 7-1.)

The national government is also given power to *tax and spend* for the common defense and general welfare. Congress can tax and spend for any purpose—education, welfare, housing, agriculture, business, urban affairs, manpower, and so forth.

At the end of Article I, Section 8, the Constitution makers added, in paragraph 18, the *"necessary and proper" clause,* which became the basis for much of the ensuing expansion of the powers of the national government. The "necessary and proper" clause states that Congress shall have power:

implied powers
powers exercised by the national government as "necessary and proper" to carry out its expressly delegated powers

> to make all laws which shall be *necessary and proper* for carrying into execution the foregoing powers [those mentioned in Article I, Section 8], and all other powers vested by this Constitution in the government of the United States, or in any department or officer thereof.

The last part of this clause makes it clear that Congress has powers that may be inferred from any of the expressly delegated powers in the Constitution.

restrictions on the states

The powers granted to the national government are accompanied by certain *restrictions* on the powers of the states, which serve to reinforce the grant of authority to the national government. These restrictions are listed in Box 7-1 but let us observe generally that the restrictions on the states take them completely out of the field of foreign affairs and partly out of military matters. In addition, the activities of the states in the economic sphere are sharply limited.

Federalism and the growth of power in Washington

The Constitution *divides* power between two separate authorities, the nation and the states, each of which can directly enforce its own laws on individuals through its own courts. This arrangement is known as *federalism*. In a disputed area, only the Constitution can determine whose authority is legitimate, and the Constitution cannot be changed without the consent of *both* the national government and three-quarters of the states.

American federalism differs from a "unitary" political system in that the central government has no legal authority to determine, alter, or abolish the power of the states. At the same time, American federalism differs from a "confederation of states," in which the national government is dependent upon its states for power. The American system *shares* authority and power constitutionally and practically.

The states are basic units in the organizational scheme of the national government. The House of Representatives apportions members to the states by population, and state legislatures draw up their districts. Every state has one House representative regardless of population. Each state elects two U.S. senators regardless of population. The president is chosen by the electoral votes of the states; each state has as many electoral votes as it has senators and House representatives. Finally, three-fourths of the states must ratify amendments to the U.S. Constitution.

Over the nation's two-hundred-year history, power has flowed toward the national government and away from the states. Major developments in the history of American federalism have contributed to national power:

federalism
the division of power between national and state governments

1. *The Supreme Court's broad interpretation of the "necessary and proper" clause.* Chief Justice John Marshall added immeasurably to national power in *McCulloch* v. *Maryland* (1819) when he broadly interpreted the "necessary and proper" clause of Article I, Section 8, of the Constitution. In approving the establishment of a national bank (a power not specifically delegated to the national government in the Constitution), Marshall wrote:

> Let the end be legitimate, let it be within the scope of the Constitution, and all means which are appropriate, which are plainly adopted to that end, which are not prohibited but consistent with the letter and the spirit of the Constitution, are constitutional.

Since then, the "necessary and proper" clause has been called the "implied powers" clause or even the "elastic" clause, suggesting that the national government can do anything not specifically prohibited by the Constitution. Given this tradition, the courts are unlikely to hold an act of Congress unconstitutional simply because no formal constitutional grant of power gives Congress the power to act.

2. *The national government's victory in the Civil War.* The Civil War was the nation's greatest crisis in federalism. Did a state have the right to oppose federal action by force of arms? This issue was decided in the nation's bloodiest war. (Combined casualties in the Civil War, military and civilian, exceeded U.S. casualties in World War II, even though the U.S. population in 1860 was only one-quarter of the population in 1940.) The same issue was at stake when the federal government sent troops to Little Rock, Arkansas, in 1957 and to Oxford, Mississippi, in 1962 to enforce desegregation; however, in these confrontations it was clear which side held the military advantage.

3. *The growth of a national economy and the broad interpretation of the interstate commerce clause.* The growth of national power under the interstate commerce clause is also an important development in American federalism. The industrial revolution created a national economy governable only by a national government. Yet until the 1930s the Supreme Court placed many obstacles in the way of government regulation of the economy. Finally, in *National Labor Relations Board* v. *Jones & Laughlin Steel Corporation* (1937), the Supreme Court recognized the principle that Congress could regulate production and distribution of goods and services for a national market under the interstate commerce clause. As a result, the national government gained control over wages, prices, production, marketing, labor relations, and all other important aspects of the national economy.

4. *The development of a national system of civil rights and their enforcement by federal courts.* Over the years, the U.S. Supreme Court has built a national system of civil rights based on the Fourteenth Amendment. This amendment rose out of the Civil War: "No *state* shall . . . deprive any person of life, liberty, or property, without due process of law; nor deny any person within its jurisdiction the equal protection of the laws." In early cases, the Supreme Court held that the general guarantee of "liberty" in the first phrase (the "due process" clause) prevents states from interfering with free speech, press, religion, and other personal liberties. Later, particularly after *Brown* v. *Board of Education of Topeka* in 1954, the Supreme Court also used the "equal protection" clause to ensure fairness and equality of opportunity throughout the nation.

5. *The growing financial power of the national government and its grant-in-aid programs for the states.* Money and power go together. The income tax (1913) gave the federal government the authority to raise large sums of money, which it spent for the "general welfare," as well as for defense. Gradually the federal government expanded its power in states and communities by use of grants-in-aid. During the Great Depression of the 1930s, the national government used its taxing and spending powers in a number

of areas formerly reserved to states and communities. Congress began grant-in-aid programs to states and communities for public assistance, unemployment compensation, employment services, child welfare, public housing, urban renewal, highway construction, and vocational education and rehabilitation. The inadequacy of state and local revenue systems contributed significantly to the increase of national power in states and communities. Federal grants-in-aid to state and local governments have expanded rapidly in recent years in both dollar amounts and the percentage of the total revenue of states and communities that comes from the federal government.

Whenever the national government contributes financially to state or local programs, the state or local officials have less discretion in using the funds than they would have otherwise (see Box 7-2). Federal grants-in-aid invariably come with congressional standards or "guidelines" to which states and communities must adhere to receive their federal money. Often Congress delegates to federal agencies the power to establish the conditions attached to grants. States or communities can reject federal grants-in-aid if they do not wish to meet federal standards, and some have done so; however, most find it difficult to do. The temptation of much-needed federal money can be a form of bribery; and the thought that other states and communities will get the federal money if they do not (although the money comes in part from federal taxes paid by their own citizens) can seem like blackmail. Thus, through the power to tax and spend for the general welfare and through the conditions

BOX 7-2 Reagan and the "new federalism"

■ The "new federalism" is a proposal for a comprehensive restructuring of federal-state relations designed to return power and responsibility to states and communities. According to President Reagan,

> Our citizens feel they have lost control of even the most basic decisions made about the essential services of government, such as schools, welfare, roads, and even garbage collection. They are right. A maze of interlocking jurisdictions and levels of government confronts the average citizen in trying to solve even the simplest of problems. They do not know where to turn to for answers, who to hold accountable, who to praise, who to blame, who to vote for or against. The main reason for this is the overpowering growth of federal grants-in-aid programs during the past few decades.[*]

The Reagan administration has attempted to consolidate hundreds of specific grant-in-aid programs for state and local governments into a few large block grant programs for broad purposes: social services; community development; elementary and secondary education; maternal and child health; community services. Congress endorsed these block grants, but the struggle between the specific grant interests (liberals and Democrats) and the consolidationists (Reagan and the Republicans) was really a draw. Many specific grant programs were merged, but many others remained independent. President Reagan also proposed to turn back to the states a variety of other federal grant-in-aid programs, including child nutrition, alcohol and drug abuse, mental health, family planning, urban mass transit, and community development. It was argued that they ought to be state and local programs and not federal responsibilities. By gradually reducing federal aid for those programs in each federal budget, the Reagan administration can achieve the turnbacks. But opposition in Congress is likely to continue many of them as federal programs for the foreseeable future.

The response of the nation's governors and mayors to these New Federalism proposals was less than enthusiastic. State and local officials generally want relief from federal guidelines, regulations, and conditions associated with specific federal grants. They usually want control over welfare, health, transportation, and community development programs in their states and cities. But they fear the financial burdens of these programs. President Reagan also proposes to end General Revenue Sharing (GRS), a program begun in 1972 in which the federal government gives state and local governments direct money grants to use as they see fit with very few strings attached. The original idea, developed in the Nixon administration, was that the federal government was better at collecting revenue, whereas state and local government was better at spending. But with the federal government running large deficits in the 1980s, it is argued that the states must raise their own revenue.

*President Ronald Reagan, State of the Union Address, January 1982.

attached to federal grants-in-aid, the national government can exercise important powers in areas originally reserved to the states.

The separation of powers

The system of separated powers in the national government—separate legislative, executive, and judicial branches—was intended by the Founding Fathers as a *bulwark against majoritarianism* and an *additional safeguard for liberty*. The doctrine of separation of legislative, executive, and judicial powers derived from the French writer Montesquieu, whose *Spirit of the Laws* was a political textbook for these eighteenth-century statesmen. *The Federalist* paper No. 51 expresses the logic of the checks and balances system:

> Ambition must be made to counteract ambition. . . . It may be a reflection on human nature, that such devices should be necessary to control the abuses of government. But what is government itself, but the greatest of all reflections on human nature? If men were angels, no government would be necessary. If angels were to govern men, neither external nor internal controls on government would be necessary. In framing a government which is to be administered by men over men, the great difficulty lies in this: you must first enable the government to control the governed; and in the next place oblige it to control itself.[1]

The concept of the separation of powers is expressed in the opening sentences of the first three articles of the Constitution:

> Art. I. All legislative powers herein granted shall be invested in the Congress of the United States. . . . Art. II. The executive power shall be vested in a president of the United States of America. . . . Art. III. The judicial power of the United States shall be vested in one Supreme Court and in such inferior courts as the Congress may from time to time ordain and establish.

There are really *four* separate decision-making bodies in the national government—a bicameral Congress, which is divided into a House of Representatives and a Senate, together with the president and the Supreme Court. Each of these bodies is chosen in a separate fashion for different terms of office. In the *original* Constitution of 1787 only the House of Representatives was directly elected by the people; each House member serves a two-year term but can be reelected as often as his constituents wish. House members (435) are apportioned to the

separation of powers
the principle of dividing governmental powers among the executive, legislative, and judicial branches

bicameral legislature
a legislature made up of two chambers or parts. The United States Congress, composed of the House of Representatives and the Senate, is a bicameral legislature

states on the basis of population. There are two U.S. senators for each state, regardless of the size of the state's population. Originally they were selected by their state legislatures, but since the adoption of the Seventeenth Amendment to the Constitution (1913), U.S. senators have been elected by the people of their states. U.S. senators are elected for six-year terms and there is no limit on the number of terms they may serve.

In the Constitution of 1787 the president was to be chosen by *electors*—prominent citizens in each state, selected as state legislatures provided. (Apparently the Founders did not believe the people should be directly involved in the choice of a president.) The *electoral college* system still remains in the Constitution, but it has been changed by custom and practice over the years. As early as 1800, presidential electors had begun running for their posts "pledged" to cast their votes for one party and candidate or another. This practice permitted popular participation in the selection of the president by enabling voters in each state to choose among electors pledged to particular candidates. The same practice holds today: voters in presidential elections actually cast their votes for slates of Democratic or Republican electors pledged to either the Democratic or Republican candidate. Each state has as many electors as it has U.S. senators and representatives combined; and the District of Columbia was given three electors in the Twenty-Third Amendment (1961). These electors compose the *electoral college*, which, according to the Constitution, actually elects the president. All a state's electors by custom cast their vote for the candidate who won their state (see Figure 7-1). But occasionally an elector violates this custom and casts a vote for someone else. Moreover, it is possible in a close election for a candidate to lose the popular-vote total nationwide but still win a majority in the electoral college. These problems have led to proposals to reform the electoral-college system, but there has been no agreement on reform.

Each of the major decision-making bodies of American government possesses important *checks and balances* (see Figure 7-2) over the decisions of the others. No bill can become law without the approval of both the House and the Senate. The president shares in legislative power through his veto and his responsibility to "give to the Congress information of the State of the Union, and recommend to their consideration such measures as he shall judge necessary and expedient." He can also convene sessions of Congress. But the appointing power of the president is shared by the Senate; so is his treaty-making power. Congress can override executive vetoes. The president must execute the laws, but to do so he must rely upon executive departments, and they must be created by Congress. Moreover, the executive branch cannot spend money that has not been appropriated by Congress. Thus the concept of separation of powers is really misnamed, for what we are really talking

electoral college
a group of persons called electors, selected by the voters in each state, that officially elects the president and vice-president

checks and balances
principle whereby each branch of the government exercises a check upon the actions of the others, preventing too great a concentration of power in any one person or group of persons

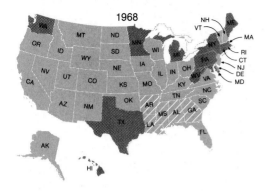

1968

Electoral votes[a]
■ Humphrey (D) 191
▨ Nixon (R) 302
▨ Wallace (American Independent) 45

[a]A North Carolina Republican elector cast his vote for George Wallace, making the official count: Nixon, 301; Humphrey, 191; Wallace, 46.

1972

Electoral votes[b]
■ McGovern (D) 17
▨ Nixon (R) 521

[b]A Virginia Republican elector cast his vote for Libertarian party candidate John Hospers, making the official count: Nixon, 520; McGovern, 17; Hospers, 1.

1976

Electoral votes[c]
■ Carter (D) 297
▨ Ford (R) 241

[c]A Republican elector from the state of Washington cast his vote for Ronald Reagan, making the official count: Carter, 297; Ford, 240; Reagan, 1.

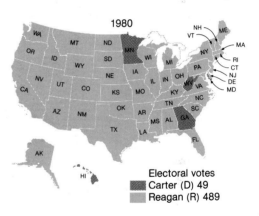

1980

Electoral votes
■ Carter (D) 49
▨ Reagan (R) 489

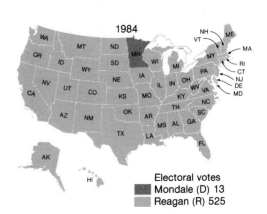

1984

Electoral votes
■ Mondale (D) 13
▨ Reagan (R) 525

FIGURE 7-1 Electoral college votes

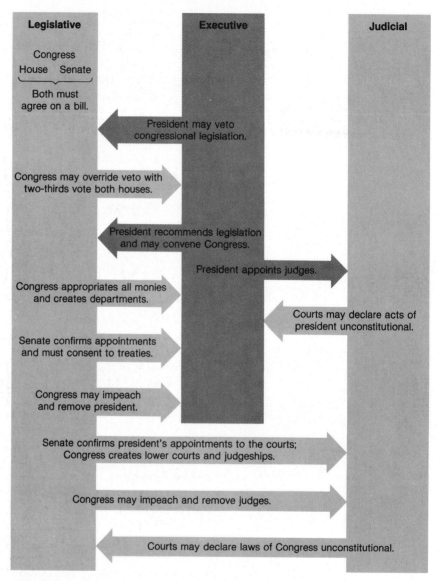

FIGURE 7-2 Checks and balances in the U.S. government

about is a *sharing*, not a separating, of power; each branch participates in the activities of every other branch.

Even the Supreme Court, which was created by the Constitution, must be appointed by the president with the consent of the Senate, and Congress may prescribe the number of judges. More important, Congress must create lower and intermediate courts, establish the number of judges, fix the jurisdiction of lower federal courts, and make "exceptions" to the appellate jurisdiction of the Supreme Court.

Perhaps the keystone of the system of checks and balances is the idea of *judicial review,* an original contribution by the Founding Fathers to the science of government. Judicial review is the power of the courts to strike down laws that they believe conflict with the Constitution. Article VI grants federal courts the power of judicial review of *state* decisions, specifying that the Constitution and the laws and treaties of the national government are the supreme law of the land, superseding anything in the constitutions or laws of any of the states. However, nowhere does the Constitution specify that the Supreme Court has power of judicial review of *executive* action or of laws enacted by *Congress.* This principle was instead established in the case of *Marbury v. Madison* in 1803, when Chief Justice John Marshall argued convincingly that the Founding Fathers had intended the Supreme Court to have the power of invalidating not only state laws and constitutions but also any laws of Congress or executive actions that came into conflict with the Constitution of the United States. Marshall reasoned (1) that the "judicial power" was given to the Supreme Court, (2) that historically the judicial power included the power to interpret the meaning of the law, (3) that the supremacy clause made the Constitution the "supreme law of the land," (4) that laws of the United States should be made "in pursuance thereof," (5) that judges are sworn to uphold the Constitution, and (6) that judges must therefore declare void any legislative act that they feel conflicts with the Constitution. Thus, the Supreme Court stands as the final defender of the fundamental principles agreed upon by the Founding Fathers against the encroachments of popularly elected legislatures and executives.

judicial review
power of the Supreme
Court or any court to
declare federal or state
laws unconstitutional

The power of the president

The responsibility for the initiation of public policy falls principally upon the president, White House staff, and executive departments. Through the power of policy initiation alone, the president has considerable impact on American politics. He sets the agenda for public decision making. His programs are presented to Congress in various presidential messages and in his budget, and he thereby largely determines what the business of Congress will be in any session. Few major undertakings get off the ground without presidential initiation; the president frames the issues, determines their context, and decides their timing.

presidential powers
chief legislator
commander in chief
chief diplomat
chief administrator
party leader
voice of the nation

On the whole, presidents of the twentieth century have exercised greater power and initiative than those of the nineteenth century, partly because of America's greater involvement in world affairs and the constant increase in the importance of military and foreign policy. The Constitution gives the president unmistakable and far-reaching powers in foreign and military affairs: he is authorized to send and receive ambassadors and to make treaties (with the advice and consent of the Senate) and is made commander in chief of the armed forces. In effect these

powers put him in almost exclusive control of foreign and military policy in the nation.

A second factor contributing to the power of the president in the twentieth century has been the growth of the executive branch, which he heads. The federal bureaucracy has become a giant power structure, and the president's constitutional powers as chief executive place him at the top of that structure. The Constitution gives the president broad, albeit vague, powers to "take care that the laws be faithfully executed" and to "require the opinion, in writing, of the principal officer of each of the executive departments upon any subject relating to the duties of their respective offices." By this clause the president has general executive authority over the 2.9 million civilian employees of the federal bureaucracy. Moreover, he has the right to appoint and remove the principal officers of the executive branch of government (the Senate consenting). Although Congress must appropriate all monies spent by executive departments, the president nonetheless has responsibility for formulating the budget, through the Office of Management and Budget (OMB), which reports directly to him. Congress may cut a presidential budget request and even appropriate more than the president asks for a particular agency or program, but by far the greatest portion of the president's budget is usually accepted by Congress.

The third reason for the importance of the presidency in the twentieth century can be traced to technological improvements in the mass media and the strengthening of the role of the president as party leader and molder of public opinion. Television brings the president directly in contact with the masses, and the masses have an attachment to him that is unlike their attachment to any other public official or symbol of government. Fred I. Greenstein has classified the "psychological functions of the presidency." First, the president "simplifies perception of government and politics" by serving as "the main cognitive 'handle' for providing busy citizens with some sense of what their government is doing." Second, the president provides "an outlet for emotional expression" through public interest in his and his family's private and public life. Third, the president is a "symbol of unity" and of nationhood (as the national shock and grief over the death of a president clearly reveals). Fourth, the president provides the masses with a "vicarious means of taking political action," in the sense that he can act decisively and effectively while they cannot do so. Finally, the president is a "symbol of social stability," in that he provides the masses with a feeling of security and guidance. Thus, for the masses, the president is the most visible elite member.[2]

The president has many sources of power (see Table 7-2); he is chief administrator, chief diplomat, commander in chief, chief of state, party leader, and voice of the people. But despite the great powers of the office, no president can monopolize policy making. The president functions within an established elite system, and he can exercise power only within its framework. The choices available to him are limited to those alternatives for which he can mobilize elite support. He cannot act outside existing consensus in the elite, outside the "rules of the game."

The power of Congress

What are the powers of Congress in the American political system? Policy proposals are initiated *outside* Congress; Congress's role is to respond to proposals from the president, executive agencies, and interest groups. Congress does not merely ratify or "rubber-stamp" decisions; it plays an independent role in the policy-making process. But this role is essentially a deliberative one, in which Congress accepts, modifies, or rejects the policies initiated by others. Congress functions as an *arbiter* rather than an *initiator* of public policy. As political scientist Robert Dahl explains:

function of Congress
arbiter of public policy

The Congress no longer expects to originate measures but to pass, veto, or modify laws proposed by the Chief Executive. It is the President, not the Congress, who determines the content and substance of the legislation with which Congress deals. The President is now the motor of the system; the Congress applies the brakes. The President gives what forward movement there is in the system; his is the force of thrust and innovation. The Congress is the force of inertia—a force, it should be said, that means not only restraint, but stability in politics.[3]

Congress is more influential in *domestic* than in foreign and military affairs. It is much freer to reject presidential proposals regarding business, labor, agriculture, education, welfare, urban affairs, civil rights, taxation, and appropriations. The president and executive departments must go to Congress for needed legislation and appropriations. Congressional committees can exercise power in domestic affairs by giving or withholding the appropriations and the legislation wanted by these executive agencies.

In the Constitution, the president and Congress share power over foreign and military affairs. The president is "Commander in Chief of the Armed Forces," but Congress "declares war." The president "sends and receives Ambassadors" and "makes treaties," but the Senate must confirm appointments and "advise and consent" to treaties. But strong presidents have generally led the nation in both war and peace. American

TABLE 7-2 Presidential powers

Chief administrator
Implement policy—"take care that laws be faithfully executed"
Supervise executive branch of government
Appoint and remove policy officials
Prepare executive budget

Chief legislator
Initiate policy—"give to the Congress information of the State of the Union and recommend to their consideration such measures as he shall judge necessary and expedient"
Veto legislation passed by Congress
Convene special sessions of Congress "on extraordinary occasions"

Party leader
Control national party organization
Control federal patronage
Influence (not control) state and local parties through prestige

Chief diplomat
Make treaties ("with the advice and consent of Senate")
Make executive agreements
Exercise power of diplomatic recognition—"to send and receive ambassadors"
Represent the nation as chief of state

Commander in chief
Command U.S. armed forces—"the President shall be Commander in Chief of the Army and the Navy"
Appoint military officials
Direct military forces
Use broad war powers

■ Watergate and the limits of presidential power ■

Election to the nation's highest office—even by an overwhelming majority—does not entitle the president to govern by himself. It only gives him the opportunity to engage in consultation, accommodation, and compromise with other elites. Richard Nixon was the only president ever to resign from the office. His forced resignation in 1974 was not merely a product of specific misdeeds associated with Watergate. It also grew out of his general isolation from established elites, his failure to cooperate with Congress and the courts, and his disregard for the general "rules of the game."

On the night of 17 June 1972, five men with burglary and wiretapping tools were arrested in the offices of the Democratic National Committee in the Watergate apartments in Washington, together with E. Howard Hunt and G. Gordon Liddy, who directed the break-in. Hunt and Liddy worked for Nixon's reelection campaign committee, and they had previously worked on Nixon's White House staff. All pled guilty and were convicted, but U.S. District Court Judge John J. Sirica believed that the defendants were shielding whoever had ordered and paid for the bugging and break-in. The *Washington Post* reported that the defendants were under pressure to plead guilty, that they were still being paid by an unnamed source, and that they had been promised cash settlements and executive clemency if they remained silent and went to jail. Judge Sirica threatened the defendants with heavy sentences, and soon James W. McCord confessed to secret payments and a cover-up.

The Senate formed a Special Select Committee on Campaign Activities—the so-called Watergate Committee—headed by Senator Sam J. Ervin, to delve into Watergate and related activities. The national press, led by the prestigious *Washington Post,* which had always been hostile to Richard Nixon, began its own "investigative reporting" and launched a series of damaging stories, reported nightly on the national television networks, involving former Attorney General John Mitchell, White House chief of staff H. R. Haldeman, and White House adviser John Ehrlichman.

President Nixon might have been able to stay in office if he had publicly repented his own actions and cooperated in the Watergate investigation by Congress and the courts. But Nixon increasingly viewed the Watergate affair as a test of his own strength and character; he perceived it as a conspiracy among liberal opponents in Congress and the news media to reverse the 1972 election outcome; he became rigid in his stance on withholding information. He came to believe he was defending the presidency itself by refusing to cooperate.

When the Senate Watergate Committee learned that the president regularly taped conversations in the oval office, it issued subpoenas for tapes that would prove or disprove charges of a cover-up. In response President Nixon chose to argue that the constitutional separation of powers permitted the president to withhold information from both Congress and the courts. He relied on the doctrine of *executive privilege*—the assertion of the president's right to keep information from either Congress or the courts if *in the opinion of the president* it was necessary to do so in the interests of national security. Nixon was not acting without precedent in his refusal to cooperate. Executive privilege had first been invoked against Congress by George Washington in 1796 and was employed by many presidents thereafter.

Eventually, the dispute over the Watergate tapes reached the Supreme Court in *The United States v. Richard M. Nixon.* The Court denied the president the power to withhold from the courts under the doctrine of executive privilege subpoenaed information, when such information was essential to a criminal investigation. The Supreme Court reaffirmed the principle established in *Marbury v. Madison* (1803), which gave the courts the power to review the actions of other branches of the government. The Court recognized the principle of executive privilege but denied that it applied to criminal cases or that the president could refuse judges access to information they needed in order to determine whether such information applied to criminal cases.

President Nixon publicly released the transcripts of the subpoenaed White House tapes in a national television broadcast in which he claimed innocence of any wrongdoing. The conversations on the tapes are rambling, inconclusive, and subject to varied interpretations. But the most common interpretation is that President Nixon approved a payoff to a convicted burglar but declined to promise him clemency.

The Judiciary Committee of the House of Representatives, chaired by Representative Peter Rodino of New Jersey, was convened in the spring of 1974 to consider a series of articles of impeachment against President Nixon. The release of the tapes failed to persuade this committee of Nixon's innocence. Indeed, they had the opposite effect. The committee passed two articles of impeachment: one accused the president of obstructing justice in the Watergate investigation; the other accused the president of misusing his executive power and disregarding his constitutional duties to take care that the laws be faithfully executed.

After the release of the tapes, the Republican members of the Judiciary Committee, who had supported the president, announced that they had changed their minds and would vote for impeachment when the articles reached the floor of the House of Representatives. Shortly thereafter, Nixon was informed by congressional leaders of his own party that impeachment by a majority of the House and removal from office by two-thirds of the Senate was assured. On 9 August 1974, President Nixon resigned his office—the first U.S. president ever to do so.

On 8 September 1974, new President Gerald R. Ford pardoned former President Richard Nixon "for all offenses against the United States which he, Richard Nixon, has committed or may have committed or taken part in" during his presidency. In accepting the pardon, Nixon expressed remorse over Watergate and acknowledged grave errors of judgment, but he did not admit personal guilt. Despite intensive questioning by the press and Congress, President Ford maintained that his purpose in granting the pardon was to end "bitter controversy and divisive national debate" and "to firmly shut and seal this book" on Watergate.

troops have been sent beyond the borders of the United States by the president on more than 150 occasions. But Congress has formally declared war only five times: the War of 1812, the Mexican War, the Spanish-American War, and World Wars I and II. Congress did not declare war in either Korea or Vietnam.

Until Vietnam no congressional opposition to undeclared war was evident. But military failure and public opposition to the war in Vietnam led Congress to try to curtail the war power of the president. Congress passed the controversial War Power Act in 1973 over a weakened President Nixon's veto. The Act specifies that the president can send U.S. forces into combat only on condition of

1. a declaration of war by Congress;
2. an armed attack on the United States or on U.S. armed forces abroad, or the imminent threat of such an attack;
3. the need to protect U.S. citizens whose lives are threatened; or
4. specific statutory authorization by Congress.

Furthermore, if the president does send U.S. troops into combat, he must report this to Congress within forty-eight hours. U.S. forces can remain in a combat situation for only sixty days unless Congress by specific legislation authorizes their continued engagement. The Act also states that Congress can withdraw troops at any time by passing a resolution in both houses, and the president cannot veto a resolution. Obviously this War Power Act raises very serious constitutional questions, but they may never be tested in court. The Act did not prevent President Ford from sending troops to Cambodia during the Mayaguez incident, or President Carter from attempting a military rescue of the Iranian-held U.S. hostages, or President Reagan from sending U.S. troops to Lebanon and Grenada.

The power of the courts

The Founding Fathers viewed the federal courts as the final bulwark against threats to individual liberty. Since *Marbury* v. *Madison* first asserted the Supreme Court's power of judicial review over congressional acts, the federal courts have struck down more than eighty laws of Congress and uncounted state laws that they believed conflicted with the

power of the courts

Constitution. *Judicial review and the right to interpret the meaning and decide the application of law* are great sources of power for judges. Some of the nation's most important policy decisions have been made by courts rather than by executive or legislative bodies. In recent years federal courts have taken the lead in eliminating segregation in public life, insuring the separation of church and state, defining relationships between individuals and law enforcers, and guaranteeing individual voters equal voice in government. Courts are an integral component of America's governmental system, for sooner or later most important policy questions are brought before them.

democracy and the Supreme Court

The undemocratic nature of judicial review has long been recognized in American politics. Nine Supreme Court justices—who are not elected to office, whose terms are for life, and who can be removed only for "high crimes and misdemeanors"—possess the power to void the acts of popularly elected presidents, Congresses, governors, and state legislators. The decision of the Founding Fathers to grant federal courts the constitutional power of judicial review of *state* decisions is easy to understand. Federal court power over state decisions is probably essential in maintaining national unity, for fifty different state interpretations of the meaning of the U.S. Constitution or of the laws and treaties of Congress would create unimaginable confusion. Thus the power of federal judicial review over state constitutions, laws, and court decisions is seldom questioned.

judicial review of state laws

However, at the national level, why should the views of an appointed court about the meaning of the Constitution prevail over the views of an elected Congress and president? Congressmen and presidents are sworn to uphold the Constitution, and it can reasonably be assumed that they do not pass laws they believe to be *unconstitutional*. Why should the Supreme Court have judicial review of the decisions of these bodies?

The answer appears to be that the Founding Fathers distrusted both popular majorities and elected officials who might be influenced by popular majorities. They believed that government should be limited so that it could not attack principle and property, whether to do so was the will of the majority or not. So the courts were deliberately insulated against popular majorities; to ensure their independence, judges were not to be elected, but appointed for life terms. Originally, it was expected that they would be appointed by a president who was not even directly elected himself and confirmed by a Senate that was not directly elected. Only in this way, the writers of the Constitution believed, would they be sufficiently protected from the masses to permit them to judge courageously and responsibly. Insulation is, in itself, another source of judicial power.

The Supreme Court is best understood as an *elite institution,* rather than as a consistently *conservative* or *liberal* institution. During the 1930s the Supreme Court was a bastion of conservatism; it attacked the economic programs of the New Deal and clung to the earlier elite philosophy of rugged individualism. In recent years the Court has been criticized as too liberal in its orientation toward racial equality, church-state relations, and individual rights before the law. The apparent paradox can be understood if we view the Court as an exponent of the dominant elite philosophy, rather than as an unchanging liberal or conservative element in national politics. When the dominant elite philosophy was rugged individualism, the Court reflected this fact, just as it reflects a liberal philosophy today. Of course, owing to the insulation of the Court even from other elites, through life terms and independence of the executive and legislative branches, there is a *time lag* between changes in elite philosophy and the Court decisions reflecting these changes. For example, Franklin D. Roosevelt became president in 1933, but the Supreme Court did not generally approve New Deal legislation until after 1937.

A liberal concern for the underprivileged in America by the Supreme Court, under the leadership of Chief Justice Earl Warren, was reflected in the development of civil rights law. The Court firmly insisted that no person in the United States should be denied equal protection of the law. It defended the right of blacks to attend integrated schools, and it upheld the power of Congress to protect blacks from being discriminated against in public accommodations, employment, voting, and hous-

judicial review of federal laws

insulation of the courts
appointed, not elected
serving life terms

the politics of the Supreme Court

the Warren Court

ing. It ruled that discrimination against any group of voters by state legislatures in the apportioning of election districts was unconstitutional. It protected religious minorities (and the nonreligious) from laws establishing official prayers and religious ceremonies in public schools. It protected defendants in criminal cases from self-incrimination through ignorance of their rights, through the subtlety of law enforcement officials in extracting confessions, and through lack of legal counsel.

the Burger Court

The elevation of Warren Burger to chief justice by Richard Nixon in 1969 did not significantly alter the commitments of the Court to end racial segregation under law, ensure equality in representation, and maintain separation of church and state. Contrary to popular expectations, the Supreme Court, with four Nixon appointees, has continued to uphold these fundamental commitments of the nation's elite. The Burger Court extended the doctrine of *Brown* v. *Board of Education of Topeka* to uphold court-ordered busing of children to end racial imbalance in schools that had a history of racial segregation under law. The Burger Court struck down state payments to church schools to pay for nonreligious instruction. Only in the area of rights of criminal defendants has the Burger Court altered the direction of Warren Court holdings. But even here the Burger Court has not reversed earlier declarations of the rights of criminal defendants; it has merely failed to extend them further.

Perhaps the most sweeping declaration of individual liberty in the Supreme Court's history was the assertion, by the Burger Court, of the constitutional right of women to have abortions. The ultimate impact of this decision on society—on population growth, the environment, and the role of women in society—may be as far-reaching as that of any decision ever rendered by the Court. Certainly this decision clearly indicates that the Supreme Court continues to be a powerful institution capable of affecting the lives of all Americans.

Political behavior in the United States

Popular participation in the political system is the very definition of democracy. Individuals in a democracy may run for public office; participate in marches and demonstrations; make financial contributions to political candidates and causes; attend political meetings, speeches, and rallies; write letters to public officials and newspapers; belong to organizations that support or oppose particular candidates and take stands on public issues; wear a political button and place a bumper sticker on their car; attempt to influence friends while discussing candidates and issues; vote in elections; or merely follow an issue or campaign in the mass media.

forms of political participation

This list of activities constitutes a ranking of the forms of political participation, in inverse order of their frequency. Those activities at the beginning of the list require greater expenditure of time and energy and greater personal commitment; consequently, far fewer people engage in

those activities (see Figure 7-3). Less than 1 percent of the American adult population ever runs for public office. Only about 5 percent are ever active in political parties and campaigns, and only about 10 percent make financial contributions. About 15 percent of the nation's autos will carry bumper stickers, even in a presidential election. A few more people claim to have written or called a public official, but this figure includes local governments and school boards. About one-third of the adult population belong to organizations, including unions, that are politically active. But fully one-third of the population are politically apathetic: they do not vote, and they are largely unaware of and indifferent to the political life of the nation.

Voter turnout is greatest in presidential elections, but even in those contests turnout is barely above 50 percent of eligible people. Voter turnout has been declining slightly over the years (see Figure 7-4). "Off-year" congressional elections—congressional elections held in years in which there is no presidential election—attract only 35 or 40 percent of eligible people to the polls. Yet in these "off-year" contests the nation chooses all of its U.S. representatives, one-third of its U.S. senators, and about one-half of its governors. Local government elections—for mayor, council members, school board, and so forth—frequently attract only one-quarter to one-third of eligible voters.

Voting is the primary form of popular participation in a democracy, and voter participation is highly valued in American political theory.

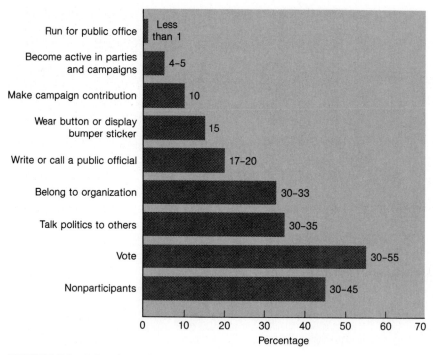

FIGURE 7-3 Political participation

Popular control of government—the control of leaders by followers—is supposed to be accomplished through the electoral process. Voting requires an individual to make not one but two decisions: the individual must choose whether to vote at all; and, if the individual decides to vote, must choose between rival parties or candidates. Both decisions are equally important; decisions about whether or not to vote can clearly influence the outcome of elections.

Voting laws in the states are now heavily circumscribed by national authority. Consider the following:

> Amendment XV—no denial of voting because of race
> Amendment XIX—no denial of voting because of sex
> Amendment XXIV—no poll taxes in federal elections
> Amendment XXVI—no denial of voting to persons eighteen years of age or older
> Civil Rights Act of 1964—no discrimination in the application of voter registration laws
> Voting Rights Act of 1965—attorney general may replace local voting officials with federal examiners on evidence of voter discrimination in southern states

The states, however, continue to administer national, state, and local elections. Most states have established a system of voting registration.

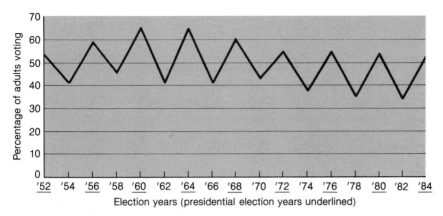

FIGURE 7-4 Voter turnout in presidential and congressional elections

Presumably, registration helps to prevent fraud and multiple voting in elections.

Democrats and Republicans—What's the difference?

Democracy is ultimately based on majority rule, and one function of political parties is to *put the majority together*. Political parties organize voters for effective political expression at the polls. Voters, in turn, use party labels to help them identify the general political viewpoints of the candidates.

Because American parties are necessarily rather loose coalitions of interests, they do not command the total loyalty of every officeholder elected under a party's banner. The fact that candidates run under a Republican or Democratic label does not clearly indicate where they will stand on every public issue. Even so, these coalitions do have considerable cohesion and historical continuity. The party label *discloses the coalition of interests and the policy views* with which candidates have generally associated themselves. At the least, the party label tells more about a candidate's politics than would a strange name on the ballot with no party affiliation attached.

Especially in two-party systems, such as we have in the United States, parties also *limit the choice of candidates* for public office and thus relieve voters of the task of choosing among dozens of contending candidates on election day. The preliminary selecting and narrowing of candidates, by conventions and primary elections, is indispensable in a large society.

Political parties help to *define the major problems and issues* confronting society. In attempting to win a majority of the voters, parties inform the public about the issues facing the nation. The comparisons made by parties during political campaigns have an important educa-

functions of political parties
organize majorities
identify candidate's coalition of interests
limit choices
define issues
criticize officeholders

tional value: voters come to "know" the opposing candidates for public office, and the problems of national interest are spotlighted.

Finally, the party *out* of office performs an important function for democratic government by *criticizing officeholders.* Moreover, the very existence of a recognized party outside the government helps to make criticism of government legitimate and effective.

criticism of the American two-party system
not enough differences

It is sometimes argued that there are few significant differences between the two main American parties. It is not uncommon in European nations to find totalitarian parties competing with democratic parties, capitalist parties with socialist parties, Catholic parties with secular parties, and so on. In contrast, in the United States both Republican and Democratic parties accept and strongly support constitutional government, with separation of powers, federalism, and judicial review. The policies of the two parties reflect the same general cultural values. In addition, both parties compete for a majority in the electorate and therefore tend to take moderate stands that will encompass the views of the largest number of voters.

ascertaining the real party differences
differing coalitions of voters
differing views of party leaders
differing voting records in Congress

If it were true that the American parties offered *no* real alternatives to the voters, then effective popular control of government through elections would be impossible. This is exactly what Marxists criticize about American democracy—that there are no differences between the American parties and no choices open to the American people. However, within the context of American political experience, the Democratic and Republican parties can be clearly differentiated. There are at least three ways in which to discern the differences: (1) by examining differences in the *coalitions of voters* supporting each party; (2) by examining differences in the *policy views of the leaders* in each party; and (3) by examining differences in the *voting records of the representatives and senators* of each party.

In ascertaining party differences according to support from different groups of voters, we must note first that major groups are seldom *wholly* within one party or the other. For example, in presidential elections all major social groups divide their votes between the parties (see Table 7-3). Yet differences between the parties are revealed in the proportions of votes given by each major group to each party. Thus the Democratic party receives a disproportionate amount of support from Catholics, Jews, blacks, lower educational and lower-income groups, younger people, blue-collar workers, union members, and big-city residents. The Republican party receives disproportionate support from Protestants, whites, higher educational and higher-income groups, older people, professionals and managers, white-collar workers, nonunion members, and rural and small-town residents.

The second way of discerning Democratic and Republican party differences involves an examination of the political opinions of the leaders of each party. Political scientist Herbert J. McClosky made a study of party differences by presenting a series of policy questions to more

TABLE 7-3 Percentage of vote by groups in presidential elections since 1964

	1964		1968			1972		1976			1980			1984	
	Johnson	Goldwater	Humphrey	Nixon	Wallace	McGovern	Nixon	Carter	Ford	McCarthy	Carter	Reagan	Anderson	Mondale	Reagan
National	61	39	43	43	14	38	62	50	48	1	41	51	7	41	59
Sex															
Male	60	40	41	43	16	37	63	53	45	1	38	53	7	37	61
Female	62	38	45	43	12	38	62	48	51	*	44	49	6	42	57
Race															
White	59	41	38	47	15	32	68	46	52	1	36	56	7	34	66
Nonwhite	94	6	85	12	3	87	13	85	15	*	86	10	2	90	9
Education															
College	52	48	37	54	9	37	63	42	55	2	35	53	10	40	59
High school	62	38	42	43	15	34	66	54	46	*	43	51	5	39	60
Grade school	66	34	52	33	15	49	51	58	41	1	54	42	3	49	50
Occupation															
Prof. & business	54	46	34	56	10	31	69	42	56	1	33	55	10	37	62
White-collar	57	43	41	47	12	36	64	50	48	2	40	51	9	40	59
Manual	71	29	50	35	15	43	57	58	41	1	48	46	5	46	53
Age															
Under 30 years	64	36	47	38	15	48	52	53	45	1	47	41	11	41	58
30–49	63	37	44	41	15	33	67	48	49	2	38	52	8	42	58
50 years & older	59	41	41	47	12	36	64	52	48	*	41	54	4	36	63
Religion															
Protestants	55	45	35	49	16	30	70	46	53	*	39	54	6	26	73
Catholics	76	24	59	33	8	48	52	57	42	1	46	47	6	44	55
Politics															
Republicans	20	80	9	86	5	5	95	9	91	*	8	86	5	7	92
Democrats	87	13	74	12	14	67	33	82	18	*	69	26	4	73	26
Independents	56	44	31	44	25	31	69	38	57	4	29	55	14	35	63
Region															
East	68	32	50	43	7	42	58	51	47	1	43	47	9	47	52
Midwest	61	39	44	47	9	40	60	48	50	1	41	51	7	38	61
South	52	48	31	36	33	29	71	54	45	*	44	52	3	36	63
West	60	40	44	49	7	41	59	46	51	1	35	54	9	40	59
Members of labor union families	73	27	56	29	15	46	54	63	36	1	50	43	5	53	45

*Less than one percent.
SOURCE: Based on data from the Gallup Poll Survey.

than 3,000 delegates to the Democratic and Republican national conventions. He found substantial differences of opinion between Democrats and Republicans on important public issues, including public ownership of natural resources, governmental regulation of the economy, egalitarianism and human welfare, tax policy, and foreign policy. On the basis of this research, McClosky concludes:

> Although it has received wide currency, especially among Europeans, the belief that the two American parties are identical in principle and doctrine has little foundation in fact. Examination of the opinions of Democratic and Republican leaders shows them to be distinct communities of co-believers who diverge sharply on many important issues. Their disagreements, furthermore, conform to an image familiar to many observers and are generally consistent with differences turned up by studies of congressional roll calls. . . . [They] grow out of their group identification and support— out of the managerial, proprietary, and high-status connections of the one, and the labor, minority, low-status, and intellectual connections of the other. . . . Democratic leaders typically display the stronger urge to elevate the low-born, the uneducated, the deprived minorities, and the poor in general; they are also more disposed to employ the nation's collective power to advance humanitarian and social welfare goals (e.g., social security, immigration, racial integration, a higher minimum wage, and public education). They are more critical of wealth and big business and more eager to bring them under regulation. Theirs is the greater faith in the wisdom of using legislation for redistributing the national product and for furnishing social services on a wide scale. Of the two groups of leaders, the Democrats are more "progressively" oriented toward social reform and experimentation. The Republican leaders, while not uniformly differentiated from their opponents, subscribe in greater measure to the symbols and practices of individualism, *laissez-faire,* and national independence. They prefer to overcome humanity's misfortunes by relying upon personal effort, private incentives, frugality, hard work, responsibility, self-denial (for both men and government), and the strengthening rather than the diminution of the economic and status distinctions that are the "natural" rewards of the differences in human character and fortunes.[4]

The third indication of party differences in the United States is the roll-call voting behavior of the representatives and senators of each party on controversial issues. Although members of the same party in Congress often have serious and lasting disagreements over important issues, it is possible to show that the *centers of gravity* of the two parties are rather widely separated in many issue areas, including governmental regulation of the economy, labor legislation, education and welfare programs, and foreign affairs.

Voters usually think of themselves as Democrats or Republicans, and their *party identification* is the single most important factor in voter decisions. Candidates and issues, two other bases of voter decisions, are influential in elections, but they do not provide the solid core of millions of party supporters who will vote for the party's nominees no matter

party identification
thinking of oneself as a Democrat or Republican and generally supporting one's party's candidates

who they are. This fact is particularly pertinent because the vast majority of candidates who appear on the ballot are unknown to the voter, especially candidates for the more obscure offices—those of county commissioner, city council member, registrar of deeds, auditor general, and so on.

People who identify themselves as Democrats outnumber those who identify themselves as Republicans by as much as two to one in national samples. Thus, if the Republican party is to win an election, it must nominate candidates who can attract Democratic voters. However, the Republican party's electoral hopes are aided by the fact that its adherents—more highly educated, higher-income, white-collar groups—tend to vote more often than the Democrats.

■ Political power and the mass media ■

Television has helped to reshape American politics. Over two-thirds of the American public report that they receive all or most of their news from television. Perhaps more important, television is the most trusted medium of communication. Television has thus become the focus of political campaigning. Candidates are no longer selected by party bosses in smoke-filled rooms. Instead of seeking meetings with party leaders, candidates now seek out professional media experts to construct a popular image for the TV screen. Campaigns are organized as media events. The media have replaced the political party as the chief link between the citizen and government.

Ronald Reagan has lived his life in front of a camera. The camera has been the principal tool of both his trades, actor and politician. Reagan's appeal to mass audiences has always been underestimated by the New York and Washington journalists and commentators. Reporters wrote down his commonplace observations and time-worn slogans. The printed messages were uninspiring. But reporters often missed Reagan's true audience appeal—his folksy, warm, comfortable, and reassuring manner and the likable personality that he projected to his audiences, whatever his words. Reagan captured the White House in 1980 in a landside victory over an incum-

bent president, Jimmy Carter. As the incumbent himself in 1984, Reagan swept to one of the largest victories ever in presidential races. Perhaps the issues in both elections—the economy, our national defenses, the standing of the United States in the world—propelled Reagan to victory in both elections. But it is also likely that Reagan's skills in political communication contributed to his winning margins.

1980—Communicating discontent

Americans take great pride in their country. They want to see their nation as strong, self-reliant, and prosperous, with a future even greater than its past. But during his presidency, Jimmy Carter talked about the limits of American resources and the limits of U.S. power in world affairs. The United States was unable to gain the release of its hostages in Iran through either diplomatic or military means. Rather than controlling its own affairs, the United States saw its economy, lifestyle, and foreign policy increasingly affected by Arab oil producers. Taxes, interest rates, and inflation were eroding the real incomes of American families. Americans were ready to shout the battle cry of the popular film *Network:* "I'm mad as hell and I'm not going to take it any more."

The task fell to Ronald Reagan to channel this discontent into a rejection of the incumbent president. Jimmy Carter, of course, did not bear the sole responsibility for Americans' accumulated discontents. But Reagan knew that the past of the United States looked better than its present, that the "good old days" never seemed better than they did in 1980. Reagan benefited from the public identification of him as the good guy in old western movies and the genial host of early television shows *G. E. Theatre* and *Death Valley Days*. His conservative political messages reinforced his image as guardian of traditional American values.

Reagan even turned his advancing age from a liability into an asset—he knew that America could be "great again." Carter mistakenly tried to portray Reagan as an unstable warmonger, on the basis of Reagan's opposition to Carter's strategic arms agreement with the Soviet Union. But Reagan's polished style as a kindly, older, soft-spoken western rancher deflected Carter's thrust.

Reagan even managed to turn some of his apparent blunders (or were they deliberate traps?) to his advantage. When he used the word *depression* instead of *recession* in a campaign speech, hordes of Carter economists explained that technically the nation was not in depression and that Reagan had misused the word. But instead of retracting it, Reagan made it a standard campaign quip: "If he [Carter] wants a definition, I'll give him one. [*Pause for audience attention.*] Recession [*Split-second pause for emphasis.*] is when your neighbor loses his job. Depression [*Same short pause.*] is when you lose yours. [*Pause for audience laughter.*] And recovery [*Pause for audience attention.*] is when Jimmy Carter loses his." [*Pause for prolonged laughter and applause.*]

Although attacked by Carter as a threat to peace, Reagan in their televised debate seemed by contrast a pleasant, smiling, reassuring figure. Carter was clearly the master of substance: he talked about programs, figures, budgets. He talked rapidly and seriously. But during the ninety minutes of debate, Reagan was the master of the stage: he was relaxed, smiling, even joking. He never raised his voice or increased the tempo, and he managed in the process to treat the president of the United States as an overly aggressive younger man, regrettably given to exaggeration. "There you go again."

Reagan never said anything of great importance. He merely asked: "Are you better off now than you were four years ago?" Simple, yet highly effective. When it was over, it was plain that Carter had been bested by a true professional in the media skills in which Carter himself had once claimed supremacy.

In the final few days before the election, the media decided to publicize the first anniversary of the Iranian hostage taking. That decision sealed Carter's fate. By reminding Americans of international humiliations, military weaknesses, and administration blunders during the Carter years, the media set the stage for the Reagan landslide. In the end, NBC announced the winner on national television before the polls had closed in the West. And Carter, who understands as well as anyone the power of the media, conceded defeat even before the voting booths were closed.

1984—Communicating confidence

Throughout Reagan's first term, whatever people thought about his tax cuts, his defense build-up, or the deficit, Reagan himself was perceived as a strong, decisive man who embodied the best of America's past. He was, above all else, a leader who commanded respect, who did not vacillate, who "stayed the course." Americans were feeling better about themselves and their country. They chanted "U-S-A" at the 1984 Los Angeles Summer Olympics and cheered the invasion of Gre-

nada. Ronald Reagan became the benefactor of this new patriotism.

Beyond Reagan's skills in political communication is the underlying perception that he is a "nice guy." He has the gift of intimacy with mass audiences, of plain speech and open feelings. Moreover, under his presidency the country was peaceful and prosperous. If he had made a mistake in sending Marines to Lebanon, he had taken personal responsibility, met the returning coffins at the airport, and ordered the Marines to withdraw. The beneficial effects of his tax cuts were real and immediate; the ill effects of his deficits were difficult to visualize and somewhere in the future. If his opponents pointed to America's problems, he could point to America's accomplishments. He could portray the voter's choice as a choice between "their government of pessimism, fear, and limits, and ours of hope, confidence, and growth."

By 1984 the television debates had become the central focus of the presidential campaign. The debates reward appearance over content and quickness of thought over thoughtfulness. A televised debate is more like a pop quiz given by selected reporters than it is a serious discussion of the issues. Reagan's advisors would have preferred that he not debate at all. The debates always seem to favor the challenger, by simply showing him in the same ring with the president. But the popularity of televised debates with 100 million viewers had gained nearly the force of a constitutional command by 1984.

In the first of the two televised debates with Democrat Walter Mondale, Reagan stumbled badly. The acquired skills of a lifetime deserted the president as he groped for words and thoughts, searching his mind and coming up empty. Mondale was respectful of the presidency, somewhat stiff and ill at ease but nonetheless clear-headed and effective in his responses to the questions. But it was not Mondale's performance that hurt Reagan, it was Reagan's own errors in preparation and performance. Instead of focusing on the broad themes of his presidency, he tried to show that he was in command of economic statistics and the details of his tax and spending programs. But his confused syntax and his lengthy mid-sentence hesitations demonstrated just the opposite. Reagan's poor performance raised the only issue that could defeat him—his age. The president had looked and sounded old. Post-debate polls showed Mondale the clear winner, and the challenger took a quick jump, although not a lead, in the voter polls.

The president decided on his own, without telling his aides, to lay the perfect trap for his questioners in the second debate. He knew the age question would be raised against him early in the debate. He memorized his lines and played the bit perfectly. When asked about his age and capacity to lead the nation he responded to a hushed audience and a waiting America in a serious dead-pan expression: "I want you to know that I will not make age an issue in this campaign. I am not going to exploit for political purposes [*pause*] my opponent's youth and inexperience." The stu-

dio audience broke into uncontrolled laughter. Even Mondale had to laugh. With a classic one-liner, the president buried the age issue, and won not only the debate but the election.

The president's performance reassured the nation that he was not too old or out of touch to handle the job. He avoided his earlier mistake of trying to reel off statistics. He was relaxed again, flashing his folksy humor, and sounding hurt rather than angry at Mondale's charges. He was once again the Great Communicator.

Later, Mondale explained his own defeat:

Modern politics requires television.

I think you know I've never really warmed up to television, and in fairness to television, it's never really warmed up to me. . . .

I like to look someone in the eye. . . . I don't believe it's possible any more to run for president without the capacity to build communications every night.

Notes

1. The Federalist papers were a series of essays by James Madison, Alexander Hamilton, and John Jay, written in 1787 and 1788 to explain and defend the new Constitution during the struggle over its ratification (*The Federalist*, New York: Modern Library, 1937).
2. Fred I. Greenstein, "The Psychological Functions of the Presidency for Citizens," in Elmer E. Cornwell, ed., *The American Presidency: Vital Center* (Chicago: Scott, Foresman, 1966), pp. 30–36.
3. Robert Dahl, *Pluralist Democracy in the United States* (Chicago: Rand McNally, 1967), p. 136.
4. Herbert J. McClosky et al., "Issue Conflict and Consensus Among Party Leaders and Followers," *American Political Science Review 54*, June 1960.

Discussion questions

1. Define political science and describe its areas of concern.
2. Describe John Locke's views on constitutionalism and constitutional government, natural law, and the social contract. Discuss the influence of Locke's ideas upon the authors of the United States Consti-

tution. Define what the Founding Fathers meant by *republican government, limited government,* and *a strong national government.*

3. Discuss the ideal and procedural meanings of democracy and the democratic values.

4. What are the foundations of national power and how does the Constitution define and limit them? Contrast expressed (delegated) powers with implied powers and identify the clause on which implied powers are based.

5. Define *federalism* and discuss the change that has taken place in the American federalist structure. Include in your discussion definitions of *grants-in-aid* and *guidelines,* as well as an identification of the delegated congressional power that has been responsible for the change in the federalist structure.

6. Discuss the Founding Fathers' rationale for structuring the government around a separation of powers. Identify the separate power structures that the Constitution created. Using the original constitutional provisions regarding elections as an illustration, describe how the Founding Fathers' philosophy conflicted with the concepts of democracy. Define what is meant by *sharing of power.*

7. Discuss the sources of presidential power and the factors contributing to the growth of that power in the twentieth century. Briefly describe how Richard Nixon overstepped the boundaries or limitations of presidential power. Comment on how the system of checks and balances and Nixon's own failure to "play by the rules of the game" contributed to Nixon's downfall.

8. Identify the sources of judicial power. Define *judicial review* and explain why the Founding Fathers were in favor of this principle. Describe how and why the courts are "insulated."

9. Discuss participation and nonparticipation in democracy. Who participates and how is it possible to participate? Identify the titles and contents of some of the congressional acts and constitutional amendments that have removed obstacles to voting.

10. Describe the functions of political parties. Compare the American two-party system with European political party systems. How is it possible to identify real party differences in America? Identify and describe the most important factor in voting behavior.

11. What has been the impact of television on politics, especially presidential elections?

CHAPTER 8

■ POWER & HISTORY

Over the ages, history seems to have had a variety of meanings for people:

> So very difficult a matter is it to trace and find out the truth of anything by history.
> *Plutarch (46–120)*
> History is little else than a picture of human crimes and misfortunes.
> *Voltaire (1694–1778)*
> Peoples and governments never have learned anything from history, or acted on principles derived from it.
> *Hegel (1770–1831)*
> The history of the world is but the biography of great men.
> *Thomas Carlyle (1795–1881)*
> The subject of history is the life of peoples and of humanity. To catch and pin down in words . . . to describe directly the life, not only of humanity, but even of a single people, appears to be impossible.
> *Tolstoy (1828–1910)*

Despite these somewhat gloomy views, and because of the opposite proof that some of these authors have provided, we believe it is possible to learn something from history, and we hope that after you have read this chapter you will agree. In it we will take a look at the tasks that historians set themselves, the various theories they have developed, and how the perspective of history can increase our understanding of power in society. After you have read this chapter, you should be able to

- describe briefly the various approaches to American history,
- describe historian Charles Beard's "economic interpretation" of the Constitution,
- describe the power elites of various periods of American history, from the American Revolution through the New Deal,
- discuss the historical reinterpretation of the black experience during the Reconstruction era.

History and social science

Can history inform the social sciences? The purpose of this chapter is not to teach American history but rather to examine the work of historians to see what contribution they can make to our understanding of power and the social sciences.

History refers to all *past human actions and events*. The study of history is the *recording, narrating, and interpreting of these events*. History includes the discovery of facts about past events, as well as the interpretation of the events. Many historians contend that their primary responsibility is the disclosure of facts about the past: the accurate presentation of what actually happened, unbiased by interpretive theories or philosophies.

But however carefully historians try to avoid bias, they cannot report *all* the facts of human history. Facts do not select and arrange themselves. The historian must select and organize facts that are worthy of interest, and this process involves personal judgment of what is important about the past. The historian's judgment about the past is affected by present conditions and by personal feelings about the future. So the past is continually reinterpreted by each generation of historians. History is "an unending dialogue" between the present and the past; it is "what one age finds worthy of note in another."

In selecting and organizing their facts, historians must consider the causes of wars and revolutions, the reasons for the rise and fall of civilizations, the consequences of great events and ideas. They cannot marshal their facts without some notion of *interrelations* among human events. Since they must consider what forces have operated to shape the past, they become involved in economics, sociology, psychology, anthropology, and political science. Historian Henry Steele Commager has observed that "no self-respecting modern historian is content merely with recording what happened; he wants to explain why it happened."[1] Thus history and social science are intimately related.

History and the American experience

There is a great temptation to romanticize national history. Many national histories are self-congratulating, patriotic exercises. Many historical biographies paint their subjects as larger-than-life figures, free of the faults of common people, who shape the course of events themselves rather than merely responding to the world in which they live. National leaders of the past—Washington, Jefferson, Jackson, Lincoln, Franklin D. Roosevelt—are portrayed as noble men, superior in character and wisdom to today's politicians. Even with the myth of the cherry tree discarded, generations of historians have looked with awe upon the gallery of national heroes as almost superhuman individuals who gallantly saved the nation.

history
the recording, narrating, and interpreting of all past human actions and events

approaches to American history
the "great man" approach
the democratic institutions approach
the western frontier approach
critical approaches

Some national histories do not rely on "great man" explanations, but instead emphasize the origin and growth of democratic institutions. Democracy is traced from its ancient Greek beginnings, through English constitutional development, to the colonies and the American constitutional system. Frequently these national histories reinforce reverence for existing political and governmental institutions. Some are written more to support than to explain the United States.

In the 1890s historian Frederick Jackson Turner argued that the main influence on American history was not the development of political institutions from English or Greek origins, or even the actions of "great men," but the impact of the western frontier upon American society. As historians explained (and occasionally exaggerated) Turner's thesis, they wrote new and even more nationalistic sagas of the American expansion. They hailed western settlement, the Indian wars, the development of transportation and communication, and the rugged individualism of the heroic democratic frontiersman.

But historians have also been critical of American institutions. At the beginning of the twentieth century, reform politicians and muckraking journalists brought a new skepticism to American life. The Progressive era was critical of the malfunctioning of many governmental institutions that had become sacred over time—and even of the Olympian position of the Founding Fathers. In 1913 Charles A. Beard created an uproar by suggesting that economic motives played a part in leading the Founding Fathers to write the Constitution.

Nevertheless, for the most part the quest for the American past has been carried on in a spirit of sentiment and nostalgia, rather than critical analysis. Historical novels, fictionalized biographies, pictorial collections, books on American regions—all appeal to our fondness for looking back to what we believe was a better era. Americans have a peculiar longing to recapture the past, to try to recover what seems to have been lost.

Power and change

Our own bias about the importance of power in society leads us to focus attention on *changing sources of power over time* in American history, and the characteristics of the people and groups who have acquired power. We contend that the Constitution itself, and the national government that it established, reflected the beliefs, values, and interests of the men of power—the elite—of the new republic. If we are to have a true understanding of the Constitution, we must investigate the political interests of the Founding Fathers and the historical circumstances surrounding the Philadelphia convention in 1787.

studying changes in sources of power over time

Power structures change over time. To understand power in society we have to explore the historical development of power relationships. Any society, to maintain stability and avoid revolution, must provide opportunities for talented and ambitious individuals to acquire power. As an expanding economy created new sources of wealth, power in the United States shifted to those groups and individuals who acquired the new economic resources. Western expansion and settlement, industrialization, immigration, urbanization, technological innovation, and new sources of wealth—all created new bases of power and new power holders.

But power in the United States has changed slowly, without any serious break in the ideas and values underlying the American political and economic system. The nation has never experienced a true revolution, in which national leadership is formally replaced by groups or individuals who do not share the values of the system itself. Instead, changes have been *slow* and *incremental*. New national leaders have generally accepted the national consensus about private enterprise, limited government, and individualism.

incremental change
slow and continuous rather than rapid or revolutionary

Historian Richard Hofstadter argues effectively that many accounts of the American past overemphasize the political differences in every era:

> The fierceness of the political struggles has often been misleading; for the range of vision embraced by the primary contestants in the major parties has always been bounded by the horizons of property and enterprise.

historical consensus
beliefs shared over time

However much at odds on specific issues, the major political traditions have shared a belief in the rights of property, the philosophy of economic individualism, the value of competition; they have accepted the economic virtues of capitalist culture as necessary qualities of man. Even when some property right has been challenged—as it was by followers of Jefferson and Jackson—in the name of the rights of man or the rights of the community, the challenge, when translated into practical policy, has actually been urged on behalf of some other kind of property.

The sanctity of private property, the right of the individual to dispose of and invest it, the value of opportunity, and the natural evolution of self-interest and self-assertion, within broad legal limits, into a beneficent social order have been staple tenets of the central faith in American political ideologies; these conceptions have been shared in large part by men as diverse as Jefferson, Jackson, Lincoln, Cleveland, Bryan, Wilson, and Hoover.[2]

Over the years, America's political leadership has been essentially conservative. Whatever the popular label of the American political and economic system—Federalist, Democrat, Whig, Republican, Progressive, Conservative, or Liberal—American leaders have remained committed to the same values and ideas that motivated the Founding Fathers. Although major changes in public policy and in the structure of American government have indeed taken place over two centuries, these changes have been *incremental* rather than revolutionary.

In the following pages we will examine how sources of power in America have gradually changed. We will trace these changes in power elites from the days of the American Revolution, through the boom of the American West and Jacksonian Democracy, to the Civil War and its aftermath—the rise of the industrial capitalist—up to the New Deal and the emergence of a liberal elite.

■ Charles Beard: The economic interpretation of the Constitution ■

Charles Beard, historian and political scientist, provided the most controversial historical interpretation of the origin of American national government in his landmark book *An Economic Interpretation of the Constitution*. Not all historians agree with Beard's interpretation—particularly his emphasis on economic forces—but all concede that it is a milestone in understanding the American Constitution. From an analysis of the economic interests of the Founding Fathers, Beard drew the following conclusions:

- The movement for the Constitution of the United States was originated and carried

through principally by four groups of personality interests which had been adversely affected under the Articles of Confederation: money, public securities, manufactures, and trade and shipping.

- The first firm steps toward the formation of the Constitution were taken by a small and active group of men immediately interested through their personal possessions in the outcome of their labors.

- No popular vote was taken directly or indirectly on the proposition to call the Convention which drafted the Constitution.

- A large propertyless mass was, under the prevailing suffrage qualifications, excluded at the outset from participation (through representatives) in the work of framing the Constitution.

■ The members of the Philadelphia Convention which drafted the Constitution were, with a few exceptions, immediately, directly, and personally interested in, and derived economic advantages from, the establishment of the new system.

■ The Constitution was essentially an economic document based upon the concept that the fundamental private rights of property are anterior to government and morally beyond the reach of popular majorities.

■ The major portion of the members of the Convention are on record as recognizing the claim of property to a special and defensive position in the Constitution.[3]

Beard argued that to understand the Constitution we must understand the economic interests of the national elite, which included the writers of the document:

Did the men who formulated the fundamental law of the land possess the kinds of property which were immediately and directly increased in value or made more secure by the results of their labors in Philadelphia? Did they have money at interest [loans outstanding]? Did they own public securities [government bonds]? Did they hold Western lands for appreciation? Were they interested in shipping and manufactures?[4]

Beard was *not* charging that the Founding Fathers wrote the Constitution exclusively for their own benefit. But he argued that they personally benefited immediately from its adoption, and they did not act only "under the guidance of abstract principles of political science." Beard closely studied old unpublished financial records of the U.S. Treasury Department and the personal letters and financial accounts of the fifty-five delegates to the Philadelphia convention. Table 8-1 sum-

TABLE 8-1 Founding Fathers classified by known economic interests

Public security interests		Real estate and land speculation	Lending and investments	Mercantile, manufacturing, and shipping interests	Plantations and slaveholdings
Major	*Minor*				
Baldwin	Bassett	Blount	Bassett	Broom	Butler
Blair	Blount	Dayton	Broom	Clymer	Davie
Clymer	Brearley	Few	Butler	Ellsworth	Jenifer
Dayton	Broom	FitzSimons	Carroll	FitzSimons	A. Martin
Ellsworth	Butler	Franklin	Clymer	Gerry	L. Martin
FitzSimons	Carroll	Gerry	Davie	King	Mason
Gerry	Few	Gilman	Dickinson	Langdon	Mercer
Gilman	Hamilton	Gorham	Ellsworth	McHenry	C. C. Pinckney
Gorham	L. Martin	Hamilton	Few	Mifflin	C. Pinckney
Jenifer	Mason	Mason	FitzSimons	G. Morris	Randolph
Johnson	Mercer	R. Morris	Franklin	R. Morris	Read
King	Mifflin	Washington	Gilman		Rutledge
Langdon	Read	Williamson	Ingersoll		Spaight
Lansing	Spaight	Wilson	Johnson		Washington
Livingston	Wilson		King		Wythe
McClurg	Wythe		Langdon		
R. Morris			Mason		
C. C. Pinckney			McHenry		
C. Pinckney			C. C. Pinckney		
Randolph			C. Pinckney		
Sherman			Randolph		
Strong			Read		
Washington			Washington		
Williamson			Williamson		

marizes his findings of the financial interests of the Founding Fathers. Beard then turned to an examination of the *Constitution* itself, in the original form in which it emerged from the Convention, to observe the *relationship between economic interests and political power.*

There are seventeen grants of power to Congress in Article I, Section 8, followed by a general grant of power to make "all laws which shall be necessary and proper for carrying into execution the foregoing powers." The first and perhaps the most important enumerated power is the power to "lay and collect taxes, duties, imposts, and excises." The *taxing power* is, of course, the basis of all other powers, and it enabled the national government to end its dependence on the states. The taxing power was of great benefit to the holders of public securities, particularly when it was combined with the provision in Article VI that "all debts contracted and engagements entered into before the adoption of this Constitution shall be as valid against the United States under this Constitution as under the Confederation." This meant that the national government would be obliged to pay off all those investors who held bonds of the United States, and the taxing power would give the national government the ability to do so on its own.

Congress was also given the power to "regulate commerce with foreign nations, and among the several states." The *interstate commerce clause,* which eliminated state control over commerce, and the provision in Article I, Section 9, which prohibited the states from taxing exports, created a free-trade area, or "common market," among the thirteen states. In *The Federalist* paper No. 11, Hamilton describes the advantages of this arrangement for American merchants:

> The speculative trader will at once perceive the force of these observations and will acknowledge that the aggregate balance of the commerce of the United States would bid fair

to be much more favorable than that of the thirteen states without union or with partial unions.

Following the power to tax and spend, to borrow money, and to regulate commerce in Article I, there is a series of *specific powers designed to enable Congress to protect money and property.* Congress is given the power to make bankruptcy laws, to coin money and regulate its value, to fix standards of weights and measures, to punish counterfeiting, to establish post offices and post roads, to pass copyright and patent laws to protect authors and inventors, and to punish piracies and felonies committed on the high seas. Each of these powers is a specific asset to bankers, investors, merchants, authors, inventors, and shippers. Obviously, the Founding Fathers felt that giving Congress control over currency and credit in America would result in better protection for financial interests than if this important responsibility were left to the states. Likewise, control over communication and transportation ("post offices and post roads") was believed to be too essential to trade and commerce to be left to the states.

All the other powers in Article I deal with *military affairs*—raising and supporting armies; organizing, training, and calling upon the state militia; declaring war; suppressing insurrections; and repelling invasions. These powers in Article I, together with the provisions in Article II making the president the commander in chief of the army and navy and of the state militia when called into the federal service, and giving the president the power to make treaties with the advice and consent of the Senate and to send and receive ambassadors—all combined to *centralize diplomatic and military affairs at the national level.* The centralization of diplomatic-military power is confirmed in Article I, Section 10, in which the states are specifically prohibited from entering into treaties with foreign nations, maintaining ships of war, or engaging in war unless actually invaded. It is clear that the Founding Fathers had little confidence in the state militia, particularly when it was under state control. Moreover, if western settlers were to be protected from the Indians, and if the British were to be persuaded to give up their forts in Ohio and open the way to American westward expansion, the national government could not rely upon state militia but must instead have an army of its own. Similarly, a strong navy was essential to the protection of American commerce on the seas (the first significant naval action under the new government was taken against the piracy of the Barbary States). Thus a national army and navy were not so much for protection against invasion (for many years the national government would continue to rely primarily upon state militia for this purpose) as for the *protection and promotion of its commercial and territorial ambitions.*

Protection against domestic insurrection also appealed to the southern slaveholders' deep-seated fear of a slave revolt. The Constitution permitted Congress to outlaw the *importation of slaves* after the year 1808. But most of the southern planters were more interested in protecting their existing property and slaves than they were in extending the slave trade, and the Constitution provided an explicit advantage to slaveholders in Article IV, Section 2 (later altered by the Thirteenth Amendment abolishing slavery):

> No person held to service or labor in one state, under the laws thereof, escaping into another, shall, in consequence of any law or regulation therein, be discharged from such service or labor, but shall be delivered up on claim of the party to whom such service or labor may be due.

Slaves were one of the most important forms of property in America at the time, and this constitutional provision was an extremely valuable protection for slaveholders. The slave trade lapsed twenty years after the Constitution was written, but slavery as a domestic institution was better safeguarded under the new Constitution than under the Articles of Confederation.

The *restrictions placed upon state legislatures* by the Constitution also provided protection to economic elites in the new nation. States were not allowed to coin money, issue paper money, or pass legal tender laws that would make any money other than gold or silver coin tender in the payment of debts. This restriction would prevent the states from issuing cheap paper money, which could be used by debtors to pay off their creditors with less valuable currency.

The Constitution also forbids states to pass any law "impairing the obligation of contracts." The structure of business relations in a free enterprise economy depends upon governmental enforcement of private contracts, and it is essential to economic elites that the government be prevented from relieving persons of their obligations to contracts. If state legislatures could relieve debtors of their contractual obligations, or relieve indentured servants of their obligations to their masters, or prevent creditors from foreclosing on mortgages, or declare moratoriums on debt, or otherwise interfere with business obligations, the interests of investors, merchants, and creditors would be seriously damaged.

Some historians disagree with Beard's emphasis on the economic motives of the Founding Fathers. For example:

> The Constitution was adopted in a society which was fundamentally democratic, not undemocratic; and it was adopted by people who were primarily middle-class property owners, especially farmers who owned realty, not just by the owners of personalty. . . . The Constitution was not just an economic document, although economic factors were undoubtedly important. Since most of the people were middle-class and had private property, practically everybody was interested in the protection of property.[5]

Moreover, in the struggle over ratification of the Constitution, it is clear that some people of prestige, reputation, and property opposed accepting the new Constitution. Influential Anti-Federalists deplored the undemocratic features of the Constitution, and their criticism about the omission of a bill of rights led directly to the inclusion of the first ten amendments. Supporters of the Constitution were forced to retreat from their demand for unconditional ratification, and they agreed to add the Bill of Rights as amendments as soon as the first Congress was convened under the Constitution.

■ Frederick Jackson Turner: The rise of the West ■

As we have noted, power relationships change over time. Industrialization, urbanization, technological change, and new sources of wealth create new bases of power and new power holders. The governmental structure of society must provide for changes in the distribution of power or suffer the threat of instability and even revolution. The political system must provide for the "circulation of elites" as new bases of power and new power holders emerge in society.

According to historian Frederick Jackson Turner, "The rise of the New West was the most significant fact in American history."[6] Certainly the American West had a profound impact on the political system of the new nation. People went west because of the vast wealth of fertile lands that awaited them there; nowhere else in the world could one acquire wealth so quickly. Because aristocratic families of the eastern seaboard seldom had reason to migrate westward, the western settlers were mainly middle- or lower-class immigrants. With hard work and good fortune, a penniless migrant could become a rich plantation owner or cattle rancher in a single generation. Thus the West meant rapid upward social mobility.

New elites arose in the West and had to be assimilated into America's governing circles. Their assimilation had a profound effect on the character of America's elite. No one exemplifies the new entrants better than Andrew Jackson. Jackson's victory in the presidential election of 1828 was not a victory of the common man over the propertied classes, but a victory of the new western elite over established Republican leadership in the East. It forced the established elite to recognize the growing importance of the West and to open their ranks to the new rich who were settled west of the Alleghenies.

Since Jackson was a favorite of the people, it was easy for him to believe in the wisdom of the masses. But "Jacksonian Democracy" was by no means a philosophy of leveling egalitarianism. The ideal of the frontier society was the self-made individual, and wealth and power won by *competitive skill* were much admired. What offended the frontierspeople was wealth and power obtained through special privilege. They believed in a *natural aristocracy,* rather than an aristocracy by birth, education, or special privilege. It was *not* absolute equality that Jacksonians demanded but a *more open elite system*—a greater opportunity for the rising middle class to acquire wealth and influence through competition.

In their struggle to open America's elite system, the Jacksonians appealed to mass sentiment. Jackson's humble beginnings, his image as a self-made man, his military adventures, his frontier experience, and his rough, brawling style endeared him to the masses. As beneficiaries of popular support, the new elite of the West developed a strong faith in the wisdom and justice of popular decisions. All the new western states that entered the Union granted universal white male suffrage, and gradually the older states fell into step. The rising elite, themselves often less than a generation away from the masses, saw in a widened electorate a chance for personal advancement that they could never have achieved under the old regime. Therefore, the Jacksonians became noisy and effective advocates of the principle that all men should have the right to *vote* and that no restrictions should be placed upon *officeholding*. They also launched a successful attack upon the congressional caucus system of nominating presidential candidates. Having been defeated in Congress in 1824, Jackson wished to sever Congress from the nominating process. In 1832, when the Democrats held their first national convention, Andrew Jackson was renominated by acclamation.

Jacksonian Democracy also brought changes in the method of selecting presidential electors. The Constitution left to the various state legislatures the right to decide how presidential electors should be chosen, and in most cases the legislatures themselves chose the electors. But after 1832 all states elected their presidential electors by popular vote. In most states the people voted for electors who were listed under the name of their party and their candidate.

The Civil War and elite division

Social scientists can gain insight into societal conflict and the breakdown of elite consensus through the study of history—particularly the history of the American Civil War. America's elite were in substantial agreement about the character and direction of the new nation during its first sixty years. In the 1850s, however, the role of blacks in American society—the most divisive issue in the history of American politics— became an urgent question that drove a wedge between elites and ultimately led to the nation's bloodiest war. The political system was unequal to the task of negotiating a peaceful settlement to the problem of slavery because America's elites were themselves deeply divided over the question.

division among the elite

It was the white elite and not the white masses of the South who had an interest in the slave and cotton culture. On the eve of the Civil War probably not more than 400,000 southern families—approximately one in four—held slaves. And many of those families held only one or two slaves each. The number of great planters—men who owned fifty or more slaves and large holdings of land—was probably not more than 7,000. Yet the views of these men dominated southern politics.

southern elite
plantation owners dependent on slave labor

The northern elite consisted of merchants and manufacturers who depended upon free labor. However, the northern elite had no direct interest in the abolition of slavery in the South. Some northern manufacturers were making good profits from southern trade, and with higher tariffs they stood a chance to make even better profits. Abolitionist activities imperiled trade relations between North and South and were often looked upon with irritation in northern social circles.

northern elite
manufacturers dependent on wage labor

Both northern and southern elites realized that control of the West was the key to future dominance of the nation. The northern elite wanted a West composed of small farmers who produced food and raw materials for the industrial and commercial East and provided a market for eastern goods. But southern planters feared the voting power of a West composed of small farmers and wanted western lands for the expansion of the cotton and slave culture. Cotton ate up the land and, because it required continuous cultivation and monotonous rounds of simple tasks, was suited to slave labor. Thus, to protect the cotton economy, it was essential to expand westward and to protect slavery in the West. The conflict over western land eventually precipitated the Civil War.

Yet despite such differences, the underlying consensus of American elites was so great that compromise after compromise was devised to maintain unity. Both northern and southern elites displayed a continued devotion to the principles of constitutional government and the protection of private property. In the Missouri Compromise of 1820, the land in the Louisiana Purchase exclusive of Missouri was divided between free territory and slave territory at 36°30′; and Maine and Missouri were admitted to the Union as free and slave states, respectively. After the war with Mexico, the elaborate Compromise of 1850 caused one of the greatest debates in American legislative history, with Senators Henry Clay, Daniel Webster, John C. Calhoun, Salmon P. Chase, Stephen A. Douglas, Jefferson Davis, Alexander H. Stephens, Robert Toombs, William H. Seward, and Thaddeus Stevens all participating. Cleavage within the elite was apparent, but it was not yet so divisive as to split the nation. A compromise was achieved, providing for the admission of California as a free state; for the creation of two new territories, New Mexico and Utah, out of the Mexican cession; for a drastic fugitive slave law to satisfy southern planters; and for the prohibition of the slave trade in the District of Columbia. Even the Kansas–Nebraska Act of 1854 was intended to be a compromise; each new territory was supposed to decide for itself whether it should be slave or free, the expectation being that Nebraska would vote free and Kansas slave. Gradually, however, the spirit of compromise gave way to divergence and conflict.

Beginning in 1856, proslavery and antislavery forces fought it out in "bleeding Kansas." Senator Charles Sumner of Massachusetts delivered a condemnation of slavery in the Senate and was beaten almost to death on the Senate floor by Congressman Preston Brooks of South Carolina. Intemperate language in the Senate became commonplace, with frequent threats of secession, violence, and civil war. In 1857 a southern-dominated Supreme Court decided, in *Dred Scott* v. *Sanford,* that the Missouri Compromise was unconstitutional because Congress had no authority to forbid slavery in any territory. Slave property, said Chief Justice Roger B. Taney, was as much protected by the Constitution as was any other kind of property. In 1859 John Brown and his followers raided

the U.S. arsenal at Harper's Ferry, as a first step to freeing the slaves of Virginia by force. Brown was captured by Virginia militia under the command of Colonel Robert E. Lee, tried for treason, found guilty, and executed. Southerners believed that Northerners had tried to incite the horror of slave insurrection, while Northerners believed that Brown died a martyr.

Yet historian Richard Hofstadter observes that even in the midst of this disastrous conflict one finds extensive evidence of attempts to maintain consensus among the elite. There were many genuine efforts at compromise and conciliation. Abraham Lincoln never attacked slavery in the South; his exclusive concern was to halt the spread of slavery in the western territories. He wrote in 1845: "I hold it a paramount duty of us in the free states, due to the union of the states, and perhaps to liberty itself (paradox though it may seem), to let the slavery of the other states alone."[7] Throughout his political career Lincoln consistently held this position. On the other hand, with regard to the western territories, he said: "The whole nation is interested that the best use shall be made of these territories. We want them for homes and free white people. This they cannot be, to any considerable extent, if slavery shall be planted within them."[8] In short, Lincoln wanted the western territories to be tied economically and culturally to the northern system. As for Lincoln's racial views, as late as 1858 he said:

Lincoln's views and slavery

> I will say, then, that I am not, nor ever have been, in favor of bringing about in any way the social and political equality of the white and black races: that I am not, nor ever have been, in favor of making voters or

jurors of negroes, nor of qualifying them to hold office, nor to intermarry with white people. . . .

And inasmuch as they cannot so live, while they do remain together there must be the position of superior and inferior, and I as much as any other man am in favor of having the superior position assigned to the white race.[9]

Lincoln's goal: to preserve the Union

Hofstadter believes that Lincoln's political posture was essentially *conservative:* he wished to preserve the long-established *order and consensus that had protected American principles and property rights* so successfully in the past. He was *not* an abolitionist, and he did *not* seek the destruction of the southern elite or the rearrangement of the South's social fabric. His goal was to bring the South back into the Union, to restore orderly government, and to establish the principle that states cannot resist national authority with force. At the beginning of the Civil War Lincoln knew that a great part of conservative northern opinion was willing to fight for the Union but might refuse to support a war to free slaves. Lincoln's great political skill was his ability to gather all the issues of the Civil War into one single overriding theme—the preservation of the Union. However, he was bitterly attacked throughout the war by radical Republicans who thought he had "no antislavery instincts."

As the war continued and casualties mounted, opinion in the North became increasingly bitter toward southern slaveowners. Many Republicans joined the abolitionists in calling for emancipation of the slaves simply to punish the "rebels." They knew that the power of the South was based on the labor of slaves. Lincoln also knew that if he proclaimed to the world that the war was being fought to free the slaves, there would be less danger of foreign intervention.

real origin of the Emancipation Proclamation

On 22 September 1862, Lincoln issued his preliminary Emancipation Proclamation. Claiming his right as commander in chief of the army and navy, he promised that "on the first day of January, . . . 1863, all persons held as slaves within any State, or designated part of a State, the people whereof shall then be in rebellion against the United States, shall be then, thenceforward, and forever free." Thus, one of the great steps forward in human freedom in this nation, the Emancipation Proclamation, did not come about as a result of demands by the people, and certainly not as a result of demands by the slaves themselves. Historian Richard Hofstadter contends that the Emancipation Proclamation was a political action taken by the president for the sake of helping to preserve the Union. It was not a revolutionary action but a conservative one.

Power and the Industrial Revolution

the rise of the industrial elite

The importance of the Civil War for the power structure of the United States lay in the commanding position that the new industrial capitalists won during the course of that struggle. Even before 1860, northern industry had been altering the course of American life; the

economic transformation of the United States from an agricultural to an industrial nation reached the crescendo of a revolution in the second half of the nineteenth century. Canals and steam railroads had been opening up new markets for the growing industrial cities of the East. The rise of corporations and of stock markets for the accumulation of capital upset old-fashioned ideas about property. The introduction of machinery in factories revolutionized the conditions of labor and made the masses dependent on industrial capitalists for their livelihood. Civil War profits compounded the capital of the industrialists and placed them in a position to dominate the economic life of the nation. Moreover, when the southern planters were removed from the national scene, the government in Washington became the exclusive domain of the new industrial leaders.

The new industrial elite found a new philosophy to justify its political and economic dominance. Drawing an analogy from Darwinian biology, Herbert Spencer undertook to demonstrate that, just as an elite was selected in nature through evolution, so also society would near perfection as it allowed a natural *social* elite to be selected by *free competition*. Spencer hailed the accumulation of new industrial wealth as a sign of "the survival of the fittest." The *social Darwinists* found in the law of survival of the fittest an admirable defense for the emergence of a ruthless ruling elite, an elite that defined its own self-interest more narrowly, perhaps, than any other in American history. It was a philosophy

social Darwinism
competition selects the best; a philosophy justifying great accumulations of wealth

that permitted the conditions of the masses to decline to the lowest depths in American history.

the industrialists acquire political power

After the Civil War, industrialists became more prominent in Congress than they had ever been. They had little trouble in voting high tariffs and hard money, both of which heightened profits. Very little effective regulatory legislation was permitted to reach the floor of Congress. After 1881 the Senate came under the spell of Nelson Aldrich, son-in-law of John D. Rockefeller who controlled Standard Oil. Aldrich served thirty years in the Senate. He believed that geographical representation in that body was old-fashioned and openly advocated a Senate manned officially by representatives from the great business "constituencies"—steel, coal, copper, railroads, banks, textiles, and so on.

the rise of the modern corporation

The corporate form of business facilitated the amassing of capital by limiting the liability of capitalists to their actual investments and thereby keeping their personal fortunes safe in the event of misfortunes to their companies. The corporate form also encouraged capitalists to take risks in expanding industrial capital through the stock market. "Wall Street," the address of the nation's busiest security market—the New York Stock Exchange—became a synonym for industrial capitalism. The markets for corporation stocks provided a vast and ready money source for new enterprises or for the enlargement and consolidation of old firms.

John D. Rockefeller
founder of the Standard Oil Company monopoly

Typical of the great entrepreneurs of industrial capitalism was John D. Rockefeller. By the end of the Civil War Rockefeller had accumulated a modest fortune in wholesale grain and meat. In 1865, with extraordinary good judgment, he invested his money in the wholly new petroleum business. He backed one of the first oil refineries in the nation and continually reinvested his profits in his business. In 1867 he and two partners—H. M. Flagler and F. W. Harkness—founded the Standard Oil Company of Ohio, which in that year refined 4 percent of the nation's output. By 1872, with monopoly as his goal, he had acquired twenty of the twenty-five refineries in Cleveland and was laying plans that within a decade would bring him into control of over 90 percent of the oil refineries of the country. Rockefeller bought up pipelines, warehouses, and factories and was able to force the railroad to grant him rebates. In 1882 he formed a giant trust, the Standard Oil Company, with a multitude of affiliates. Thereafter, the Standard Oil Company became a prototype of American monopolies. As Rockefeller himself put it: "The day of combination is here to stay. Individualism has gone, never to return." But a series of antitrust cases inspired by President Theodore Roosevelt resulted in the Supreme Court decision *United States v. Standard Oil Co.* (1911), which forced the Rockefellers to split the company into several parts: the Exxon Corporation (which is still the largest industrial corporation in America), Standard Oil of California, Standard Oil of Ohio, Standard Oil of Indiana, Atlantic Richfield, and Mobil.

The New Deal and the emergence of "the liberal establishment"

The economic collapse of the Great Depression undermined the faith of both rich and poor in the idea of "social Darwinism." Following the stock market crash of October 1929, and in spite of assurances by President Herbert Hoover that prosperity lay "just around the corner," the American economy virtually stopped. Prices dropped sharply, factories closed, real estate values declined, new construction practically ceased, banks went under, wages were cut drastically, unemployment figures mounted, and welfare rolls swelled.

impact of the Great Depression

The election of Franklin Delano Roosevelt to the presidency in 1932 ushered in a new era in American political philosophy. The Great Depression did *not* bring about a revolution; it did *not* result in the emergence of new elites; but it did have an important impact on the *thinking* of America's governing circles. The economic disaster that had befallen the nation caused the elite to consider the need for economic reform. The Great Depression also reinforced the notion that the elite must acquire a greater public responsibility. The victories of fascism in Germany and communism in the Soviet Union and the growing restlessness of the masses in the United States made it plain that *reform and regard for the public welfare* were essential to the continued maintenance of the American political system and the dominant place of the elite in it.

new era in elite thinking
reform and welfare to preserve American democracy

Roosevelt sought to elaborate a New Deal philosophy that would permit government to devote much more attention to the public welfare than did the philosophy of Hoover's somewhat discredited "rugged individualism." The New Deal was not a revolutionary system but rather a

Roosevelt and the New Deal
to reform capitalism, not replace it

necessary *reform* of the existing capitalist system. In the New Deal, the American elite accepted the principle that the entire community, through the agency of the national government, has a *responsibility for mass welfare*. Roosevelt's second inaugural address called attention to "one-third of a nation, ill housed, ill clad, ill nourished." Roosevelt succeeded in preserving the existing system of private capitalism and avoiding the threats posed to the established order by fascism, socialism, communism, and other radical movements.

Historian Richard Hofstadter comments on Roosevelt's liberal, public-regarding philosophy:

> At the beginning of his career he took to the patrician reform thought of the progressive era and accepted a social outlook that can best be summed up in the phrase "noblesse oblige." He had a penchant for public service, personal philanthropy, and harmless manifestos against dishonesty in government; he displayed a broad easy-going tolerance, a genuine liking for all sorts of people; he loved to exercise his charm in political and social situations.[10]

Roosevelt's personal philosophy was soon to become the prevailing ethos of the new liberal establishment.

the origins of liberalism

Thus, liberalism in the United States today is a product of elite response to economic depression at home and the rising threats of fascism and communism abroad. Its historical origin can be traced to elite efforts to *preserve* the existing political and economic system through reform. This historical perspective on the liberal tradition gives us a better understanding of the origins of change and reform within society. In a broader view, the historical perspective expands our understanding of society in general, and, as we hope this chapter has shown, can indeed contribute to our understanding of the nature and uses of power in society. In the case study that follows, we will examine the revisions that the historical perspective must sometimes undergo.

■ Reconstruction and black history ■

The ideal history, completely objective and dispassionate, is really an illusion. Consciously or unconsciously, all historians are biased. There is bias in their choice of subject, in their selection of material, in their organization and presentation of the material, and, inevitably, in their interpretation of it.

Let us consider the historical interpretation of black experience in America, particularly of black experience in the Reconstruction era following the Civil War. Only a few years ago historians viewed the Reconstruction Congress as vindictive and sinful. The period as a whole was considered destructive, oppressive, and corrupt. Military rule was imposed upon the South. "Carpetbaggers" and "scallywags" confiscated the property of helpless southerners and retarded the economic progress of the South for decades. Maladministration and corruption in the federal government were portrayed as being greater than ever before in American history. The role of blacks in the Reconstruction years was regarded with ridicule: it was implied that blacks were pushed into positions of authority by spiteful military rulers in order to humiliate proud southern whites. The accomplishments of blacks during this period were overlooked. Finally, it was suggested that the separation of the races—segregation—was the "normal" pattern of southern life. The belief was fostered that blacks and whites in the South had never known any other pattern of life than slavery and segregation.

A new awareness of black history in recent years has resulted in a thoroughgoing reinterpretation of the Reconstruction era. Historian C. Vann Woodward's work led the way in bringing new light to this important period. Woodward recorded the progress of blacks during Reconstruction, described the good-faith efforts of the Reconstruction Congress to secure equality for black Americans, and explained the reimposition of segregation in terms of class conflict among whites. (Alex Haley's popular book *Roots,* together with the dramatic television series based on it, is another example of historical interpretation. Whereas many older histories of the pre–Civil War South romanticized plantation life, *Roots* described the cruelties and brutality of slavery.)

A revised view of Reconstruction: Black progress.

When the radical Republicans (as opposed to the moderate faction within the party) gained control of Congress in 1867, blacks momentarily seemed destined to attain their full rights as U.S. citizens. Under military rule southern states adopted new constitutions that awarded the vote and other civil liberties to blacks. Black men were elected to state legislatures and to the U.S. Congress. In 1865 nearly 10 percent of all federal troops were black. The literacy rate among blacks rose rapidly as hundreds of schools set up by the federal government's Freedmen's Bureau began providing education for ex-slaves.[11]

The first black actually to serve in Congress was Hiram R. Revels of Mississippi,

who in 1870 took over the Senate seat previously held by Confederate President Jefferson Davis. In all, twenty-two southern blacks served in Congress between 1870 and 1901. All were elected as Republicans; thirteen were former slaves. Many of those men made substantial contributions to Reconstruction policy. Robert B. Elliott, of South Carolina, won national fame when he delivered a two-hour speech on behalf of the Civil Rights Act of 1875. The last black congressman under Reconstruction from the South was George H. White, of North Carolina, who finally left Congress in 1901.

The accomplishments of the Reconstruction Congress were considerable. Even before the radical Republicans gained control, the Thirteenth Amendment, which abolished slavery, had become part of the Constitution. But it was the Fourteenth and Fifteenth Amendments and the important Civil Rights Act of

1875 that attempted to secure a place for the blacks in the United States equal to that of whites. The wording of the Fourteenth Amendment was explicit:

> No state shall make or enforce any law which shall abridge the privileges or immunities of citizens of the United States; nor shall any state deprive any person of life, liberty, or property, without due process of law; nor deny to any person within its jurisdiction the equal protection of the laws.

The Civil Rights Act of 1875 declared that all persons were entitled to the full and equal enjoyment of all public accommodations—inns, public conveniences, theaters, and other places of public amusement. In this act the Reconstruction Congress committed the nation to a policy of nondiscrimination in all aspects of public life.

But by 1877 support for Reconstruction policies began to crumble. In what has been described as the "Compromise of 1877," the national government agreed to end military occupation of the South, thereby giving up its efforts to rearrange southern society and lending tacit approval to white supremacy in that region. In return, the southern states pledged their support for the Union, accepted national supremacy, and enabled the Republican candidate, Rutherford B. Hayes, to assume the presidency following the much-disputed election of 1876 in which his opponent, Samuel Tilden, had received a majority of the popular vote.

The development of the white supremacy movement. The withdrawal of federal troops from the south in 1877 did not bring about an instant change in the status of the blacks. Southern blacks voted in large numbers well into the 1880s and 1890s. Certainly we do not mean to suggest that discrimination was nonexistent during that period. Perhaps the most debilitating of all segregation—that in the public schools—appeared

immediately after the Civil War under the beneficent sanction of Reconstruction authorities. Yet segregation took shape only gradually, and largely as the result of political and economic conflicts that divided southern whites.

Segregation was closely associated with the rise of *populism*—a movement purporting to represent the interests of the common people—in the South. Interestingly, the earliest southern populists attempted to enlist blacks in a coalition of white and black poor people against the wealthy plantation owners. However, they soon came to realize that this strategy was bound to fail, since racial prejudice was greatest among the poor whites to whom their appeal was directed. These were the classes most subject to deep-rooted fears of the black man. The planters, realizing that the populists had erred in their strategy, were able to discredit the early populists by fanning the flames of racial hatred, thus driving a wedge between poor blacks and poor whites. Alarmed by the populists' successes in the 1880s and 1890s (especially after the formation of the Populist party in 1891), the wealthy soon raised the cries of "Negro domination" and "white supremacy," thereby galvanizing the racial fears of southern whites of all classes. The planters of the rich lowland counties needed an issue—even better, a scapegoat—to oppose the growing influence of white farmers from the mountainous counties. Soon the Populists realized that they would have to dissociate themselves from blacks and adopt the white supremacy position.

The first objective of the *white supremacy movement* was to disenfranchise blacks. The standard devices developed for achieving this feat were the literacy test, the poll tax, the white primary, and various forms of intimidation. Following the disenfranchisement of blacks, the white supremacy movement established segregation and discrimination as public policy by the adoption of a large number of

"Jim Crow" laws, designed to prevent the mingling of whites and blacks (Jim Crow was a stereotype Negro in a nineteenth-century song-and-dance show). Between 1900 and 1910 laws were adopted by southern state legislatures requiring segregation of the races in streetcars, in hospitals, in prisons, in orphanages, and in homes for the aged and indigent. A New Orleans ordinance decreed that white and black prostitutes confine their activities to separate districts. In 1913 the federal government itself adopted policies that segregated the races in federal office buildings, cafeterias, and restroom facilities. Social policy followed (indeed, exceeded) public policy. Little signs reading "White Only" or "Colored" appeared everywhere, with or without the support of law.

Response of blacks to segregation.
Many early histories of Reconstruction paid little attention to the response of blacks to the imposition of segregation. But there were at least three distinct types of response: (1) accommodation and acceptance of a subordinate position in society, (2) participation in the formation of a black protest movement, and (3) migration out of the South to avoid some of the consequences of white supremacy.

The foremost black advocate of accommodation to segregation was the well-known black educator Booker T. Washington. Washington enjoyed wide popularity among both white and black Americans. He was an adviser to two presidents (Theodore Roosevelt and William Howard Taft) and was highly respected by white philanthropists and government officials. In his famous Cotton States' Exposition speech in Atlanta in 1895, Washington assured whites that blacks were prepared to accept a separate position in society:

> As we have proved our loyalty to you in the past, in nursing your children, watching by the sickbed of your mothers and fathers, and often following them with tear-dimmed eyes to their graves, so in the future, in our humble way, we shall stand by you. . . . In all things that are purely social we can be as separate as the fingers, yet one as the hand in all things essential to mutual progress.[12]

Booker T. Washington's hopes for black America lay in a program of self-help through education. He himself had attended Hampton Institute in Virginia, where the curriculum centered around practical trades for blacks. Washington obtained some white philanthropic support in establishing his own Tuskegee Institute in Tuskegee, Alabama, in 1881. His first students helped build the school. Training at Tuskegee emphasized immediately useful vocations, such as farming, preaching, and blacksmithing. Washington urged his students to stay in the South, to acquire land, and to build homes, thereby helping to eliminate ignorance and poverty among their fellow blacks. One of Tuskegee's outstanding faculty members was George Washington Carver, who researched and developed uses for southern crops. Other privately and publicly endowed black colleges were founded that later developed into major universities, including Fisk and Howard (both started by the Freedmen's Bureau) and Atlanta, Hampton, and Southern.

While Washington was urging blacks to make the best of segregation, a small band of blacks were organizing themselves behind a declaration of black resistance and protest that would later rewrite American public policy. The leader of this group was W. E. B. Du Bois, a brilliant historian and sociologist at Atlanta University. In 1905 Du Bois and a few other black intellectuals met in Niagara Falls, Canada, to draw up a black platform intended to "assail the ears" and sear the consciences of white Americans. In rejecting moderation and compromise, the Niagara statement proclaimed: "We refuse to allow the impression to remain that the Negro American assents to inferiority, is submissive under oppression and apologetic before insults." The platform listed the major injustices perpetrated against blacks since Reconstruction: the loss of voting rights, the imposition of Jim Crow laws and segregated public schools, the denial of equal job opportunities, the existence of inhumane conditions in southern prisons, the exclusion of blacks from West Point and Annapolis, and the failure on the part of the federal government to enforce the Fourteenth and Fifteenth Amendments. Out of the Niagara meeting came the idea for a nationwide organization dedicated to fighting for blacks, and on 12 February 1909, the one-hundredth anniversary of Abraham Lincoln's birth, the National Association for the Advancement of Colored People (NAACP) was founded.

Du Bois himself was on the original board of directors of the NAACP, but a majority of the board consisted of white liberals. In the years to follow, most of the financial support and policy guidance for the association was provided by whites rather than blacks. However, Du Bois was the NAACP's first director of research and the editor of its magazine, *Crisis*. The NAACP began a long and eventually successful campaign to establish black rights through legal action. Over the years, hundreds of court cases were brought at the local, state, and federal court levels on behalf of blacks denied their constitutional rights.

World War I provided an opportunity for restive blacks in the South to escape the worst abuses of white supremacy by migrating en masse to northern cities. In the years 1916 to 1918, an estimated half-million blacks moved to the North to fill the labor shortage caused by the war effort. Most migrating blacks arrived in big northern cities only to find more poverty and segregation. But at least they could vote and attend better schools, and they were not obliged to step off the sidewalk into the gutter when a white man approached.

The progressive "ghettoization" of black Americans—their migration from the rural South to the urban North and their increasing concentration in central-city ghettos—had profound political, as well as social, implications. The ghetto provided an environment conducive to collective mass action. Even as early as 1928, the black residents of Chicago were able to elect one of their own to the House of Representatives. The election of Oscar de Priest, the first black congressman from the North, signaled a new turn in American urban politics by announcing to white politicians that they would have to reckon with the black vote in northern cities. The black ghettos would soon provide an important element in a new political coalition that was about to take form—namely, the Democratic party of Franklin Delano Roosevelt.

The increasing concentration of blacks in northern ghettos in large, politically competitive, "swing" states provided black voters with new political power—not only to support the Democratic party coalition in national politics but also to elect black men to local public office. Today black mayors serve, or have served, in cities as diverse as Los Angeles, Detroit, Gary, Atlanta, and Newark. Thus, this particular case of "revisionist" history helps social scientists to understand how blacks coped with segregation and emerged from this experience with new power, unity, and purpose.

Notes

1. Henry Steele Commager, *The Study of History* (Columbus, Ohio: Merrill, 1965), p. 79.
2. Richard Hofstadter, *The American Political Tradition and the Men Who Made It* (New York: Vintage Books, 1956), p. viii.
3. Charles Beard, *An Economic Interpretation of the Constitution* (New York: Macmillan, 1913), pp. 324–325.
4. Ibid., p. 73.
5. Robert E. Brown, *Charles Beard and the Constitution* (Princeton, N.J.: Princeton University Press, 1956), p. 200.
6. Frederick Jackson Turner, "The West and American Ideals," in *The Frontier in American History* (New York: Holt, 1921).
7. Richard Hofstadter, *The American Political Tradition* (New York: Knopf, 1948), p. 109.
8. Ibid., p. 113.
9. Ibid., p. 116.
10. Ibid., pp. 323–324.
11. For a general history of Reconstruction politics, see C. Vann Woodward, *Reunion and Reaction* (Boston: Little, Brown, 1951); also see C. Vann Woodward, *The Strange Career of Jim Crow* (New York: Oxford University Press, 1957).
12. Quoted in Henry Steele Commager, ed., *The Struggle for Racial Equality: A Documentary Record* (New York: Harper & Row, 1967), p. 19.

Discussion questions

1. Describe the various approaches to studying history. Comment on the strengths or weaknesses of each.
2. What were Charles Beard's two main approaches to understanding the Constitution? Describe briefly how the following constitutional provisions were of immediate benefit to the nation's elite: taxing power; interstate commerce clause; congressional powers to protect money and property; power to raise an army and navy; Article IV, Section 2, which required the return of runaway slaves and indentured servants; restrictions on state legislatures; prevention of laws impairing obligation of contracts. Discuss the criticisms of Beard's interpretation of the Constitution.
3. Describe the power elite that was created by expansion into the American West. What factors contributed to the emergence of this elite, and what was its power base? Identify the factor that significantly contributed to the assimilation of this elite into American governing circles. Describe the philosophy of this new elite and the impact that it had on both the elite system and the electoral system.

4. Describe the economic interests of northern and southern elites on the eve of the Civil War. What were their points of conflict and of agreement? Discuss at least one of the compromises these elites attempted. Describe Lincoln's attitude toward slavery and his attempts at preserving consensus. Why was the Emancipation Proclamation a conservative, rather than a revolutionary, document?

5. Describe the power elite that emerged in the aftermath of the Civil War. What factors contributed to the rise of this elite? Discuss the philosophy that this elite adopted, as well as the influence that this elite had on Congress.

6. Discuss the impact that the Great Depression had on both elite and nonelite philosophy, and the kind of elite thinking that developed in this era. What foreign influences had an impact on this new thinking? Briefly describe Franklin Delano Roosevelt's New Deal philosophy.

7. Show how historical interpretations of the same historical events can radically differ by contrasting earlier interpretations of the Reconstruction era with the more recent interpretations of historian C. Vann Woodward.

Finally, classical liberalism, as a *political* ideology, is closely related to *capitalism* as an *economic* ideology. Capitalism asserts the individual's right to own private property and to buy, sell, rent, and trade in a free market. The economic version of freedom is the freedom to make contracts, to bargain for one's services, to move from job to job, to join labor unions, to start one's own business. Capitalism and classical liberal democracy are closely related as economic and political systems. Capitalism stresses individual rationality in economic matters; freedom of choice in working, producing, buying, and selling; and limited governmental intervention in economic affairs. Liberal democracy emphasizes individual rationality in voter choice; freedom of speech, press, and political activity; and limitations on governmental power over individual liberty. In liberal politics individuals are free to speak out, to form political parties, and to vote as they please—to pursue their political interests as they think best. In liberal economics, individuals are free to find work, to start businesses, and to spend their money as they please—to pursue their economic interests as they think best. The role of government is restricted to protecting private property, enforcing contracts, and performing only those functions and services that cannot be performed by the private market.

classical liberalism and capitalism
political freedom and economic freedom related

Modern liberalism: Governmental power to "do good"

Modern liberalism rationalizes and justifies much of the growth of governmental power in the United States in the twentieth century. Modern liberalism retains the fundamental commitment to *individual dignity.* But it emphasizes the importance of *social* and *economic security* of a whole population as a prerequisite to individual self-realization and self-development. Classical liberalism looked with suspicion on government as a potential source of "interference" with personal freedom; but modern liberalism looks upon the *power of government as a positive force* to be used to contribute to the elimination of social and economic conditions that adversely affect people's lives and impede their self-development. The modern liberal approves of the use of governmental power to ensure the general social welfare and to correct the perceived ills of society.

governmental power
a positive force in protecting the individual

Modern liberals believe they can change people's lives through the exercise of governmental power: end discrimination, abolish poverty, eliminate slums, ensure employment, uplift the poor, eliminate sicknesses, educate the masses, and instill humanitarian values in everyone. The prevailing impulse is to *do good,* to perform public services, and to assist the least fortunate in society, particularly the poor and the black. Modern liberalism is impatient with what it sees as slow progress through individual initiative and private enterprise toward the solution of socioeconomic problems, so it seeks to use the power of the national government to find *immediate* and *comprehensive* "solutions" to society's troubles.

reform of capitalism

Modern liberalism is frequently critical of certain aspects of capitalism, but it proposes to *reform* capitalism rather than replace it with socialism. Modern liberalism continues to recognize the individual's right to own private property, but it imposes on the property owner social and economic obligations that are designed to reduce capitalism's hardships. It assumes that business will be privately owned, but subject to considerable governmental regulation. Thus the government intervenes to ensure fair labor standards, minimum wages, healthy working conditions, consumer protection, and so forth. Modern liberalism stresses the utility of government fiscal policies—taxing and spending—for maintaining full employment and economic stability. Modern liberals are committed to a significant *enlargement* of the public (governmental) sector of society—in matters having to do with education, welfare, housing, recreation facilities, transportation, urban renewal, medicine, employment, child care, and so on. Modern liberalism envisions a larger role for government in the future—setting new goals, managing the economy, meeting popular wants, and drastically redirecting national resources away from private wants toward public needs.

reduction of extreme inequalities

Modern liberalism places much greater emphasis on the value of equality than does classical liberalism. Classical liberalism stresses the value of equality of opportunity: individuals should be free to make the most of their talents and skills, but differences in wealth or power that are a product of differences in talent, initiative, risk taking, and skill are accepted as natural. In contrast, modern liberalism contends that *individual dignity and equality of opportunity depend in some measure upon reduction of absolute inequality* in society. Modern liberals believe that true equality of opportunity cannot be achieved where there are significant numbers of people suffering from hunger, remediable illness, or extreme hardships in the conditions of life. They believe that the existence of opportunities to "rise" in employment, housing, education, and the like depends upon a certain degree of absolute equality. Thus modern liberalism supports government efforts to reduce extreme inequalities in society.

Conservatism: The insights of Edmund Burke

conservatism and liberalism

In the United States today "conservatism" is associated with classical liberalism. Conservatives in this country retain the early liberal commitment to individual freedom from governmental controls; maximum personal liberty; reliance upon individual initiative and effort for self-development, rather than governmental programs and projects; a free-enterprise economy with a minimum of governmental intervention; and rewards for initiative, skill, risk, and hard work, in contrast to government-imposed "leveling" of income. These views are consistent with the

early classical liberalism of Locke, Jefferson, and the nation's Founding Fathers. The result, of course, is a confusion of ideological labels: Conservatives today charge modern liberals with abandoning the principles of individualism, limited government, and free enterprise, and today's conservatives claim to be the true "liberals" in society.

Modern conservatism does indeed incorporate much of classical liberalism, but conservatism also has a distinct ideological tradition of its own. Indeed, conservatism had its origins in *reaction* to the excesses of early liberalism, particularly the radical liberalism of the French Revolution. The first important statement of modern conservatism is found in Edmund Burke's assessment of French liberalism, *Reflections on the Revolution in France,* written in 1790.

Conservatism is not as optimistic as liberalism about human nature. Traditionally, conservatives realized that human nature includes elements of irrationality, intolerance, extremism, ignorance, prejudice, hatred, and violence. Thus they were more likely to place their faith in *law* and *tradition* than in the popular emotions of mass movement. Edmund Burke recognized selfish and irrational human motives. He believed that without law or tradition, people would exist in a jungle of violence, terror, and chaos—a jungle in which only the most powerful would survive by cunning, deceit, and violence. If law and tradition were discredited and exclusive reliance placed upon rationality, the fabric that holds society together would be weakened. Without the protection of law and tradition, people and societies are vulnerable to terror and violence. The absence of law does not mean freedom, but rather, exposure to the tyranny of terrorism and violence.

conservatism and human nature

Conservatives doubt the ability of governmental planners to solve all of society's problems. Edmund Burke believed that reason was a valuable and distinctive human gift, but he challenged the views of

doubts about government

liberals that the answers to every human problem were already at hand or could easily be discovered. In Burke's eyes this attitude was unpardonable conceit, and he was convinced that the intellectual arrogance of liberal reformers could lead society into chaos. Conservatives since Burke have doubted the rational powers of governmental bureaucracies. They tend to think that societies are held together not exclusively by government programs and policies but also by *traditional morality* and *force of habit,* and that the progress of civilization depends as much on the *maintenance of social order* as on governmental planning.

preference for evolutionary change

Conservatism sets forth an *evolutionary* view of social progress. Burke believed that real progress in society was the outcome of continuous social change over a prolonged period of time. Revolutionary change is far more likely to set back society than to improve it. But over time, people can experiment in small ways with incremental changes; continued from generation to generation, this process of evolutionary change leads to a progressive improvement in the condition of humanity. *No government* possesses the wisdom to resolve all problems, but the cumulative experience of society does produce certain workable arrangements for the amelioration of social ills. Gradual progress is possible, but only if people do not destroy the painfully acquired wisdom of the past in favor of new, untried utopian solutions that jeopardize the well-being of society.

tradition and morality as guides

Conservatives hold that people are rational beings, but that they are also victims of passion. Irrational drives and impulses—hatred, prejudice, intolerance, violence—are constantly at war with rational judgment and humane feelings. Without the guidance of law, tradition, and morality, people would soon come to grief by the unruliness of their passions, destroying both themselves and others in pursuit of selfish gain. Rationalism is far from a sufficient guide to action; law, tradition, and morality are also needed for the realization of human purposes. Left to their own instincts, without the benefit of the accumulated wisdom of ages, and without institutions to channel and modify their aggressive instincts, people will degenerate to savagery. *Strong institutions*—family, church, and community—are needed to repress selfish and irrational impulses of individuals and to inculcate civilized ways of life.

family, church, and community

Fascism: The supremacy of race and nation

the supremacy of the nation over the individual

Fascism is an ideology that asserts the supremacy of the nation or race over the interests of individuals or groups—in the words of Benito Mussolini: "Everything for the state; nothing against the state; nothing outside of the state." The state is the embodiment of a unifying, ethical "ideal" that stands above the materialistic class interest of a Marxist or the selfish individualism of the liberals.

the organic state

Fascism perceives the state as not merely a governmental bureaucracy but the organic life of a whole people. According to Mussolini, "The

BOX 9-1 Americans: Middle of the road

■ Most Americans think of themselves as "middle of the road," rather than as "liberal" or "conservative." Of course, it is difficult to know exactly what people mean when they do describe themselves as liberals or conservatives. These terms mean different things to different people. We cannot be sure that all the people asked in public opinion surveys to describe their own views attach the same meaning to those terms as do social scientists. Nonetheless, more people chose to call themselves "middle of the road" than either "liberal" or "conservative." People describing themselves as "conservative" clearly outnumber people describing themselves as "liberal." Indeed, in recent years the conservatives' lead over the liberals has widened. Figure 9-1 graphs these comparative trends.

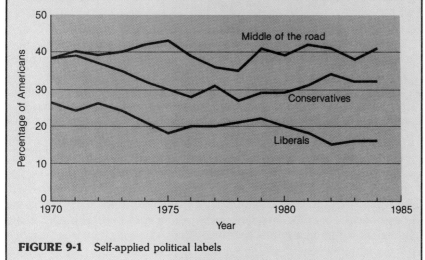

FIGURE 9-1 Self-applied political labels

Italian nation is an organism having ends, life, and means of action superior to those of the separate individuals or groups of individuals which compose it." In *Mein Kampf,* written prior to his assumption of power, Adolf Hitler added to the concept of an organic state, with his idea of the *Volk* (people) in which race and nation are united.

"Volk"
race and nation united

> The highest purpose of the volkish State is the care for the preservation of those racial primal elements which, supplying culture, create the beauty and dignity of a higher humanity. We, as Aryans, are therefore able to imagine a state only to be the living organism of a nationality which not only safeguards the preservation of that nationality, but which, by a further training of its spiritual and ideal abilities, leads it to the highest freedom.[2]

The central ideal of the *Volk,* then, is that of a racial folk or an "organic people" with a life, will, and purpose of its own.

the goal of the fascist state
the superior human being

The *goal* of the fascist state is not the welfare of the mass of people but the *development of a superior type of human being*. The goal is the cultivation of the best qualities of a people—bravery, courage, creativity, genius, intelligence, and strength. Fascism values the superior individual who rises out of the mire of mass mediocrity—and the superior nation that rises above the vast anthill of humankind. If life is a struggle for existence in which the fittest survive, then strength is the ultimate virtue and weakness is a fault. Good is that which survives and wins; bad is that which fails. Socialism, communism, and democracy mean the worship of mediocrity and the hatred of excellence; not the superior person but the majority person becomes the ideal and the model; everyone comes to resemble everyone else. These ideologies submerge what is best and noble in the people. All of this degrades the race and contradicts the theory of evolution. In contrast, fascism admires heroism in individuals and nations. War frequently brings out the best in a nation: unity, bravery, strength, and courage.

triumph of "will" over "reason"

Fascism asserts the superiority of "will" over "reason." The great deeds of history were performed not by reason but by heroic will. Peoples are preserved *not* by rational thought but by racial intuition. They rise to greatness when their will to power surmounts physical and worldly handicaps. Happiness is a poor motive in comparison with hero-ism, self-sacrifice, duty, and discipline. This irrationalism derives from a belief that life is too difficult, too complex, and too changeable to be reduced to a rational formula—that nature is driven by many forces, as yet unknown to science, that can be understood only by intuition and genius. The one universal law is that of the survival of the fittest. The fascist hero is the opposite of the democratic common man. He lives dangerously and is prepared to meet disaster. He does not wish to be mediocre, but instead superior in everything he does. He creates his own rules and tramples down the opposition.

Fascism offers itself as a *merger of nationalism and socialism.* Prior to World War II, fascism in Italy and in Germany put itself forward as a socialist regime adopted to national purposes. The party of Adolf Hitler was the National Socialist party or "Nazi" party. Since under fascism the nation is an organic whole, the economy ought to be *cooperative* rather than competitive. Every class and every interest ought to work together for the *good of the nation.* Thus national socialism was designed to ap-peal not only to the working class but also to the lower-middle class—the small shopkeepers and salaried employees—who suffer from inflation and depression and who are fearful of the prospect of being degraded to the ranks of the proletariat, a fate that Marxism had promised them. A program of national socialism involves *complete control* of the national economy by the national government in the national interest. Against the rights of liberty or equality, national socialism established the duties of *service, devotion, and discipline.* As an extreme form of nationalism, fas-cism identified internationalism with cowardice and lack of honor. In-deed, fascism depended for its driving force on sentiments of national patriotism.

a "cooperative" economy

The power structure of a fascist regime is totalitarian. The unity of the fascist state requires "one people, one party, one leader." The fas-cist believes that a natural, superior, self-made leadership will emerge to provide intelligence and direction to the nation. The Nazi elite emerges from political combat as the fittest and most deserving of political sur-vival; there is no interest in mass vote counting. A Nazi leadership repre-sents *das Volk* simply by embodying more clearly and explicitly its will to power. At the head of the fascist elite is the leader—*Il Duce* in Italy or *Der Fuehrer* in Germany—in whose name everything is done, who is said to be "responsible" for all, but whose acts can nowhere be called into question. The leader is neither a scholar nor a theorist, but a charismatic man of action. Fascism strives for a *totality of power* in which all sectors of society—education, labor, art, science—are incorporated into the state and serve the purposes of the state. No sphere of social activity is free from national scrutiny and control. All society's resources are viewed as resources of the state.

a totalitarian power structure

Marxism: "Workers of the world, unite"

the roots of socialism and communism

Liberalism began as an eighteenth-century revolt against the aristocracy of a feudal system. Socialism represents a nineteenth-century revolt against the privileged wealth of a capitalist system. Communism is a particularly violent strain of the larger ideological movement of socialism. Both socialism and communism arose out of the Industrial Revolution and the *social evils* it generated. Even though the Industrial Revolution led to a rapid rise in standards of living in western Europe, what impressed many early observers of this revolution was the economic inequalities it engendered. Throughout much of the nineteenth century, the only beneficiaries of the new industrialism seemed to be the successful manufacturers, bankers, merchants, and speculators; the lot of the slum-dwelling working classes showed little improvement. This was a bitter disappointment to the humanitarian hopes of many who had earlier embraced liberalism in the expectation that the rewards of economic progress would be shared by everyone. It appeared that liberalism and capitalism had simply substituted an aristocracy of wealth for an aristocracy of birth.

early utopian socialism

The first stirrings of socialism date back to the days of the French Revolution itself. Although the majority of French revolutionists were liberals whose aim it was to establish *equality of opportunity,* there were already a few who wished to establish *absolute equality* of wealth and income. The rise of Napoleon appeared to check the growth of socialism for a time, but a number of *utopian socialists* continued to develop schemes to replace the free market system with cooperative, egalitarian communities. Much of this effort was directed toward founding small communistic communities that were self-sufficient and organized on a cooperative basis, with profits from labor distributed equally among the members of the community. This socialism was mild and philanthropic; it was neither political nor violent. Utopian socialism and communal living never amounted to a strong political movement or a full-fledged ideology. The man who finally made socialism an effective ideology and a successful political movement was Karl Marx.

Karl Marx

Like many other socialists, Karl Marx (1818–1883) was an upper-middle-class intellectual. He was educated at the University of Berlin and began his career as a professor of philosophy. When his radicalism barred academic advancement, he turned to journalism and moved to Paris. There he met Friedrich Engels, a wealthy young intellectual who supported Marx financially and collaborated with him on many of his writings. It was Marx's humanitarian sympathy for industrial workers, not his personal experience in a factory, that led him to devote his activities to the cause of the working classes. The *Communist Manifesto* (1848) was a political pamphlet—short, concise, and full of striking phrases. It provided an ideology to what had previously been no more than scattered protest against injustices. The *Manifesto* set forth the key ideas of Marxism, which would be developed twenty years later in great detail in a lengthy work, *Das Kapital*.

Economic determinism.   Communism believes that the nature of the economy, or "modes of production," is basic to all the rest of society. The mode of production determines the class structure, the political system, religion, education, family life, law, and even art and literature. Thus the mode of production determines the basic social structure of society, and the rest is simply "superstructure," which is also molded by the prevailing economic arrangements. For example, the economic structure of feudalism creates a class structure of a privileged aristocracy and a suffering serfdom. The economic structure of capitalism creates a class structure of a wealthy *bourgeoisie* (a property-owning class of capitalists) who control the government and exercise power over the *proletariat* (the propertyless workers).

economic determinism
the nature of the economy determines the social structure

Class struggle.   The first sentence of the *Communist Manifesto* exclaims, "The history of all hitherto existing society is the history of class struggles." These class struggles are created by the mode of production; the class that owns the mode of production is in the dominant position and *exploits* the other classes. Such exploitation creates antagonism, which gradually increases until it bursts into revolution. The means of production in the Middle Ages was land, and the aristocracy that owned the land controlled government and society. The Industrial Revolution created a new class, the bourgeoisie, which rose to importance because it owned the means of production—money, machines, and factories. But just as the aristocracy was supplanted by the bourgeoisie, so the bourgeoisie will in the course of time be superseded by the proletariat. The capitalist exploits the worker to the point at which the worker is forced to revolt against the oppressors and overthrow the capitalist state.

class struggle
the basic conflict in any society

Theory of surplus value.   According to Marx, *labor* is the only source of value. Labor is the one thing common to all commodities and gives each commodity its value. As Marx put it, "All wealth is due to labor, and therefore, to the laborer, all wealth is due." Although laborers deserve the full value of the commodity they make, under capitalism they receive only a small part of it, just enough for their subsistence. The rest, which Marx called *surplus,* is taken by the capitalists for their own enrichment. Thus the capitalist system is a gigantic scheme for exploiting the workers by confiscating the surplus value they have created. The practical solution, of course, is to make it impossible for capitalists to exploit workers by establishing "collective ownership of all means of production, distribution, and exchange." In other words, the proletariat

theory of surplus value
labor is the only source of value, and profits belong to the workers

must eliminate the capitalist and take over all the tools of production, distribution, and exchange so that the surplus value will not flow to the capitalist.

Inevitability of revolution. Not only did Marx predict the coming of the proletariat revolution, but he also sought to show that such a revolution was inevitable. According to the *Communist Manifesto,* "What the bourgeoisie produces, above all, is its own grave-diggers. Its fall and the victory of the proletariat are equally inevitable." As capitalists try to maximize their profits, the rich become richer and the poor become poorer. Moreover, competition squeezes out small capitalists, and ownership is gradually concentrated in the hands of fewer and fewer capitalists. As exploitation increases, and as more petty capitalists are forced into the ranks of the proletariat, both the strength and the antagonism of the proletariat increase. The proletariat develops a working-class consciousness and ultimately rises up against the exploiters. As capitalists drive wages down to maximize profits, capitalism becomes plagued by a series of crises or depressions, each one worse than the one before. As wages are forced ever lower, capitalists soon cannot sell their products because of the lower purchasing power of the proletariat, and depression follows. Further, as capitalists introduce more machinery, the demand for labor declines, and unemployment rises. The result of these internal contradictions in capitalism is a great deal of human misery, which eventually explodes in revolution. Thus, in their drive for profit, capitalists really dig their own grave by bringing the revolution ever closer.

Dictatorship of the proletariat. Although Marx claimed that the coming of the revolution is inevitable, he nonetheless urged the workers to organize for revolutionary action. The *Communist Manifesto* closes with the words, "The proletarians have nothing to lose but their chains. They have a world to win. Working men of all countries, unite!" The capitalists will never peacefully give up their ruling position. Only a violent revolution will place the proletarians in power. When the proletarians come to power, they, like ruling classes before them, will set up a state of their own—a dictatorship of the proletariat—to protect their class interests. Unlike governments of the past, however, which served oppressive minorities, the proletariat dictatorship will be a government by and for the great majority of workers. It will seize the property of the capitalist majority and place ownership of the modes of production in the hands of the proletariat. The bourgeoisie will be eliminated as a class.

Withering away of the state. Since class differences depend on ownership of the modes of production, the result of *common ownership* will be a one-class, or *classless,* society. Since the purpose of government is to assist the ruling class in exploiting and oppressing other classes, once a classless society is established the government will have no purpose and will gradually "wither away." In the early stages of the revolution the rule of distribution will be "from each according to his ability, to each according to his work." But after the victory of communism and the establishment of a full classless society, the rule of distribution will be "from each according to his ability, to each according to his need." After the elimination of classes, society will be peaceful and cooperative, and there will no longer be any need for coercion. Government and its coercive powers will disappear forever.

classless society of peace and cooperation will emerge and the need for government will disappear

Socialism: From private enterprise to public ownership

There is a bewildering variety of definitions of socialism. Communists employ the term as a label for societies that have experienced successful communist revolutions and are in the process of developing a communist society. Occasionally critics of governmental programs in the United States label as "socialist" any program or policy that restricts free enterprise in any way. Socialism is also frequently confused with egalitarianism—governmental efforts to achieve absolute equality or "leveling" of wealth or income. But fundamentally, socialism means *public ownership of the means of production, distribution, and service.* Socialists agree on one point: private property in land, buildings, factories, and stores must be transformed into social or collective property. The idea of *collective ownership* is the core of socialism.

socialism
collective ownership

Socialism shares with communism a *condemnation of the capitalist system* as exploitive of the working classes. Communists and socialists agree on the evils of industrial capitalism—the exploitation of labor, the concentration of wealth, the insensitivity of the profit motive to human needs, the insecurities and sufferings brought on by the business cycle, the conflict of class interests, and the propensity of capitalist nations to involve themselves in war. In short, most socialists agree with the criticisms of the capitalist system set forth by Marx.

socialism and communism
condemnation of capitalism

However, socialists are committed to the *democratic process* as a means of replacing capitalism with collective ownership of economic enterprise. They generally reject the desirability of revolution as a way to replace capitalism and instead advocate peaceful constitutional roads to socialism. Moreover, socialists have rejected the idea of a socialist "dictatorship"; they contend that the goal of socialism is a *free society* embodying the democratic principles of freedom of speech, press, assembly, association, and political activity. They frequently claim that socialism in the economic sector of society is essential to achieving democracy and equality in the political sector of society. In other words, they believe that true democracy cannot be achieved until wealth is widely distributed and the means of production are commonly owned.

democratic socialism
replacing capitalism through democratic processes

BOX 9-2   Capitalism and socialism in the world

■ In reality all modern economics use some combination of capitalist and socialist economic organization. In primarily capitalist countries like the United States, the government protects private property, provides some public goods, and regulates and taxes business. In socialist countries, government ownership and central control of the economy exist side by side with a small but often significant free market. Socialist governments forbid free markets in most goods (the Soviet Union refers to most market activities as "economic crimes"), although small "black markets" are allowed.

The chart below presents a rough classification of governments in the world today according to their reliance on capitalist or socialist economic organization.

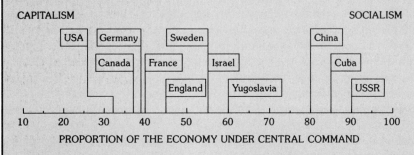

CAPITALISM   SOCIALISM

USA	Germany		Sweden		China
Canada	France		Israel		Cuba
	England		Yugoslavia		USSR

10   20   30   40   50   60   70   80   90   100

PROPORTION OF THE ECONOMY UNDER CENTRAL COMMAND

- Productive resources owned by private individuals and firms
- Workers employed by private individuals and firms or self-employed
- Investment undertaken by private individuals and firms in search of profit
- Allocation of goods by market forces
- Income determined by market forces that reward productivity and ownership

- Productive resources owned by government
- Workers employed by government
- Investment ordered by government planners according to their own goals
- Allocation of goods by government planners according to their own goals
- Income determined by government planners who may seek to reward productivity or achieve equality or any other goals they desire

Wealth must be redistributed in such a way as to make it possible for all persons to share in the benefits created by society. Redistribution means a transfer of ownership of all substantial economic holdings to the government. But the transfer must be accomplished in a democratic fashion, rather than by force or violence; and a socialist society must be governed as a true democracy.

Socialists are generally committed to an *evolutionary* approach to the achievement of common ownership of an economic enterprise. They reject the necessity of violent revolution or civil war. They are prepared for a gradual evolutionary restructuring of society—a restructuring that can take place within the framework of liberal democratic traditions. Socialists are ready to *cooperate* with liberal parties to achieve improvements in the conditions of the working classes—to mitigate the conditions of the impoverished, maintain full employment, regulate economic cycles, extend social security, eliminate discrimination, and expand educational and cultural opportunities for the masses. Unlike communists, they envision a gradual change from private to public ownership of property. Thus socialists may begin by "nationalizing" the railroads, the steel industry, the automobile industry, privately owned public utilities, or other specific segments of the economy. Nationalization involves governmental seizure of these industries from private owners, perhaps accompanied by some form of compensation. Many socialists realize that support for collective ownership must not rest exclusively on a single class. Socialists have learned through hard experience that their programs have to have the approval of a *wide* segment of the public, and not merely the working class. See Box 9-2 for a comparison of capitalist and socialist economies.

democratic socialist programs

■ Marxism-Leninism in the Soviet Union ■

The task fell to Lenin to reinterpret Marxism as a revolutionary ideology, to carry out a successful communist revolution, and to construct a communist state in the Soviet Union after the 1917 Revolution. Lenin contributed a great deal to communist ideology—so much so that contemporary communist ideology is frequently referred to as *Marxism-Leninism.*

From the Russian standpoint in 1917, Marxism was a discouraging doctrine because its hopes for the future were based on conditions that were supposed to emerge in the later stages of industrialism. Marx believed that the communist revolution would occur when capitalism itself had produced a class of factory workers that would be large enough to overcome its capitalist rulers. But this theory did not apply in pre-World War II Russia, which was still a semifeudal society of peasants and landlords, with only a small number of factory workers and an even smaller number of capitalists. Lenin, however, believed that Russia could skip the capitalist stage of

revolution and move directly from a feudal order to a communist society. His belief was based on the decay of the Russian state after decades of inefficient despotism under the czarist regime. To Lenin the Russian political system appeared so weak that it could be destroyed by a relatively small, disciplined, hard-core group of professional revolutionaries.

The totalitarian party. According to Lenin, the *key to a successful revolution* was the creation of a new and revolutionary type of totalitarian political party composed of militant professional revolutionaries. This party would be organized and trained like an army to obey the commands of superior officers. While western European socialist parties were gathering millions of supporters in relatively democratic organizations, Lenin constructed a small, exclusive, well-disciplined, elitist party. First he described such a party in an early pamphlet, entitled *What Is to Be Done;* then he proceeded to organize it. Under his skilled leadership the Communist party of the Soviet Union became the first modern totalitarian party.

Lenin could justify the creation of a highly disciplined party elite on the basis of Marx's ambiguous attitudes toward democracy. Marx's idea of a *dictatorship of the proletariat,* and his phrase the *vanguard of the proletariat,* seemed to suggest an *elitist* view of the revolutionary process. Lenin seized upon these and amplified them into an elitist and totalitarian notion of a communist party. According to Lenin the Communist party is the true "vanguard of the proletariat"—the most advanced and class-conscious sector of the proletariat, which has an exclusive right to act as spokesperson for the proletariat as a whole and to exercise the dictatorial powers of the proletariat over the rest of society. There is no need to ask who speaks for the masses, or even who speaks for the proletariat; the Communist party *is* the voice of the proletariat and it can legitimately exercise dictatorial powers in the name of the proletariat.

The theory of imperialism.   Lenin also tried to come to grips with two dilemmas: Why were capitalist societies still flourishing in the twentieth century, contrary to Marx's prediction? And why was the condition of the working classes improving, rather than deteriorating? Lenin's theory of *imperialism* was an attempt to answer these embarrassing questions. According to Lenin, when advanced capitalist countries were unable to find home markets for their products because of depressed worker income, they were obliged to turn outward and to seize colonial markets. This maneuver enabled them, for the time being at least, to expand without forcing the wages of their own workers down to subsistence level. By "exporting poverty abroad" they managed to keep their own workers relatively prosperous, thus delaying the development of true proletariat class consciousness in their own countries. Lenin believed that the

whole world was being divided into exploiters and exploited, with backward nations providing the surplus labor for more advanced nations. To shore up the shaky foundations of capitalism, capitalist nations were continually obliged to strive for fresh colonial markets. Of course, they were thus brought into bitter conflict with one another in their attempt to expand their respective empires. The final state of capitalism, therefore, would assume the form of *imperialist warfare* as rival capitalist nations engaged in a struggle to control colonial markets. To Lenin, World War I was proof that this advanced stage of capitalist decay had been reached and the worldwide capitalist system was ready for destruction. The idea of worldwide imperialism and exploitation also helped to explain why revolutionary activities in economically backward regions could be successful despite the absence of industrial capitalism. Since the inhabitants of these regions were the most cruelly exploited of all the world's workers, the revolution need not begin in the industrial heartland, but would arise at the colonial periphery.

Communism in one country.   After Lenin came to power in the Soviet Union, he found himself no longer in the position of revolutionary leader; he was the leader of a nation. Should the Soviet Union direct its energies toward immediate worldwide revolution, as envisioned by Marx? Or should it avoid confrontation with the Western world until it became a strong and self-sufficient nation? Gradually abandoning the original hopes for an immediate world revolution, Lenin and his successor, Stalin, turned to the task of creating "communism in one country." With the Communist party more firmly and centrally disciplined than ever, the Soviet leaders turned to the achievement of rapid industrialization through a series of five-year plans designed to convert a backward agrarian country into a modern industrial nation. The sweeping industrialization, brought about by the repression and terror of a totalitarian regime, came at great cost to the people. The Stalinist period saw brutality, oppression, imprisonment, purges, and murders—later officially admitted by the Soviet leaders. The Soviet regime held down the production of consumer goods in order to concentrate on development of heavy industry. As costly and ruthless as it was, the effect of this policy was the modernization of the Russian economy in the course of a single generation. In part, the ideology of communism made it possible to call upon the people for tremendous sacrifices for the good of the communist state.

Neither Marx nor Lenin proved successful as a political prophet. The state never "withered away" in communist Russia. Indeed, to maintain the communist government, a massive structure of coercion—informants, secret police, official terrorism, and a giant prison system—was erected. (The brutality of the system is described by Nobel Prize-winning author and former Soviet political prisoner Aleksandr Solzhenitsyn in *The Gulag Archipelago*.) At the same time the overall goal of world revolution, while never abandoned by the Soviet leadership, was compromised by the "realities" of world power. Particularly after the death of Stalin, the Soviet Union gradually restored its ties with the Western world. Among the factors that improved relations between ideologically opposed powers were (1) the unspeakable implications of nuclear weapons, which created a balance of terror and provided both sides with a reason to limit conflict; (2) a gradual rise in the standard of living in the Soviet Union and a relaxation of forced industrialization; and (3) the threat of an increasingly powerful Communist China on the eastern border of the USSR, which compelled the Soviet leadership to seek support against a militant revolutionary rival.

The USSR deviated from earlier interpretations of Marxism-Leninism in other ways. More and more, the Soviets have turned to the *principle of material interest*—larger rewards for better labor and management performance—indicating that they are realistic enough to accept a capitalist notion when it is in their interest to do so. Another change involves greater decentralization in industry, along with less reliance on centralized state direction. It is becoming more difficult for the central party apparatus to control the increasingly sophisticated managerial and professional elite required in an advanced technological society. Finally, there has been some decline in terrorism since the Stalinist period, although the Soviet leadership has proved that it can oscillate easily between cruel orthodoxy and relaxed experimentation as it suits its purposes.

Despite these changes, Marxist-Leninist ideology still plays a very important role in the Soviet Union today. There is no lack of interest in the continuing indoctrination of the citizenry in Marxism-Leninism—in schools, factories, collective farms, universities, the military, and social organizations.

Flaws in the Marxist theory. Marxism as a political ideology has reshaped the modern world. More than half of the world's population lives under political regimes that call themselves "communist" or "socialist." Yet Marxism as a scientific approach to understanding history and society is clearly inadequate. Let us summarize some of the more serious flaws in Marxism:

1. Capitalism has given the American people the world's highest standard of living—a standard of living that is clearly the envy of people living under socialist and communist regimes. Capitalism does *not* inevitably depress the condition of workers. On the contrary, workers in the United States own their own homes, automobiles, appliances, and other material luxuries, and the middle class has grown rather than diminished over time. Industrial workers in modern

capitalist nations have received larger and larger shares of national income, and standards of living have increased rapidly. Labor under capitalism is *not* becoming progressively miserable and downtrodden.

2. Governments in capitalist nations have responded to the pressures of organized labor and the masses of voters to provide a wide variety of health, education, and welfare programs. It is difficult to argue that U.S. national leadership has reflected only the interest of a ruling capitalist class, in view of vast governmental programs and expenditures for social security, welfare, fair labor standards, protection for union organizations, public education, and so forth. Furthermore, these programs have been financed on a progressive income tax structure that takes a larger proportion in taxation from the income of high-income persons than from low-income persons. In short, there are many examples of government programs and policies in capitalist nations that conflict with the interests of capitalists.

3. Capitalist nations have more complex social structures than the simple bourgeois-proletarian distinction of Marxism. There are many crosscutting social, political, economic, religious, and racial interests and allegiances in a modern industrial society. For example, Marx assumed that the interests of farm populations would be the same as those of factory workers, but in most nations farm populations have resisted communism. In the United States, industrial workers have been neither class conscious nor revolutionary. Ironically, support for Marxism is greater among upper-middle-class intellectuals than among industrial workers.

4. Marxism does not recognize the difference between dictatorship and democracy. The idea of a "dictatorship of the proletariat" justifies suppression, terrorism, violence, purges, imprisonment, and murder when directed against "enemies of the people." After the revolution has occurred, and the proletariat has emerged victorious, there is no reason for political parties, or opposition candidates, or dissent of any kind. In a communist society only the party of the working class—the Communist party—is permitted to exist.

5. Marxism predicts the "withering away" of the state in a communist society, but in fact communist governments have become giant bureaucracies that oversee every aspect of life and society.

Notes

1. William L. Shirer, *The Rise and Fall of the Third Reich* (New York: Simon and Shuster, 1960), p. 959.
2. Adolph Hitler, *Mein Kampf* (New York: Reynal and Hitchcock, 1939), p. 595.

Discussion questions

1. Define ideology and describe its relationship to power. Discuss the ways in which ideology can control people's behavior. Identify the characteristics of modern ideologies.

2. Compare and contrast classical liberalism and modern liberalism. What is the attitude of each of these ideologies toward the individual? What is their approach to governmental power, the concept of equality, and the capitalist system?
3. Explain the confusion that arises from the ideological labels of *conservative* and *modern liberal*.
4. Describe the goal of the fascist state. What should the attitudes of a "good" fascist be toward "happiness" and rational thought, and toward the economy and the power structure?
5. Trace the development of socialism and communism. Discuss what Marx meant by economic determinism; class struggle; the theory of surplus value; the inevitability of revolution; the dictatorship of the proletariat; and the withering away of the state.
6. Define *socialism* and discuss how this ideology differs from communism.
7. Describe how Lenin adapted the ideology of Marxism to conditions in the Soviet Union. Describe Lenin's totalitarian party and his theory of imperialism. Discuss the "communism in one country" created by Lenin and Stalin. How was the ideology of communism used during Stalin's regime, and what rather recent changes have the goals and methods of Soviet communism undergone?
8. Describe some of the more serious flaws in Marxist theory.

CHAPTER 10

■ POWER, RACE, & SEX

Power is exercised when some individuals or groups are kept powerless by law or by custom. The long history of slavery and segregation in America is a history of the exercise of power by a white majority over a black minority—first through the institution of slavery, later through laws that segregated the races and imposed an inferior position upon blacks.

The United States has a long history of protest. The nation was in fact born as a protest against the injustices of colonialism—against powerlessness and the lack of a "voice" in controlling its own affairs. Despite that heritage, America's women and racial minorities have had a long and continuing fight against the inequalities imposed on them by their nation's laws and customs.

In 1776 Abigail Adams wrote to her husband John, who was then a delegate to the Continental Congress, cautioning him and his fellow delegates that when framing the new nation's laws they should "Remember the Ladies. . . . Do not put such unlimited power into the hands of the Husbands." She added, probably in jest, "If perticuliar care and attention is not paid to the Ladies we are determined to foment a Rebelion, and will not hold ourselves bound by any Laws in which we have no voice, or Representation."[1] The "Ladies" did not find that voice until 1920, when the Nineteenth Amendment finally guaranteed women the right to vote. And the struggle for sexual equality continues today.

In this chapter we will explore the struggles and triumphs of both blacks and women in the United States, as well as some of the inequalities that these groups suffer. After you have read it, you should be able to

- ■ discuss the civil rights movement of the 1950s and 1960s and the changes in the laws that it brought about,

- describe the inequalities against which American blacks and women have protested,
- describe the philosophy of nonviolent direct action advocated by Martin Luther King, Jr.,
- discuss the controversy over "affirmative action" goals and time-tables,
- describe the historical obstacles to black political participation, as well as recent black gains in political power,
- describe economic inequality between the sexes and various theories purporting to explain sexual inequality,
- describe the Supreme Court's reasoning in *Roe* v. *Wade* regarding the constitutionality of abortion.

Racism and the American experience

The Thirteenth Amendment abolished slavery in the United States. The Fifteenth Amendment guaranteed that the right to vote would not be denied or abridged on account of race, color, or "previous condition of servitude." The Fourteenth Amendment declared:

> No state shall make or enforce any law which shall abridge the privileges or immunities of citizens of the United States; nor shall any state deprive any person of life, liberty, or property, without due process of law; nor deny to any person within its jurisdiction the equal protection of the laws.

All three of these amendments were passed by Congress and ratified soon after the Civil War. Their language and historical context leave little doubt that their purpose was to secure for blacks a place in American society equal to that of whites. Yet for a full century these promises went unfulfilled. Segregation became the social instrument by which blacks were "kept in their place"—that is, denied social, economic, educational, and political equality—and the vast majority of blacks remained at the bottom of the social and economic structure of American society.

Segregation was supported by a variety of social practices and institutions. In many states "Jim Crowism" followed blacks throughout life: birth in a segregated hospital ward, education in a segregated school, residence in segregated housing, employment in a segregated job, eating in segregated restaurants, and burial in a segregated graveyard. Segregation was enforced by a variety of private sanctions, from the occasional lynching mobs to country club admission committees. But government was a principal instrument of segregation both in the southern and the border states of the nation. (School segregation laws in the United States in 1954 are shown in Figure 10-1.) In the northern states government was seldom used to enforce segregation, but it was also seldom used to prevent it. The results were often quite similar.

Jim Crow
laws and social customs requiring separation of the races

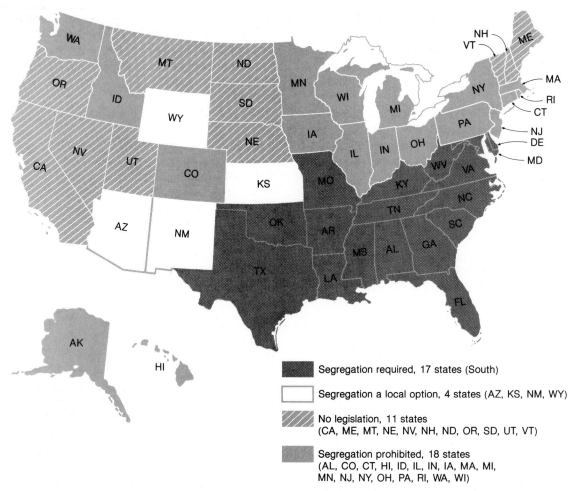

Segregation required, 17 states (South)

Segregation a local option, 4 states (AZ, KS, NM, WY)

No legislation, 11 states
(CA, ME, MT, NE, NV, NH, ND, OR, SD, UT, VT)

Segregation prohibited, 18 states
(AL, CO, CT, HI, ID, IL, IN, IA, MA, MI,
MN, NJ, NY, OH, PA, RI, WA, WI)

FIGURE 10-1 Segregation laws in the United States in 1954

"separate but equal"
interpreting the equal
protection clause of the
Fourteenth Amendment
to allow segregation of
the races if facilities were
equal (1895–1954)

The constitutional argument made on behalf of segregation—that the phrase "equal protection of the laws" did not prohibit the enforced separation of races so long as the races were treated equally—became known as the *separate-but-equal doctrine.* In 1896 the Supreme Court, in *Plessy* v. *Ferguson,* made this doctrine the official interpretation of the equal-protection clause, thus giving segregation constitutional approval.

The initial goal of the civil rights movement was the elimination of direct *legal segregation.* First, discrimination and segregation practiced by governments had to be prohibited, particularly in voting and public education. Then direct discrimination in all segments of American life, private as well as public—in transportation, theaters, parks, stores, restaurants, businesses, employment, and housing—came under attack. It is important to understand, however, that the elimination of direct lawful discrimination does not in itself ensure *equality*. The civil rights laws of the national government did not affect conditions of equality in the United States as directly as we might suppose. The problem of racial inequality—inequality between blacks and whites in income, health, housing, employment, education, and so on—is more than a problem of direct legal discrimination. Nevertheless, the first important step toward equality was the elimination of *lawful* segregation.

Led by Roy Wilkins, executive director of the National Association for the Advancement of Colored People (NAACP), and Thurgood Marshall, chief counsel for the NAACP (who was later to become the first black Supreme Court justice), the newly emerging civil rights movement of the 1950s pressed for a court decision that direct lawful segregation violated the guarantee of "equal protection of laws" of the Fourteenth Amendment. The civil rights movement sought a complete reversal of the "separate but equal" interpretation of *Plessy* v. *Ferguson;* it wanted a decision that laws separating the races were *unconstitutional*.

The civil rights group chose to bring suit for desegregation in Topeka, Kansas, where segregated black and white schools *were* equal with respect to buildings, curricula, qualifications and salaries of teachers, and other tangible factors. The object was to prevent the Court from ordering the admission of a black person because tangible facilities were not equal, and to force the Court to review the doctrine of segregation itself.

On 17 May 1954, the Court rendered its decision in *Brown* v. *Board of Education of Topeka, Kansas:*

> Segregation of white and colored children in public schools has a detrimental effect upon the colored children. The impact is greater when it has the sanction of law, for the policy of separating the races is usually interpreted as denoting the inferiority of the Negro group. A form of inferiority affects the motivation of a child to learn. Segregation with the sanction of law, therefore, has a tendency to retard the educational and mental development of Negro children and to deprive them of some of the benefits they would receive in a racially integrated school system. Whatever may have been the extent of psychological knowledge of the time of *Plessy* v. *Ferguson,* this finding is amply supported by modern authority. Any language in *Plessy* v. *Ferguson* contrary to this source is rejected.[2]

The Supreme Court's decision in *Brown* was symbolically very important. Although it would be many years before any significant numbers of black children would attend previously all-white schools, the decision by the nation's highest court stimulated black hopes and expectations. Indeed, *Brown* started the modern civil rights movement. The black psychologist Kenneth Clark writes: "This [civil rights] movement would probably not have existed at all were it not for the 1954 Supreme

initial civil rights goal
eliminating segregation by law

Brown v. Board of Education of Topeka, Kansas
landmark Supreme Court decision declaring that segregation itself violates the equal protection clause of the Fourteenth Amendment (1954)

Court school desegregation decision which provided a tremendous boost to the morale of blacks by its *clear* affirmation that color is irrelevant to the rights of American citizens."[3]

The impact of segregation *by law* has diminished over time, especially in comparison with the continuing impact of *de facto* segregation in large cities. Racial isolation occurs when schools are predominantly white or black as a result of segregated housing patterns and neighborhood schools, rather than as a result of direct lawful discrimination. The U.S. Civil Rights Commission reported that even when segregation was "de facto"—that is, not a product of direct discrimination—the adverse effects on black students were still significant.[4] However, ending de facto segregation requires changes in the prevailing concept of "neighborhood schools." Schools would no longer be a part of the neighborhood or the local community, but rather part of a larger citywide or areawide school system. Students would be assigned to schools on the basis of race, in order to maintain "racial balance." Inner-city students would be bused to the suburbs, and suburban students would be bused to the core city. If a federal district court in any city finds that any actions by governments or school officials have contributed to racial imbalances (for example, drawing school district attendance lines), the judge may order busing within the city to overcome any racial imbalances produced by official action. In recent years an increasing number of northern cities have come under federal district court orders to improve racial balances in their schools through busing.

However, in *Millikan* v. *Bradley* (1974) the Supreme Court decided by a 5-to-4 vote that *the Fourteenth Amendment does not require busing across city–suburban school district boundaries* to achieve integration.[5] Where central-city schools are predominantly black, and suburban schools are predominantly white, cross-district busing is not required, unless it is shown that some official action brought about the segregation. The Supreme Court threw out a lower federal court order for massive busing of students between Detroit and fifty-two suburban school districts. Although Detroit city schools are 70 percent black, none of the Detroit-area school districts segregated students *within* their own boundaries. Chief Justice Burger, writing for the majority, said:

> The constitutional right of the Negro respondents residing in Detroit is to attend a unitary school system in that district. Unless petitioners drew the district lines in a discriminatory fashion, or arranged for the white students residing in the Detroit district to attend schools in Oakland or Macomb counties, they were under no constitutional duty to make provisions for Negro students to do so.

In a strong dissent, Justice Thurgood Marshall wrote:

> In the short run it may seem to be the easiest course to allow our great metropolitan areas to be divided up each into cities—one white, the other black—but it is a course, I predict, our people will ultimately regret.

---

racial isolation or de facto school segregation
racial segregation resulting from housing patterns and neighborhood schools

---

busing
ending racial imbalances in schools by areawide assignments of pupils and busing them outside their home neighborhoods

---

Millikan v. Bradley
Supreme Court refuses to order city–suburban cross-district busing

This important decision means that largely black central cities, surrounded by largely white suburbs, will remain de facto segregated because there are not enough white students living within the city to achieve integration.

The Civil Rights Act of 1964

As long as the civil rights movement was combating *governmental* discrimination, it could employ the U.S. Constitution as a weapon in its arsenal. The Constitution governs the actions of governments and government officials. Since the Supreme Court and the federal judiciary are charged with the responsibility of interpreting the Constitution, the civil rights movement could concentrate on *judicial* action to accomplish its objective of preventing governmental discrimination. But the Constitution does *not* directly govern the activities of private individuals. Thus, when the civil rights movement turned its attention to combating *private* discrimination, it had to carry its fight into the *legislative* branch of government. *Only* Congress could restrict discrimination practiced by private owners of restaurants, hotels, and motels, private employers, and other individuals who were not government officials.

private discrimination
the need for legislative action

Before 1964 Congress had been content to let other agencies, including the president and the courts, struggle with the problem of civil rights. Yet Congress could not long ignore the nation's most pressing domestic issue. The civil rights movement had stepped up its protests and demonstrations and was attracting worldwide attention with organized sit-ins, freedom rides, picketing campaigns, boycotts, and mass

background

■ Martin Luther King, Jr.: The power of protest ■

The civil rights movement invented new techniques for minorities to gain power and influence in American society. *Mass protest* is a technique by which groups seek to obtain a bargaining position for themselves that can induce desired concessions from established power holders. It is a means of acquiring a bargaining leverage for those who would otherwise be powerless. The protest may challenge established groups by threatening their reputations (where they might be harmed by unfavorable publicity), their economic position (where they might be hurt by a boycott), their peace and quiet (where noise and disruption might upset their daily activities), or their security (where violence or the threat of violence is involved).

The protest technique appeals to powerless minorities who have little to bargain with except their promise *not* to protest. Once the protest has begun—or even before it has begun, if the *threat* of protest is made credible—the minority can promise not to protest in exchange for the desired concessions. Perhaps more important, mass protest frequently motivates members of established elites, who have the political resources the protesters lack, to enter the political arena on behalf of the protesters.

The nation's leading exponent of *nonviolent* protest was Dr. Martin Luther King, Jr. Indeed, King's contributions to the development of a philosophy of nonviolent, direct-action protest on behalf of blacks won him international acclaim and the Nobel Peace Prize in 1964. King first came to national prominence in 1955 when he was only twenty-five years old; he led a year-long bus boycott in Montgomery, Alabama, to protest discrimination in seating on public buses. In 1957 he formed the Southern Christian Leadership Conference (SCLC) to provide encouragement and leadership to the growing nonviolent protest movement in the South.

In 1963 a group of Alabama clergymen petitioned Martin Luther King, Jr., to call off mass demonstrations in Birmingham, Alabama. King, who had been arrested in the demonstrations, replied in his famous "Letter from Birmingham Jail":

You may well ask, "Why direct action? Why sit-ins, marches, etc.? Isn't negotiation a better path?" You are exactly right in your call for negotiation. Indeed, this is the purpose of direct action. Nonviolent direct action seeks to create such a crisis and establish such creative tension that a community that has constantly refused to negotiate is forced to confront the issue. It seeks to so dramatize the issue that it can no longer be ignored. . . .

You express a great deal of anxiety over our willingness to break laws. . . . One may well ask, "How can you advocate breaking some laws and obeying others?" The answer is found in the fact that there are *unjust* laws. I would be the first to advocate obeying just laws. One has not only a legal but a moral responsibility to obey just laws. Conversely, one has a moral responsibility to disobey unjust laws. . . .

In no sense do I advocate evading or defying the law as the rabid segregationist would do. This would lead to anarchy. One who breaks an unjust law must do it *openly, lovingly* (not hatefully as the white mothers did in New Orleans when they were seen on television screaming "nigger, nigger, nigger") and with a willingness to accept the penalty. I submit that an individual who breaks a law that conscience tells him is unjust, and willingly accepts the penalty by staying in jail to arouse the conscience of the community over its injustice, is in reality expressing the very highest respect for law.[6]

Nonviolent direct action is a technique requiring direct mass action against laws regarded as unjust, rather than court litigation, political campaigning, voting, or other conventional forms of democratic political activity. Mass demonstrations, sit-ins, and other nonviolent direct-action tactics usually result in violations of state and local laws. For example, persons remaining at a segregated lunch counter after the owner orders them to leave are usually violating trespass laws. Marching in the street frequently entails the obstruction of traffic and results in charges of "disorderly conduct" or "parading without a permit." Mass demonstrations often involve "disturbing the peace" or refusing to obey the lawful orders of a police officer. Even though these tactics are nonviolent, they do entail *disobedience to civil law.*

Civil disobedience is not new to American politics. Its practitioners have played an important role in American history, from the patriots who participated in the Boston Tea Party, to the abolitionists who hid runaway slaves, to the suffragists who paraded and demonstrated for women's rights, to the labor organizers who picketed to form the nation's major industrial unions, to the civil rights marchers of recent years. Civil disobedience is a political tactic of minorities. (Since majorities can more easily change laws through conventional political activity, they seldom have to disobey them.) It is also a tactic attractive to groups wishing to change the social status quo significantly and quickly.

The political purpose of nonviolent direct action and civil disobedience is to call attention or "to bear witness" to the existence of injustices. Only laws regarded as unjust are broken, and they are broken openly, without hatred or violence. Punishment is actively sought rather than avoided since punishment will further emphasize the injustices of the law. The object of nonviolent civil disobedience is to stir the conscience of an apathetic majority and to win support for measures that will eliminate the injustices. By accepting punishment for the violation of an unjust law, persons practicing civil disobedience demonstrate their sincerity. They hope to shame the majority and to make it ask itself how far it will go to protect the status quo.

Clearly the participation of the mass news media, particularly television, contributes immeasurably to the success of nonviolent direct action. Breaking the law makes news; dissemination of the news calls the attention of the public to the existence of unjust laws or practices; the public sympathy is won when injustices are spotlighted; the willingness of the demonstrators to accept punishment provides evidence of their sincerity; and the whole drama lays the groundwork for changing unjust laws and practices. Cruelty or violence directed against the demonstrators by the police or other defenders of the status quo plays into the hands of the demonstrators by stressing the injustices they are experiencing.

Perhaps the most dramatic application of nonviolent direct action occurred in Birmingham, Alabama, in the spring of 1963. Under the direction of Martin Luther King, Jr., the SCLC chose Birmingham as a major site for desegregation demonstrations during the centennial year of the Emancipation Proclamation. Birmingham was by its own description the "Heart of Dixie"; it was the most rigidly segregated large city in the United States. King believed that if segregation could be successfully challenged in Birmingham, it might begin to crumble throughout the South. Thousands of black people, including school children, staged protest marches in Birmingham from 2 to 7 May. In response, police and firefighters under the direction of Police Chief "Bull" Connor attacked the demonstrators with fire hoses, cattle prods, and police dogs—all in clear view of national television cameras. Pictures of police brutality were flashed throughout the nation and the world, doubtless touching the consciences of many white Americans. The demonstrators conducted themselves in a nonviolent fashion. Thousands were dragged off to jail, including King. (It was at this time that King wrote his "Letter from Birmingham Jail," explaining and defending nonviolent direct action.)

The most massive application of nonviolent direct action was the great "March on Washington" in August 1963, during which more than two hundred thousand black and white marchers converged on the nation's capital. The march ended in a formal program at the Lincoln Memorial in which Martin Luther King, Jr., delivered his most eloquent appeal, entitled "I Have a Dream."

> I still have a dream. It is a dream deeply rooted in the American dream. I have a dream that one day this nation will rise up and live out the true meaning of its creed: "We hold these truths to be self-evident, that all men are created equal."

Another very significant application of nonviolent direct action occurred in Alabama in the spring of 1965 during the SCLC-organized march from Selma to Montgomery to protest voting inequities. The Selma marchers convinced Congress that its earlier legislation was inadequate to the task of securely guaranteeing the right to vote for all Americans. In response to the march, Congress enacted the *Voting Rights Act of 1965,* which threatened federal intervention in local voting matters to a degree never before attempted. The act authorized the attorney general, upon evidence of voter discrimination in southern states, to replace local registrars with federal examiners, who were authorized to abolish literacy tests, to waive poll taxes, and to register voters under simplified federal procedures. The impact of the Voting Rights Act of 1965 can be observed in increased black voter registration figures in the South and election of blacks to state legislatures in every southern state and to many city and county offices as well.

On 4 April 1968 Martin Luther King, Jr., was shot and killed by a white man in Memphis, Tennessee. The murder of the nation's leading advocate of nonviolence was a tragedy affecting all Americans. Before his death, King had campaigned in Chicago and other northern cities for an end to de facto segregation of blacks in ghettos and the passage of *fair housing legislation* prohibiting discrimination in the sale or rental of houses and apartments. But King appeared to be having less success in achieving this goal than in his previous efforts to effect change. "Fair housing" legislation had consistently failed in Congress; there was no mention of discrimination in housing even in the comprehensive Civil Rights Act of 1964; and the prospects of a national fair housing law were unpromising at the beginning of 1968. With the assassination of Martin Luther King, Jr., however, the mood of the nation and of Congress changed dramatically. Many people came to feel that Congress should pass a fair housing law as a tribute to the slain civil rights leader.

The *Civil Rights Act of 1968* prohibited the following forms of discrimination:

Refusal to sell or rent a dwelling to any person because of his race, color, religion, or national origin.

Discrimination against a person in the terms, conditions, or privileges of the sale or rental of a dwelling.

Indication of a preference or discrimination on the basis of race, color, religion, or national origin in advertising the sale or rental of a dwelling.

Despite its successes, nonviolent direct action does pose problems. If undertaken too frequently or directed against laws or practices that are not really serious injustices, it may have the effect of alienating the majority, whose sympathies are so essential to the success of the movement. A favorable outcome can be achieved by actions that arouse the conscience of a majority against the injustice or that discomfort a majority to the point that it is willing to grant the demands of the minority rather than experience further discomfort. But actions that provoke hostility or a demagogic reaction from the majority merely reduce the opportunities for progress. Whereas nonviolent direct action may be effective against direct discrimination or an obvious injustice, the strategy is less successful against very subtle discrimination or de facto segregation. Few Americans approve of direct discrimination or cruelty against a nonviolent minority, and direct-action tactics that spotlight such injustice can arouse the conscience of the white majority. But the white majority is less likely to become conscience-stricken over subtle forms of discrimination, segregation, or inequalities that are not the immediate product of direct discrimination.

marches. After the massive "March on Washington" in August 1963, led by Martin Luther King, Jr., President Kennedy asked Congress for the most comprehensive civil rights legislation it had ever considered. After Kennedy's assassination, President Johnson brought heavy pressure upon Congress to pass the bill as a tribute to the late president. The Civil Rights Act of 1964 finally passed both houses of Congress by better than a two-thirds vote and with the overwhelming support of members of both the Republican and Democratic parties. It can be ranked with the Emancipation Proclamation, the Fourteenth Amendment, and *Brown* v. *Board of Education* as one of the most important steps toward full equality for blacks in America.

The Act includes the following key provisions:

provisions

[Title II]   It is unlawful to discriminate against or segregate persons on the grounds of race, color, religion, or national origin in any place of public accommodation, including hotels, motels, restaurants, movies, theaters, sports arenas, entertainment houses, and other places offering to serve the public. This prohibition extends to all establishments whose operations affect interstate commerce or whose discriminatory practices are supported by state action. Private clubs are specifically exempted.

[Title V]   The U.S. Commission on Civil Rights, first established by the Civil Rights Act of 1957, shall be empowered (1) to investigate deprivations of the right to vote, (2) to collect and study information regarding discrimination in the United States, and (3) to make reports to the president and Congress as necessary.

[Title VI]   Each federal department and agency shall take appropriate action to end discrimination in all programs or activities receiving federal financial assistance in any form. These actions may include the termination of assistance.

[Title VII]   It shall be unlawful for any firm or labor union employing or representing twenty-five or more persons to discriminate against any individual in any fashion because of his or her race, color, religion, sex, or national origins; an Equal Employment Opportunity Commission shall be established to enforce this provision by investigation, conference, conciliation, or civil action in federal court.

Power and powerlessness in the black ghetto

"colonialism" in black ghettos

Powerlessness in black ghettos is reflected in a comparison of ghettos with the "colonies" of an earlier era. Ghetto residents feel that they have little control over the institutions in their own communities; businesses, schools, welfare agencies, police departments, and most other important agencies are controlled from the outside. Often the agents of these institutions—the store managers, clerks, teachers, welfare workers, and police officers—are whites who live outside the ghetto. Thus the important institutions of the ghetto are staffed and controlled almost entirely by outsiders; hence the analogy with colonialism. Sociologist Kenneth Clark writes:

> The dark ghetto's invisible walls have been erected by white society, by those who have power, both to confine those who have *no* power and to perpetuate their powerlessness. The dark ghettos are social, political, educational, and—above all—economic colonies. Their inhabitants are subject peoples, victims of the greed, cruelty, insensitivity, guilt, and fear of their masters.[7]

powerlessness as a cause of frustration and violence

In analyzing urban riots, the National Advisory Commission on Civil Disorders also referred to powerlessness, this time as a contributing cause to both urban social disorders and the rise of militant mass movements:

> Many Negroes have come to believe that they are being exploited politically and economically by the white "power structure." Negroes, like people in poverty everywhere, in fact lack the channels of communication, influence, and appeal that traditionally have been available to ethnic minorities within the city and which enabled them—unburdened by color—to scale the walls of the white ghettos in an earlier era. The frustrations of powerlessness have led some to the conviction that there is no effective alternative to violence as a means of expression and redress, as a way of "moving the system." More generally, the result is alienation and hostility toward the institutions of law and government and the white society which controls them. This is reflected in the reach toward radical consciousness and solidarity reflected in the slogan "Black Power."[8]

Thus the ghetto provides an environment that encourages appeals to racial consciousness, black solidarity, and black power. In a book entitled *Black Power: The Politics of Liberation in America*, Stokely Carmichael and Charles V. Hamilton write:

Black Power . . . is a call for black people in this country to unite, to recognize their heritage, to build a sense of community. It is a call for black people to begin to define their own goals, to lead their own organizations and to support those organizations. It is a call to reject the racist institutions and values of this society. . . .

Black people must lead and run their own organizations. Only black people can convey the revolutionary idea—and it is a revolutionary idea—that black people are able to do things themselves. . . .

It does not mean merely putting black faces into office.[9]

One prominent theme in black politics is the necessity of *fostering black pride and dignity.* One of the worst effects of segregation and discrimination is that members of the minority group begin to doubt their own worth as human beings. Black leaders therefore endeavor to develop a positive image toward blackness. Carmichael and Hamilton write:

Throughout this country, vast segments of the black communities are beginning to recognize the need to assert their own definitions, to reclaim their history, their culture; to create their own sense of community and togetherness. There is a growing resentment of the word "Negro," for example, because this term is the invention of our oppressor: it is *his* image of us that he describes. Many blacks are now calling themselves African-Americans, Afro-Americans or black people because that is *our* image of ourselves.[10]

An important political theme of black militancy is a general *condemnation of white society as "racist."* This condemnation of racism in society

themes in the black power movement
black pride and dignity
condemnation of institutional racism
the failure of liberal reform
black leadership and self-reliance
rejection of integration into white society
black power on campus

extends far beyond individual acts of bigotry (for example, the bombing of a black church) to encompass nearly all the institutions of white society. It is argued that the institutions of American society are inherently racist because blacks are kept segregated in slums, because black unemployment is twice as great as white unemployment, because black incomes are only half of those of whites, because the infant mortality rate among blacks is twice that among whites, because the educational level of blacks is below that of whites, and so on. In other words, the condition of blacks is itself considered sufficient proof of the racism of established institutions.

The black militant condemnation of existing social values and institutions as racist leads to a *rejection of the ideal of coalition with white liberals.* White liberals want to reform the system, whereas black radicals want to do away with it. Whereas "limited, short-term coalitions on relatively minor issues" are possible, "such approaches seldom come to terms with the roots of institutional racism." In addition to black militants' concern that most white liberals are insufficiently radical in their politics, there is the fear that black people will be "absorbed or swallowed up" in white-controlled liberal organizations. There is the fear that white liberals will use black people to further white liberal objectives, claiming all the while that these objectives coincide with the aspirations of black people.

This line of reasoning inevitably leads to the conclusion that *black organizations must be led by black people* rather than by white people. The participation of whites in black organizations should be limited to "supportive roles" involving "specific skills and techniques," as, for example, the special knowledge of lawyers. The black militants do not welcome the participation of the

> many young, middle-class, white Americans [who], like some sort of Pepsi generation, have wanted to "come alive" through the black community and black groups. They have wanted to be where the action is—and the action has been in those places. They have sought refuge among blacks from the sterile, meaningless, irrelevant life in middle-class America. They have been unable to deal with the stifling, racist, parochial, split-level mentality of their parents, teachers, preachers, and friends. . . . The black organizations do not need this kind of idealism, which borders on paternalism.[11]

The emphasis on black pride and solidarity, as well as the hostility toward existing social values and institutions, frequently leads to a *rejection of integration.* To the militants, integration means assimilation into the white middle-class society that they so vigorously condemn. It means the loss of black identity and the submersion of black culture in the prevailing culture of the white society. Thus the black power movement is closely identified with "black separatism." If the prevailing values and institutions of white society were radically altered or abolished, then perhaps genuine racial integration would be possible. The black power movement generally does not envision a separate black nation but merely asserts that black pride and black solidarity are preconditions for bringing about the kinds of social conditions necessary for genuine integration. The kind of integration pictured by advocates of black power is one in which the black masses will become an integral part of a radically different society, rather than one in which individual black people will be absorbed into the existing culture.

At many colleges and universities, black students have organized clubs whose activities frequently reflect black power philosophy. These students have demanded greater emphasis on black history and culture, including the establishment of black studies curricula; they have demanded that more black students be accepted for admission; they have demanded that universities hire more black faculty. The black student unions have stressed black consciousness and black pride among their members.

Black political power

The Fifteenth Amendment (1870), ratified after the Civil War, stated that "the right of citizens in the United States to vote shall not be denied or abridged by the United States or by any state on account of race, color, or previous condition of servitude." Immediately after the adoption of this amendment, blacks in the South began to participate in political life. (See the case study "Reconstruction and black history" in Chapter 8.) But their political power declined after 1877 when southern Democrats regained control of state governments. Social pressure, threats of violence, and the terrorist tactics of the Ku Klux Klan combined to dissuade blacks from voting. Southern states passed laws that effectively deprived blacks of the right to vote.

This was the era of the *white primary* and the *"grandfather clause."* By using the ruse that party primaries were private, southern whites were allowed to exclude blacks. Indeed, it was not until 1944 in *Smith v. Allwright* that the U.S. Supreme Court finally declared the white primary a violation of the Fifteenth Amendment, reasoning that the political party was actually performing a state function in holding a primary election, not acting as a private group. Grandfather clauses, also later declared unconstitutional, prevented persons from voting unless they could prove that their grandfathers had voted before 1867.

Another device to prevent blacks from voting was the *poll tax,* requiring the payment of a fee in order to vote. This practice assured the exclusion of poor blacks from the political process. It wasn't until the passage of the Twenty-Fourth Amendment, ratified in 1964, that the poll tax as a precondition to voting was eliminated. Literacy tests and other barriers were also used in the South to prevent blacks from voting. Frequently, literacy tests asked potential voters to interpret (not just read) complicated texts, such as sections of the state constitution, to the

white primary
state primary elections for white voters only; outlawed in 1944

grandfather clause
intended to disenfranchise black voters, it allowed the vote only to those who could prove their grandfathers had voted before 1867

poll tax
a special tax paid as a qualification for voting; outlawed in national elections and by the Twenty-Fourth Amendment, and declared unconstitutional in 1966

satisfaction of local registrars. Voters were sometimes asked to recite from memory parts of the Constitution. At times prospective voters even had to pass "good character" tests.

In 1965, Martin Luther King, Jr., took action to change all that. Selma, the county seat of Dallas County, Alabama, was chosen as the site to dramatize the voting rights problem. In Dallas County only 2 percent of eligible blacks had registered to vote by the beginning of 1965. King organized a fifty-mile march from Selma to the state capital in Montgomery. He didn't get very far. Acting on orders of Governor George Wallace to disband the marchers, state troopers did so with a vengeance—with tear gas, night sticks, and whips. Once again the national government was required to intervene to force compliance with the law. President Johnson federalized the National Guard and the march continued. During the march the president went on television to address a special joint session of Congress urging passage of new legislation to assure blacks the right to vote.

The Selma march resulted in the Voting Rights Act of 1965. The Act had two major provisions. The first one outlawed discriminatory voter registration tests like the literacy test. The second authorized federal registration of persons and federally administered voting procedures in any political subdivision or state that discriminated electorally against a particular group. As a result of that act and its extensions and of the large-scale voter registration drives in the South, the number of blacks registered to vote climbed dramatically, until by 1980 55.8 percent of blacks of voting age in the South were registered.

Today there is a total of more than 5,000 black elected officials, including 20 black members of Congress (see Table 10-1), more than 300 state legislators, more than 3,000 local officials, and 1,500 in various local school districts. Some of the largest cities in the United States have had black mayors: Chicago, Los Angeles, Philadelphia, Atlanta, and Detroit. President Carter's 1977 appointment of Andrew Young as ambassador to the United Nations was widely heralded as a major breakthrough for blacks in high office. Young was an early member of the Southern Christian Leadership Conference; Young was beaten and jailed in Birmingham in 1963 with Martin Luther King, Jr. Young later resigned from the ambassadorship in a disagreement with the Carter White House over his public statements, which frequently conflicted with Carter's announced policies. Young was later elected mayor of Atlanta.

Sexual inequality and the economy

Sex roles involve power relationships. The traditional American family was patriarchal, and many cultural practices continue to reflect male dominance. (See the section headed "Power and Sex" in Chapter 3.) Men still hold most of the major positions in industry, finance, universities, the military, politics, and government. Authority in most families

TABLE 10-1   Blacks and women in Congress, 1947–1986

Congress	Senate (100)		House (435)	
	Blacks	Women	Blacks	Women
80th (1947–1948)	0	1	2	7
81st	0	1	2	9
82nd	0	1	2	10
83rd	0	3	2	12
84th	0	1	3	16
85th	0	1	4	15
86th	0	1	4	16
87th	0	2	4	17
88th	0	2	5	11
89th	0	2	6	10
90th	1	1	5	11
91st	1	1	9	10
92nd	1	2	12	13
93rd	1	0	15	14
94th	1	0	15	19
95th	1	2	16	18
96th	0	1	16	16
97th	0	2	17	19
98th	0	2	21	21
99th (1985–1986)	0	2	20	22

still rests with the man. Today more than half of all married women work; more than half of women with children under six years of age work (see Figure 10-2). The numbers of working wives and mothers are increasing each year. Nonetheless, stereotyped sex roles continue to assign domestic service and child care to women, whether they work or not, and human achievement, interest, and ambition to men.

Despite these increases in the number and proportion of working women, the nation's occupational fields are still divided between traditionally male and female jobs. Most of the women who have entered the

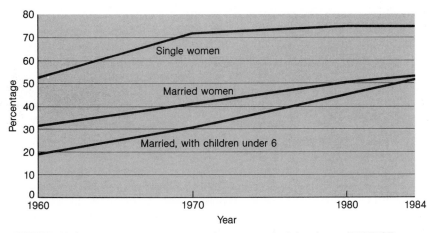

FIGURE 10-2   Increasing participation of women in the labor force. (SOURCE: *Statistical Abstract of the United States, 1985*, p. 399.)

■ Jesse Jackson: Chasing rainbows

Jesse Jackson inspired millions of blacks in 1984 as no other black leader had done since Martin Luther King, Jr. Jackson was not the first black to run for president. (That distinction belongs to Representative Shirley Chisholm, of New York, who ran for the Democratic nomination in 1972.) But Jackson demonstrated conclusively that a black could be a serious contender for the presidency. His vision was a Rainbow Coalition of "the desperate, the damned, the disinherited, the disrespected, and the despised," but the rainbow never attracted any colors except black.

Jackson was born and raised in the segregated South. His mother "Miss Helen" married Charles Jackson when Jesse was a small boy, and Jackson adopted him. Jesse attended the all-black school of Greenville, South Carolina, where he excelled in sports. He played quarterback on the state championship team and won a football scholarship to the University of Illinois. But Jackson's first experiences far from home on a predominantly white campus were unhappy ones. He learned that a black had no real chance of playing quarterback at the University of Illinois in the early 1960s. So he returned to the South, to black North Carolina A&T University at Greensboro. He played four years as quarterback at A&T and was student body president as well. More important, Jackson led the North Carolina A&T students in a successful campaign of marches and sit-ins to desegregate downtown Greensboro. Jackson became one of the nation's youngest recognized civil rights leaders.

Like many black leaders before him, Jackson chose the ministry as a vocation. But while completing his divinity studies at Chicago Theological Seminary, he was chosen by Martin Luther King, Jr., to lead the Southern Christian Leadership Conference's "Operation Breadbasket" in Chicago. This activity was part of King's effort in the late 1960s to bring the civil rights movement north to the urban ghettos and to spotlight the economic problems confronting blacks. Jackson was in Memphis with King on the day King was assassinated in 1968.

Jackson transformed the SCLC Operation Breadbasket in Chicago into his own independent organization—Operation PUSH (People United to Save Humanity). Jackson preached the values of hard work, dedication, and self-confidence to ghetto youth: "I am somebody!" PUSH also threatened boycotts against large corporations whose employment policies were not in its judgment sufficiently "affirmative." Jackson negotiated "trade agreements" with Coca-Cola, Heublein, and Burger King to hire and promote more blacks.

Yet Jackson captured the aspirations for power and self-determination of millions of blacks from the rural South to the northern urban ghettos. He pushed himself into national black leadership, stepping over the more experienced black politicans—Andrew Young of Atlanta, Tom Bradley of Los Angeles, Wilson Goode of Philadelphia. But those leaders were eventually swept along by the feelings of racial pride that Jackson's campaign unleashed.

The Jackson campaign turned out millions of new black voters. Jackson had very little money to spend and no real organization. But with his gifted oratory and his flair for the dramatic, he commanded free television news coverage nearly every day. He accomplished at least three objectives: increasing black voter registration, heightening black political awareness and skills, and making the Democratic Party more responsive to black concerns. The passion and pride he stirred among black masses were real. Jesse Jackson became the preeminent black political leader in the United States.

labor force over the past fifteen years have done so because of the expansion of the service sector of our economy (trade, finance, travel, government). Women continue to dominate the traditional "pink-collar" jobs (see Table 10-2). Women have made important inroads in traditionally male white-collar occupations—doctors, lawyers, and engineers, for example—although men still remain in the majority in these professions. However, women have only begun to break into the "blue-collar" occupations traditionally dominated by men. Blue-collar jobs usually pay more than pink-collar jobs. This circumstance accounts for much of the earnings gap between men and women that we examined in Chapter 3 (see especially Figure 3-1). Box 10-1 describes the controversy over the handling of this wage gap by government classification of traditionally male and female jobs according to their "comparable worth."

TABLE 10-2   Women's occupations

	Percentage female	
	1960	1983
"White collar"		
Women are increasingly entering white-collar occupational fields traditionally dominated by men:		
Architects	3	13
Computer analysts	11	28
College and university teachers	28	36
Engineers	1	6
Lawyers and judges	4	16
Physicians	10	16
"Pink collar"		
Women continue to be concentrated in occupational fields traditionally dominated by women:		
Nurses		96
Elementary school teachers		83
Librarians		87
Secretaries		99
Receptionists		97
Bookkeepers		91
Bank tellers		91
Child care workers		97
"Blue collar"		
Women continued to be largely shut out of blue-collar occupational fields traditionally dominated by men:		
Police		1
Mechanics		3
Construction workers		2
Miners		2
Motor vehicle operators		9
Truck drivers		3
Heavy equipment operators		2

SOURCE: *Statistical Abstract of the United States, 1985*, pp. 402–403.

BOX 10-1   The "comparable worth" controversy

■ Federal laws guarantee equal pay for men and women doing the same work. Ever since passage of the Civil Rights Act of 1964, pay differences between men and women in the same job have been illegal. Yet, overall, women continue to earn less than men; the average woman in the work force today earns about 64 percent of the pay of the average man.* Most of this "wage gap" is a product of the concentration of women in traditionally lower-paid "pink-collar" occupations.

The initial efforts of the feminist movement were directed toward getting more women into traditionally male occupational fields; success would automatically narrow the "wage gap." But these efforts require time: many years are required to recruit and train women as doctors, lawyers, or engineers. Moreover, efforts to recruit more women into blue-collar jobs have been only marginally successful.

Recently some feminist organizations have adopted a new approach to the elimination of the wage gap—the demand that pay levels be determined by the "comparable worth" of various jobs rather than by the labor market. *Comparable worth* means more than paying men and women equally for the same work; it means paying the same wages for jobs of comparable value to the employer. Comparable worth means that traditionally male and female jobs would be evaluated according to their "worth" to the employer, perhaps by considering responsibilities, effort, and knowledge and skill requirements. Jobs adjudged to be "comparable" would be paid equal wages. For example, the work of a secretary might be adjudged comparable in value to the work of a mechanic.

Comparable worth requires that a government agency, or perhaps the courts, determine for both private employers and government employers the value of various jobs. Decisions by the agencies would replace the determination of wage rates by the labor market. Many feminist groups charge that the labor market is really a "dual market" in which women's work is valued less than men's work.

Comparable worth raises problems of implementation: Who would decide what wages for various jobs should be? How would comparable worth be decided? What standards would be used to determine worth? If government agencies set wage rates by law instead of the free market, would a black (illegal) market for labor arise? What penalties would be imposed on employers or employees who worked for wages different from those set by the government?

The U.S. Equal Employment Opportunity Commission has rejected the notion of comparable worth and has declined to set wages for traditionally male and female occupations. However, a number of state governments have undertaken to review their own pay scales to determine if traditionally female occupations are underpaid. The state of Washington was ordered by a federal judge to equalize salaries in traditionally male and female state jobs and to pay back wages to many of its female workers. However, a federal appeals court reversed this order in 1985, declaring that salary differences in different occupations were not evidence of sexual discrimination and that governments had no obligation under current law to correct the labor market.

*Nancy Rytina, "Comparing Annual and Weekly Earnings," *Monthly Labor Review,* April 1983, p. 36.

The roots of sexual inequality

How much of male dominance can be attributed to *biology* and how much to *culture?* Many scholars deny that biological differences necessitate any distinctions between male and female in domestic service or child-care responsibilities, or authority in the family, or economic roles in society, or political or legal rights. They contend that existing sex differences are culturally imposed upon women from earliest childhood. The very first item in personality formation is the assignment of sex roles (you are a boy, you are a girl) and the encouragement of "masculine" and "feminine" traits. Aggression, curiosity, intelligence, initiative, and force are encouraged in the boy; passivity, refinement, shyness, and virtue are encouraged in the girl. Girls are supposed to think in terms of domestic and child-care roles, while boys are urged to think of careers in industry and the professions. Deeply ingrained symbols, attitudes, and practices are culturally designated as "masculine" or "feminine" behaviors ("What a big boy!" "Isn't she pretty!"). There are masculine and feminine subjects in school: science, technology, and business are male; teaching, nursing, and secretarial studies are female. Boys are portrayed in roles in which they master their environment; girls, in roles in which they admire the accomplishments of men. It is this *cultural* conditioning that leads a woman to accept a family- and child-centered life and an inferior economic and political role in society—not her *physiology.*

inequality as a product of cultural conditioning

Many writers have complained about the social-psychological barriers to a woman's full human development. There is a double standard of sexual guilt in which women are subject to greater shame for any sexual liaison, whatever the circumstances. The family and society inculcate greater sexual inhibitions in women, sometimes leading to an inabil-

inequality as a product of social-psychological barriers

ity to enjoy sex fully. Yet, while denied sexual freedom herself, the woman is usually obliged to seek advancement through the approval of men. She may try to overcome her powerlessness by using her own sexuality, perhaps at the cost of her dignity and self-respect. The prevailing male attitude is to value women for their sexual traits rather than their qualities as human beings. Women are frequently portrayed as "sex objects" in advertising, magazines, and literature. They are supposed to entertain, please, gratify, and flatter men with their sexuality; it is seldom the other way around. There is even evidence of self-rejection among women that is similar to that encountered among minority groups: female children are far more likely to wish they had been born boys than male children are to wish they had been born girls.[12] The "cult of virginity" continues as a traditional sign that the new husband's "property" is received "unused." The power aspects of sex roles are also ingrained in male psychology. Young men are deemed feminine (inferior) if they are not sufficiently aggressive, physical, or violent.

inequality as a product of physiological differences

In contrast to these arguments about *culturally* imposed sex roles, other observers have contended that *physiological* differences between men and women account for differential sex roles. The woman's role in the reproduction and care of the young is biologically determined. To the extent that she seeks to protect her young, she also seeks family arrangements that will provide maximum security and support for them. Men acquire dominant positions in industry, finance, government, and so forth, largely because women are preoccupied with family and child-care tasks. Men are physically stronger than women, and their role as economic providers is rooted in this biological difference. Whether there are any biologically determined mental or emotional differences between men and women is a disputed point, but the possibility of such differences exists. Thus differential sex roles may be partly physical in origin.

The power of women's protest movements

Women in the United States have made great progress in acquiring equal rights over the years. The earliest active "feminist" organizations grew out of the pre-Civil War antislavery movement. The first generation of feminists, including Lucretia Mott, Elizabeth Cady Stanton, Lucy Stone, and Susan B. Anthony, learned to organize, to hold public meetings, and to conduct petition campaigns as abolitionists. After the Civil War, the feminist movement concentrated on winning civil rights and the franchise for women. The suffragettes employed mass demonstrations, parades, picketing, and occasional disruptions and civil disobedience — tactics not dissimilar to those of the civil rights movement of the 1960s. The more moderate wing of the American suffrage movement became the League of Women Voters; in addition to women's vote, they sought protection of women in industry, child welfare laws, honest election practices, and the elimination of laws discriminating against the rights of women.

The culmination of the early feminist movement was the passage in 1920 of the Nineteenth Amendment to the Constitution:

> The right of citizens of the United States to vote shall not be denied or abridged by the United States or by any state on account of sex.

The movement was also successful in changing many state laws that abridged the property rights of the married woman and otherwise treated her as the "chattel" (property) of her husband. But active feminist politics declined after the goal of women's voting rights had been achieved.

Renewed interest and progress in women's rights came with the civil rights movement of the 1960s. The Civil Rights Act of 1964 prevents discrimination on the basis of sex, as well as race, in employment, salary, promotion, and other conditions of work. The Equal Employment Opportunity Commission (EEOC), the federal agency charged with eliminating discrimination in employment, has established guidelines barring stereotyped classifications of "men's jobs" and "women's jobs." State laws and employer practices that differentiate between men and women in terms of hours, pay, retirement age, and so on, have been struck down. Under active lobbying from feminist organizations, federal agencies, including the U.S. Office of Education and the Office of Federal Contract Compliance, have established affirmative-action guidelines for government agencies, universities, and private businesses doing work for the government. These guidelines set goals and timetables for employers to alter their work force to achieve higher percentages of women at all levels.

For many years feminist activity focused on the Equal Rights Amendment (ERA) to the Constitution, which would have struck down *all* existing legal inequalities in state and federal laws between men and women. The proposed amendment stated simply:

> Equality of rights under the law shall not be denied or abridged by the United States or by any state on account of sex.

ERA passed the Congress easily in 1972 and was sent to the states for the necessary ratification by three-fourths (thirty-eight) of them. The amendment won quick ratification by half of the states, but a developing "Stop-ERA" movement slowed progress after 1976. Both the ERA and Stop-ERA movements were led by women; they fought their battles over ratification in state legislatures across the nation. Despite an extension of time by Congress, ERA fell three states short of the necessary thirty-eight in 1982. Throughout the debates over ratification of ERA, opinion polls reported a large majority of Americans favoring it. Opponents argued that it might eliminate many legal protections for women—financial support by husbands, an interest in the husband's property, exemp-

political equality
Nineteenth Amendment (1920)

equality in employment
Civil Rights Act of 1964

ERA
Equal Rights Amendment

tion from military service, and so forth. In addition to these specific objections, the opponents of ERA and the feminist movement also charged that they weaken the family institution and demoralize women who wish to devote their lives to their family and children. Supporters of ERA argue that only a constitutional amendment can guarantee women full equality and that such a guarantee should be a part of the fundamental laws of the land.

changing mores and medical advances

Women are also acquiring greater power over their own lives by means of a series of social and medical developments. Increased physiological understanding and improved sexual technique have contributed to an assertion of feminine sexuality. Advances in birth control techniques, including "the pill," have freed women's sexuality from the reproductive function. Legal abortions in early months of pregnancy are now a recognized constitutional right. Women can now determine for themselves whether and when they will undertake childbirth and child rearing.

Abortion and the law

Abortion can dramatically affect a nation's birth rate, its population growth, and ultimately the whole structure and quality of life. For years, abortions in the United States for any purpose other than saving the life of the mother were criminal offenses under state laws. Then in the late 1960s about a dozen states acted to permit abortion in cases of rape or incest, or to protect the physical health of the mother, and in some cases the mental health as well. However, relatively few abortions were performed under those laws because of the red tape involved—review of each case by several concurring physicians, approval of a hospital board, and so forth.

Abortion is a highly sensitive issue. It is not an issue that can be compromised. The arguments touch on fundamental moral and religious principles. Proponents of abortion argue that a woman should be permitted to control her own body and should not be forced by law to have unwanted children. They cite the heavy toll in lives lost in criminal abortions and the psychological and emotional pain of an unwanted pregnancy. Opponents of abortion generally base their belief on the sanctity of life, including the life of the unborn child, which they insist deserves the protection of law—"the right to life." Many believe that the killing of an unborn child for any reason other than the preservation of the life or health of the mother is murder.

Roe v. Wade

Perhaps the most significant decision about the future of the nation's population was the Supreme Court's momentous ruling in *Roe v. Wade* (1973), which recognized abortion as a *constitutional* right of women. In this historic decision the Court determined that the fetus is not a "person" within the meaning of the Constitution, and therefore the

fetus's right to life is not guaranteed by law. Moreover, the Court held that the liberties guaranteed by the Fifth and Fourteenth Amendments encompass the woman's decision on whether or not to terminate her pregnancy. The Supreme Court decided the criminal abortion laws that prohibited abortions in any state of pregnancy except to save the life of the mother were unconstitutional; that during the first three months of pregnancy the abortion decision must be left wholly to the woman and her physician; that during the second three months of pregnancy the state may not prohibit abortion, but only regulate procedures in ways reasonably related to maternal health; and that only in the final three months of pregnancy may the state prohibit abortion except when abortion is necessary for the preservation of life or health of the mother. In this sweeping decision the Supreme Court established abortion not merely as permissible under law but as a constitutional right immune to the actions of popularly elected legislatures.

■ The *Bakke* case—Affirmative action or reverse discrimination? ■

Aside from busing, perhaps the most sensitive issue affecting relations between blacks and whites in the United States today is the question of how to achieve real equality in education, jobs, and income. The civil rights movement of the 1960s opened new opportunities for black Americans. But equality of *opportunity* is not the same as *absolute* equality. The problem of inequality today is usually identified as continued disparities in the incomes, educations, and occupations of blacks and whites.

What public policies should be pursued to achieve equality in the United States? Is it sufficient that government eliminate discrimination, guarantee equality of opportunity for blacks and whites, and apply "color-blind" standards to both blacks and whites? Or should government take "affirmative action" to overcome the results of past unequal treatment of blacks—preferential or compensatory treatment that would favor black applicants for university admissions and scholarships, job hiring and promotion, and other opportunities for advancement in life?

The earlier emphasis of government policy was, of course, nondiscrimination. Although special recruiting techniques, special training, and encouragement of university applicants were stressed, equal employment opportunity "was not a program to offer special privilege to any one group of persons because of their particular race, religion, sex or national origin."[13] There were no quota systems for black applicants that might result in the selection of less qualified blacks over more highly qualified whites for schools, jobs, or promotions.

Increasingly, however, the goal of the civil rights movement shifted from the traditional aim of equality of opportunity through nondiscrimination alone to absolute equality through "goals and timetables" established by affirmative action. Although carefully avoiding the term *quota,* the notion of affirmative action tests the success of equal employment opportunity by observing whether blacks achieve admissions, jobs, and promotions in proportion to their numbers in the population.

Federal policy has been ambiguous—perhaps deliberately so. There has been a question about whether quotas that give preference to blacks because of their race violate the Fourteenth Amendment's guarantee of "equal protection of the laws" to all citizens. Yet federal officials have generally measured progress in affirmative action in terms of the number of blacks admitted, employed, or promoted. The pressure to show progress and retain federal financial support can result in preferential treatment of blacks and "reverse discrimination" against whites with equal or better qualifications.

Affirmative action also puts pressure on traditional measures of qualifications—test scores and educational achievement. Blacks have argued that these measures are not good predictors of performance on the job or in school and that they are biased in favor of white culture. State and local governments, schools, colleges, and universities, and private employers have been under pressure to drop these standards.[14] But how far can any school, agency, or employer go in dropping traditional standards? It is not difficult to drop educational requirements for sanitation workers, but what about physicians, surgeons, attorneys, pilots, and others whose skills directly affect health and safety?

The more perplexing question, however, has been whether affirmative action programs discriminate against whites and thus violate the equal protection clause of the Fourteenth Amendment.

In 1972, after several years of premedical courses and volunteer work in a hospital, Allan Bakke, a thirty-two-year-old white who was also a Vietnam veteran, applied to the University of California–Davis Medical School. He was rejected two years in a row. He later learned that his college grades and medical aptitude test scores ranked well above those of many who had been accepted. All who had been accepted with lower scores were black or Mexican American. Bakke filed a lawsuit arguing that the university had discriminated against him because of race—a violation of the Fourteenth Amendment's guarantee of "equal protection of the law." The university, which accepted 100 applicants to medical school per year, admitted that it set aside sixteen places for "disadvantaged students"—a category that never included any whites. Candidates for those sixteen positions were placed in a separate admissions pool and competed only against each other. White applicants with grade point averages below 2.5 (out of a possible 4.0) were always rejected, but many minority students were accepted with averages as low as 2.1 and 2.2. Bakke's average was 3.5.

The university argued that using race as a favorable criterion was in the best interest of the state and the nation. By increasing the number of minority students, the university hoped eventually to improve medical care among the poor and the black. Minority doctors would also provide "role models" for young blacks, giving them something to aspire to in their career development. The university contended that its separation of black and white candidates was "benign" discrimination (meant to help) rather than "invidious" (meant to hurt).

The California Supreme Court, however, believed that the affirmative action program at the University of California–Davis was a quota system based on race and therefore denied white applicants the "equal protection of the laws" guaranteed by the Fourteenth Amendment. The California court said that the purpose of the equal protection clause of

the Fourteenth Amendment, "to secure equality of treatment for all, is incompatible with the premise that some races may be afforded a higher degree of protection against unequal treatment than others." The California court upheld Bakke and told the university to find other ways of increasing minority enrollments—such as instituting remedial programs and aggressive recruiting techniques, and increasing the number of students accepted—ways that do not discriminate against whites.

The university appealed the California court's decision to the U.S. Supreme Court, and the Supreme Court rendered its important judgment on affirmative action programs in *Regents of the University of California* v. *Bakke* (1978).

The Supreme Court divided over the case five to four, with Justices Burger, Powell, Stewart, Rehnquist, and Stevens in the majority and Justices Brennan, White, Marshall, and Blackmun dissenting. The majority held that the affirmative action program at the University of California–Davis Medical School violated Allan Bakke's rights to "equal protection of the law" under the Fourteenth Amendment. They also held that the program violated Title VI of the Civil Rights Act of 1964 because Bakke was "subjected to discrimination under a program receiving federal financial assistance." The Supreme Court ordered the university to admit Bakke to medical school; Bakke was admitted in the fall of 1978 and began his studies six years after his original application.

The Supreme Court was careful to specify the discriminatory aspects of the university's affirmative action program:

> The Davis special admission program involves the use of an explicit racial classification. . . . It tells applicants who are not Negro . . . that they are totally excluded from a specific percentage of seats. . . . No matter how strong their qualifications . . . they [whites] are never afforded the chance to compete with

applicants from the preferred groups for the special admission seats.

However, the Supreme Court went on to describe how an affirmative-action program *could* be constitutional:

> Race or ethnic background may be deemed a "plus" in a particular applicant's file, . . . [as long as] it does not insulate the individual from comparison with all other candidates for the available seats.

The Supreme Court generally approved of the goal of achieving racial and ethnic diversity in the student body.

In short, the U.S. Supreme Court indicated: (1) that affirmative-action programs that set aside specific numbers or percentages of positions for minorities violate the "equal protection" rights of majority candidates; but (2) that affirmative-action programs that consider race or ethnic origin as one of many factors in a competition and do not exclude anyone from competing for all available positions do not necessarily violate the constitutional rights of majority candidates.

Thus, the *Bakke* case sets some limits on affirmative-action programs, but it still permits schools to consider race as a "plus" factor in competition for admission. In later cases, notably *United Steelworkers of America* v. *Weber* (1979), the Supreme Court upheld affirmative-action programs. This fact suggests that the Supreme Court will look closely at such programs to ensure that they deal fairly with all groups. We can expect additional cases to come before the Supreme Court in search of a clearer definition of the differences between "affirmative action" and "reverse discrimination."

Notes

1. L. H. Butterfield, Marc Friedlander, and Mary-Jo Kline, eds., *The Book of Abigail and John* (Cambridge, Mass.: Harvard University Press, 1975), p. 121.
2. *Brown* v. *Board of Education of Topeka, Kansas,* 347 U.S. 483 (1954).
3. Kenneth Clark, *Dark Ghetto: Dilemmas of Social Power* (New York: Harper & Row, 1965), p. 75.
4. United States Commission on Civil Rights, *Racial Isolation in the Public Schools,* 2 vols. (Washington, D.C.: U.S. Government Printing Office, 1967).
5. *Millikan* v. *Bradley,* 418 U.S. 717 (1974).
6. A public letter by Martin Luther King, Jr., Birmingham, Alabama, 16 April 1963; the full text is reprinted in Thomas R. Dye and Brett Hawkins, eds., *Politics in the Metropolis* (Columbus, Ohio: Merrill, 1967), pp. 100–109.
7. Clark, *Dark Ghetto,* p. 11.
8. National Advisory Commission on Civil Disorders, *Report* (Washington, D.C.: U.S. Government Printing Office, 1968), p. 205.
9. Stokely Carmichael and Charles V. Hamilton, *Black Power: The Politics of Liberation in America* (New York: Random House, 1967), pp. 44, 46.

10. Ibid., p. 37.
11. Ibid., p. 83.
12. Goodwin Watson, "Psychological Aspects of Sex Roles," in *Social Psychology, Issues and Insights* (Philadelphia: Lippincott, 1966), p. 477. See also Philip Goldberg, "Are Women Prejudiced Against Women?" *Transaction,* April 1968.
13. David H. Rosenbloom, "The Civil Service Commission's Decision to Authorize the Use of Goals and Timetables in Federal Equal Employment Opportunity Programs," *Western Political Quarterly* 26, June 1973.
14. Frank J. Thompson, "Bureaucratic Responsiveness in the Cities: The Problem of Minority Hiring," *Urban Affairs Quarterly* 10, September 1974.

Discussion questions

1. Identify the initial goal of the civil rights movement. Discuss the Supreme Court case that marked the first step in attaining that goal and the constitutional amendment upon which the civil rights movement based its arguments. Why was the Supreme Court unable to implement its decision by itself?
2. Define *de facto segregation.* What obstacles exist to the elimination of de facto segregation?
3. Identify the key provisions of the Civil Rights Act of 1964.
4. Describe "nonviolent direct action" as advocated by Martin Luther King, Jr., its political purpose, and factors important to its success.
5. Describe how King and his followers were instrumental in the passage of the Voting Rights Act of 1965 and the Civil Rights Act of 1968. Briefly describe the content of each act.
6. Discuss the meaning of powerlessness in the ghetto. Include in your discussion an explanation of the analogy between life in the ghetto and "colonialism."
7. Discuss the themes of the black power movement.
8. Describe the purpose of affirmative-action programs. How does affirmative action differ from "color-blind" standards?
9. Describe some of the early obstacles to blacks' acquisition of political power.
10. Discuss the "cultural" and "biological" explanations of male dominance in society. Describe some of the important landmarks for women's protest movements, including the Supreme Court's ruling in *Roe* v. *Wade.* What factors have contributed to women's acquiring greater power over their lives?
11. Discuss the *Bakke* case. How may affirmative action conflict with the concept of equality of opportunity? How may it be in violation of the Fourteenth Amendment?

CHAPTER 11

■ POVERTY & POWERLESSNESS

Captain John Smith's ultimatum to his starving band of settlers in Jamestown in 1609 that "he who would not work must not eat" is probably the first recorded American welfare policy statement. It reflects an attitude that prevailed for many years: if one were poor in the United States, one deserved to be poor. This view was reinforced by the belief in America as the land of unbounded opportunity; by the ideal of rugged individualism and a firmly rooted belief in the individual's right to property; by the growing nation's need for the labor of every able-bodied person; by a peculiar blending of Calvinism and commercialism that turned poverty into a moral failing; and by the expanding economy of the nineteenth century and the social Darwinism that justified the social evils of that era. It was not until the frontier had finally and forever closed and the Great Depression of the 1930s had reduced many of the prosperous to the ranks of the paupers that there was any discernible change in the American attitude toward poverty. When poverty exists in the midst of plenty, as it does today in the United States, it is more difficult for the poor to bear.

In this chapter we will explore various definitions of poverty, as well as some of the recent efforts of those in positions of power to lift the poverty-stricken from their positions of powerlessness. After you have read it, you should be able to

- discuss various definitions of poverty and describe the characteristics of the poor,
- discuss the theory of a subculture of poverty and its implications for social policy,
- describe the strategies of the Social Security Act of 1935 and the current welfare system,

- describe the relationship between poverty and powerlessness and what groups can be expected to lobby for the poor in Washington,
- describe the "social safety net" and the welfare policies under President Reagan,
- describe the changing age composition of the American population and how this will affect social security in the future.

Poverty in the United States

Conflict over poverty begins with conflict over the definition of poverty and differing estimates of its extent in the United States. Proponents of large-scale government programs for the poor, on the one hand, frequently make broad definitions of poverty and high estimates of the number of poor people. They view the problem as a persistent one, even in an affluent society. They contend that millions suffer from hunger, exposure, and remediable illness, and that some people starve to death. Their definition of the problem of poverty practically mandates immediate and massive governmental programs to assist the poor.

conflict over the nature and extent of poverty in the United States

On the other hand, opponents of large-scale governmental antipoverty programs frequently minimize the number of poor in America. They see poverty diminishing over time, without major public programs. They view the poor in the United States as considerably better off than the middle class was fifty years ago—and even wealthy by the standards of most other societies in the world. They deny that Americans need to suffer from hunger, exposure, remediable illness, or starvation if they make use of the services and facilities available to them. Their definition of the problem of poverty minimizes the need for massive public programs to fight poverty.

According to the U.S. Social Security Administration, there are about 34 million poor people (those below the official poverty level) in the United States, or approximately 14 percent of the population (see Figure 11-1). The poverty level is set by the Social Security Administra-

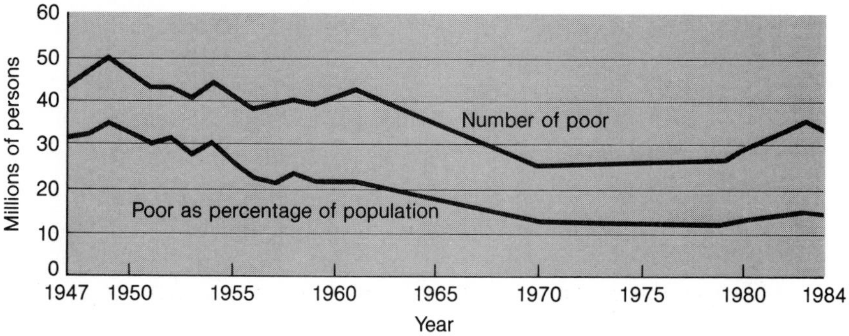

FIGURE 11-1 Poverty in the United States. (SOURCE: *Statistical Abstract of the United States, 1985*, p. 454.)

official definition of poverty
government estimates each year of the minimum costs required to maintain families of various sizes

liberal objections to official definition of poverty

conservative objections to official definition of poverty

tion. It is derived by a calculation of the minimum costs required to maintain families of different sizes. The dollar amounts change each year to take into account the effect of inflation. In 1984 the poverty line for a family of four was an income of approximately $10,609 (see Figure 11-2).

This official definition of poverty emphasizes *subsistence levels;* it seeks to describe poverty objectively as lack of enough income to acquire the minimum necessities of life. Liberals frequently view the subsistence definition of poverty as insensitive to a variety of needs—including entertainment, recreation, and the relief of monotony. Items that were "luxuries" a generation ago are now considered "necessities." John Kenneth Galbraith writes:

> People are poverty-stricken when their income, even if adequate for survival, falls markedly behind that of the community. Then they cannot have what the larger community regards as the minimum necessary for decency; and they cannot wholly escape, therefore, the judgment of the larger community that they are indecent.[1]

Liberals also note that the official definition *includes* cash income from welfare and social security. Without this government assistance, the number of poor would be much higher.

Conservatives also challenge the official definition of poverty: it does not include the value of family assets. People (usually older people) who own their own houses and automobiles may have incomes below the poverty line yet not suffer any real hardship. (More than 50 percent of

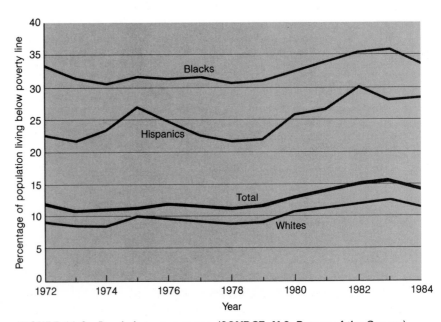

FIGURE 11-2 People living in poverty. (SOURCE: U.S. Bureau of the Census.)

the official "poor" own their own homes and more than 65 percent own automobiles.) Many persons who are ranked as poor do not think of themselves as "poor people"—students, for example. More important, the official definition of poverty *excludes* "in-kind" (noncash) benefits provided by government, benefits that include, for example, free medical care under Medicaid and Medicare, food stamps, public housing, and school lunches. If these benefits were "costed out" (that is, calculated as cash income), there might be far fewer persons classified as poor. The U.S. government itself estimates that if all government benefits to the poor are costed out, the percentage of poor in the country is about 10 percent rather than the official 15 percent.[2] Box 11-1 discusses the categories of people that make up "the poor."

Poverty as relative deprivation

It is possible to define poverty as *relative deprivation*. This definition is not tied to any *absolute* level of subsistence or deprivation. Instead, it characterizes poverty as a sense of deprivation that some people feel because they have less income or fewer material possessions than most other Americans. Even with a fairly substantial income, it is possible to feel relative deprivation in a very affluent society when commercial advertising in the mass media portrays the "average American" as having a high level of consumption and material well-being.

relative deprivation
feeling of deprivation caused by comparison with others

Today the poor in the United States are wealthy by the standards that have prevailed through most of history and that still prevail over large areas of the world. Nonetheless, millions of American families are considered poor, both by themselves and by others, because they have less income than most other Americans. Actually they are not any more deprived, even relative to the nonpoor, than in the past. But they *feel* more deprived; they perceive a wide gap between themselves and an affluent middle class of Americans, and they do not accept the gap as legitimate. Blacks are heavily overrepresented among the poor, and the civil rights movement made blacks acutely aware of their position in American society relative to whites. The black revolution contributed to a new awareness of the problem of poverty in terms of differences in income and conditions of life. Eliminating poverty when it is defined as relative deprivation really means achieving *equality* of income and material possessions.

increased awareness of inequalities in society

Let us try systematically to examine poverty as relative deprivation. Table 11-1 divides all American families into five groups—from the lowest one-fifth, in personal income, to the highest one-fifth—and shows the percentage of total family personal income received by each group over the years. (If perfect income equality existed, each fifth would receive 20 percent of all family personal income, and it would not even be possible to rank fifths from highest to lowest.) The poorest one-fifth received 3.5 percent of all family personal income in 1929; in 1980,

measuring inequality
percentage of total national income received by each fifth of income earners

---

BOX 11-1   Who are the poor?

■ Poverty occurs in many different kinds of families and in all environmental settings, as the following table shows.

Population, by categories, with income below poverty level (based on total population)

	Percent of total in category	
	1983	*1984*
Total population	15.0%	14.4%
White population	12.2	11.5
Black population	35.7	33.8
Over age 65	14.2	12.4
Families with male head	9.8	9.2
Families with female head	36.2	34.5

SOURCE: U.S. Bureau of the Census.

First, blacks are three times more likely to experience poverty than whites; the percentage of the black population of the United States falling below the poverty line was 33.8 in 1984, compared to 11.5 percent of the white population. (However, most poor people are white—24.2 million whites, compared to 9.5 million blacks—even though the percentage of poor among blacks is greater.) Second, female-headed families experience poverty far more frequently than male-headed families; 34.5 percent of all female-headed families live below the poverty line, compared to only 9.2 percent of families with both husband and wife present.

Until recently, the aged experienced more poverty than the working-age population. However, continuing increases in social security benefits have reduced poverty among the aged to the point that there is *less* poverty among the aged than among the general population. The aged are *not* poor, despite the linkage suggested by the popular phrase "the poor and the aged." Moreover the aged (persons over 65) are much wealthier than the nonaged, with a large proportion owning homes and automobiles debt free and having savings in banks.

however, this group had increased its percentage of all family personal income to 5.2. (Most of the increase occurred during World War II.) The highest one-fifth received 54.4 percent of all family personal income in 1929; in 1980, however, the percentage had declined to 41.5. This was the only income group to lose in relation to other income groups. The middle classes improved their relative income position even more than

TABLE 11-1 Percent distribution of family personal income, by quintiles, and top 5 percent of consumer units, selected years, 1929–1980

Quintiles	1929	1936	1941	1944	1947	1950	1955	1960	1965	1970	1975	1980
Lowest	3.5%	4.1%	4.1%	4.9%	5.0%	4.5%	4.8%	4.8%	5.2%	5.4%	5.4%	5.2%
Second	9.0	9.2	9.5	10.9	11.0	12.0	12.3	12.2	12.2	12.2	11.8	11.6
Third	13.8	14.1	15.3	16.2	16.0	17.4	17.8	17.8	17.8	17.6	17.6	17.5
Fourth	19.3	20.9	22.3	22.2	22.0	23.4	23.7	24.0	23.8	23.9	24.1	24.1
Highest	54.4	51.7	48.8	45.8	46.0	42.7	41.3	41.2	40.9	40.9	41.1	41.5
Total	100.0	100.0	100.0	100.0	100.0	100.0	100.0	100.0	100.0	100.0	100.0	100.0
Top 5 Percent ratio	30.0	26.5	24.0	20.7	20.9	17.3	16.4	15.9	15.5	15.6	15.5	15.6

SOURCE: U.S. Bureau of the Census, *Statistical Abstract of the United States, 1980* (Washington, D.C.: U.S. Government Printing Office, 1981), p. 453.

the poor. Another measure of income equalization over time is the decline in the percentage of income received by the top 5 percent. The top 5 percent received 30 percent of all family personal income in 1929 but only 15.6 percent in 1980.

Nevertheless, it is unlikely that income differentials will ever disappear completely—at least not in a society that rewards skill, talent, risk taking, and ingenuity. If the problem of poverty is defined as relative deprivation—that is, *inequality*—then it is not really capable of solution. Regardless of how well off the poor may be in absolute terms, there will always be a lowest one-fifth of the population receiving something less than 20 percent of all income. Income differences may decline, but *some* differences will remain, and even minor differences can acquire great importance and hence pose a "problem."

relative deprivation
insoluble problem

Poverty as powerlessness

Powerlessness is the inability to control the events that shape one's life. The poor lack economic resources and are hence largely dependent on others for the things they need. Their lack of power derives from their *dependency*. But powerlessness is also an attitude—a feeling that no matter what one does it will have little effect on one's life. An *attitude* of powerlessness *reinforces* the *condition* of powerlessness among the poor. Their experiences generate feelings of meaninglessness, hopelessness, lack of motivation, distrust, and cynicism. Constant defeat causes many of the poor to retreat into a self-protective attitude characterized by indifference and a pervasive sense of futility.

powerlessness
the inability to control the events that shape one's life

The poor often feel *alienated*—separated from society—because of their lack of success in obtaining important life goals. Persons who are blocked consistently in their efforts to achieve life goals are most likely to express powerlessness and alienation. These attitudes in turn become barriers to effective self-help, independence, and self-respect. Poverty can lead to apathy and aimlessness and a lack of motivation.

alienation
a feeling of separation from society

To be *both* black and poor in a predominantly white and affluent society magnifies feelings of powerlessness and alienation. Social psychologists are not always certain about the processes by which social inequalities are perceived or how these perceptions influence attitudes and behaviors. But black sociologist Kenneth B. Clark has provided some interesting insights into "the psychology of the ghetto."

self-hatred and self-doubt
victims of poverty begin to blame themselves and see themselves as inferior

Professor Clark argues that human beings who live apart from the rest of society, who do not share in society's affluence, and who are not respected or granted the ordinary dignities and courtesy accorded to others will eventually begin to doubt their own worth. All human beings depend on their experiences with others for clues to how they should view and value themselves. Black children who consistently see whites in a superior position begin to question whether they or their family or blacks in general really deserve any more respect from the larger society than they receive. These doubts, Clark maintains, become the seeds of "a pernicious self- and group-hatred, the Negro's complex and debilitating prejudice against himself."

experiments showing impact of racism and poverty on very young children

Clark observed that when black children as young as three years old were shown white and black dolls, or were asked to color drawings of children to look like themselves, many of them rejected the black dolls as "dirty" or "bad" and colored the picture of themselves a light color or even a bizarre shade like purple. The observations suggest that many black children suffer from serious injury to their sense of self-worth at a very young age. The results of their sense of inferiority are revealed when these children begin school—a lack of confidence in themselves as students, a lack of motivation to learn, behavior problems, and a gradual withdrawal or growing rebellion. Lack of success in school, coupled with poor teaching and poor ghetto schools, tends to reinforce the experience of inferior achievement.

> In Negro adults the sense of inadequate self-worth shows up in a lack of motivation to rise in their jobs or fear of competition with whites; and a sense of impotence in civil affairs, demonstrated in lethargy toward voting, or community participation, or responsibility for others, in family instability and the irresponsibility rooted in hopelessness.[3]

the search for self-esteem in the poor whose environment leads to aggressive and self-destructive behavior

But all human beings search for self-esteem. According to Clark, teenage blacks often pretend to knowledge about illicit activities and to sexual experiences that they have not really had. Many use as their models the petty criminals of the ghetto, with their colorful, swaggering style of cool bravado. The inability to succeed by the standards of the wider society leads to a peculiar fascination with individuals who successfully defy society's norms. Some young black men seek their salvation in aggressive and self-destructive behavior. Because the larger society has rejected them, they reject—or at least appear to reject—the values of that society.

Professor Clark believes that the explanation for violence and crime in the ghetto lies in the conscious or unconscious belief of many young blacks that they cannot hope to win meaningful self-esteem through the avenues available to middle-class whites, so they turn to "hustling"— pimping, prostitution, gambling, or drug dealing. They are frequently scornful of what they consider the hypocrisy and dishonesty of the larger society. They point to corruption among respected middle-class whites, including the police force.

Poverty and discrimination have also taken their toll on black family life. Professor Clark observed that under the system of slavery, the only source of family continuity was through the female; children were dependent on their mothers rather than their fathers. Segregation relegated the black male to menial and subservient jobs. He could not present himself to his wife and children as a consistent wage earner.

family instability

> His doubts concerning his personal adequacy were therefore reinforced. He was compelled to base his self-esteem instead on a kind of behavior that tended to support a stereotyped picture of the Negro male—sexual impulsiveness, irresponsibility, verbal bombast, posturing, and compensatory achievement in entertainment and athletics, particularly in sports like boxing in which athletic prowess could be exploited for the gain of others.[4]

Many black women were obliged to hold the family together—to set its goals and encourage and protect boys and girls. Many young black males had no strong father figure upon which to model their behavior. Many established temporary liaisons with a number of women. The result was a high rate of illegitimacy and family instability.

Is there a culture of poverty?

It is sometimes argued that the poor have a characteristic lifestyle or "culture of poverty" that assists them in adjusting to their world. Like other aspects of culture it is passed on to future generations, setting in motion a self-perpetuating cycle of poverty. The theory of the poverty cycle is as follows: deprivation in one generation leads, through cultural impoverishment, indifference, apathy, or misunderstanding of their children's educational needs, to deprivation in the next generation. Lacking the self-respect that comes from earning an adequate living, some young men cannot sustain responsibilities of marriage and so they hand down to their children the same burden of family instability and female-headed households that they themselves carried. Children born into a culture of alienation, apathy, and lack of motivation learn these attitudes themselves. Thus the poor are prevented from exploiting any opportunities that are available to them.

the culture-of-poverty thesis
the idea that a lifestyle of poverty, alienation, and apathy is passed on from one generation to another

It is probably more accurate to talk about a *subculture* of poverty. The prefix *sub* is used because most of the poor subscribe to the "mid-

dle-class American way of life," at least as a cultural ideal and even as a personal fantasy. Most poor people do not reject American culture but strive to adapt its values to the realities of economic deprivation and social disorganization in their own lives.

the culture of poverty as "present-orientedness"
the inability to plan or sacrifice for the future

Another view of the "culture of poverty" emphasizes the "present-orientedness" of many poor people. Professor Edward C. Banfield argues that the culture of poverty is primarily an effect produced by extreme present-orientedness rather than a lack of income or wealth. Individuals caught up in the culture of poverty are unable to plan for the future, to sacrifice immediate gratifications in favor of future ones, or to exercise the discipline that is required to get ahead. Banfield admits that some people experience poverty because of involuntary unemployment, prolonged illness, death of the breadwinner, or some other misfortune. But even when severe, this kind of poverty is not self-perpetuating. It ends once the external cause of it no longer exists. According to Banfield, other people will be poor no matter what their "external" circumstances are. They live in a culture of poverty that continues for generations because they are psychologically unable to provide for the future. Improvements in their circumstances may affect their poverty only superficially. Even increased income is unlikely to change their way of life. The additional money will be spent quickly on nonessential or frivolous items. This culture of poverty may involve no more than 10 or 20 percent of all families who live below the poverty line, but it generally continues regardless of what is done in the way of remedial action.[5]

Opponents of the idea of a culture of poverty argue that this notion diverts attention from the *conditions* of poverty that foster family instability, present-orientedness, and other ways of life of the poor. The question is really whether the conditions of poverty create a culture of poverty or vice versa. Reformers are likely to focus on the conditions of poverty as the fundamental cause of the social pathologies that afflict the poor. They note that the idea of a culture of poverty can be applied only to groups who have lived in poverty for several generations. It is not relevant to those who have become poor during their lifetime because of sickness, accident, or old age. The cultural explanation basically involves *parental transmission of values and beliefs,* which in turn determines behavior of future generations. In contrast, the situational explanation of poverty involves social conditions—differences in financial resources— that operate directly to determine behavior. In this view the conditions of poverty can be seen as affecting behavior directly, as well as *indirectly* through their impact upon succeeding generations. Perhaps the greatest danger in the idea of a culture of poverty is that poverty in this light can be seen as an unbreakable, puncture-proof cycle, which may lead to a relaxation of efforts to ameliorate the conditions of poverty. In other words, a "culture" of poverty may become an excuse for inaction.[6]

Whether or not there is a culture of poverty is a perplexing question. The argument resembles the classic exchange between F. Scott Fitzgerald and Ernest Hemingway. When Fitzgerald observed, "The rich are different from you and me," Hemingway retorted, "Yes, they have more money." Observers who believe that they see a distinctive lower-class culture will say, "The poor are different from you and me." But opponents may reply, "Yes, they have less money." In other words, are the poor poorly educated, underskilled, poorly motivated, "delinquent," and "shiftless" because they are poor, or are they poor because they are poorly educated, underskilled, unmotivated, "delinquent," and "shiftless"? The question is a serious one because it has important policy implications.

If one assumes that the poor are no different from other Americans, then one is led toward policies that emphasize "opportunity" for individuals rather than drastic changes in the environment. If the poor are like other Americans, it is necessary only to provide them with the ordinary means to achievement of the desires of other Americans—for example, job training programs, good schools, and perhaps some counseling to make them aware of opportunities that are available to them. The intervention that is required to change their lives, therefore, is one of supplying a means of achieving a level of income that most Americans already enjoy. It can be argued that this kind of thinking—the denial that a subculture of poverty exists—influenced many of the programs of the Johnson administration's "War on Poverty." The goal of the War on Poverty was not to provide resources directly that would end poverty but to provide opportunities so that people could achieve their own

poverty
a result of current social conditions or parental transmission?

do the poor have a separate culture or simply less money that most other Americans?

policy implications
if the poor need only money, then simply help them prepare to earn it
if poverty is a subculture, then policy should emphasize "cultural enrichment" programs for the very young

escape from poverty. The assumption behind the programs was that the poor would respond to these opportunities in the same way most middle-class Americans would respond.

If, however, one believes in the notion of a subculture of poverty, it is necessary to devise a strategy to interrupt the transmission of lower-class cultural values from generation to generation. The strategy must try to prevent the socialization of young children into an environment of family instability, lack of motivation, crime and delinquency, and so forth. One rather drastic means to accomplish this would be simply to remove the children from lower-class homes at a very early age and raise them in a controlled environment that transmits the values of the conventional culture rather than of the subculture of poverty. Perhaps a less harsh version of this same idea would involve special day-care centers and preschool programs to remedy cultural deprivation and disadvantage; these programs would be oriented toward bringing about cultural change in young children through "cultural enrichment."

The subculture of poverty has another policy implication: if one believes that such a subculture exists, then one must also conclude that little can be done to help people escape from poverty until after there has been sufficient change in their conditions of life to permit them to take advantage of opportunity programs. According to this line of reasoning, you cannot change people without changing their environment; the poor cannot be changed by schooling, or manpower training, or programs to develop better attitudes while they are still poor. The emphasis on "self-help"—education, information, job training, participation—is incomplete and misleading unless it is accompanied by a program aimed at directly altering the conditions of poverty. Hence, it is argued that a *guaranteed minimum income* is required to bring the poor up to a level where they will be able to take advantage of educational and training information and other opportunity programs.

Strategies in public welfare policy

Social Security Act
alleviative and preventive

social insurance
compulsory savings for all with legal entitlement to benefits

In the Social Security Act of 1935 the federal government undertook to establish a basic framework for welfare policies at the federal, state, and local levels in America. This act embodied both an alleviated strategy (public assistance) and a new preventive strategy (social insurance). The *social insurance* concept was designed to *prevent* poverty resulting from individual misfortune—unemployment, old age, death of the family breadwinner, or physical disability. Social insurance was based on the same notion as private insurance: the sharing of risks, the setting aside of money for a rainy day, and legal entitlement to benefits upon reaching retirement or upon occurrence of specific misfortunes. Social insurance was *not* to be charity or public assistance. Instead, it relied on people's (compulsory) financial contribution to their own protection.

One of the key features of the Social Security Act is the Old-Age, Survivors, Disability, and Health Insurance (OASDHI) program; this is a compulsory social insurance program financed by regular deductions from earnings, which gives individuals the legal right to benefit in the event that their income is reduced by old age, death of the head of the household, or permanent disability (see Figure 11-3). OASDHI is not public charity but a way of compelling people to provide insurance against loss of income. Another feature of the Social Security Act was that it induced states to enact unemployment compensation programs. Unemployment compensation is also an *insurance* program, only in this case the costs are borne solely by the employer. In 1965 Congress amended Social Security to add comprehensive medical care for persons over sixty-five—"Medicare." Medicare provided for prepaid hospital insurance for the aged under Social Security, and low-cost voluntary medical insurance for the aged under federal administration. Medicare, too, is based upon the insurance principle: individuals pay for their medical insurance during their working years and enjoy its benefits after age sixty-five. Thus the program resembles private medical hospital insurance, except that it is compulsory.

major social insurance programs
Social Security
unemployment compensation
Medicare

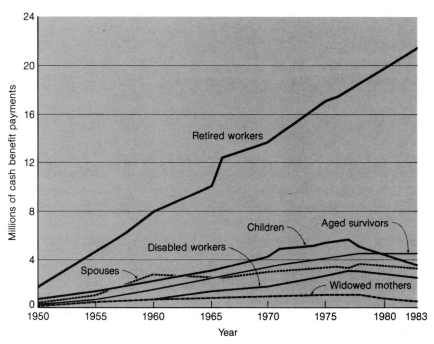

FIGURE 11-3 Social Security—OASDHI Cash Benefits, by Type of Beneficiary. (SOURCE: U.S. Bureau of the Census, *Social Indicators III.* Washington, D.C.: U.S. Government Printing Office, 1980; *Statistical Abstract of the United States, 1985,* p. 364.)

*social insurance ver-
sus public assistance*

social insurance
contributions required
all are entitled to benefits

public assistance
financed out of tax
  revenues
benefits paid only to persons who are poor

*major public assist-
ance cash programs*
SSI
AFDC
general assistance

*major public assist-
ance "in-kind"
programs*
food stamps
school lunches
Medicaid
public housing

The distinction between the *social insurance* program and a *public assistance* (welfare) program is an important one that has on occasion become a major political issue. If the beneficiaries of a government program are required to have made contributions to it before claiming any of its benefits, and if they are entitled to the benefits regardless of their personal wealth, the program is said to be financed on the *social insurance* principle. If the program is financed out of general tax revenues, and if the recipients are required to show that they are poor before claiming its benefits, the program is said to be financed on the *public assistance* principle.

In addition to the insurance programs mentioned above, the federal government undertook in the Social Security Act to provide public assistance payments to certain needy persons to alleviate the conditions of poverty. The strategy of public assistance is clearly *alleviative*. There is no effort to prevent poverty or to attack its causes; the idea is simply to provide a minimal level of subsistence to certain categories of needy persons. The federal government, under its Supplemental Security Income (SSI) program, directly aids three categories of recipients: the aged, the blind, and the disabled. The federal government, under its Aid to Families with Dependent Children (AFDC) program, gives money to the states to assist them in providing welfare payments to families with children under eighteen. Welfare aid to persons who do not fall into any of these categories but who, for one reason or another, are poor is referred to as *general assistance* and is paid for entirely from state funds. SSI, AFDC, and general assistance all provide cash benefits.

The federal government also provides many "in-kind" (noncash) welfare benefits.[7] The Food Stamp program was begun in 1965; originally the poor were allowed to purchase food stamps at large discounts and use the stamps to buy food at stores; after 1977 the stamps were distributed free. Free school lunches (and in some cities breakfasts as well) are made available to children of the poor by federal payments to school districts. In 1965, Congress also authorized federal funds to enable states to guarantee medical services to all public assistance recipients. This program is known as "Medicaid." Unlike Medicare, Medicaid is a welfare program designed for needy persons; no prior contributions are required, but recipients of Medicaid must be eligible for welfare assistance. In other words, they must be poor. Finally, the federal government assists cities in providing low-cost public housing for the poor.

The welfare mess

On the whole, the social insurance programs of the government are popular: Social Security, unemployment compensation, and Medicare. But the various cash and in-kind public assistance programs have not been very popular. They are disliked by national, state, and local legislatures who must vote the large appropriations for them; they are resented by the taxpayers who must bear their increasing burdens; they are denounced by officials and caseworkers who must administer them; they are often accepted with bitterness by those who were intended to benefit from them.[8]

Dependence on public assistance in the United States *increased* at a very rapid rate in the 1970s (see Table 11-2). Only since 1980 have welfare rolls begun to level off. Certainly our public assistance programs have not succeeded in reducing dependency. In the last decade the number of welfare recipients has more than doubled, and public assistance costs have quadrupled. Interestingly, it is not programs for the aged, blind, or disabled, or even the general assistance programs, that have incurred the greatest burdens. It is the Aid to Families with Dependent Children (AFDC) program that is the largest, most expensive, and most rapidly growing of all cash welfare programs—and the most controversial.

The rise in welfare rolls began during a period of high unemployment. However, the continued rise cannot be attributed to economic depression, but is simply due to the fact that more and more people are applying for public assistance. Despite increased dependence on welfare and the growing burden of welfare costs, many of the nation's poor do *not* receive public assistance. There were 25 million poor people in America in 1976, yet only 16 million persons on welfare rolls. Many of the nation's poor are *working poor,* who are ineligible for welfare assistance because they hold jobs, even though the jobs pay very little. A low-income family, headed by the father, is not eligible to receive AFDC payments if the father is working, regardless of how poor the family may be.

Not only does welfare fail to assist all the nation's poor, it does not provide enough to those it does assist to raise them out of poverty.

criticisms of public assistance

TABLE 11-2 Growth of public assistance cash programs (in millions of recipients)

	Total	AFDC	SSI*	General assistance
1950	6.0	2.2	3.0	0.9
1955	5.8	2.2	2.8	0.7
1960	7.0	3.1	2.8	1.2
1965	7.8	4.4	2.8	0.7
1970	10.4	6.7	3.0	0.8
1975	16.5	11.4	4.3	0.8
1980	15.2	11.1	4.1	1.0
1983	15.8	10.8	3.9	1.1

*Prior to 1974, SSI was separated into programs for the aged, blind, and disabled. These are combined in the table.
SOURCE: U.S. Bureau of the Census, *Statistical Abstract of the United States, 1985* (Washington, D.C.: U.S. Government Printing Office, 1985), and past issues.

Although welfare benefits differ from state to state, in every state the level of benefits falls *well below* the recognized poverty line.

State administration of welfare has resulted in wide *disparities among the states* in eligibility requirements and benefit levels. For example, in 1980 average AFDC monthly payments ranged from a high of $389 per family in Hawaii to a low of $84 per family in Mississippi.

Operating policies and administration of welfare have produced a whole series of problems. For one thing, they have contributed to the *disintegration of family life.* Until recently, most states denied AFDC benefits if a man was living with his family, even though he had no work. This denial was based on the assumption that an employable man in the household meant that children were no longer "dependent" on the state. Thus, if a man lived with his family, he could watch them go hungry; if he abandoned them, public assistance would enable them to eat. Moreover, it was easier for an unmarried mother to get on welfare rolls than it was for a married mother (who had to prove she was not receiving support from her husband). These rules have now been relaxed, but it is still more difficult for whole families to get on public assistance than it is for fatherless families.

Welfare policies and administration have also acted as *deterrents to work*. In most states, if a recipient of assistance takes a full job, assistance checks are reduced or stopped. If the recipient is then laid off, it may take some time to get back on the welfare roll. In other words, employment is uncertain, while assistance is not. More important, the jobs available to most recipients are low-paying jobs that do not produce much more income than assistance, particularly when transportation, child care, and other costs of working are considered. All these facts may discourage the welfare recipient from seeking work.

Although such problems are serious, it is well to note that some of the charges leveled against public assistance are unfounded. For example, there are very few individuals for whom welfare has become "a permanent way of life." The median length of time on AFDC is less than three years; only one-tenth of the persons aided have been receiving assistance for more than ten years. The number of "welfare chiselers"— able-bodied employable adults who prefer public-assisted idleness to work—is probably quite small. Most recipients are either women or children, or aged, blind, or disabled; few employable men are on welfare rolls. The work alternative for the large numbers of AFDC mothers is fraught with problems—child care, lack of skills, lack of work experience, and so on. It might be more costly to society to prepare these women for work than to support them.

Power in Washington for the poor

The poor are not represented in Washington in the same fashion as other groups in society. The poor themselves rarely write letters to

payments to the states or communities for general functions such as health, welfare, social service, and community development; states and communities are free to decide for themselves what specific programs will be supported with block grant money. The Reagan administration believed that time and money could be saved by relocating decision making outside Washington. But frequently the total dollar amount of a block grant was smaller than the amount used in the past to fund all the programs consolidated into the block grant program. Thus block grants are also a way to hold down federal spending.

Despite the Reagan administration's efforts to cut federal spending, actual federal spending for social welfare continues to climb (see Figure 11-4).

The politics of Social Security reform

Political obstacles to rational Social Security reform are awesome. The 36 million people receiving Social Security benefits are the largest blocks of recipients of any government program. They are especially sensitive to talk of "reform" that suggests any reduction in their benefits. Mostly elderly, these persons vote more regularly than any other age

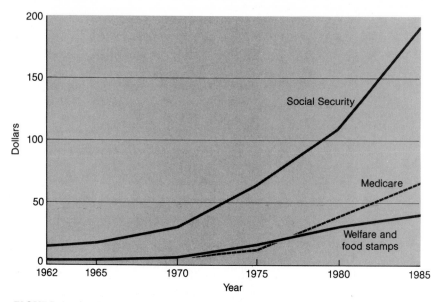

FIGURE 11-4 Government spending for social welfare.

category. They want to keep the Social Security program financially sound, but they do not want to give up any benefits, including annual cost-of-living increases.

Many reforms have been proposed for the Social Security system in order to ensure its continued solvency:

1. Congress has responded to immediate shortfalls in revenues by increasing the Social Security tax and taxable wage base. Raising payroll taxes even higher than current levels not only is politically distasteful but may also undermine support for Social Security by adding to the burdens of current workers.

2. Most Social Security benefits to the elderly are exempted from personal income taxes. Retirees whose only source of income was Social Security should not pay any taxes, but retirees with other income sources might be required to do so. (In 1982 Congress allowed Social Security benefits for persons earning more than $20,000 to be taxed.)

3. Congress may eventually be forced to contribute to Social Security from general tax revenues. (The first movement in this direction came with Medicare in 1965, when Congress agreed to pay part of the cost through general tax revenues and part through Social Security taxes.)

4. Congress could allow persons over sixty-five to continue working without losing their Social Security benefits. Their wages would be subject to Social Security taxes and at least part of their benefits would be recovered.

proposals to save Social Security
raise Social Security taxes
tax benefits
use general tax revenues
encourage elderly to continue to work
reduce automatic cost-of-living increases
raise retirement age
lower benefits for early retirement

5. Congress could readjust the automatic cost-of-living increases for Social Security recipients. Older Americans are *not* necessarily poor and most do not have the high expenses of younger workers who are buying homes and raising children. A COLA (cost of living adjustment) that rose more slowly than the official Consumer Price Index might better reflect the real needs of the elderly.

6. Congress could gradually increase the age at which individuals can retire and receive full Social Security benefits. If the retirement age were gradually moved from sixty-five to sixty-seven years of age, recipient payment would be delayed and the system could be financed on roughly the same basis as it is today. When Social Security was begun in 1935 the average life span was about sixty—five years *less* than the legal retirement age. Today the average life span is closer to seventy-five—ten years *more* than the Social Security retirement age. (In 1982 Congress called for an increase in the retirement age from sixty-five to sixty-seven but not until after the year 2000.)

7. Congress could reduce the benefits of persons retiring early at age sixty-two to 30 or 50 percent of regular benefits instead of the 80 percent currently allowed.

Currently Social Security and Medicare contributions ("FICA" deductions from wages) are 7.5 percent on the first $37,800 of earnings, to be matched by 7.5 from employers, for a total of 15 percent of payrolls. This means that Social Security taxes are higher for many middle- and low-income earners than federal income taxes. These taxes have become a major burden for most working Americans.

■ The graying of America ■

America is "graying," not "greening," as indicated in a popular book of several years ago. The proportion of the population that is over sixty-five is steadily increasing. By the year 2030—less than fifty years from now—more than 20 percent of the population will be over sixty-five, compared with about 11 percent today (see Figure 11-5). Most of these people will be dependent on social security and Medicare for their income and medical care. However, because of low fertility rates among today's young people (fewer births among women of childbearing age), there will be a relatively small work force to provide support for a large, dependent, elderly population. Today the "dependency ratio" is one elderly person for every three workers, but by 2030 we will have one elderly person for every two workers. The burden of social security and Medicare will be much greater than it is today.

The aged today. In the 1980 census there were nearly 26 million people age sixty-five or over in the United States; this is 11.1 percent of the population. The aged are mostly women: 16 million women and only 10 million men. At age sixty-five, women have an added life expectancy of 18.4 years and men have 14.0 remaining years. The median income of the aged is about half the median

countered stiff competition for jobs in the 1970s and 1980s. During the baby boom, women averaged 3.5 births during their lifetime. Today the birth rate is only 1.8 births per woman; this is less than the 2.1 figure required to keep the population from declining. The baby-boom generation will be retiring beginning in 2010, and by 2030 they will constitute more than 20 percent of the population. Changes in lifestyle—less smoking, more exercise, better weight control—may increase the aged population even more. So, too, may medical advances extend life expectancy.

Social Security and Medicare.

Under current financing the Social Security system, including Medicare, will go broke—if not now, sometime in the early years of the next century. Medicare costs are rising very rapidly: as people live longer they require greater medical care. The "old old"—persons who are 80 and over—may grow from 22 percent of the aged today to 35 percent in 2030.

Social Security was begun in 1935 as a "trust fund" with the expectation that a reserve would be built up from "social insurance"

income of younger adults. About 15 percent of the aged live below the poverty line.

The aged in the future. The "baby boom" from 1945 to 1960 produced a large generation of people who crowded schools and colleges in the 1960s and 1970s and en-

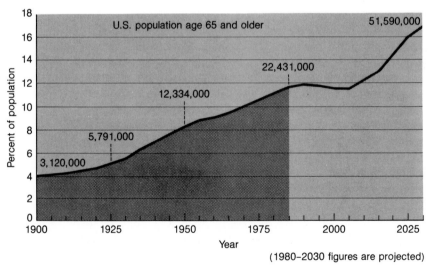

FIGURE 11-5 The graying of America. (SOURCE: Department of Commerce, Bureau of the Census.)

premiums" (taxes) from working persons. The reserve would earn interest, and the interest and principal would be used in later years to pay benefits. Benefits for individuals would be in proportion to their contributions. But it turned out not to work that way at all. The social insurance system is now financed on a pay-as-you-go, rather than a reserve, system. Political pressure to raise benefit levels while keeping payments low reduced the reserve to a very minor role in social security finance. Today, the income from all social insurance premiums (taxes) matches the outgo in Social Security benefits. Today's generation of workers is paying for the benefits of the last generation, and it is hoped that this generation's benefits will be financed by the next generation of workers.

Since current workers must pay for the benefits of current retirees and other beneficiaries, the "dependency ratio" becomes an important component of evaluating the future of Social Security.

Notes

1. John Kenneth Galbraith, *The Affluent Society* (New York: New American Library, 1958), p. 251.
2. *Statistical Abstract of the United States, 1985,* p. 459.
3. Kenneth B. Clark, *Dark Ghetto: Dilemmas of Social Power* (New York: Harper & Row, 1965), p. 67.
4. Ibid., p. 70.
5. Edward C. Banfield, *The Unheavenly City* (Boston: Little, Brown, 1968), ch. 6.
6. Jack L. Roach and Orville R. Gursslin, "An Evaluation of the Concept Culture of Poverty," *Social Forces* 45 (March 1967): 384–392.
7. For a description of all the various federal welfare programs, see A. Levitan, *Programs in Aid of the Poor in the 1980s* (Baltimore: Johns Hopkins University Press, 1980).
8. However, for the view that these in-kind welfare programs have helped reduce poverty, see Sheldon Danzinger and Robert Plotnick, *Has the War on Poverty Been Won?* (New York: Academic Press, 1980).

Discussion questions

1. Discuss the criteria used by the U.S. Social Security Administration to define the poverty line. Describe the emphasis of this official definition of poverty on subsistence levels. What are the criticisms of this definition of poverty?
2. Identify the groups of people who experience poverty in greater proportions than the national average.
3. Discuss the definition of poverty as relative deprivation, or inequality. Explain why it seems unlikely that this type of poverty will ever be eliminated.
4. Discuss the relationship between poverty and feelings of powerlessness. What are the feelings of the poor about themselves? What are

their attitudes toward the larger society? Describe some of the forms of personal adjustment to poverty and the effect of poverty and discrimination on family life.

5. What is meant by the expression *culture of poverty?* Comment on Edward C. Banfield's view of the culture of poverty as "present-orientedness." What are the policy implications of a culture of poverty? Discuss the arguments of those who oppose the idea of a culture of poverty.

6. Identify the two basic strategies that are embodied in the Social Security Act of 1935. Differentiate between social insurance programs and public assistance programs in terms of who pays, who benefits, and when they benefit. Give examples of each type of program and specify the type of strategy they express.

7. Discuss the criticisms of current public assistance (welfare) programs.

8. Who lobbies in Washington for the poor?

9. What is meant by the "social safety net?" What changes in welfare policy were initiated by the Reagan administration?

10. What changes are occurring in the age composition of the nation's population? What do these changes mean for Social Security? How can the Social Security program be preserved?

CHAPTER 12

■ POWER, CRIME & VIOLENCE

More than 2,000 years ago Aristotle wrote of the problem of crime that "the generality of men are naturally apt to be swayed by fear rather than by reverence, and to refrain from evil rather because of the punishment that it brings, than because of its own foulness." Power must be exercised by society for the very basic purposes of maintaining order and protecting the citizenry. The way that a society exercises that power obviously has enormous implications for the lives of all who live in it. Nazi Germany and Stalinist Russia are but two examples of how the unconstrained use of police power can turn the lives of citizens into nightmares. A free democratic society must struggle with maintaining a balance between its exercise of police power and its safeguarding of individual freedom. In this chapter we will examine America's struggles with this problem. We will also examine the violence that has been a part of most of the important social movements in American history.

After you have read Chapter 12, you should be able to

- describe the current status of crime and punishment in the United States as evidenced by crime rates, the constitutional rights of defendants, and judicial decisions regarding defendants' rights and capital punishment,
- describe the current legal status of various potentially harmful substances: alcohol, tobacco, marijuana, cocaine, and heroin,
- describe the basic protections afforded to persons accused of crime,
- discuss the history of violence in the United States and some of the social-psychological explanations of violence,
- discuss violence as a form of political protest,
- discuss the constitutional issues arising from capital punishment.

Power and individual freedom

Thomas Hobbes
freedom is not the absence of law; law is required to protect individual freedom
governments are formed for collective self-protection

For thousands of years people have wrestled with the question of balancing social power against individual freedom. How far can individual freedom be extended without undermining the stability of a society, threatening the safety of others, and risking anarchy? The early English political philosopher Thomas Hobbes (1588–1679) believed that society must establish a powerful "Leviathan"—the state—in order to curb the savage instincts of human beings. A powerful authority in society was needed to prevent people from attacking each other for personal gain—"war of every man against every man" in which "notions of right and wrong, justice and injustice, have no place." According to Hobbes, without law and order there is no real freedom. The fear of death and destruction permeates every act of life: "Every man is enemy to every man"; "Force and fraud are the two cardinal virtues"; and "The life of man [is] solitary, poor, nasty, brutish, and short." Freedom, then, is *not* the absence of law and order. On the contrary, law and order are required if there is to be any freedom in society at all.[1]

dilemma of free government:
a government strong enough to protect its citizens may threaten their liberty

To avoid the brutal life of a lawless society—where the weak are at the mercy of the strong—people form governments and endow them with powers to secure peace and self-preservation. Hobbes believed that "the social contract"—the agreement of human beings to establish governments and grant them the powers to maintain peace and security—is a collective act of self-preservation. People voluntarily relinquish some of their individual freedom to establish a powerful government that is capable of protecting them from their neighbors as well as from foreign aggressors. This government must be strong enough to maintain its own existence or it cannot defend the rights of its citizens. But what happens when a government becomes too strong and infringes the liberties of its citizens? People agree to abide by law and accept restrictions on their personal freedom for the sake of peace and self-preservation; but how much liberty must be surrendered to secure an orderly society? This is the *classic dilemma of free government:* people must create laws and governments to protect freedom, but the laws and governments themselves restrict freedom.

The problem of crime

crime rates
reported serious crimes per 100,000 people

Crime rates are the subject of a great deal of popular discussion. Very often they are employed to express the degree of social disorganization or even the effectiveness of law enforcement agencies. Crime rates are based on the Federal Bureau of Investigation's *Uniform Crime Reports,* but the FBI reports themselves are based on figures supplied by state and local police agencies. The FBI has succeeded in establishing a uniform classification of the number of serious crimes per 100,000 people that are known to the police—murder and nonnegligent manslaughter, forcible rape, robbery, aggravated assault, burglary, larceny and theft, including auto theft (see Table 12-1).

We should be cautious in interpreting official crime rates. They are really a function of several factors: the diligence of police in detecting crime, the adequacy of the system for reporting and tabulating crime, and the amount of crime itself.

The official FBI crime rate rose very dramatically in the United States in the twenty years prior to 1980. Increases occurred in both violent crime—murder, rape, robbery and assault (see Figure 12-1)—and nonviolent crime—burglary, larceny, and theft. Certainly some of the increase was a result of improved reporting. As more people insure their property, they file more police reports in order to make insurance claims. The introduction of computers and sophisticated police data collection systems may also have contributed to the increases. But unquestionably crime itself was also on the rise.

Recently, however, the crime rate has declined slightly. We can only speculate about possible reasons for this modest success: (1) police are becoming more effective, with better training and equipment; (2) business and industry are installing protective technology (steering locks on autos, for example), and they are hiring more private security guards; or, more likely, (3) the most "crime-prone" age group, persons fifteen to twenty-four years old, is no longer increasing as a percentage of the population.

Police statistics vastly understate the real amount of crime. Citizens *do not report* many crimes to police. The National Opinion Research Center of the University of Chicago asked a national sample of individuals whether they or any member of their household had been a victim of crime during the past year. This survey revealed that the actual amount of crime is several times greater than that reported by the FBI. There are more than twice as many crimes committed as are reported to the police. The number of forcible rapes was more than three and one-half times the number reported; burglaries were three times, aggravated assaults and larcenies were more than double, and robbery was 50 per-

FBI classification
criminal homicide
forcible rape
robbery
assault
burglary
larceny
auto theft

underreporting of crime

TABLE 12-1 Crime rate—Number of offenses known to police per 100,000 persons

Year	Total	Criminal homicide	Forcible rape	Robbery	Assault	Burglary	Larceny	Auto theft
1960	1,126	5.0	10	60	85	502	283	182
1965	1,516	5.0	12	71	110	653	410	255
1970	3,985	7.9	19	172	165	1,025	2,079	457
1972	3,961	9.0	22	180	187	1,141	1,994	426
1976	5,266	8.8	26	196	229	1,439	2,921	446
1980	5,931	10.2	37	248	292	1,697	3,164	500
1983	5,159	8.3	34	214	273	1,334	2,866	429

SOURCE: U.S. Bureau of the Census, *Statistical Abstract of the United States, 1985* (Washington, D.C.: U.S. Government Printing Office, 1985), p. 166.

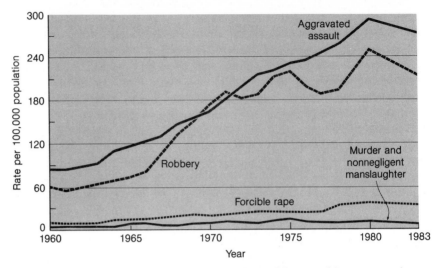

FIGURE 12-1 Violent crimes reported to the Federal Bureau of Investigation, by type. (SOURCE: U.S. Bureau of the Census, *Social Indicators III.* Washington, D.C.: U.S. Government Printing Office, 1980; *Statistical Abstract of the United States, 1985,* p. 167.)

cent greater than the reported rate. Only auto theft statistics were reasonably accurate, indicating that most people call the police when their cars are stolen.

Interviewees gave a variety of reasons for their failure to report crimes to the police. The most common reason was the belief that police

could not be effective in dealing with the crime. This is a serious commentary on police protection in the United States today (see Box 12-1). Other reasons included the feeling that the crime was "a private matter" or that the victim did not want to harm the offender. Fear of reprisal was

---

BOX 12-1   What police do

■ At least three important functions in society are performed by police: law enforcement, keeping the peace, and furnishing services. Actually, law enforcement may take up only a small portion of a police officer's daily activity, perhaps only 10 percent.[a] The service function is far more common—attending accidents, directing traffic, escorting crowds, assisting stranded motorists, handling drunks, and so on. The function of peace-keeping is also very common—breaking up fights, quieting noisy parties, handling domestic or neighborhood quarrels, and the like. It is in this function that police exercise the greatest discretion in the application of the law. In most of these incidents, it is difficult to determine blame. Participants are reluctant to file charges and police must use personal discretion in handling each case.

Police are on the front line of society's efforts to resolve conflict. Indeed, instead of a legal or law enforcement role, the police are more likely to adopt a peacekeeping role. Police are generally lenient in their arrest practices; that is, they use their arrest practice less often than the law allows.[b] Rather than arresting people, the police prefer first to reestablish order. Of course, the decision to be more or less lenient in enforcing the law gives the police a great deal of discretion—the police exercise decision-making powers on the streets.

What factors influence police decision making? Probably the first factor to influence police behavior is the attitude of the other people involved in police encounters. If a person adopts an acquiescent role, displays deference and respect for the police, and conforms to police expectations, he is much less likely to be arrested than a person who shows disrespect or uses abusive language toward police.[c] This is not just an arbitrary response of police. They learn through training and experience the importance of establishing their authority on the streets.

[a] James Q. Wilson, *Varieties of Police Behavior* (Cambridge: Harvard University Press, 1968), p. 18.
[b] See Donald J. Black, "Social Organization of Arrest," in William B. Sanders and Howard C. Davidstel, eds., *The Criminal Justice Process* (New York: Holt, Rinehart & Winston, 1976).
[c] Stuart A. Sheingold, "Cultural Cleavage and Criminal Justice," *Journal of Politics* 40 (November 1978), 865–897.

mentioned much less frequently, usually in cases of assaults and family crimes.

> **deterring crime**
> *in changing behavior, certainty of punishment is more important than severity but likelihood of punishment for crime is small*

The current system of criminal justice is certainly no serious deterrent to crime. Most behavioral research suggests that it is not the *severity* of punishment but rather its *certainty* that affects behavior. In other words, crime is more likely to be deterred by making punishment sure than by making it severe. However, the best available estimates of the ratio between crime and punishment suggest that the likelihood of an individual's being jailed for a serious crime is less than one in a hundred (see Figure 12-2). Most crimes are not even reported by the victim. Police are successful in clearing only about one in five reported crimes by arresting the offender. The judicial system convicts only about one in four of the persons arrested and charged; others are not prosecuted, handled as juveniles, found not guilty, or permitted to plead guilty to a lesser charge and released. Only about half of the convicted felons are given prison sentences.

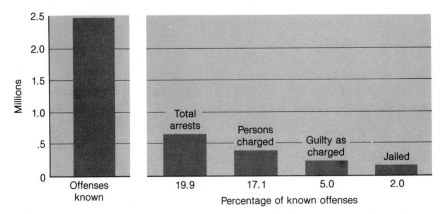

FIGURE 12-2 Law enforcement in relation to crime. (Actual crime is estimated to be two and a half times the known offenses. If the base were actual crime, the percentages would be less than half those appearing in the figure. Thus, persons jailed as a percentage of actual crime is less than 1 percent.) (SOURCE: U.S. Bureau of the Census, *Statistical Abstract of the United States, 1980*. Washington, D.C.: U.S. Government Printing Office, 1981.)

The constitutional rights of defendants

> **habeas corpus**
> *police may not hold a defendant without showing cause before a judge*

Guarantee of the writ of habeas corpus. An ancient right in common law is the right to obtain a *writ of habeas corpus*, a court order directing a public official who is holding a person in custody to bring the prisoner into court to explain the reasons for the confinement. If a judge finds that the prisoner is being unlawfully detained, or that there is not sufficient evidence that a crime has been committed or that the prisoner could have committed it, the judge orders the prisoner's immediate release.

Prohibition of bills of attainder and of ex post facto laws. Protection against bills of attainder and against ex post facto laws was, like the guarantee of habeas corpus, considered so fundamental to individual liberty that it was included in the original text of the Constitution. A *bill of attainder* is a legislative act that inflicts punishment without judicial trial. An *ex post facto law* is a retroactive criminal law that works to the detriment of the accused—for example, a law that makes an act a criminal one *after* the act is committed, or a law that increases the punishment for a crime and applies it *retroactively.*

bill of attainder
a legislative act that inflicts punishment without a trial

ex post facto law
making an act criminal after it is committed or retroactively increasing punishment

Prohibition of "unreasonable" searches and seizures. The Fourth Amendment provides: "The right of the people to be secure in their persons, houses, papers, and effects, against unreasonable searches and seizures, shall not be violated, and no warrants shall issue but upon probable cause, supported by oath or affirmation, and particularly describing the place to be searched, and the persons or things to be seized." The requirement that the things to be seized must be described in the warrant is meant to prevent "fishing expeditions" into an individual's home and personal effects on the possibility that some evidence of unknown illegal activity might crop up. An exception to the requirement for a warrant is made if the search is "incident to a lawful arrest." A "lawful arrest" can be made by the police if they have "probable cause" to believe a person has committed a felony or if a misdemeanor is committed in their presence; a search of the person and the person's property is permitted without a warrant at the time of such an arrest.

unreasonable search
search without lawful warrant by judge, unless "incident to a lawful arrest"

Freedom from self-incrimination. Although the Fifth Amendment establishes a number of procedural guarantees, perhaps the most widely quoted clause of that amendment guarantees that no person "shall be compelled in any criminal case to be a witness against himself." The sentence "I refuse to answer that question on the ground that it might tend to incriminate me" is, today, a household expression. Freedom from self-incrimination has its origins in English resistance against torture and confession. It now embodies the ideas that individuals should not be forced to contribute to their own prosecution and that the burden of proof of guilt is on the state. The constitutional protection against self-incrimination applies not only to accused persons in their own trials but also to witnesses testifying in any public proceedings, including criminal trials of other persons, civil suits, congressional hearings, or other investigations. The silence of an accused person cannot be interpreted as guilt; the burden of proving guilt rests with the prosecution.

freedom from self-incrimination
no physical or psychological force can be used to obtain confession or incriminating evidence from a defendant

The right to counsel. The right to avoid self-incrimination is closely connected with the right to counsel, as provided in the Sixth Amendment, because counsel may advise the accused to remain silent and claim protection against self-incrimination. The Sixth Amendment states: "In all criminal prosecutions, the accused shall enjoy . . . the assistance of counsel for his defense." An accused individual has the right to ask for counsel before answering any police questions. If the person in custody is indigent and requests counsel, the police must see that counsel is provided.

right to counsel
the right to an attorney in all criminal cases

Guarantee of a fair jury trial. Trial by jury is guaranteed in both the original text of the Constitution and the Fifth Amendment: "In all criminal prosecutions, the accused shall enjoy the right to a speedy and public trial, by an impartial jury . . . and to be informed of the nature and cause of the accusation; to be confronted with the witnesses against him; to have compulsory process for obtaining witnesses in his favor. . . ." The requirement of a "speedy" trial protects the accused from long pretrial waits; but the accused may ask for postponements in order to prepare a defense. A "public" trial prevents secret proceedings, and "impartial" means that each juror must be able to judge the case objectively. Discrimination in the selection of the jury is forbidden. The guarantee of a fair trial can be violated if sensational pretrial publicity or an unruly courtroom hinders the jury from making an unbiased verdict. By old canon law a jury consisted of twelve persons, and the vote of the jurors had to be unanimous. This is still the requirement in most cases, but recently the Supreme Court indicated that unanimity might not be required in some cases.

fair jury trial
public
speedy
unbiased

unanimous jury not required in all cases

The burden of proof rests with the prosecution. It is up to the prosecution to convince a jury "beyond reasonable doubt" that the accused is guilty. Witnesses must appear in person against the accused. The accused or the counsel for the accused has the right to cross-examine those witnesses and may present witnesses on behalf of their own case. The accused may even obtain a "summons" to compel people to testify at the trial. If a guilty verdict is rendered, the defendant may appeal any errors in the trial to a higher court.

burden of proof on prosecution
"beyond reasonable doubt"

Protection against double jeopardy. The Fifth Amendment states: "Nor shall any person be subject for the same offense to be twice put in jeopardy of life or limb. . . ." Once a person has been tried for a particular crime and the trial has ended in a decision of not guilty, that person cannot be tried again for the same crime. However, this right does not prevent a new trial if the jury cannot agree on a verdict (a "hung jury"), or if the verdict is reversed by an appeal to a higher court because of a procedural error. Moreover, an individual may be tried by

no double jeopardy
if found not guilty, a person cannot be tried again for the same crime

different jurisdictions on slightly different charges stemming from the same act.

Protection against excessive bail.   Arrested persons are considered innocent until tried and found guilty. They are entitled to go free prior to trial unless their freedom would unreasonably endanger society or unless there is reason to believe that they would not appear for trial. Bail is supposed to ensure that the accused will appear. Bail may be denied for major crimes, but most accused persons are entitled to be released on bail pending their trial. Bail must not be "excessive," although there are no fixed standards for determining what "excessive" is.

bail
money held by court to ensure that defendant will appear for trial

Landmark decisions.   The Warren Court—the Supreme Court of the 1950s and 1960s, under the guidance of Chief Justice Earl Warren—greatly strengthened the rights of accused persons in criminal cases. Several key decisions, which were the result of split votes, drew heavy criticism from law enforcement officers and others as hamstringing police in their struggle with lawlessness. These decisions include:

Mapp v. *Ohio* (1961), barring the use of illegally seized evidence in criminal cases by applying the Fourth Amendment guarantee against unreasonable searches and seizures. Even if the evidence seized proves the guilt of the accused, it cannot be presented in a trial.

Gideon v. *Wainwright* (1963), ruling that equal protection under the Fourteenth Amendment requires that free legal counsel be appointed for all indigent defendants in all criminal cases.

Escobedo v. *Illinois* (1964), ruling that suspects are entitled to confer with counsel as soon as police investigation focuses on them, or once "the process shifts from investigatory to accusatory."

Miranda v. *Arizona* (1966), requiring that police, before questioning suspects, must inform them of all their constitutional rights, including the right to counsel (appointed free, if necessary) and the right to remain silent. Although suspects may knowingly waive these rights, the police cannot question suspects who at any point ask for a lawyer or indicate "in any manner" that they do not wish to be questioned (see Figure 12-3).

To what extent these decisions have really hampered efforts to halt the rise in crime in America is very difficult to ascertain. The Supreme Court under Chief Justice Burger has not reversed any of these landmark decisions. Whatever progress is made in law enforcement, therefore, will have to be made within the current definition of the rights of defendants. It is important to note that Chief Justice Burger's recommendations for judicial reform center on the speedy administration of justice and not on changes in the rights of defendants.

DEFENDANT	LOCATION

SPECIFIC WARNING REGARDING INTERROGATIONS

1. YOU HAVE THE RIGHT TO REMAIN SILENT.
2. ANYTHING YOU SAY CAN AND WILL BE USED AGAINST YOU IN A COURT OF LAW.
3. YOU HAVE THE RIGHT TO TALK TO A LAWYER AND HAVE HIM PRESENT WITH YOU WHILE YOU ARE BEING QUESTIONED.
4. IF YOU CANNOT AFFORD TO HIRE A LAWYER ONE WILL BE APPOINTED TO REPRESENT YOU BEFORE ANY QUESTIONING, IF YOU WISH ONE.

SIGNATURE OF DEFENDANT	DATE

WITNESS	TIME

☐ REFUSED SIGNATURE   SAN FRANCISCO POLICE DEPARTMENT   PR.9.1.4

FIGURE 12-3 The "Miranda card" used by San Francisco police to inform suspects of their rights at the time of arrest.

Crime and the courts

Chief Justice Warren E. Burger has argued persuasively that rising crime in the United States is due partly to inadequacies in our system of criminal justice. "The present system of criminal justice does not deter criminal conduct," he said in a special State of the Federal Judiciary

message. "Whatever deterrent effect may have existed in the past has now virtually vanished."[2] He urged widespread reforms in law enforcement, courts, prisons, probation, and parole.

A major stumbling block to effective law enforcement is the current plight of U.S. judicial machinery:

Congestion on court dockets that delays the hearing of cases for months or even years. Moreover, actual trials are now twice as long on the average as they were ten years ago.

Increased litigation in the courts. Not only are more Americans aware of their rights but more of them are also using *every* avenue of appeal. Seldom do appeals concern the suit or the innocence of the defendant; usually they focus on procedural matters.

Excessive delays in trials. "Defendants, whether guilty or innocent, are human; they love freedom and hate punishment. With a lawyer provided to secure release without the need for a conventional bail bond, most defendants, except in capital cases, are released pending trial. We should not be surprised that a defendant on bail exerts a heavy pressure on his court-appointed lawyer to postpone the trial as long as possible so as to remain free. These postponements—and sometimes there are a dozen or more—consume the time of judges and court staffs as well as of lawyers. Cases are calendared and reset time after time while witnesses and jurors spend endless hours just waiting."[3]

Excessive delays in appeals. "We should not be surprised at delay when more and more defendants demand their undoubted constitutional right to trial by jury because we have provided them with lawyers and other needs at public expense; nor should we be surprised that most convicted persons seek a new trial when the appeal costs them nothing and when failure to take the appeal will cost them freedom. Being human a defendant plays out the line which society has cast him. Lawyers are competitive creatures and the adversary system encourages contention and often rewards delay; no lawyer wants to be called upon to defend the client's charges of incompetence for having failed to exploit all the procedural techniques which we have deliberately made available."[4]

Excessive variation in sentencing. Some judges let defendants off on probation for crimes that would draw five- or ten-year sentences by other judges. Whereas flexibility in sentencing is essential in dealing justly with individuals, perceived inconsistencies damage the image of the courts in the public mind.

Excessive "plea bargaining" between the prosecution and the defendant's attorney, in which the defendant agrees to plead guilty to a lesser offense if the prosecutor will drop more serious charges.

Crime and drugs

variation in laws regarding substances
alcohol, tobacco, marijuana, cocaine, heroin

Laws in the United States treat various drugs quite differently, even though all of these drugs have harmful effects. Alcohol and cigarettes are legal products, although the Office of the Surgeon General of the United States has undertaken educational campaigns to reduce their use, and Congress has banned the advertising of liquor and tobacco on radio and television. Marijuana has been "decriminalized" in several states, making its use or possession a misdemeanor comparable to a traffic offense; a majority of states, however, have retained criminal sanctions against marijuana, and its manufacture and distribution are prohibited everywhere. The potential for drug abuse is found in many prescription medicines—amphetamines, barbiturates, and tranquilizers. These may not be sold anywhere in the United States without a medical prescription. The use and possession of cocaine is a criminal offense everywhere in the United States, yet this drug is increasingly popular, particularly among the upper and upper-middle classes. Heroin is a physically addictive drug, but its use in the United States is declining somewhat,[5] in part perhaps because of worldwide law enforcement activity.

It is difficult to estimate the various forms of drug use. According to the U.S. National Institute on Drug Abuse, there are 12 to 14 million "problem drinkers," or about 6 percent of the population. There are an estimated 65 million cigarette smokers, or about 33 percent of the population (significantly less than the 45 percent of the population who smoked cigarettes in the 1940s and 1950s). An estimated 16 million, or about 7 percent of the population, are regular users of marijuana, although many more have smoked it at least once. Recent estimates of cocaine use have leaped upward to 10 million, or about 5 percent of the population. There are an estimated one-half million users of heroin in the country.[6]

Marijuana. The medical evidence on the health effects of marijuana is mixed; conflicting reports have been issued about whether or not it is more dangerous than alcohol.[7] The manufacture and sale of marijuana is illegal in all U.S jurisdictions. "Decriminalizing" marijuana does not make its production or sale legal, but it makes its possession (generally of an ounce or less) a civil offense, much like a traffic offense. In 1973 Oregon became the first state to decriminalize marijuana possession and use.

As marijuana use increased in the 1960s and 1970s, very often the children of the elite were swept up in drug busts. The late Senator Philip Hart of Michigan was quoted in Senate committee: "One of my children is one of the statistics you have here. He's a minor and he's been 20 days in jail for a stub this big, and that's all the education I needed to convince me we are topsy-turvy on this."[8] The result was that in the 1970s marijuana laws were relaxed and most prosecutors and judges took a more lenient attitude toward marijuana users. Most Americans oppose legalization of marijuana, but a majority believe that "the possession of small amounts" should not be "treated as a criminal offense."[9]

Heroin.   Since the Harrison Narcotic Act of 1916, heroin use has been considered a major law enforcement problem. In contrast, in Great Britain since 1920 heroin use has been considered a medical problem, and heroin is dispensed to addicted patients through physicians in the National Health Service. Heroin addiction in the United States is estimated to be greater than in Great Britain, as is the number of crimes committed by addicts. Over the years in the United States the extent of heroin addiction has varied with the success or failure of law enforcement. During the 1930s and 1940s with strong federal law enforcement efforts (almost one-third of all federal prisoners in 1928 were violators of the Harrison Act), heroin use declined. It rose again in the 1960s, but in the early 1970s the United States succeeded in pressing the Turkish government to ban opium poppy growing. Law enforcement officials in the United States and France succeeded with their "French Connection" efforts to destroy a major drug smuggling syndicate, and use declined somewhat.

Cocaine.   In recent years cocaine has replaced heroin as the major drug smuggled into the United States. The burgeoning market for cocaine currently challenges law enforcement efforts. Cocaine is not regarded as physically addictive, although the psychological urge to continue use of the drug is strong. It is made from coca leaves and imported into the United States. Its high cost and celebrity use have gained it favor in upper-class circles, although there is yet to be any strong effort to "decriminalize" it. The health problems associated with its continuous use are fairly serious, as reported by the National Institute on Drug Abuse.[10] The power of the coca leaf has been known for hundreds of years: Coca-Cola originally contained cocaine, though the drug was removed from the popular drink in 1903.

Trafficking.   Crime associated with drug trafficking is a serious national problem, whatever the health effects of various drugs. The world of drug trafficking is fraught with violence. Sellers rob and murder buyers and vice versa; neither can seek the protection of police or courts in their dealings with each other. Though some citizens might wish simply to allow dealers to wipe each other out, the frequency with which innocent bystanders are killed must be considered.

Violence in American history

Violence is not uncommon in American society. The nation itself was founded in armed revolution, and violence has been a *source of power* and a *stimulus to social change* ever since. Violence has been

violence as a source of power and change

associated with most of the important movements in American history: the birth of the nation (revolutionary violence), the freeing of the slaves and the preservation of the union (Civil War violence), the westward expansion of the nation (Indian wars), the establishment of law and order in frontier society (vigilante violence), the organization of the labor movement (labor–management violence), the civil rights movement (racial violence), and attempts to deal with the problems of cities (urban violence). History reveals that the patriot, the humanitarian, the pioneer, the lawman, the laborer, the black man, and the urban dweller have all used violence as a source of power. Despite pious pronouncements against it, Americans have frequently employed violence even in their most idealistic endeavors.

Perhaps the most famous act of organized mob violence occurred in 1773 when a group of "agitators" in Boston, Massachusetts, illegally destroyed 342 chests of tea. The early Revolutionary War fighting in 1774 and 1775, including the battles of Lexington and Concord, was really a series of small guerrilla skirmishes designed more to intimidate Tories than to achieve national independence. The old American custom of tarring and feathering was a product of the early patriotic campaign to root out Tories. Aside from the regular clash of Continental and British armies, a great deal of violence and guerrilla strife occurred during the Revolution. Savage guerrilla forays along the eastern coast resulted in the killing of thousands of Tory families and the destruction of their property. The success of this violence enshrined it in our traditions.

After the Revolutionary War many armed farmers and debtors resorted to violence to assert their economic interests. If taxes owed to the British government and debts owed to the British merchants could be denied, why not also the taxes owed to state governments and the debts owed to American merchants? In several states debtors had already engaged in open rebellion against tax collectors and sheriffs. The most serious rebellion broke out in the summer of 1786 in Massachusetts, when a band of insurgents, composed of farmers and laborers, captured courthouses in several western districts of that state and momentarily held the city of Springfield. Led by Daniel Shays, a veteran of Bunker Hill, the insurgent army posed a direct threat to the governing elite of the new nation. Shays' Rebellion, as it was called, was put down by a small mercenary army paid for by well-to-do citizens who feared that a wholesale attack on property rights was imminent. The growing domestic violence in the states contributed to the momentum leading to the Constitutional Convention of 1787, where propertied men established a new central government with the power to "ensure domestic tranquility," guarantee "the republican form of government," and protect "against domestic violence." Thus the Constitution itself reflects a concern of the Founding Fathers about domestic violence.

The Civil War was the bloodiest war the United States ever fought. Total casualties of the northern and southern armies equaled American casualties in World War II—but when the Civil War occurred, the nation was only one-third as large as it was during the latter conflict. There were few families that did not suffer the loss of a loved one during the Civil War. In addition to military casualties, the toll in lives and property among civilians was enormous. A great deal of domestic violence also occurred both before and after the war. In 1856 the brutal events surrounding the "bleeding Kansas" issue took place. In 1859 came John Brown's raid at Harper's Ferry, meant to start the freeing of the slaves in Virginia. Brown's capture, trial for treason, and execution made him a hero to many abolitionists, though Southerners believed that he had tried to incite slave uprisings. The guerrilla war that took place in the West during the Civil War has seldom been equaled for savagery; the fearsome Kansas Jayhawkers traded brutalities with Confederate guerrillas headed by William Quantrell. Later, western bandits, including Frank and Jesse James and the Younger brothers, who had fought as Confederate guerrillas, continued their forays against banks and railroads and enjoyed considerable popular prestige and support. Moreover, after the war, racial strife and Ku Klux Klan activity became routine in the old Confederate states. The Ku Klux Klan was first employed to intimidate the Republicans of the Reconstruction era by violence and threats, and later to force blacks to accept the renewed rule of whites.

Unquestionably the longest and most brutal violence in American history was that between whites and Indians. It began in 1607 and continued with only temporary truces for nearly three hundred years, until the final battle at Wounded Knee, South Dakota, in 1890. The norms of Indian warfare were generally more barbaric than those in other types of warfare, if such a thing is possible. Women and children on both sides were deliberately and purposefully killed. Torture was accepted as a customary part of making war. Scalping was a frequent practice among both Indians and Indian-fighters.

Vigilante violence (taking the law into one's own hands) arose as a response to a typically American problem: the absence of effective law and order in the frontier region. Practically every state and territory west of the Appalachians had at one time or another a well-organized vigilante movement. The first vigilante movement appeared in 1767-1769 in South Carolina, where the vigilantes were known as *regulators*—a term later used by San Francisco vigilantes in the 1850s. Vigilantes were frequently backed by prominent men; many later became senators, representatives, governors, judges, businessmen, and even clergymen. Like Indian-fighters, vigilantes became great popular heroes. Antithief and antirustling associations flourished in the West until World War I. Vigilantes often undertook not only to establish law and order but also to regulate the morals of the citizens—punishing drunks, vagrants, ne'er-do-wells, and occasional strangers.

Violence was also a constant companion of the early labor movement in the United States. Both management and strikers resorted to violence in the struggles accompanying the Industrial Revolution. In 1887 in the bitter railroad strike in Pittsburgh, Pennsylvania, an estimated sixteen soldiers and fifty strikers were killed, and locomotives, freight cars, and other property were destroyed. The famous Homestead strike of 1892 turned Homestead, Pennsylvania, into an open battlefield. The Pullman strike of 1893 in Chicago resulted in twelve deaths and the destruction of a great deal of railroad property. In 1914 Ludlow, Colorado, was the scene of the famous Ludlow Massacre, in which company guards burned a miner tent city and killed nearly a hundred persons, including women and children. The Molly Maguires were a secret organization of Irish miners who fought their employers with assassination and mayhem. The last great spasm of violence in the history of American labor came in the 1930s with the strikes and plant takeovers ("sit-down strikes") that accompanied the successful drive to unionize the automobile, steel, and other mass-production industries.

The long history of racial violence in the United States continues to plague the nation. Slavery itself was accompanied by untold violence. It is estimated that one-third to one-half of the blacks captured in African slave raids never survived the ordeal of forced marches to the sea, with thirst, brutalities, and near starvation the rule; the terrible two-month voyage in filthy holds packed with squirming and suffocating humanity; and the brutal "seasoning" whereby African blacks were turned into slaves. Nat Turner's slave insurrection in 1831 resulted in the deaths of fifty-seven white persons and the later execution of Turner and his followers. Following the end of slavery the white-supremacy movement employed violence to reestablish the position of whites in the southern social system. Racial violence directed against blacks—whippings, torture, and lynching—was fairly common from the 1870s to the 1930s. During World War II serious racial violence erupted in Detroit. Black and white mobs battled each other in June 1943, causing thirty-five deaths and hundreds of injuries, more than a thousand arrests, and finally the dispatching of federal troops to restore order.

Political assassinations have not been uncommon. Four presidents (Lincoln, Garfield, McKinley, and Kennedy) have fallen to assassins' bullets, and others were the intended objects of assassination. Only Lincoln was the target of a proven assassination conspiracy; the other presidential victims were the prey of presumably free-lance assassins in varying states of mental instability. In the 1930s Senator Huey P. Long of Louisiana was murdered, and a bullet narrowly missed President Franklin Delano Roosevelt and killed Mayor Anton Cermak of Chicago, who was standing near the president. The wave of political assassinations in more recent years, which cut down John F. Kennedy, Robert F. Kennedy, and Martin Luther King, Jr., crippled George C. Wallace, and threatened the life of Ronald Reagan, may represent a "contagion phenomenon," unstable individuals being motivated to violence by highly publicized and dra-

matic acts of violence. But an even grimmer possibility is that political assassination may become a persistent feature of American society.

Social-psychological perspectives on violence

Social psychologists have various explanations of violence. One explanation relies heavily on learning theory (stimulus–response theory); we shall refer to this as the *frustration-aggression* explanation. Another relies on Freudian notions of instinctual behavior in the "unlocking" of inhibitions; we shall call this the *aggressive-instinct* explanation. Yet another explanation focuses on the violence that is triggered when rising hopes and expectations outstrip the ability of the system to fulfill them. We shall refer to this as the *relative-deprivation* explanation.

The frustration-aggression explanation is perhaps the most popular explanation of social violence—of political turmoil, racial conflict, urban disorders, even crime and juvenile delinquency. More than thirty years ago psychologist John Dollard and several colleagues at Yale University set forth the proposition that "aggression is always the result of frustration."[11] They argued, "The occurrence of aggressive behavior always presupposes the existence of frustration and, contrariwise, the existence of frustration always leads to some form of aggression." Frustration occurs when there is a blocking of ongoing, goal-directed activity, and it evokes a characteristic reaction—aggression—whereby the individual seeks to reduce the emotional anxiety produced by this blocking. Aggression helps to lessen frustration brought on by the blocking of the

contrasting explanations of violence
frustration and aggression
aggressive instincts
relative deprivation

the frustration-aggression explanation
goal-directed activity is blocked, resulting in anxiety
aggression may reduce anxiety but fails to satisfy original need
displaced aggression is directed against something other than the cause of the frustration
suicide may be aggression turned against the self

original need, but it fails to satisfy the original need. The aggressive behavior merely copes with the emotional reaction to the blocking. The degree of frustration is affected by the intensity of the original need and by the degree of expectation that the goal-directed activity would be successful. Aggressive behavior is a function of this degree of frustration, which in turn is determined by the strength of the original need, the degree of interference with its satisfaction, and the number of times its satisfaction has been blocked. Minor frustrations added together can produce a stronger aggressive response than would normally be expected from a frustrating situation that appears immediately before aggression. Thus frustration can build up over time.

Acts of physical violence are the most obvious forms of aggression. But other forms include fantasies of "getting even," forays against the frustrating persons (stealing from them or cheating them, spreading malicious rumors about them, or making verbal assaults), and generalized destructive outbursts. Dollard contended that frustration and aggression can characterize group action as well as individual action: "Remonstrative outbursts like lynchings, strikes, and certain reformist campaigns are clearly forms of aggression as well." Aggression is generally directed at the person or object that is perceived as causing the frustration, but it may also be *displaced* to some altogether innocent source, or even toward the self, as in masochism, martyrdom, and suicide. The act of aggression is presumed to reduce the emotional reaction to frustration. Aggression turned against the self may occur when other forms of expression are strongly inhibited.

explanations of violence related to political ideology

The frustration-aggression explanation of violence is frequently espoused by political liberals because it implies that violence is best avoided by eliminating barriers to the satisfaction of human needs and wants. In other words, liberals believe that violence can be reduced if human needs and wants are satisfied and aggression-producing frustration is reduced. In contrast, if it should turn out that aggressive behavior is innate, then no amount of satisfaction of needs or wants would eliminate it. Only strong inhibiting forces would be able to cope effectively with innate aggressive instincts. This is frequently the view of political conservatives.

the aggressive-instinct explanation
instinct for aggression is genetically based
civilization has inhibited the expression of aggressive instincts
"safe" outlets for aggression may release instinctual drive

The research on the innate aggressive tendencies of organisms—human beings as well as animals, fish, and birds—suggests that aggressive behavior may be deeply rooted in human genetic history. In his interesting book *On Aggression*, eminent zoologist Konrad Lorenz argues that aggressive behavior is rooted in the long human struggle for survival.[12] The human being is by nature an aggressive animal. The external stimulus that seems to produce aggressive behavior only "unlocks" inhibitory processes, thereby "releasing" instinctual aggressive drives. Aggressive behavior is not just a reaction to some external condition but an inner force or instinct that is let loose by the stimulus. "It is the spontaneity of the (aggressive) instinct that makes it so dangerous." Aggressive behavior "can explode without demonstrable external stimulation" merely because inner drives for aggression have not been discharged through some previous behavior. Lorenz believes that "present day civilized man suffers from insufficient discharge of his aggressive drive." Civilization has inhibited people from expressing themselves aggressively; for the greatest part of human history, people released their aggressive drives in hunting, killing, and the struggle for survival. Now, however, these drives must be checked. The instincts that helped people to survive millions of years in a primitive environment today threaten their very existence. Lorenz believes that frustrations are, at best, an unimportant source of aggression. According to this formulation, an excellent way to prevent people from engaging in aggression is to provide them with "safe" ways of venting their aggressive urges. For example, competitive, body-contact sports provide "safe" outlets; even observing their activities, as in the case of televised professional football, affords some release of aggressive drives.

A number of experimental psychologists disagree with Lorenz's proposed remedy for aggression. Laboratory experiments have indicated that attacks on supposedly safe targets do not lessen, and can even increase, the likelihood of later aggression. Angry people may perhaps feel better when they can attack a safe target, but their aggressive tendencies are not necessarily reduced thereby. For example, recent laboratory studies have demonstrated that giving children an opportunity to play aggressive games does not decrease the attacks they will later make upon another child, but in fact actually increases the strength of subsequent attacks.[13] These studies do not rule out the notion of innate determinants of aggression; indeed, there is today among social psychologists much greater recognition of the role of inherent determinants of human behavior. However, it is clear that other factors—such as fear of punishment or learning to respond in nonaggressive ways to frustrations—can prevent the human potential for violence from being realized.

Another explanation of violence centers in the "relative deprivation" of individuals and groups. Relative deprivation is the discrepancy between people's expectations about the goods and conditions of life to which they feel justifiably entitled and what they perceive to be their chances of getting and keeping them. Relative deprivation is not merely a complicated way of saying that people are deprived and therefore angry because they have less than they want. Rather, it focuses on (1) what people think they deserve, not just what they want in an ideal sense, and (2) what they think they have a chance of getting, not just what they have. According to this theory, it is *relative* deprivation that creates aggression.

Relative deprivation is an expression of the distance between current status and levels of expectation. According to this explanation, neither the wholly downtrodden (who have no aspirations) nor the very

a contrary view
learning can contribute to aggression

the relative-deprivation explanation
individual and group
  expectations and
  entitlements
perceived chances of actually obtaining benefits
focus on difference
  between current status
  and expectation
poverty itself does not
  inspire violence, but
  rather, differences be-
  tween conditions and
  expectations
"revolution of rising

expectations": violence occurs when expectations rise faster than conditions

well off (who can satisfy their aspirations) represent a threat to civil order; that threat arises from those whose expectations about what they deserve outdistance the capacity of society to satisfy them. Often rapid increases in expectations are the product of symbolic or token improvements in conditions. This situation leads to the apparent paradox of the eruption of violence and disorder precisely when conditions are getting better. Hope, not despair, generates civil violence and disorder. As Bowen and Masotti observe, "The reason why black Americans riot is because there has been just enough improvement in their condition to generate hopes, expectations, or aspirations beyond the capacity of the system to meet them."[14]

The political counterpart of this explanation of violence is frequently referred to as *the revolution of rising expectations.* Poverty-stricken people who have never dreamed of owning automobiles, television sets, or new homes are not frustrated merely because they have been deprived of these things; they are frustrated only after they have begun to hope that they can obtain them. Once they have come to believe that they can get them and have anticipated having them, the inability to fulfill their anticipations is a frustrating experience. The dashing of hopes is more likely to breed violence than privation itself. Political scientist James C. Davies has employed this type of reasoning in developing a theory of revolutions.[15] Revolutions do not arise because people are subjected to long severe hardships. Revolutions occur when there is a sudden, abrupt thwarting of hopes and expectations that had begun to develop during the course of gradually improving conditions. Thus modernization in traditionally backward societies is associated with a great increase in political instability. Hope outstrips reality, and, even though conditions are improving in society as a whole, many people become frustrated.

Violence as political protest

Violence can also be interpreted as a form of political protest. For example, riots in big-city black ghettos may express the hostility many blacks feel toward established authority. To be sure, this form of political protest is a criminal one. And it may be irrational and self-defeating. The majority of casualties in ghetto riots—the dead, the injured, and the arrested—are rioters themselves. Much of the property that is destroyed belongs to ghetto residents. Many businesses and other conveniences will never again venture into the ghetto. Moreover, riots may harden the attitudes of whites toward blacks. Certainly violence itself cannot solve the complicated social problems facing the ghetto. Nonetheless, not all riots were "senseless" or without political purpose.

The view that ghetto riots were a form of political protest is supported by evidence indicating that a large percentage of the black population in the ghetto supported the riots. For example, a survey in Watts, California, after the 1965 riot determined that roughly one-fifth of blacks in that ghetto actually participated in the riot and more than one-half of the residents supported the activities of the rioters.[16] Interviewers found that 58 percent of the Watts residents felt that the long-run effect of the riot would be favorable; 84 percent said that whites were now more aware of black problems; 62 percent regarded the riot as a black protest. In the eyes of a large proportion of blacks, riots were a legitimate protest against white society, and this protest was expected to produce improvement in the condition of the blacks. Of those blacks who claimed that riots had a political purpose, each cited one or more of the following "purposes": (1) to call attention to black problems; (2) to express black hostility to whites; and (3) to serve as an instrument for improving conditions, ending discrimination, and communicating with the "power structure."[17]

Stokely Carmichael once remarked, "Violence is as American as apple pie." And the uncomfortable fact is that the most important social movements in American history *have* been accompanied by violence. Frequently, the American political system is moved by crises when it is not moved by anything else. The civil rights protest movement sought to create *nonviolent* crises that would impel the system to end discrimination. But many black militants argue that white America will not respond to black demands for full equality until whites feel their own physical well-being directly threatened.

political purposes of violence
call attention to perceived injustices
express hostility
communicate and bargain with persons in power

Violence as subculture

Another explanation of violence centers in the cultural characteristics of lower-class city life. Political scientist Edward C. Banfield argues *against* the notion that urban riots are always a form of black political protest or a result of rage and frustration over racial discrimination. He contends that the causes of rioting are complex and deeply rooted in the culture of lower-class life. In his view there are four principal motives in riot behavior, each of which implies a corresponding type of riot:

diverse motives for participation in violence
excitement and thrills
theft and profit
indignation and frustration
advancement of political purposes

The rampage. This is an outbreak of animal—usually young, male animal—spirits. Young men are naturally restless, in search of excitement, thrills, "action." . . . The rampage begins not because the incident made the rampagers angry (although they may pretend that) but because they were looking for an excuse (signal?) to rampage. . . .

The foray for pillage. Here the motive is theft, and here also boys and young adults of the lower class are the principal offenders. Stealing is ordinarily most conveniently done in private, of course, but when disasters—earthquakes, fires, floods, power failures, blizzards, enemy invasions, police strikes—interrupt law enforcement it may be done as well or better in public. . . .

The outburst of righteous indignation. Here the rioters are moved by indignation at what they regard, rightly or wrongly, as injustice or violation of the mores that is likely to go unpunished. . . .

The demonstration. Here the motive is to advance a political principle or ideology or to contribute to the maintenance of an organization. The riot is not a spontaneous, angry response to an incident. Rather, it is the result of the prearrangement by persons who are organized, have leaders, and who see it as a means to some end. The word "demonstration" is descriptive, for the event is a kind of show staged to influence opinion. Those who put it on are usually middle or upper class, these being the classes from which the people who run organizations and espouse political causes are mostly drawn.[18]

Professor Banfield contends that all these motives may be operating in any particular disorder. Some individuals participate "for the fun of it," others to steal liquor and cigarettes and television sets, still others out of some momentary rage and a felt injustice, and a few (probably a tiny minority) for political purposes.

television as an "accelerating cause"

Banfield believes that television is an "accelerating cause" in riots and disorders. He contends that sensational television coverage of riots helps to recruit rampagers and pillagers. Moreover, television informs urban dwellers that they can throw a great city into turmoil by hurling rocks, smashing windows, and setting fires. Once the possibility of such action has been established, the probability of someone's taking it is very much increased. Thanks to television, the knowledge that riots are a possibility is widely disseminated. Finally, the probability of rioting is increased when spokespeople give legitimacy on television to rioting. The knowledge that "everybody is doing it" is transformed into the idea that "it can't be wrong." By explaining riots, commentators tend to justify them and hence to encourage them. Many civil rights leaders predicted that violence would occur if reforms were not implemented at a faster pace. The riots, of course, made these predictions much more credible. But as Martin Luther King, Jr., acknowledged, "A prediction of violence can sometimes be an invitation to it." Thus explanations and predictions of disorder made rioting appear to be more natural, normal, and hence justifiable.

Professor Banfield believes that society must brace itself for a certain amount of violence:

> It is naïve to think that efforts to end racial injustice and to eliminate poverty, slums, and unemployment will have an appreciable effect upon the amount of rioting that will be done in the next decade or two. . . . Boys and young men of the lower classes will not cease to "raise hell" once they have adequate job opportunities, housing, schools, and so on. Indeed, by the standards of any former time, they have these things now. . . . As for the upwardly mobile and politically minded Negro who has a potential for outbursts of righteous indignation and for demonstrations, even serious and successful efforts at reform are likely to leave him more rather than less angry. The faster and farther the Negro rises the more impatient he is likely to be with whatever he thinks prevents his rising still faster and still farther.[19]

▪ The death penalty

One of the more heated debates in correctional policy today concerns capital punishment. Opponents of the death penalty argue that it is "cruel and unusual punishment," and is thus in violation of the Eighth Amendment of the Constitution. They contend that nations and states that have abolished the death penalty have not experienced higher homicide rates, and hence there is no concrete evidence that the death penalty discourages crime. They also argue that the death penalty is applied unequally. A large proportion of those executed have been poor, uneducated, and nonwhite.

In contrast, there is a strong sense of justice among many Americans that demands retribution for heinous crimes—a life for a life. A mere jail sentence for a multiple murderer or a rapist-murderer seems unjust compared with the damage inflicted upon society and the victims. In most cases, a life sentence means less than ten years in prison, under the current parole and probation policies of many states. Convicted murderers have been set free, and some have killed again. Moreover, prison guards and other inmates are exposed to convicted murderers who have "a license to kill" because they are already serving life sentences and have nothing to lose by killing again.

For nearly 200 years there was general agreement that death was not "cruel" or "unusual" unless it was carried out in a particularly bizarre or painful fashion. Most executions were by hanging; the electric chair was introduced in the 1920s as a "humane" alternative, and the gas chamber followed in some states. (Today, Texas employs a "lethal injection.") Before 1972, the death penalty was officially approved by thirty states; only fifteen

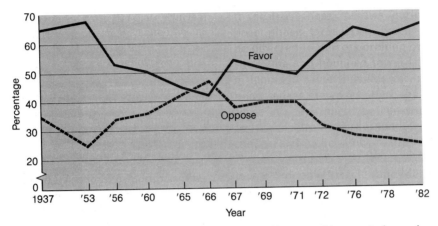

FIGURE 12-4 Public opinion on the death penalty. (Question: "Are you in favor of the death penalty for persons convicted of murder?") SOURCE: *The Gallup Report* (April 1981), p. 19.

states had abolished capital punishment. Federal laws also retained the death penalty. However, no one had actually suffered the death penalty since 1967, because of numerous legal tangles and direct challenges to the constitutionality of capital punishment.

In *Furman* v. *Georgia* (1972) the Supreme Court ruled that capital punishment *as then imposed* violated the Eighth and Fourteenth Amendments in that it constituted cruel and unusual punishment and denied due process of law. The decision was made by a five-to-four vote of the justices, and the reasoning in the case is very complex. Only two justices—Brennan and Marshall—declared that capital punishment itself is cruel and unusual. The other three justices in the majority—Douglas, White, and Stewart—felt that death sentences had been applied unfairly; a few individuals were receiving the death penalty for crimes for which many others were receiving lighter sentences. These justices left open the possibility that capital punishment would be constitutional if it were specified for certain kinds of crime and applied uniformly.

After this decision, a majority of states rewrote their death penalty laws to try to ensure fairness and uniformity of application.

Generally, these laws mandate the death penalty for murders committed during rape, robbery, hijacking, or kidnapping; murders of prison guards; murder with torture; and multiple murders. Two trials must be held—one to determine guilt or innocence and another to determine the penalty. At the second trial evidence of "aggravating" and "mitigating" factors is presented; if there are aggravating factors but no mitigating factors, the death penalty is mandatory.

In a series of cases in 1976 (*Gregg* v. *Georgia, Profitt* v. *Florida, Jurek* v. *Texas*), the Supreme Court finally held that "the punishment of death does not invariably violate the Constitution." The Court upheld the death penalty with the following rationale: the men who drafted the Bill of Rights accepted death as a common sanction of crime. It is true that the Eighth-Amendment prohibition against cruel and unusual punishments must be interpreted in a dynamic fashion, reflecting changing moral values. But the decisions of more than half of the nation's state legislatures to reenact the death penalty since 1972, as well as the decisions of juries to impose the death penalty on more than 450 persons under these new laws, were evidence that "a large proportion of American society continues to regard it as an appropriate and necessary criminal sanction." Moreover, said the Court, the social purposes of retribution and deterrence justify the use of the death penalty. This ultimate sanction is "an expression of society's moral outrage at particularly offensive conduct."

The Court reaffirmed that *Furman v. Georgia* (1972) only struck down the death penalty where it was inflicted in "an arbitrary and capricious manner." The Court upheld the death penalty in states where the trial was a two-part proceeding, the second part of which provided the judge or jury with relevant information and standards for deciding whether to impose the death penalty. The

Court approved the consideration of "aggravating and mitigating circumstances." The Court also approved of automatic review of all death sentences by state supreme courts to ensure that the sentence was not imposed under the influence of passion or prejudice, that aggravating factors were supported by the evidence, and that the sentence was not disproportionate to the crime.

In the early 1960s public support for the death penalty was declining and opposition growing. However, with increases in crime rates after 1965, opinion trends reversed and support for the death penalty rose. Today supporters outnumber opponents by a wide margin (see Figure 12-4).

Notes

1. Thomas Hobbes, *Leviathan,* edited by Michael Oakeshott (New York: Crowell-Collier, 1962).
2. Chief Justice Warren E. Burger, address on the State of the Federal Judiciary to the American Bar Association, 10 August 1970.
3. Ibid.
4. Ibid.
5. Richard C. Schroeder, *The Politics of Drugs,* 2nd ed. (Washington, D.C.: Congressional Quarterly, Inc., 1980), p. 80.
6. National Institute on Drug Abuse, *National Survey on Drug Abuse* (Washington, D.C.: U.S. Government Printing Office, 1978).
7. For a summary of this evidence and references to the relevant health literature, see Schroeder, *The Politics of Drugs,* Chapter 4.
8. Ibid., p. 19.
9. *The Gallup Report* (July 1980), p. 15.
10. National Institute on Drug Abuse, op. cit., Chapter 9.
11. John Dollard et al., *Frustration and Aggression* (New Haven, Conn.: Yale University Press, 1939), p. 1.
12. Konrad Lorenz, *On Aggression* (New York: Harcourt Brace Jovanovich, 1966).
13. For an excellent review of the implications of laboratory studies on frustration and aggression, see Leonard Buckewitz, "The Study of Urban Violence," in Louis H. Masotti and Don R. Bowen, eds., *Riots and Rebellion* (Beverly Hills, Calif.: Sage, 1968).
14. Don R. Bowen and Louis H. Masotti, "Civil Violence: A Theoretical Overview," in Masotti and Bowen, eds., *Riots and Rebellion,* pp. 24–25.

15. James C. Davies, "Toward a Theory of Revolution," *American Sociological Review* 27, 1962.
16. Governor's Commission on the Los Angeles Riots, *Violence in the City—An End or a Beginning?* (Sacramento: Office of the Governor, State of California, 1965), pp. 3–5. The commission was headed by John A. McCone, former director of the Central Intelligence Agency.
17. National Advisory Commission on Civil Disorders, *Report* (Washington, D.C.: U.S. Government Printing Office, 1968), p. 4.
18. Edward C. Banfield, *The Unheavenly City* (Boston: Little, Brown, 1970), pp. 187–91.
19. Ibid., pp. 205–06.

Discussion questions

1. Discuss the "classic dilemma" of a free government and Thomas Hobbes's ideas regarding the need for a powerful state.
2. Discuss crime rates. How are they used, how are they determined, and what factors contribute to their inaccuracy? What is their current trend?
3. Suppose you have just been arrested by the police. Describe how the following constitutional rights of defendants would be of use to you: guarantee of the writ of habeas corpus; prohibition of bills of attainder and of ex post facto laws; prohibition of "unreasonable" searches and seizures; freedom from self-incrimination; the right to counsel; guarantee of a fair jury trial; protection against double jeopardy; protection against excessive bail.
4. Choose two of the following cases that were decided by the Warren Court and discuss how each of them strengthened the rights of accused persons in criminal cases: *Mapp v. Ohio* (1961); *Gideon v. Wainwright* (1963); *Escobedo v. Illinois* (1964); *Miranda v. Arizona* (1966).
5. Discuss the judicial stumbling blocks to law enforcement that Chief Justice Warren E. Burger outlined in his State of the Federal Judiciary message. What are some of the difficulties that the *police* may encounter in their law enforcement function?
6. Describe the major drug threats confronting the United States today. What is the legal status of various potentially harmful substances—alcohol, tobacco, marijuana, cocaine, and heroin?
7. Discuss the history of violence in the United States. Using at least three specific eras or social movements as examples, describe the type of violence that was used and the kind of social change that was its goal.
8. Discuss two of the following social-psychological explanations of violence: the frustration-aggression explanation; the aggressive-instinct explanation; the relative-deprivation explanation.

9. Contrast the interpretation of violence as a form of political protest with Edward Banfield's "fun" or "profit" explanation of violence.
10. Discuss the arguments for and against capital punishment. Describe the 1972 Court decision regarding the constitutionality of capital punishment and the changes in state laws that followed it. Discuss the reasoning of the justices in the 1976 Court decision on capital punishment.

CHAPTER 13

■ POWER & COMMUNITY

It has always been fashionable in the United States to deplore life in big cities. Thomas Jefferson believed that cities were the source of human vice and that only a rural and small-town America could maintain democracy. When the first census of the United States was taken in 1790, only 5 percent of the American people lived in cities, whereas today three-quarters of our population live in large urban clusters known as metropolitan areas. We have changed from a rural society to an urban society. We are trying to cope with the social, psychological, economic, and political problems of urban life. We are particularly concerned with the deterioration of older central cities, the creation of black ghettos in large cities, "white flight" to the suburbs, and financial and governmental problems posed by growth and decline in metropolitan areas.

In this chapter we will describe where Americans live and the impact of urban life on social relations, psychological states of mind, government, and power relations. After you have read it, you should be able to

- describe changes over the past decade in central cities and suburbs of metropolitan areas and in nonmetropolitan areas,
- identify the social characteristics associated with urban life,
- discuss suburbanization and increasing separation of black central cities from white suburbs in large metropolitan areas,
- discuss the social psychology of urban life,
- describe various structures of government found in American cities,
- describe "community power structures" and how they may vary from one city to another.

■ 326

Where Americans live

Three out of four Americans live in population clusters called metropolitan areas. Most of the nation's population increase is occurring in the suburbs of these metropolitan areas. Approximately 44 percent of all Americans live in the suburbs of metropolitan areas, 32 percent live in central cities, and 24 percent live outside metropolitan areas (see Table 13-1).

What is a metropolitan area? Briefly, it consists of a central city of 50,000 or more persons together with the surrounding suburbs, which are socially and economically tied to the central city. The Census Bureau calls a metropolitan area a "Standard Metropolitan Statistical Area" (SMSA) and defines it as a city of 50,000 or more persons together with adjacent counties that have predominantly urban industrial populations with close ties to the central city (see Figure 13-1). The nation's twenty-five largest SMSAs are listed in Table 13-2 together with their growth rates.

Very few large *central cities* are growing in size. Those metropolitan areas that are still growing are growing because their *suburbs* are growing. Suburbanization is due to technological advances in transportation—the automobile and the expressway. In the nineteenth century, industrial workers had to live within walking distance of their places of employment. Hence, the nineteenth-century American city crowded large masses of people into relatively small central areas, often in tenement houses and other high-density neighborhoods. But new modes of transportation—first the streetcar, then the private automobile, and finally the expressway—eliminated the necessity for workers to live close to their jobs. Now one can spend one's working hours in a central business district office or industrial plant and pass one's evenings in a residential suburb miles away. The same technology that led to the suburbanization of residences has also influenced commercial and industrial

SMSA
metropolitan statistical area, a city of 50,000 or more, plus surrounding urban population

central city versus suburban growth

TABLE 13-1 Population growth in cities and suburbs of metropolitan areas in the United States

| | Total U.S. population | Metropolitan area | | | Outside metropolitan areas |
		Total	Central cities	Suburbs	
1980					
Population (thousands)	226,500	172,000	72,500	99,400	54,600
Percentage of U.S. total	100.0	75.9	32.0	43.9	24.1
1970					
Population (thousands)	203,185	155,500	72,000	83,500	47,800
Percentage of U.S. total	100.0	76.5	35.4	41.1	23.5

SOURCE: *Statistical Abstract of the United States, 1985*, p. 17.

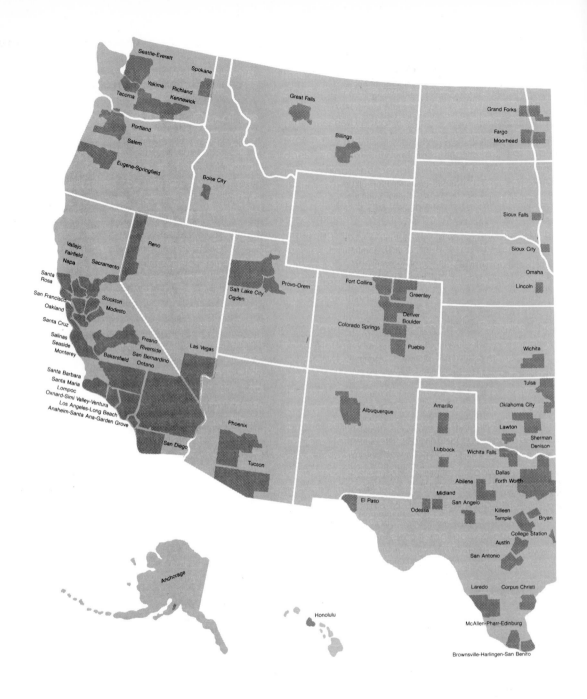

location. Originally industry was tied to waterways or railroads for access to supplies and markets. Its dependence has been reduced by the development of motor truck transportation, the highway system, and the greater mobility of the labor force. Now many industries can locate in the suburbs, particularly light industries, which do not require extremely

FIGURE 13-1 Standard metropolitan statistical areas. (SOURCE: U.S. Bureau of the Census.)

heavy bulk shipment that can be handled only by rail or water. When industry and people move to the suburbs, commerce follows. Giant suburban shopping centers have sprung up to compete with downtown stores. Thus metropolitan areas are becoming decentralized as people, business, and industry spread over the suburban landscape.

TABLE 13-2   The nation's largest standard metropolitan statistical areas (figures in thousands)

Rank	SMSA	1980	1970	% Change
1	New York, NY–NJ	9,080	9,973	− 8.9
2	Los Angeles–Long Beach, CA	7,445	7,041	+ 5.7
3	Chicago, IL	7,057	6,974	−11.9
4	Philadelphia, PA–NJ	4,700	4,824	− 2.6
5	Detroit, MI	4,344	4,435	− 2.0
6	San Francisco–Oakland, CA	3,226	3,109	+ 3.7
7	Washington, D.C.–MD–VA	3,045	2,910	+ 4.6
8	Dallas–Ft. Worth, TX	2,964	2,377	+24.7
9	Houston, TX	2,891	1,999	+44.6
10	Boston, MA	2,759	2,899	− 5.1
11	Nassau–Suffolk, NY	2,603	2,555	+ 1.9
12	St. Louis, MO–IL	2,344	2,410	− 2.8
13	Pittsburgh, PA	2,260	2,401	− 5.9
14	Baltimore, MD	2,166	2,071	− 4.6
15	Minneapolis–St. Paul, MN	2,109	1,965	+ 7.3
16	Atlanta, GA	2,010	1,595	+26.0
17	Newark, NJ	1,963	2,057	− 4.8
18	Anaheim–Santa Ana–Garden Grove, CA	1,925	1,421	+14.4
19	Cleveland, OH	1,895	2,063	− 8.1
20	San Diego, CA	1,859	1,357	+36.9
21	Denver–Boulder, CO	1,615	1,239	+30.3
22	Seattle, WA	1,600	1,424	+12.3
23	Miami, FL	1,573	1,267	+24.1
24	Tampa–St. Petersburg, FL	1,550	1,088	+42.4
25	Riverside–San Bernardino, CA	1,538	1,139	+35.0

SOURCE: U.S. Bureau of the Census, *Statistical Abstract of the United States, 1980* (Washington, D.C.: U.S. Government Printing Office, 1981).

The sociology of urban life

What is the impact of urbanism on the way people interact? To deal with this question, sociologists first had to formulate a sociological definition of urbanism—one that would identify those characteristics most affecting social life. Sociologist Louis Wirth provided a classic definition of urbanism more than three decades ago: "For sociological purposes a city may be defined as a relatively large, dense, and permanent settlement of socially heterogeneous individuals."[1] Thus, according to Wirth, the distinguishing characteristics of urban life were *number, density,* and *heterogeneity*—large numbers of people living closely together who are different from one another.

Large numbers of people involve a great range of individual variation. The modern economic system of the metropolis is based on a highly specialized and complex division of labor. We are told that in the simple farm community a dozen occupations exhausted the job opportunities available to people. In an agricultural economy nearly everyone was a farmer or was closely connected to or dependent on farming. But in the modern metropolis there are tens of thousands of different kinds of jobs. An industrial economy means highly specialized jobs; hence the

sociological theory of urbanism

urbanism distinguished by numbers, density, and heterogeneity

heterogeneity of urban populations. Different jobs result in different levels of income, dress, and styles of living. People's jobs shape the way they look at the world and their evaluations of social and political events. To acquire a job, one attains a certain level and type of education that also distinguishes one from those in other jobs with other educational requirements. Differences in educational level in turn produce a wide variety of differences in opinions, attitudes, and styles of living. Urban life concentrates people with all these different economic and occupational characteristics in a very few square miles.

Ethnic and racial diversities are also present. A few decades ago opportunities for human betterment in the cities attracted immigrants from Ireland, Germany, Italy, Poland, and Russia; today the city attracts blacks, Puerto Ricans, and rural families. These newcomers bring with them different needs, attitudes, and ways of life. The "melting pot" tends to reduce some of the diversity over time, but the pot does not melt people immediately, and there always seem to be new arrivals.

Increasing the numbers of people in a community limits the possibility that each member of the community will know everyone else personally. Multiplying the number of persons with whom an individual comes into contact makes it impossible for that individual to know everyone very well. The result is a "segmentalization of human relationships," in which an individual comes to know *many* people but only in highly *seg-*

heterogeneity
diversity in occupation, income, education ethnic and racial diversity

segmental relationships

knowing many people, but only in their partial roles

---

utilitarian relationships
interaction with others as a means to an end

---

anomie
a sense of social isolation and loss of personal recognition and self-worth

---

primary groups
family and neighborhood groups known personally

---

secondary groups
interest or voluntary groups

---

social control in urban society based more on formal institutions than on social groups

---

social mobility
movement from one social status to another

---

physical mobility
movement from one location to another

---

both kinds of mobility greater in urban than in rural societies

mental, partial roles. According to Wirth, "The contacts of the city may indeed be face to face, but they are nevertheless impersonal, superficial, transitory, and segmental. The reserve, the indifference, and the blasé outlook that urbanites manifest in their relationships may thus be regarded as devices for immunizing themselves against the personal claims and expectations of others."[2] Moreover, urban dwellers frequently interact with others by utilizing them as means to an end, thus giving a *utilitarian* quality to interpersonal relations.

Large numbers mean a certain degree of freedom for the individual from the control of family groups, neighbors, churches, and other community groups. But urbanism also contributes to a sense of *anomie*—a sense of social isolation and a loss of the personal recognition, self-worth, and feeling of participation that comes with living in a small integrated society. The social contacts of urban dwellers are more anonymous than those of rural dwellers; they interact with persons who have little if any knowledge of their life histories.

Rural life emphasized *primary group ties*—interactions within the extended family. Many sociologists believe that urban life emphasizes *secondary group ties*—interactions among members of age and interest groups rather than among families and neighbors. Urban life is said to center around voluntary associations and secondary group memberships—crowds, recreational groups, civic clubs, business groups, and professional and work groups. Sociologists believe that urban dwellers have a greater number of interpersonal contacts than rural dwellers and that urban dwellers are more likely to interact with people as occupants of specific social roles. In contrast, rural dwellers are more likely to interact with individuals as full personalities.

Urban society also presents problems of social control. The anomie of urban life is believed to weaken social mores and social group controls. External controls through a series of formal institutions, such as laws, and organizations, such as the courts and the police, become more essential. Thus *social control* in the cities depends in large degree on *formal mechanisms.* But laws generally express the minimum behavioral standard, and urban life involves a much wider range of behavior than rural life. Moreover, laws do not always succeed in establishing minimum standards of behavior; crime rates increase with increases in urbanism.

Another characteristic of urban life is *mobility,* or ease of movement. Urban mobility is both *physical* (from one geographic area to another) and *social* (from one position of social status to another). Rural communities are more stable than urban communities in both respects. Traditionally rural dwellers were more likely to stay near the place of their birth. In contrast, urbanites frequently move from city to city, or from one section of a city to another. Social mobility is also greater in the city, because of the wider range of economic opportunities there. Moreover, urban dwellers are judged far less by their family backgrounds (which are unknown) than by their own appearances, occupational accomplishments, incomes, and lifestyles. Although mobility creates opportunities for individuals, it weakens the sense of community. City dwellers do not think of their city as a community to which they belong but rather as a place they happen to live—a geographical entity commanding little personal allegiance.

Urban life presents a serious problem in *conflict* management. Since a metropolitan area consists of a large number of different kinds of people living closely together, the problem of regulating conflict and maintaining order assumes tremendous proportions. Persons with different occupations, incomes, and educational levels are known to have different views on public issues. The way that persons well equipped to compete for jobs and income in a free market view government housing and welfare programs may differ from the way that others not so well equipped view them. People at the bottom of the social ladder look at police—indeed, governmental authority in general—differently from the way those on higher rungs do. Persons who own their homes and those who do not own their homes regard taxation in a different light. Families with children and those without children have different ideas about school systems. And so it goes. Differences in the way people make their living, in their income and educational levels, in the color of their skin, in the way they worship, in their style of living—all are at the roots of political life in the metropolis.

political conflict
heterogeneity of urban life presents greater potential for conflict among diverse peoples

Thus sociological theory provides us with a series of characteristics to look for in urban life:

summary

large numbers of people
population density
social and economic heterogeneity
ethnic and racial diversity
numerous but superficial, segmental, utilitarian relationships
impersonality and anonymity
greater interaction in secondary groups
reliance on formal mechanisms of social control
physical and social mobility
greater potential for conflict

Not all these characteristics of urban life have been documented. Indeed, in a highly industrialized and urbanized society such as the United States, it is difficult to discern any differences between rural and urban dwellers. Furthermore, urban dwellers display a great range and variation in styles of life; some reflect the "typical" style described by sociological theory, and others do not. Many retain their commitment to the extended family, and many city neighborhoods are stable and socially cohesive communities. Despite the plausibility of the hypothesis that urban life leads to anonymity, impersonality, and segmentalization in social relationships, it is hard to prove systematically that urban dwellers are getting more impersonal or anonymous than are rural dwellers.

weaknesses of early theory

Finally, sociologists can no longer focus upon central-city lifestyles in describing urban living. We must now take account of suburban life-styles, since more people live in suburbs than in central cities. And the suburban way of life is in many ways quite different from the way of life described in early sociological theory.

The suburban trend

why people move to the suburbs
seeking amenities
neighbors like themselves
small-scale communities
"escape" social problems
of cities

One explanation of the suburbanization of America is that people strive to avoid many of the unpleasant characteristics of urban life. The move to the suburbs is in part generated by a desire to get away from the numbers, density, and heterogeneity of big-city life, the problems created by large numbers of people—the crowds, dirt, noise, smog, congestion, gas fumes, crime, and delinquency. People move to the sub-urbs seeking amenities—more land on which to build their own homes, enjoy backyard recreation, and give their children more room in which to play; they want sunshine, fresh air, quiet, privacy, and space.

Moreover, people often move to the suburbs to place physical dis-tance between themselves and those whose cultures and lifestyles are different from theirs—the poor, the black, the lower class. They seek to replace the *heterogeneity* of big-city life with the *homogeneity* of the small suburban community—congenial neighbors, people like them-selves, who share their interest in good schools, respectable neighbor-hoods, and middle-class lifestyles. The suburban community, with a local government small in scale and close to home, represents a partial es-cape from the anonymity of mass urban life. Suburbanites identify their communities by reference to their suburban homes—Scarsdale or Mineola; they do not feel much identification with the "New York-Northeastern New Jersey Standard Metropolitan Statistical Area." A separate suburban government and a separate school district provide suburbanites with a sense of personal effectiveness in the management of public affairs.

Suburbs offer escape from the worst problems of urban life—racial conflict, crime, violence, poverty, slums, drugs, congestion, pollution, and so forth. A move to the suburbs permits a family, for the time being at least, to avoid the problems of poor schools, deteriorating housing, expanding welfare rolls, muggings and robberies, and violence and riot-ing in the central cities. Yet at the same time suburbanites retain the positive benefits of urban life. The city offers economic opportunity—high-paying jobs, openings for highly skilled professionals and techni-cians, and upward social and economic mobility. This is the reason most people come to the city in the first place. The big city also offers theater and entertainment, professional sports, civic and cultural events, special-ized shops and stores, and a host of other attractions. Suburban living allows people to enjoy the advantages of urban life while avoiding some of its hardships.

Of course, it is not really possible to argue that the major social problems of urban society—racial conflict, poverty, drugs, crime, under-education, slum housing, and so on—are problems of central cities and not of suburbs. John C. Bollens and Henry J. Schmandt in *The Metropolis* addressed themselves to this point very effectively:

Is "escape" possible?

> Some myopic defenders of suburbia go so far as to say that the major socioeconomic problems of urban society are problems of the central city, not those of the total metropolitan community. Where but within the boundaries of the core city, they ask, does one find an abundance of racial strife, crime, blight of housing, and welfare recipients? Superficially, their logic may seem sound, since they are in general correct about the prevalent spatial location of these maladies. Although crime and other social problems exist in suburbia, their magnitude and extent are substantially less than in the central city. But why in an interdependent metropolitan community should the responsibility for suburbanites be any less than that of the central city dwellers? Certainly no one would think of contending that residents of higher income neighborhoods within the corporate limits of the city should be exempt from responsibility for its less fortunate districts. What logic then is there in believing that neighborhoods on the other side of a legal line can wash their hands of social disorders in these sections?
>
> . . . No large community can hope to reap the benefits of industrialization and urbanization and yet escape their less desirable byproducts. The suburbanite and the central city resident share the responsibility for the total community and its problems. Neither can run fast enough to escape involvement sooner or later.[3]

Perhaps the most frequently mentioned reason for a move to the suburbs is the "kids." Family after family lists consideration of its young as the primary cause for the move to suburbia. The city is hardly the place for most child-centered amenities. A familistic or child-centered lifestyle can be identified in certain social statistics. There are proportionately more children in the suburbs than in the central cities; a larger proportion of suburban mothers stay at home to take care of the children; and a larger proportion of suburban families are housed in single-family homes. A nonfamilistic lifestyle is characteristic of the central city, where there are proportionately fewer children, greater numbers of employed mothers, and more apartment dwellers.

family lifestyles

But the most important difference between cities and suburbs is their contrasting *racial composition*. Although blacks constitute only 12 percent of the total population of the United States, they are rapidly approaching a numerical majority in many of the nation's largest cities. Blacks are already in the majority in Washington, Atlanta, and Newark, and they make up more than 40 percent of the population of Detroit, Baltimore, St. Louis, New Orleans, Oakland, Birmingham, and Gary. They are nearing a third of the population of Chicago, Philadelphia, Cleveland, Memphis, Columbus, and Cincinnati.

racial composition

The concentration of blacks in large central cities is a product of the availability of low-priced rental units in older, run-down sections of central cities and of discriminatory housing practices of private owners and developers. Of course, underlying the concentration of blacks in run-down sectors of central cities is a lack of sufficient income to purchase housing in suburbs or in better city neighborhoods. The poverty and

black "ghettos"

unemployment that contribute to the concentration of blacks in "ghettos" are in turn a product of inadequate training and education, low aspiration levels, and often a lack of motivation. And problems in education and motivation are themselves related to a breakdown in family life, delinquency, and crime. Thus urban blacks face a whole series of interrelated problems in addition to discrimination: poverty, slum housing, undereducation, lack of job skills, family troubles, lack of motivation, delinquency, and crime. It is difficult to talk about any one of these problems without reference to them all.

The migration of blacks into cities, particularly in the North, has been accompanied by a heavy out-migration of whites fleeing to the suburbs for a variety of reasons. The total populations of many large central cities have remained stagnant in recent years or even declined slightly; black population percentages have increased because black in-migration has compensated for white out-migration.

Many whites have fled to the suburbs to get away from concentrations of black people in central cities. One reason suburbanites may want to remain politically separate from the central cities is so they can more easily resist "invasion" by blacks. However, as blacks gain majorities in central cities, they too may resist metropolitan governmental consolidation in order to avoid dilution of their political power through merger with white suburbs. The restriction of suburban home sales to whites only and the generally higher costs of suburban homes and property have made it difficult or impossible for blacks to follow whites to the suburbs in any significant number.

emerging patterns
black cities, white suburbs

Thus American life is becoming more, not less, segregated. These population statistics clearly show that the United States is building racial ghettos in its large central cities and surrounding them with white middle-class suburbs. As the exodus to the suburbs continues, cities are becoming bereft of their middle-class, white, high-income, high-taxpaying populations. Increasingly, nonwhite, low-income, low-education, unskilled, nonfamilistic populations are being concentrated in the central cities. Hence, the problems of these people (racial imbalance, crime, violence, inadequate education, poverty, slum housing) have also been concentrated in the central cities. By moving to the suburbs, white middle-class families not only separate themselves from blacks and poor people but also place physical distance between themselves and the major social problems that confront metropolitan areas.

The nation's fifty largest cities are shown in Table 13-3, together with their rate of growth (or decline). It is interesting to note that most of the growing cities are located in the "Sunbelt"—the lower tier of states from California through Arizona, New Mexico, and Texas, to the south-

growth of "Sunbelt" cities; decline of "Frostbelt" cities

TABLE 13-3   U.S. cities: Growth and decline (figures in thousands)

Rank	City	1980	1970	% Change
1	New York, NY	7,071	7,895	−10.4
2	Chicago, IL	3,005	3,369	−10.8
3	Los Angeles, CA	2,966	2,811	+ 5.5
4	Philadelphia, PA	1,688	1,949	−13.4
5	Houston, TX	1,594	1,233	+29.4
6	Detroit, MI	1,203	1,514	−20.5
7	Dallas, TX	904	844	+ 7.1
8	San Diego, CA	875	697	+25.5
9	Baltimore, MD	786	905	−13.1
10	San Antonio, TX	785	654	+20.0
11	Phoenix, AZ	764	584	+30.8
12	Honolulu, HI	762	630	+20.9
13	Indianapolis, IN	700	736	− 4.8
14	San Francisco, CA	678	715	− 5.2
15	Memphis, TN	646	623	+ 3.7
16	Washington, DC	637	756	−15.7
17	San Jose, CA	636	459	+38.5
18	Milwaukee, WI	636	717	−11.2
19	Cleveland, OH	573	750	−23.6
20	Columbus, OH	564	540	+ 4.4
21	Boston, MA	562	641	−12.3
22	New Orleans, LA	557	593	− 6.0
23	Jacksonville, FL	540	504	+ 7.1
24	Seattle, WA	493	530	− 6.9
25	Denver, CO	491	514	− 4.4
26	Nashville, TN	455	426	+ 6.8
27	St. Louis, MO	453	622	−27.2
28	Kansas City, KS	448	507	−11.6
29	El Paso, TX	425	322	+31.9
30	Atlanta, GA	425	495	−14.1
31	Pittsburgh, PA	423	520	−18.6
32	Oklahoma City, OK	403	368	+ 9.5
33	Cincinnati, OH	385	453	+15.0
34	Fort Worth, TX	385	393	− 2.0
35	Minneapolis, MN	370	434	−14.7
36	Portland, OR	366	379	− 3.4
37	Long Beach, CA	361	358	− 0.8
38	Tulsa, OK	360	330	+ 9.1
39	Buffalo, NY	357	462	−23.7
40	Toledo, OH	354	383	− 7.6
41	Miami, FL	346	334	+ 3.6
42	Austin, TX	345	253	+36.3
43	Oakland, CA	339	361	− 6.1
44	Albuquerque, NM	331	244	+35.6
45	Tucson, AZ	330	262	+25.9
46	Newark, NJ	329	381	−13.6
47	Charlotte, NC	314	241	+30.2
48	Omaha, NB	311	346	−10.1
49	Louisville, KY	298	361	−18.2
50	Birmingham, AL	284	300	− 5.3

SOURCE: U.S. Bureau of the Census, *Statistical Abstract of the United States, 1980* (Washington, D.C.: U.S. Government Printing Office, 1981).

eastern United States, including Florida. The greatest population losses are found in the cities of the Northeast and the Midwest.

The psychology of urban life—Calling Aunt Sally

Is city life really more impersonal than life in a small town?

One of the more persistent views of life in big cities is that social relations are impersonal, indifferent, and unfriendly. It has been argued that because city dwellers daily come into close contact with thousands of strangers on the streets, in stores, at work, and at play, city dwellers unconsciously develop superficial, transitory, and impersonal modes of social interaction.[4] Since it is impossible to know personally all or even most of the people we come into contact with each day in the city, we learn to deal with fellow city dwellers with reserve, if not indifference. In contrast, in small towns and rural areas, we see other people less frequently, but we know most of those whom we see on a personal basis. We can all think of personal stories of ill treatment in big cities, but is there really any systematic evidence to support the view that big-city dwellers are habitually indifferent to others? Unfortunately, there is.[5]

an experiment in social psychology

One interesting test of the urban indifference theme, conducted by social psychologists, is the "Aunt Sally call." Experimenters randomly call big-city and small-town dwellers and ask to speak to "Aunt Sally." When the respondent tells the experimenter that a wrong number has been reached, the experimenter says: "Oh, I'm sorry. But this is my last dime and I'm at the airport [in a city, or "bus stop" in a town]. Could you do me a favor and call my aunt for me and let her know my plane [or bus] has come in early? She is supposed to pick me up here." If the respondent agrees, the experimenter gives a local phone number where another experimenter waits to see if the respondent actually calls. One test of this technique produced the results shown in Table 13-4.[6]

Scholars do not always agree on whether it is big-city life itself that creates impersonality or whether it is mobility, rapid change, and social disorganization. Some social psychologists link urban life to a wide variety of personal problems and social pathologies: mental illness, sexual deviance, crime and delinquency, suicide, high death rates, alcoholism and drug abuse, and violence in politics. Marshall Clinard traces social disorganization to urbanization: "Urbanism with mobility, impersonality,

TABLE 13-4 Calling Aunt Sally: "Could you do me a favor and call my aunt for me . . . ?"

Response	*Big-city percentage*	*Small-town percentage*
1. Subject hangs up	35	10
2. Subject hears request, refuses to help	15	20
3. Subject fulfills request	30	45
4. Subject offers assistance beyond what is requested	20	25
	100	100

individualism, materialism, norm and role conflicts, and rapid social change appears to be associated with higher incidence of deviant behavior."[7] However, other scholars believe that there is no necessary relationship between urbanization and personal or social problems. It is true that rapid change and social disorganization are associated with social deviance, but these conditions may occur in rural as well as urban areas and in big cities as well as small towns. In other words, it is not city life itself that produces deviance, but rather mobility, social change, poverty, racism, unemployment, ignorance, and ill health.

many possible causes of impersonality

Governing urban communities

Local government is not mentioned in the U.S. Constitution. Although we regard the American federal system as a mixture of federal, state, and *local* governments, from a constitutional point of view local governments are really a part of state governments. Communities have no constitutional right to self-government; all their governmental powers legally flow from state governments. Local government—cities, townships, counties, special districts, and school districts—are creatures of the states, subject to the obligations, privileges, powers, and restrictions that state governments impose upon them. The state, either through its constitution or its laws, may create or destroy any or all units of local government. To the extent that local governments can collect taxes, regulate their citizens, and provide services, they are actually exercising *state* powers delegated to them by the state in either its constitution or its laws.

Local governments are creatures of state governments; all their powers legally flow from state governments.

The fifty states have created 82,000 local governments (see Table 13-5). What do they all do? Different units of government are assigned different responsibilities by each of the states, so it is difficult to generalize about what each of these types of local government is supposed to do. Indeed, even in the same state there may be overlapping functions and responsibilities assigned to cities, counties, school districts, and special districts.

Nevertheless, let us try to make some generalizations about what each of these types of government does, realizing, of course, that in any

functions of rural counties

TABLE 13-5 Number of local governments in the United States

	1952	1962	1972	1977	1982
Counties	3,052	3,043	3,044	3,042	3,041
Municipalities	16,807	17,997	18,517	18,862	19,076
Townships	17,202	17,144	16,991	16,822	16,734
School districts	67,355	34,678	15,781	15,174	14,851
Special districts	12,340	18,323	23,885	25,962	28,588
Total (including states and national government)	116,756	91,185	78,269	79,913	82,290

SOURCE: U.S. Bureau of the Census, *Census of Government*, 1982.

urban counties
cities
school districts
townships
special districts

specific location the pattern of governmental activity may be slightly different:

Counties: rural—keep records of deeds, mortgages, births, marriages; assess and levy property taxes; maintain local roads; administer elections and certify election results to state; provide law enforcement through sheriff; maintain criminal court; maintain a local jail; administer state welfare programs.

Counties: urban—most of same functions as rural counties (except police and court systems, which often become city functions), together with planning and control of new subdivisions; mental health; public health maintenance and public hospitals; care of the aged; recreation, including parks, stadiums, and convention centers; and perhaps some city functions.

Cities—provide the "common functions" of police, fire, streets, sewage, sanitation, and parks; over half of the nation's large cities also provide welfare services and public education. (In other cities welfare is handled by county governments or directly by state agencies, and education is handled by separate school districts.)

School districts—organized specifically to provide public elementary and secondary education; community colleges may be operated by county governments or by special districts with or without state support.

Townships—generally subdivisions of counties with the same responsibilities as their county.

Special districts—may be as large as the Port Authority of New York with more than $1 billion in diversified assets. However, special districts are usually established for mass transit, soil conservation, libraries, water and irrigation, mosquito control, sewage disposal, airports, and so on.

forms of city government
mayor-council
commission
council-manager

American city government comes in three structural packages. There are some adaptations and variations from city to city, but generally one can classify the form of city government as mayor-council, commission, or council-manager. Approximately 51 percent of American cities have the mayor-council form of government; 6 percent have the commission form; and 43 percent have the council-manager form. Figure 13-2 shows the general organization of two of these three forms of government.

Mayor-council. The nation's largest cities tend to function under the *mayor-council* plan. This is the oldest form of American city government and is designed in the American tradition of separation of powers between legislature and executive. One may also establish subcategories of strong- or weak-mayor forms of mayor-council government. A strong mayor is one who is the undisputed master of the executive agencies of city government and who has substantial legislative powers in the form of budget making, vetoes, and opportunity to propose legislation. Only a few cities make the mayor the sole elected official among city executive officers; it is common for the mayor to share powers with other elected officials—city attorney, treasurer, tax assessor, auditor, clerk, and so on. Yet many mayors, by virtue of their prestige, persuasive abilities, or role as party leader, have been able to overcome most of the weaknesses of their formal office.

In recent years large cities have been adding to the formal powers of their chief executives. Cities have augmented the mayors' roles by providing them with direction over budgeting, purchasing, and personnel controls; and independent boards, commissions, and individual council members have relinquished administrative control over city departments in many cities. Moreover, many cities have strengthened their mayors' position by providing them with a chief administrative officer (CAO) to handle important staff and administrative duties of supervising city departments and providing central management services.

Commission.   The *commission* form of city government gives both legislative and executive powers to a small body, usually consisting of five members. The commission form originated at the beginning of the century as a reform movement designed to end a system of divided responsibility between mayor and council. One of the commission members is nominally the mayor, but he or she has no more formal powers than the other commissioners. The board of commissioners is directly responsible for the operation of city departments and agencies. In practice one commission member will become responsible for the management of a specific department, such as finance, public works, or public safety. As long as the council members are in agreement over policy, there are few problems; but when commissioners differ among themselves and develop separate spheres of influence in city government, city government becomes a multiheaded monster, totally lacking in coordination. The results of the commission form of government were generally so disastrous that the reform movement abandoned its early support of this form of government in favor of the council-manager plan.

Council-manager.   The *council-manager* form of government revived the distinction between legislative "policy making" and executive "administration" in city government. Policy-making responsibility is vested in an elected council, and administration is assigned to an appointed professional administrator known as a manager, chosen by the council and responsible to it. All departments of the city government operate under the direction of the manager, who has the power to hire and fire personnel within the limits set by the merit system. The council's role in administration is limited to selecting and dismissing the city manager. The plan is based on the ideas that policy making and administration are separate functions and that the principal task of city govern-

Wards

Other officials

Mayor

Council

Treasurer

Mayor-Council form

ment is to provide the highest level of services at the lowest possible costs—utilities, streets, fire and police protection, health, welfare, recreation, and so on. Hence, a professionally trained, career-oriented administrator is given direct control over city departments.

The city in history

The United States developed an anticity bias in its rural beginnings

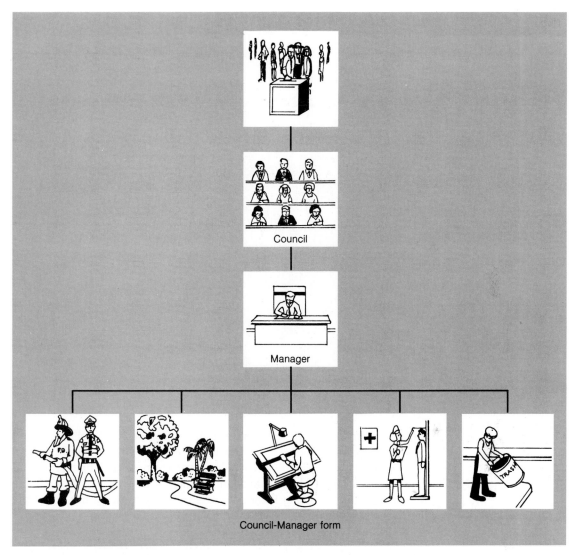

Council

Manager

Council-Manager form

FIGURE 13-2 Forms of city government. (SOURCE: National Municipal League. Reproduced by permission.)

and retained that bias long after it became a nation of city dwellers. Lewis Mumford and other urbanologists profess to see the roots of today's urban ills in this national trait.

When the first census was taken in 1790, a mere 5 percent of the nation's 4 million people lived in cities; there were only 24 towns with populations of 2,500 or more. A strong anticity bias was already ingrained in the national character. In an age when technological progress was giving rise to the first industrial centers in Europe, the American

from a rural to an urban America

social and economic outlook was decidedly agrarian. Most politicians and citizens distrusted cities, which Thomas Jefferson believed were not conducive to the exercise of virtue. Jefferson's warning notwithstanding, American cities steadily increased in population. The lure of urban life is reflected in the following Census Bureau figures showing the country's five most populous cities in 1820, 1870, 1950, and 1980.

1820		*1870*	
New York	152,000	New York	1,478,000
Philadelphia	65,000	Philadelphia	674,000
Baltimore	63,000	St. Louis	311,000
Boston	43,000	Chicago	299,000
New Orleans	27,000	Baltimore	267,000

1950		*1980*	
New York	7,896,957	New York	7,071,000
Chicago	3,620,962	Chicago	3,005,000
Philadelphia	2,071,605	Los Angeles	2,966,800
Los Angeles	1,970,338	Philadelphia	1,688,200
Detroit	1,849,568	Houston	1,594,100

First as seaports, then as trading and manufacturing centers, cities in the United States grew in response to economic needs. "Villages expanded into towns; towns became metropolises," historian Lewis Mumford wrote in *The City in History*.

economic needs fuel growth

> Between 1820 and 1900, the destruction and disorder within cities was like that of a battlefield. . . . Industrialism, the main creative force of the nineteenth century, produced the most degraded urban environment the world had yet seen. . . . Men built in haste, and had hardly time to repent of their mistakes before they tore down their original structures and built again, just as heedlessly. The newcomers, babies, or immigrants, could not wait for new quarters: they crowded into whatever was offered. It was a period of vast urban improvisation: makeshift hastily piled upon makeshift.[8]

By the late nineteenth century most large American cities had become socially and economically stratified. The affluent lived in their posh neighborhoods, comfortably isolated from the poor in their ethnic ghettos, whereas the middle classes tended to move to the less-expensive outlying areas. As populations spread, many central cities simply annexed those areas to which the middle class had gravitated. New York, for example, added more than 250 square miles in 1891, and in 1941 Boston doubled its area. Some states established automatic annexation procedures. By 1920, however, political opposition to the absorption of fringe areas mounted, and large cities, especially in the congested Northeast, found themselves unable to keep pace, through annexation or consolidation, with suburban migration.

social stratification in cities

During the 1920s general prosperity and the increasing number of automobiles gave new impetus to the growth of the suburbs. In that decade, the suburban populations around the seventeen largest U.S. cities rose by nearly 40 percent, while the rate of growth for most cities fell sharply. But until the 1940s, the central city remained the focal point of business and industry; the surrounding suburbs were primarily commuter villages.

Automobiles encourage suburban growth.

Following World War II suburbia began to take on the character of a retreat from the city, its congestion, and its poor. Highways, built largely with federal money, carried ex-urbanites to conclaves far beyond city limits. The suburbs filled with families moving outward from urban cores and inward from rural regions. From the early 1950s on, the suburbanization of America was the country's dominant growth pattern.

Government highway construction encourages suburban growth.

The downward spiral that gripped most central cities in the wake of the exodus to suburbia prompted the federal government to undertake the rebuilding of slum areas by feeding large subsidies of public money into the normal operations of the private market. The first federal urban-renewal effort was authorized by the Housing Act of 1949. The act called for the public acquisition of land by negotiation or condemnation and its resale to private contractors for redevelopment. The program's two main objectives were

Government begins urban renewal efforts for central cities in Housing Act of 1949.

1. to eliminate substandard housing through slum clearance and the reconstruction of blighted areas,
2. to stimulate housing construction and community development sufficiently to remedy the housing shortage.

From its beginning in 1949 through its high point during the Johnson administration, urban renewal was the subject of intense debate. Critics found fault with the practical effect on those who are displaced by redevelopment. "The federal renewal programs allow those in control . . . to change one kind of neighborhood into another kind by destroying the old buildings and replacing them with new ones," wrote Martin Anderson in 1964.[9] "The people who are most seriously affected by the program come from low-income minority groups that for various reasons do not or cannot attempt to correct the injustices to which they are subjected."

successes and failures

Although high-rise public housing has been denounced as a failure, the restoration of old homes in the inner city by affluent young homebuyers is regarded as one of today's success stories. The trend toward renovation is attributed largely to economics—it has become cheaper to buy an old house and repair it than to build or buy a new one. The buyer typically is an unmarried person or a young couple without children, either one of whom prefers city living but wants to own a house.

community develop- ment block grants

In the Community Development Act of 1974, Congress consolidated federal grants for housing and urban renewal in a community development *block grant* program. Cities receive direct federal monies to use as they think best to renew and redevelop blighted areas. The federal government generally monitors what cities do with these monies, but Washington no longer must approve specific projects.

Many cities are encouraging migration into urban neighborhoods by making available low-cost city-owned houses to noncommercial buyers who agree to refurbish them and live in them for a specified period. Under special "urban homesteading" programs, such houses have been sold for as little as a dollar. But the redevelopment of some urban districts has not been without its problems, especially the displacement of the poor, who are often forced to move as rents and taxes in renovated areas rise along with property values.

Although cities welcome affluent returnees, settlement has generally been confined to a few areas. So far local governments have been slow to generate plans to curtail speculation or distribute investment evenly in center cities to protect poor residents from being victimized by redevelopment.

■ Community power structures ■

Who runs this town? Do the elected public officials actually make the important decisions? Or is there a "power structure" in this community that really runs things? If so, who is in the power structure? Are public officials "errand boys" who carry out the orders of powerful people who operate "behind the scenes"? Or are community affairs decided by democratically elected officials acting openly in response to the wishes of many different individuals and groups? Is city government of the people, by the people, and for the people? Or is it a government run by a small "elite," with the masses of people largely apathetic and uninfluential in public affairs? Do people who make the important decisions in business and banking also make the important decisions in urban renewal, public works, education, taxation, public charity, land development, and so on? Or are there different groups of people making decisions in each of these areas, with little or no overlap except for elected officials?

Social scientists have differed in their answers to these questions. Some social scientists, to whom we shall refer as *elitists,* believe that power in American communities is concentrated in the hands of relatively few people, usually top business and financial leaders. They believe that this elite is subject to relatively little influence from the masses of people. Other social scientists, to whom we shall refer as *pluralists,* believe that power is widely shared in American communities among many leadership groups who represent segments of the community and who are held responsible by the people through elections and group participation. Interestingly, both elitists and pluralists seem to agree that decisions are made by small minorities in the community. Elitists describe a single structure of power, with a single leadership group making decisions on a variety of issues, whereas pluralists describe multiple structures of power, with different groups active in different issues and a great deal of competition, bargaining, and sharing of power among the elite.[10]

Power in "Middletown."   One of the earliest studies of American communities, the classic study of Middletown, conducted by Robert and Helen Lynd in the mid-1920s and again in the mid-1930s, tended to confirm a great deal of elitist thinking about community powers.[11] The Lynds found in Muncie, Indiana, a monolithic power structure dominated by the owners of the town's largest industry. Community power was firmly entrenched in the hands of the business class, centering on but not limited to the "X family."[12] The power of this group was based on its control over the economic life in the city, particularly its ability to control the extension of credit. The city was run by a "small top group [of] wealthy local manufacturers, bankers, the local head managers of . . . national corporations with units in Middletown, and . . . one or two outstanding lawyers." Democratic procedures and governmental institutions were so much window dressing for business control. The Lynds described the typical city official as a "man of meager calibre" and as "a man whom the inner business control group ignore economically and socially and use politically." Perhaps the most famous quotation from the Lynds' study was a comment by a Middletown man made in 1935:

> If I'm out of work, I go to the X plant; if I need money I go to the X bank, and if they don't like me I don't get it; my children go to the X college; when I get sick I go to the X hospital; I buy a building lot or house in the X subdivision; my wife goes downtown to buy X milk; I drink X beer, vote for X political parties, and get help from X charities; my boy goes to the X YMCA and my girl to their YWCA; I listen to the word of God in X subsidized churches; if I'm a Mason, I go to the X Masonic temple; I read the news from the X morning paper; and, if I'm rich enough, I travel via the X airport.[13]

Noted sociologist W. Lloyd Warner studied Morris, Illinois, in the 1940s, and he describes a power structure somewhat similar to that encountered by the Lynds in Muncie.[14] Sociologist August B. Hollingshead studied the same town, and his findings substantially confirmed those of Warner.[15] (Sociologists seem to prefer to disguise the names of towns they are studying: Warner called the town Jonesville, whereas Hollingshead called it Elmtown.)

Power in "Regional City." One of the most influential elitist studies of community politics was sociologist Floyd Hunter's *Community Power Structure*, a study of Atlanta, Georgia.[16] According to Hunter, no one man or family or business dominated "Regional City" (a synonym for Atlanta), as might be true in a smaller town. Instead, Hunter described several tiers of influentials, with the most important community decisions reserved for a top layer of the business community. Admission to the innermost circle was based primarily on one's position in the business world. These top decision makers were not formally organized but conferred informally and passed down decisions to government leaders, professional personnel, civic organizations, and other "front men." Hunter explained that the top power structure concerned itself only with major policy decisions; there were other substructures—economic, governmental, religious, educational, professional, civic, and cultural—that communicated and implemented the policies at the top levels. These substructures

> are subordinate, however, to the interests of the policy makers who operate in the economic sphere of community life in Regional City. The institutions of the family, church, state, education, and the like take their sustenance from economic institutional sources and are thereby subordinate to this particular institution more than any other. . . . Within the policy forming groups the economic interests are dominant.[17]

Top power holders seldom operated openly. "Most of the top personnel in the power group are rarely seen in the meetings attended by the associational understructure personnel in Regional City."[18]

In Hunter's description of community decision making, decisions tend to flow *down* from top policy makers, composed primarily of business and financial leaders, to civic, pro-

fessional, and cultural association leaders, religious and education leaders, and government officials, who implemented the program; and the masses of people have little direct or indirect participation in the whole process. Policy does not go *up* from associational groupings or from the people themselves. According to Hunter, elected public officials are clearly part of the lower-level institutional substructure, which "executes" policy rather than formulating it. Finally, Hunter found that this whole structure is held together by "common interests, mutual obligations, money, habit, delegated responsibilities, and in some cases, by coercion and force."

Power in New Haven. Perhaps the most influential of the pluralist community studies was Robert A. Dahl's *Who Governs?*, a detailed analysis of decision making in New Haven, Connecticut. Dahl chose to examine sixteen major decisions on redevelopment and public education in New Haven and on nominations for mayor in both political parties for seven elections. Dahl found a polycentric and dispersed system of community power in New Haven, in contrast to Hunter's highly monolithic and centralized power structure. Influence was wielded from time to time by many individuals, each exercising power over some issues but not over others. When the issue was one of urban renewal, one set of individuals was influential; in public education, a different group of leaders was involved. The business elite, who were said by Hunter to control Atlanta, were only one of many different influential groups in New Haven. According to Dahl,

> The economic notables, far from being a ruling group, are simply one of many groups out of which individuals sporadically emerge to influence the politics and acts of city officials. Almost anything one might say about the influence of the economic notables could be said with equal justice about a half a dozen other groups in the New Haven community.[19]

The mayor of New Haven was the only decision maker who was influential in most of the issue areas studied, and his degree of influence varied from issue to issue.

> The mayor was not at the peak of a pyramid but at the center of intersecting circles. He rarely commanded. He negotiated, cajoled, exhorted, beguiled, charmed, pressed, appealed, reasoned, promised, insisted, demanded, even threatened; but he most needed support and acquiescence from other leaders who simply could not be commanded. Because he could not command them, he had to bargain.[20]

Studying community power. Only by comparing structures of power and decision-making processes in a wide variety of communities can social scientists learn the actual extent of elitism or pluralism in American community life. Some communities may have concentrated, pyramidal structures of power, whereas others have diffused, multicentered power arrangements. For example, it is very likely that decision making in Atlanta is much more centralized than decision making in New Haven, Connecticut.

The key to understanding community power lies in identifying different types of community power structures and then relating them to social, economic, and political conditions in communities. For example, we may find that large communities with a great deal of social and economic diversity, a competitive party system, and a variety of well-organized competing interest groups tend to have *pluralistic* decision-making systems. On the other hand, small communities with a homogeneous population, a single dominant industry, nonpartisan elections, and few competing organizations may have power structures resembling the *elite* model.

Notes

1. Louis Wirth, "Urbanism as a Way of Life," *American Journal of Sociology* 44, July 1938.
2. Ibid., p. 24.
3. John C. Bollens and Henry J. Schmandt, *The Metropolis* (New York: Harper & Row, 1965), pp. 249–250.
4. Louis Wirth, "Urbanism as a Way of Life," *American Journal of Sociology* 44, 1938; Georg Simmel, *The Sociology of Georg Simmel,* Kurt Wolff, ed. (New York: Free Press, 1950).
5. See, for example, S. Milgram, "The Experience of Living in Cities," *Science* 167, 1970; A. Lowin et al., "The Pace of Life and Sensitivity to Time in Urban and Rural Settings," *Journal of Social Psychology* 83, 1971; C. Korte and N. Kerr, "Response to Activistic Opportunities under Urban and Rural Conditions," *Journal of Social Psychology* 32, 1975.
6. Derived from figures provided by Charles Korte, "The Impact of Urbanization on Social Behavior," *Urban Affairs Quarterly* 12, September 1976.
7. Marshall Clinard, *Sociology and Deviant Behavior* (New York: Holt, Rinehart & Winston, 1968), p. 96.

8. Lewis Mumford, *The City in History* (London: Penguin Books, 1966), p. 11.

9. Martin Anderson, *The Federal Bulldozer* (New York: McGraw-Hill, 1967), p. 9

10. This literature is so voluminous that it seems appropriate to cite only some of the major summary pieces: Thomas J. Anton, "Power, Pluralism, and Local Politics," *Administrative Science Quarterly* 7, March 1963; Lawrence Herson, "In the Footsteps of Community Power," *American Political Science Review* 55, December 1961; Peter Bachrach and Morton S. Baratz, "Two Faces of Power," *American Political Science Review* 56, December 1962; Peter Bachrach and Morton C. Baratz, "Decisions and Nondecisions," *American Political Science Review* 57, September 1963; Herbert Kaufman and Victor Jones, "The Mystery of Power," *Public Administration Review* 14, Summer 1954; Nelson Polsby, *Community Power and Political Theory* (New Haven: Yale University Press, 1963); Robert Presthus, *Men at the Top* (New York: Oxford University Press, Inc., 1964); Robert Dahl, *Who Governs?* (New Haven: Yale University Press, 1961); Floyd Hunter, *Community Power Structure* (Chapel Hill: The University of North Carolina Press, 1953); Robert Agger, Daniel Goldrich, and Bert Swanson, *The Rulers and the Ruled* (New York: John Wiley & Sons, Inc., 1965); other citations are given in notes following.

11. Robert S. Lynd and Helen M. Lynd, *Middletown* (New York: Harcourt Brace & World, 1929); and *Middletown in Transition* (New York: Harcourt Brace & World, 1937).

12. The "X family," never identified in the Lynds' books, was actually the Ball family, glass manufacturers. Today it is headed by E. F. Ball, Chairman of the Board of the Ball Corporation, Ball Brothers' Foundation, Ball Memorial Hospital, Muncie Aviation Corp., and Muncie Airport, Inc., and a director of the American National Bank and Trust of Muncie, Borg-Warner Corp., Indiana Bell Telephone Co., Merchants National Bank of Muncie, and Wabash College. Ball State University in Muncie is named for the family.

13. *Middletown in Transition,* p. 74.

14. W. Lloyd Warner et al., *Democracy in Jonesville* (New York: Harper & Row, 1949).

15. August B. Hollingshead, *Elmtown's Youth* (New York: John Wiley & Sons, Inc., 1949).

16. Floyd Hunter, *Community Power Structure* (Chapel Hill: The University of North Carolina Press), 1969.

17. Ibid., p. 94.

18. Ibid., p. 90.

19. Robert A. Dahl, *Who Governs?* (New Haven: Yale University Press, 1961), p. 72.

20. Ibid., p. 204.

Discussion questions

1. Describe overall growth and decline in central cities, suburbs, and nonmetropolitan areas of the United States. What is an SMSA?
2. According to sociologist Louis Wirth, what are the distinguishing characteristics of urban life?
3. Why do people choose to live in suburbs? What is meant by the statement "American life is becoming more, not less, segregated"?
4. How can we test the hypothesis that urban life is more impersonal than rural or small-town life?
5. What are the governmental functions of counties (rural and urban), cities, school districts, townships, and special districts?
6. What are the most common forms of city government?
7. Describe governmental programs designed to revive declining central cities.
8. What is meant by "elitist" and "pluralist" descriptions of community power structures?

CHAPTER 14

■ POWER & THE INTERNATIONAL SYSTEM

Since the earliest recorded times, and no doubt before, people have been fighting wars. They have fought them for *every* conceivable reason—and even for some reasons that may seem *inconceivable*. They have fought to defend themselves or to subjugate others; they have fought for territorial, economic, or political gain; they have fought for ideological reasons and for leaders whose sole reason was to secure a place for themselves in history; they have fought class wars and race wars; they have undoubtedly even fought just for excitement and glory. But in our age the threat of a nuclear holocaust makes it imperative that the world's superpowers avoid war. Nuclear war can have no meaning today, no reason worth the annihilation of civilization as we know it.

In this chapter we will explore some of the means, past and present, by which people have sought to avoid war. After you have read it, you should be able to

- discuss the meaning of sovereignty and describe the nature of international law,
- discuss the concepts of a balance of power, collective security, and regional security,
- discuss the concepts of deterrence and "MAD" and the means by which these policies are implemented,
- discuss the "minibalances of power" and the reasons why it is necessary for the superpowers to maintain conventional armed forces.

Relations among nations

The distinguished political scientist Hans Morgenthau wrote:

> International politics, like all politics, is a struggle for power. Whatever the ultimate aims of international politics, power is always the immediate aim. Statesmen and peoples may ultimately seek freedom, security, prosperity, or power itself. They may define their goals in terms of a religious, philosophic, economic, or social ideal. . . . But whenever they strive to realize their goal by means of international politics, they are striving for power.[1]

international politics
the worldwide struggle
for power

In brief, we are reminded that the struggle for power is global—it involves all the nations and peoples of the world, whatever their goals or ideals.

There are nearly 200 nations in the world today. Of these nations 154 are members of the United Nations. Others are too small or too poor to claim membership in that body. Yet all the nations of the world—inside and outside the UN, whatever their size, location, culture, politics, economic system, or level of technological development—claim *sovereignty*. Sovereignty means formal, legal power over internal affairs, freedom from external intervention, and political and legal recognition by other nations. Sovereignty is a legal fiction, of course: many nations have difficulty controlling their internal affairs; they are constantly meddling in each other's internal affairs and even trampling on each other's political and legal authority. Nonetheless, the *struggle* to achieve sovereignty is an important force in world politics, particularly among nations that were once colonies of other nations. The demand for national control over internal affairs and freedom from outside interference is frequently heard among the newer nations of Asia and Africa. But muffled cries for sovereignty are also heard from inside communist "satellite" nations of the Soviet Union.

sovereignty
legal power over internal
affairs, freedom from
external intervention, and
legal recognition by other
nations

Although sovereignty is highly valued by all nations, it creates an international system in which no authority—not even the United Nations—is given the power to make or enforce rules binding on all nations. There is *no world government*. Nations cooperate with each other only when it is in their own interest to do so. Nations can make treaties with each other, but there is no court to enforce the treaties, and they can be (and are) disregarded when it becomes advantageous for a nation to do so.

There is a series of customs and principles among nations—known as *international law*—that help to guide relations among nations. But international "law" is also a fiction: there is no international "police force" to enforce the law, and it is frequently broken or ignored. An International Court (at The Hague, the Netherlands) exists to decide conflicts according to international law, but nations do not have to submit to the authority of this court and can, if they wish to, ignore its decisions. The United Nations, as we shall see, is largely a debating society. The UN has no real power to enforce its resolutions, unless one or more

international law
a legal fiction that guides
relations among nations

nations (acting in their own self-interest) decide to try to enforce a UN resolution with their own troops, or contribute troops to a joint "UN force." But "UN forces" are really the forces of sovereign nations that have voluntarily decided to contribute troops to enforce a particular resolution.

international politics as a serious game

The international system can be viewed as a global game of power that is played continuously. All the players pursue different goals against all the other players. Some players are more powerful than others, and

occasionally players team up against each other. (Some team up willingly, while others are coerced into doing it.) Periodically, fights break out, but there is no referee with enough power to stop the fighting (unless one or more stronger players step in to restrain the fighting nations). The players belong to a club called the United Nations, where they sit around and quarrel about the game. But the players never agree to a referee or to rules of the game for fear that a referee or rules might interfere with their own style of play. The game has been played for centuries. No one really knows all the goals that each player seeks (although we all know that power is the key instrument in achieving any goal). Yet all the players are deadly serious and play to win.

Bringing order to international relations

The instability and insecurity of "the global game of power" have led to many attempts over the centuries to bring order to the international system. Indeed, wars among nations have averaged one every two years,[2] and if "civil wars" and "indirect aggressions" are counted, the rate of armed conflict is even greater.[3]

The balance-of-power system. One method of trying to bring order to international relations is the *balance-of-power* system. The nineteenth century saw a deliberate attempt to stabilize international relations by creating a system of alliances among nations that was designed to balance the power of one group of nations against the power of another and thus to discourage war. If the balance worked, war would be avoided and peace would be assured. For almost an entire century, from the end of the Napoleonic Wars (1815) to World War I (1914), the balance-of-power system appeared to be at least partially effective in Europe. But an important defect in the balance-of-power system is that a small conflict between two nations that are members of separate alliances can draw all the member nations of each alliance into the conflict.

the balance-of-power system, 1815–1914

This defect in the balance-of-power system can result in the rapid expansion of a small conflict into a major war between separate alliances of nations. Essentially this is what happened in World War I, when a minor conflict in the Balkan nations resulted in a very destructive war between the Allies (England, France, Russia, and eventually the United States) and the Central Powers (Germany, Austria-Hungary, and Turkey).

the Allies and the Central Powers

Indeed, World War I proved so destructive (10 million men were killed on the battlefield between 1914 and 1918) that there was a worldwide demand to replace the balance of power system with a new arrangement—"collective security."

Collective security. *Collective security* originally meant that *all* nations would join together to guarantee each other's "territorial integrity and existing political independence" against "external aggression" by any nation.[4] This concept resulted in the formation of the League of Nations in 1919. However, opposition to international involvement was so great in the United States after World War I that after a lengthy debate in the Senate, the United States refused to join the League of Nations. More important, the League of Nations failed completely to deal with rising militarism in Germany, Japan, and Italy in the 1930s. During that decade, Japan invaded Manchuria, Italy invaded Ethiopia, and Germany invaded Czechoslovakia; and the League of Nations failed to prevent any of these aggressions. Fascism in Germany and Italy and militarism in Japan went unchecked. The result was a war even more

efforts at collective security

the League of Nations

devastating than World War I: World War II cost more than 40 million lives, both civilian and military.

Yet, even after World War II, the notion of collective security remained an ideal of the victorious Allied powers—especially the United States, Great Britain, the Soviet Union, France, and China. The Charter of the United Nations was signed in 1945. The new organization included fifty-one members. The UN provided for (1) a Security Council with eleven members, five of them being permanent members (the United States, the USSR, Britain, France, and China) and having the power to veto any action by the Security Council; (2) a General Assembly composed of all the member nations, each with a single vote (except the USSR, which obtained three votes by claiming that Byelorussia and the Ukraine were independent); (3) a secretariat headed by a secretary-general with a staff at UN headquarters in New York; and (4) several special bodies to handle specialized affairs—for example, the Economic and Social Council, the Trusteeship Council, and the International Court at The Hague.

The Security Council has the "primary responsibility" for maintaining "international peace and security." For this reason the world's most powerful nations—the United States, the USSR, Great Britain, France, and China—have permanent seats on the council and veto powers over all but procedural matters. The General Assembly has authority over "any matter affecting the peace of the world," although it is supposed to defer to the Security Council if the council has already taken up a particular matter. No nation has a veto in the General Assembly; every nation has one vote, regardless of its size or power. Most resolutions can be passed by a majority vote.

Since 1945 the United Nations has disappointed all but its most ardent admirers. It has grown to a membership of 154 nations, but the vast majority of those nations are headed by authoritarian regimes of one kind or another. The western democracies are badly outnumbered. Nonetheless, the United States, because of its wealth, pays the largest share of UN expenses. In the General Assembly, the prevailing voice is that of small, authoritarian regimes, usually backed by communist powers. The votes of tiny populations headed by absolute dictators count for just as much as the votes of large democracies, including the United States. "One man, one vote" does not operate in the UN; the rule is "one country, one vote." Moreover, the UN has been ineffective in dealing with many major international disputes. This is true largely because parties to these disputes have no confidence in the UN and decline to bring their problems to it. Except on rare occasions (in Korea and, at times, in the Middle East), member nations of the UN have failed to commit their troops to enforce UN decisions. Finally, in recent years, antiwestern and antidemocratic speeches in the General Assembly have become common.

the United Nations
General Assembly
Security Council
secretary-general
specialized bodies
veto powers

problems at the United Nations

Regional security. The general disappointment with the United Nations as a form of collective security gave rise as early as 1950 to a different approach: *regional security.* In response to aggressive Soviet moves in Europe,[5] President Harry S. Truman created the North Atlantic Treaty Organization (NATO). In the NATO treaty the United States made a specific commitment to defend Western Europe in the event of a Soviet attack. Indeed, fifteen Western nations agreed to collective *regional security:* they agreed that "an armed attack against one or more . . . shall be considered an attack against them all." Moreover, a joint NATO military command was established with a U.S. commanding officer (the first was General of the Army Dwight D. Eisenhower) to command and coordinate the defense of Western Europe. After the formation of NATO, the Soviets made no further advances into Western Europe, and NATO remains today as a deterrent to Soviet expansion in the area. The Soviets themselves, in response to NATO, drew up a comparable treaty among their own Eastern European satellite nations—"the Warsaw Pact."

These regional security agreements—NATO and the Warsaw Pact—remind us more of the nineteenth-century *balance-of-power* alliances than of the true concept of *collective security.* The original notion of collective security envisioned agreement among *all* nations, whereas NATO and the Warsaw Pact are similar to the older systems of separate alliances.

regional security

NATO and the Warsaw Pact

The superpowers balance. Collective security and balance-of-power concepts have been overshadowed by the confrontation of the world's two "superpowers"—the United States and the Soviet Union. Indeed, international conflicts throughout the world—in the Middle East, Africa, Latin America, Southeast Asia, and elsewhere—are usually affected by some aspect of the superpower struggle. The superpowers are distinguished from the rest of the world by their capacity to destroy each other with nuclear weapons. Other nations—Great Britain, France, China, India, South Africa, and Israel—may possess nuclear weapons, but none can deliver the kind of devastating blow that could destroy a large industrial society.

the superpower balance

Peace and deterrence

To maintain peace and protect the national interests, the United States today relies primarily on the notion of *deterrence.* In a general sense, deterrence means that war and overt aggression can best be prevented by making the consequences of such acts clearly unacceptable to rational leaders of other nations.

deterrence and the prevention of war
peace is maintained by the threat of retaliation against potential attackers

Assured-destruction deterrence. The policy of *assured destruction* is based on the notion that one can dissuade a potential enemy from war or aggression only by maintaining the capacity to destroy the enemy's society even *after* one has suffered a well-executed surprise attack by the enemy. Assured-destruction deterrence assumes that the worst may happen—a surprise first strike against our own offensive forces. It emphasizes our *second-strike capability*—the ability of our forces to survive a surprise attack by the enemy and then to inflict an unacceptable level of destruction on the enemy's homeland. Assured-destruction deterrence, then, requires (1) that the United States maintain the *capability* to destroy an enemy even after absorbing a full-scale surprise attack (second-strike capability); (2) that the United States *communicate* its second-strike capability to the enemy (deterrence is achieved only if the enemy *knows* that you have the capacity to deliver unacceptable damage even after absorbing a first strike); (3) that the United States make its threat *credible* (the enemy must believe that you would in fact retaliate if attacked); and (4) that the enemy is a *rational* decision maker (only an irrational enemy would go to war knowing that it would result in the destruction of his society).

Deterrence, then, is a *psychological* concept: it is not enough for a nation to be confident of its own capability; the potential aggressor must be clearly aware of that nation's capabilities and intentions. Capacities and intentions must be fully communicated to the enemy. Hence, U.S. policy makers regularly publicize the strength and size of U.S. strategic forces.

But advertising numbers of missiles, or warheads, or megatonnage is not enough either. The key component of assured-destruction deterrence is the *survivability* of an effective strike force *after* a successful surprise attack by the enemy—that is, second-strike capability.

The triad. American defense policy currently relies on a "triad" of land-based missiles, submarine-launched missiles, and manned bombers to provide its assured-destruction deterrence. This combination of forces is believed to be a more effective deterrent than reliance on any single weapons system, because the diversity and multiplicity of forces makes it difficult for an enemy to develop a "first-strike capability"—the capability of destroying all three retaliatory systems simultaneously and thereby avoiding our "second-strike retaliation" (see Box 14-1).

In striving for assured-destruction deterrence, both the United States and the USSR have developed long-range intercontinental ballistic missiles (ICBMs) that can travel between the United States and the USSR in less than forty minutes. They are dispersed in underground "hardened" silos—concrete structures designed and constructed so that they can be destroyed only by a large explosion very nearby. They are far enough apart so that a single explosion, regardless of its size, can destroy no more than one missile silo. Thus, for an attacker to eliminate with confidence the defender's entire force on a first strike, he would have to evade early detection of his own missile firings (otherwise the

---

second-strike capability
the ability to retaliate even after absorbing an enemy's first strike

deterrence as a psychological concept
to maintain peace, you must let potential enemies know of your retaliatory capability

the key concept
survivability of forces

triad
separate land-based and submarine-launched missiles and manned aircraft to ensure survivability and discourage potential enemies from attempting a first strike

retaliatory systems
ICBMs
SLBMs
manned bombers
cruise missiles

BOX 14-1　The balance of military power

■ The overall military balance between the United States and the Soviet Union includes *strategic* nuclear forces, *intermediate* nuclear forces deployed in Europe, and *conventional* army, navy, and air forces (see Table).

Balance of forces: United States and USSR

	U.S.		USSR	
Strategic nuclear forces				
ICBMs				
Numbers	1,030		1,398[a]	
Warheads	2,130		6,400	
SLBMs				
Numbers	616		980	
Warheads	5,536		2,000	
Bombers, strategic	248		143[b]	
Intermediate nuclear forces in Europe				
Launchers	572[e]		375	
Warheads	572[e]		1,125	
Armed forces				
Personnel (in millions)	2.1		3.7	
Army				
Divisions	17		193[c]	
Deployment		5 Europe		30 Eastern Europe
		1 South Korea		65 European USSR
		11 U.S.		16 Central USSR
		(including Rapid		30 Southern USSR
		Deployment		52 China Border
		Forces)		4 Afghanistan
Tanks	12,023		51,000	
Artillery and Missiles	5,140		34,000	
Helicopters	9,000		3,450	
Marines				
Divisions	3		[d]	
Aircraft	436		[d]	
Air Force				
Combat Aircraft	3,700		4,430	
Navy				
Major Combat Surface				
Ships	192		293	
Attack Submarines	95		201	
Aircraft Carriers	14		3	
Aircraft	1,450		839	

[a]Including 308 "heavy" SS-18.
[b]Plus an additional 130 "Backfire" bombers, capable of strategic attack on the U.S.
[c]At full strength, Soviet combat divisions include about 8,000 men, compared to 14,000–16,000 men in U.S. combat divisions.
[d]USSR has small "Naval Infantry" units assigned to fleets; these units have no separate air support units.
[e]Not yet fully deployed.
SOURCE: International Institute for Strategic Studies. *The Military Balance 1984–85* (London: Institute for Strategic Studies, 1984).

Evaluating the strategic nuclear balance between the United States and the USSR requires the comparison of very different types of forces. The Soviets rely primarily on large land-based ICBMs; they outnumber the United States in ICBMs by 1,398 to 1,030. Moreover, their larger ICBMs can carry many more nuclear warheads than those of the United States—6,400 to 2,130. The United States relies primarily on submarine-based SLBMs. The Soviet Union has more SLBMs at sea (980 to 616), but the U.S. technological superiority in this field enables us to place more warheads on these missiles (5,536 to 2,000). The United States still retains some of its old, large, slow-flying B-52 bombers, with its newer B-1 supersonic bombers beginning to enter service. The Soviet supersonic "Backfire" bomber has been deployed since the early 1970s.

In Europe, the Soviets established clear superiority in intermediate nuclear forces by deploying their triple-warhead, mobile SS-20 missile in the late 1970s. In 1979 the NATO alliance agreed to deploy 108 U.S. Pershing II intermediate nuclear missiles and 464 ground-launched cruise missiles (GLCM) if the Soviets refused in arms talks to withdraw their SS-20s. This NATO deployment began in 1984.

The USSR has a vast superiority over the United States in numbers of ground combat troops, tanks, and artillery. However, the USSR must defend its eastern boundaries against possible Chinese incursion, and this diverts nearly one-third of Soviet ground combat forces. The Soviets must also use military forces to keep the populations of Eastern European nations in subjection. Nearly 20 percent of Soviet ground combat forces appear to be used to control the populations of Poland, Hungary, East Germany, Rumania, Bulgaria, and Czechoslovakia, and additional troops are required to occupy Afghanistan. Thus it can be argued that the USSR needs a larger ground combat capability than the United States.

However, the overwhelming numerical superiority of the USSR in ground combat troops, tanks, and artillery clearly exceeds that nation's need to protect itself from the Chinese and to maintain control of its Eastern European satellite nations. It is this *excess* capability that worries U.S. and NATO military commanders.

American conventional arms—tactical, aircraft, conventional bombs, tanks, antitank missiles, artillery, and battlefield missiles—are technologically equal or superior to Soviet conventional arms. But the USSR produces so many more conventional arms than the United States that the Soviets can send advanced arms to various nations in the Middle East, Asia, and Africa without depleting their own armies.

The United States currently maintains an armed force of 2.1 million, compared to 3.7 million for the Soviet Union. The Soviet Union spends about 15 percent of its gross national product on defense, compared to 6 percent for the United States. (However, since the GNP of the United States is larger than that of the Soviet Union, the ratio of Soviet to U.S. defense spending is somewhat closer.) If current trends in defense spending continue in both nations, eventually the Soviets will gain superiority in all aspects of war-making power.

defender's missiles would be fired before the attacker's missiles arrived) and either accurately target each of the defender's missile silos or else fire several warheads at each silo to ensure a hit.

Another approach to assured-destruction deterrence is to place missiles in submarines. Submarines with submarine-launched ballistic missiles (SLBMs) are difficult to detect, follow, and destroy. The coordinated destruction of this deterrent on a first strike is very unlikely with the technology presently available.

The third approach to assured-destruction deterrence is the development of advanced manned bomber forces. Bombers are safe only when they are in the air, and keeping a large bomber force in the air at all times is expensive. However, given sufficient warning, bombers can be effective. An advanced bomber (the B-1) flies at supersonic speeds (over 2,000 miles per hour); it is small, yet carries a heavy payload of nuclear weapons; its guidance system allows it to fly very low to escape radar detection; and it can launch nuclear warheads in air-to-surface missiles without having to fly over the target area. However, at present the United States relies primarily on an older and slower bomber—the B-52—which was developed in the 1950s. Manned bombers are flexible: they can change targets in flight; they can be recalled if the alert is an error; and they can be used in conventional, nonnuclear wars if needed.

Cruise missiles add to the deterrent effect of manned aircraft. Cruise missiles are low-flying, inexpensive, unmanned missiles that carry nuclear warheads and can be launched from aircraft, ships or submarines in large enough numbers to saturate enemy air defenses. A single B-52 can carry ten cruise missiles.

A balance of terror: "MAD"

If *both* sides have assured-destruction deterrence—that is, second-strike capability—then *neither* side is likely to begin a nuclear war. Mutual assured destruction, or "MAD," refers to this kind of balance of power. However, if either side should lose its second-strike capability, this would upset the balance by providing an incentive for the other side to proceed with a first strike of its own, knowing that it would not suffer any serious consequences.

MAD
a type of stability

threats to stability
MIRV
missile accuracy

Mutual assured destruction represents *stability* in the international balance of power. MAD envisions a balance of terror—each side is restrained from war because of the knowledge of the terrible consequences that the other side can inflict upon it even after an attack. In other words, peace is maintained because of the terrible consequences to both sides in the event of war.

Research and technological advancement are constant threats to stability. For example, both the United States and the USSR have developed a multiple independently targeted reentry vehicle (MIRV) for its land-based and submarine-launched missiles. MIRV enables *each* missile to launch three, six, or ten separate warheads at separate targets while still high in space over the enemy's homeland. MIRV multiplies by three to ten times the number of warheads that can be delivered by SLBMs or ICBMs. MIRV permits either side to aim multiple warheads at a single ICBM site to ensure its destruction. It reduces the "survivability" of ICBMs and threatens second-strike capability. Thus MIRV tends to "destabilize" the MAD balance.

Another threat to stability is the improved accuracy of ICBMs and SLBMs on both sides. Improved accuracy means that hardened silos can be destroyed in a first strike, thus reducing second-strike capability. The United States now recognizes that its land-based ICBMs are vulnerable to an accurate Soviet first strike.

To maintain second-strike assured-destruction deterrence against an accurate MIRVed ICBM attack, it is essential that the United States maintain a strong *submarine deterrent force* equipped with underwater-launched missiles. Accurate MIRVed missiles have a potential first-strike capability against land-based missiles and aircraft, but they have no ability to attack missile-carrying submarines lurking in the depths of the oceans. The United States is currently building a new, larger (twenty-four missiles each with MIRVed warheads) *Trident* submarine force, to replace the *Polaris* submarine force. These submarine forces may become major stabilizing elements in the nuclear war game in the 1990s and beyond.

stabilizing elements
Trident
intelligence

Satellite reconnaissance is another major stabilizing force in the nuclear war game. Good intelligence reduces uncertainty about offensive and defensive capabilities and hence reduces the likelihood of war through miscalculation. One result of the U.S. space program was the development of "spy-in-the-sky" satellites capable of constant photo reconnaissance of enemy territory. These satellites can take amazingly detailed pictures from outer space. It is now virtually impossible for the enemy to develop offensive or defensive weapons without the president's knowing about it as soon as construction begins. The development of "spy-in-the-sky" satellites has also made arms limitations agreements easier, because with its space photography each nation can identify cheating.

Strategic arms limitation

Following the election of Richard Nixon as president in 1968, the United States, largely guided by former Harvard professor Henry Kissinger (National Security Advisor to the president and later Secretary of State) began negotiations with the Soviet Union over strategic nuclear arms. In 1972, the United States and the USSR concluded two and one-half years of talks about limiting the strategic arms race. The agreement that resulted from the first Strategic Arms Limitation Talk (SALT I) consists of a treaty limiting antiballistic missiles (ABMs) and an agreement placing a numerical ceiling on offensive missiles.

SALT I

The ABM treaty limits each side to one ABM site for defense of its national capital and one ABM site for defense of an offensive ICBM field. The total number of ABMs permitted is 200 for each side, 100 at each location. (The USSR has one ABM site defending Moscow; the United States deactivated its only site in 1975.) Both sides agreed not to build large-scale ABM systems to defend their own cities. This means that each agreed to curtail its damage limitation efforts. Satellite reconnaissance makes the SALT agreement self-enforcing; without satellite

the ABM treaty

photography the question of inspection would have doomed negotiations. Each nation holds the population of the other as hostage (a "stabilizing" condition) as long as neither develops a credible first-strike capability.

the offensive arms agreement

Under the offensive arms agreement, each side was frozen at the total number of offensive missiles completed or under construction. Both sides could construct new missiles if they dismantled an equal number of older missiles. Both sides were limited to the number of missile-carrying submarines operational or under construction at the time of the agreement. Both sides could replace older submarines and missiles, as long as their number remained unchanged. Each nation agreed not to interfere in the satellite intelligence-gathering activities of the other nation. There were no limitations on MIRV. There are no limitations on bombers. There are no limitations on advanced research on totally new weapons systems like the cruise missile. Both nations pledged to continue efforts at further arms control—the SALT II talks.

SALT II

The United States and the Soviet Union signed the lengthy and complicated SALT II treaty in 1979. But President Carter failed to win the necessary support in the Senate to ratify the treaty. President Reagan opposed the SALT II treaty's terms, which included the following:

A total limit of 2,250 strategic nuclear launchers—ICBMs, SLBMs, bombers, and long-range cruise missiles—for each side.

A limit of 1,320 on the total number of missiles that could be MIRVed.

A ban on new types of ICBMs, with an exception of one new type of ICBM for each side.

A limit of ten MIRVed warheads on any ICBM, fourteen MIRVed warheads on any SLBM.

Ceilings on the size and weight of missiles.

Advance notification of test launches.

Agreement not to interfere with electronic or satellite reconnaissance or use deliberate concealment of weapons testing or deployment.

opposition

Opposition to the treaty in the United States centered on several points:

The Soviets were allowed to keep 314 very heavy SS-18 missiles for which the United States has no equivalent.

The United States was required to count its old B-52s against its limit of 2,250 launchers, whereas the Soviets were not required to count their newer, faster "Backfire" bombers.

Questions were raised about the ability to verify numbers of MIRVs on a missile, as well as size and weight limitations.

More important, opponents of the treaty worried that the American public would relax its defense efforts if the treaty were signed. The Soviets had moved ahead during SALT I to build more and bigger missiles. Perhaps the Soviets were only interested in SALT agreements as a means of slowing U.S. defense efforts while they raced ahead.

When the Soviet Union invaded Afganistan, President Carter withdrew the SALT II treaty from Senate consideration. But both President Carter and, later, President Reagan announced that the U.S. would abide by the provisions of the unratified SALT II treaty as long as the Soviet Union did so. President Reagan continued negotiations with the Soviets in a new effort to secure reductions in the numbers, sizes, and nuclear warheads of missiles allowed in SALT II.

The Soviet Union walked out of the arms talks in December 1983 and launched a massive propaganda "peace offensive." The Soviet moves were designed to divide the U.S. from its European allies and to slow or halt the rebuilding of U.S. defense that had begun under President Carter and was continuing under President Reagan. But the United States's European allies remained firm and continued the European deployment of U.S. nuclear missiles. President Reagan was reelected in 1984 promising continued U.S. efforts to maintain its strategic defenses, and he announced a new research program in space-based nuclear defense (see this chapter's case study: "'Star Wars' and the Superpowers"). In early 1985 the Soviets announced their willingness to resume talks over nuclear arms.

The Geneva talks between the United States and the Soviet Union cover three broad topics:

1. Strategic nuclear weapons (land-based and submarine-based missiles and bombers capable of attacking the homelands of each nation);
2. Intermediate nuclear forces (European-based nuclear weapons);
3. Space weapons (missile defenses based in space, as well as ground-based, antiballistic missiles).

The Soviets insisted that all three of these topics had to be considered "in their interrelatedness," implying that the Soviets would not agree to any reductions in nuclear arms unless the U.S. gave up its research in space defenses.

Minibalances of power

Although the balance of power between the world's two superpowers—the United States and the Soviet Union—overshadows world events, smaller areas of the world are also confronted with the problem of achieving stability by balancing the power of conflicting local forces.

We have labeled this process of achieving local stability by balancing the forces of smaller nations as *minibalances of power.*

It is difficult to achieve stability in all parts of the world, not only because of the large number of nations involved, each with its own goals, but also because of frequent intervention by the superpowers on one side or the other. This type of intervention, coupled with local hostilities, makes local war a common occurrence in areas of Africa, Asia, and the Middle East. The danger of superpower intervention is, of course, *escalation*—the growth of a local conflict into a larger war, perhaps even a nuclear war between the superpowers themselves.

escalation

Vietnam. Indochina, which had been a French colony, was occupied by Japanese troops during World War II. Before Allied troops reached Indochina, an independent native Democratic Republic of Vietnam was proclaimed in September 1945, with the revolutionary Communist leader Ho Chi Minh as premier. By December 1946 the French Army had organized itself for an invasion of Vietnam and the recovery of the lost colony. Ho Chi Minh requested U.S., British, and even Nationalist Chinese support against the French, but the Allies instead supported the French. Eight years of bloody war ensued, ending in the defeat of a sizable French force at Dien Bien Phu.

Representatives of the Democratic Republic of Vietnam and the French met at Geneva in 1954 and agreed to a cease-fire along a temporary military demarcation line at the seventeenth parallel, separating Communist North Vietnam from Western-supported South Vietnam. Both sides agreed that the line did not constitute a political or territorial boundary, but they promised not to introduce foreign troops or military bases anywhere in Vietnam, Laos, or Cambodia. The Communist North Vietnamese established their capital in Hanoi in the North, while the anticommunist South Vietnamese rallied in Saigon in the South.

When the North Vietnamese moved south in large numbers to support Communist "Viet Cong" units fighting the South Vietnamese government, the United States gave heavy military and economic assistance to "save" South Vietnam from communism. In February 1965 President Lyndon Johnson sent American ground combat units into action in South Vietnam and began bombing military targets in North Vietnam. The president explained that the U.S. military effort was necessary because of our commitment to the South Vietnamese, who were victims of North Vietnam's aggression. But years of fighting, the commitment of a half million men to Vietnam, and the loss of over 50,000 American lives failed to achieve victory. On 31 March 1968 President Johnson announced an end to U.S. bombing in North Vietnam, issued a new call for negotiations, and withdrew from the presidential race. The North Vietnamese agreed to hold discussions with the United States in Paris, but even while discussions were under way, the war continued unabated, with heavy civilian and military casualties on both sides.

The Nixon administration began a slow withdrawal from a situation that looked more and more like a disaster for American policy. However, to cover our withdrawal, Nixon mounted a brief but large-scale attack into Cambodia in 1970. Finally, after renewed heavy bombing of the North Vietnamese capital of Hanoi, the North Vietnamese signed the Paris Peace Agreement in early 1973. The agreement called for an end to fighting, with all forces holding areas they controlled, a withdrawal of all U.S. troops, and the return of U.S. prisoners held by the North Vietnamese. The Paris Peace Agreement lasted only two years; after American troops were withdrawn, the North Vietnamese launched a massive and successful attack on the South, leading to a complete collapse of the South Vietnamese government in 1975. Communist forces took over all of Vietnam, Laos, and Cambodia. The presidency, weakened by Watergate and lacking the support of Congress, was helpless. The American public was disgusted with the long and costly jungle war. The United States did nothing. A few refugee survivors were helped to find homes in America, but the war in Vietnam ended in American defeat.

China. President Nixon's decision to seek a reconciliation with the communist People's Republic of China, suddenly and dramatically revealed in 1971, signaled a new American effort to balance Soviet power in the world. In 1979 the Carter administration opened full diplomatic relations with the People's Republic of China and cut off U.S. relations with the noncommunist government of the Republic of China on Taiwan. The new policy caused anxiety in the Soviet Union by shifting the balance of power in the world community. It was Secretary of State Henry Kissinger's view that the United States should, by taking advantage of the growing split between China and the Soviet Union, play a power-balancing role between these communist giants. The United States and China have grown closer in recent years, even though U.S. support of independent Taiwan presents an obstacle to improved relations. Nonetheless, the Soviet Union is disturbed by U.S.–China cooperation and very upset about the possibility of the United States selling arms to China.

The Middle East. In 1948, immediately after Britain withdrew from its old League of Nations "mandate" to govern Palestine and the United Nations recognized the new nation of Israel, the Arab-Israeli conflict broke out into open warfare. Although vastly outnumbered, the Israelis were successful in their War of Independence. Palestinian Arabs who were displaced from Israel were never integrated into surrounding Arab nations, but were instead kept in squalid camps in Egypt, Jordan, and Syria. These camps nourished the growth of a Palestinian Liberation Organization (PLO) dedicated to the elimination of the state of Israel and willing to use political, military, and terrorist means to accomplish their goal.

In 1956, after Egyptian President Nasser seized the British-built and -owned Suez Canal, a combined force of British, French, and Israeli forces captured the canal, with Israelis doing most of the fighting in the Sinai Desert. The United States, seeking to maintain its influence in the oil-rich Arab world, forced a return of the canal and of all captured lands to Egypt. Nonetheless, Egypt and Syria turned increasingly to the Soviet Union for military aid (although Lebanon and Jordan did not). In 1967 Egypt and Syria, heavily armed by the Russians, raced their armies to the Israeli frontier. But in the Six-Day War in a lightning military strike, the Israelis, though heavily outnumbered, defeated the forces of Egypt, Syria, and Jordan. The Israeli border expanded to the Suez Canal in the west, the Jordan River in the east, and the Golan Heights in the northeast. The Israelis asked for a permanent peace agreement that would recognize the right of Israel to exist, but the defeated Arabs, having received a rapid influx of new Russian arms, refused to negotiate under any conditions.

By 1973 the Arabs were prepared for another major military attack on Israel—the fourth in twenty-five years. The Yom Kippur War resulted in yet another defeat for the Arab nations, but this time the Israelis suffered a greater loss of men and material than they had in previous wars. The Yom Kippur War also resulted in the direct involvement of the United States in negotiations. The Arab nations placed a temporary embargo on oil shipped to the United States as a way of forcing the United States to pressure Israel into concessions. When Egyptian armies were threatened with annihilation in the desert and the Syrian capital of Damascus was under Israeli attack, the Soviets prepared to send in their own troops. A direct confrontation with the Soviets was avoided only when Henry Kissinger succeeded in getting the Israelis to pull back. Kissinger was later able to obtain additional limited Israeli withdrawals and demilitarized zones in the Sinai and Golan areas. Indeed, Kissinger began to win the Egyptians away from the Soviets and to move Israel and the Arab states closer to a permanent peace.

President Anwar Sadat of Egypt surprised the world in 1977 by announcing that he was prepared to go to Jerusalem and talk with Israel's Prime Minister Menachem Begin in an effort to achieve a permanent peace. This announcement changed the long-standing Arab policy of refusing even to recognize the existence of Israel. The subsequent talks between Egypt and Israel did not bring immediate peace. "Hardline" Arab states, such as Iraq, Libya, Algeria, and Syria, and the militant Palestinian Liberation Organization (PLO) denounced the Egyptian–Israeli talks. However, with the forces of the Arab nations and Israel reasonably balanced, the atmosphere for peace in the Middle East improved. President Carter succeeded in moving Egypt and Israel closer to peace in talks with President Sadat of Egypt, and Prime Minister Begin of Israel at the presidential conference site at Camp David, Maryland.

The signing of a peace treaty by Anwar Sadat and Menachem Begin (the "Camp David agreement") in 1979 brought a brief promise of hope to the embattled Middle East. The Israelis agreed to a gradual withdrawal of all occupied Egyptian lands (the Sinai) and to open negotiations regarding the future of Arabs living in the Israeli-controlled areas of the West Bank of the Jordan River and the Gaza Strip. In exchange, Egypt agreed to recognize the right of Israel to exist and to exchange ambassadors. But even this limited agreement was denounced by other Arab states. Egypt and Israel have continued to abide by the Camp David agreement, despite the assassination of Anwar Sadat in 1981.

For many years Lebanon had been the most advanced Arab nation and its capital Beirut the most cosmopolitan city in the Middle East. Its Christian Arabs shared power with its Moslem Arabs in a delicately balanced constitution. But Palestinian refugees destabilized the Christian–Moslem balance in Lebanon; the PLO became a separate government in Lebanon and launched many attacks on Israel from its bases in southern Lebanon. In 1984 Israel launched an attack on PLO forces in Lebanon that carried Israeli troops to the outskirts of Beirut. Syrian air forces were destroyed in the battle, but Syrian and Israeli ground troops avoided direct contact. The PLO was severely damaged, but other Moslem groups in Lebanon joined in a bloody guerrilla campaign against the Israeli occupiers. Israel eventually withdrew from Lebanon and the country became a battleground in which many separate armed Christian and Moslem sects engaged in sporadic fighting against each other.

Hostilities in the Middle East run deep, and the Soviets continue to stir unrest. Conflicts over the boundaries of Israel, over the future of the city of Jerusalem, and over the future of the Palestinian people appear unresolvable. The United States continues to try to maintain a balanced approach toward Israel and the "moderate" Arab states—Egypt, Saudi Arabia, and Jordan.

▪ "Star Wars" and the superpowers ▪

For more than forty years, since the terrible nuclear blasts of Hiroshima and Nagasaki in 1945, the world has avoided nuclear war. Peace has been maintained by deterrence—by the threat of devastating nuclear attacks that would be launched in retaliation to an enemy's first strike. Although the balance of terror has kept the peace, many scholars, soldiers, and citizens have tried to think of a better way of avoiding nuclear war. Instead of deterring war through fear of retaliation, perhaps we should seek a technological defense against nuclear missiles, one that will eventually render them "impotent and obsolete."

According to President Reagan,

Our nuclear retaliating forces have deterred war for 40 years. The fact is, however, that we have no defense against nuclear ballistic missile attack. . . . In the event that deterrence failed, a president's only recourse would be to surrender or to retaliate. Nuclear retaliation, whether massive or limited, would result in the loss of millions of lives. . . .

If we apply our great scientific and engineering talent to the problem of defending against ballistic missiles, there is a very real possibility that future presidents will be able to deter war by means other than threatening devastation to any aggressor—and by a means which threatens no one. . . .

Emerging technologies offer the possibilities of nonnuclear options for destroying missiles and the nuclear warheads they carry in all phases of their flight. New technologies may be able to permit a layered defense by providing: sensors for identifying and tracking missiles and nuclear warheads; advanced ground and spaceborne intercepters and directed energy weapons to destroy both missiles and nuclear warheads; and the technology to permit the command control and communication necessary to operate a layered defense . . . .[6]

President Reagan's Strategic Defense Initiative (SDI) is a research program designed to explore means of destroying enemy nuclear missiles in space before they could reach their targets. Following the president's initial announcement of SDI in March 1983, the press quickly labeled the effort "Star Wars." SDI or "Star Wars" is only a research program. The Soviets have two small ABM systems permitted by SALT I, and the United States has successfully experimented with destroying a single object in space. But at present neither side can stop any significant portion of the other side's missiles once they have been fired. For many years to come, deterrence will continue to rest on fear of retaliation.

As a broad research program, the SDI is not yet based on any single type of ballistic missile defense. A *boost phase defense* might attempt to destroy enemy missiles shortly after they are launched. Sophisticated battle management satellites might keep watch over known Soviet missile fields. Antimissiles might be placed in orbit over Soviet missiles, ready

to destroy those missiles during their initial boost phase. Or lasers or particle beams might be directed to mirrors orbiting over Soviet missile fields and bounced toward Soviet missiles in flight. If Soviet missiles escape these early boost phase defenses, perhaps *a layered defense* in space might be constructed in an effort to destroy missiles and warheads while they are traveling toward the United States. Defensive missiles or beams would have to locate, identify, track, and destroy perhaps thousands of separate missiles and warheads. Finally, those enemy warheads that survive a layered defense in space might be attacked in the *terminal phase* of their flight. Antiballistic missile defense might be set up specifically to defend expected targets—for example, the capital and command centers of our own offensive missile sites. (Currently the Soviet Union has two ABM systems permitted under SALT I, one defending Moscow and one defending its offensive ICBM fields; the United States has no operating ABM systems.)

These new missile defenses will require the development of highly sophisticated computers able to recognize and track Soviet missiles and direct laser beams or antimissiles to them. Note that missile defenses need *not* be nuclear. It does not require a nuclear weapon to destroy a missile; a missile can be destroyed if it can be hit by a laser beam or by the force of collision with another missile. This is a major attraction of the SDI proposal. It holds out the possibility of defending the United States without relying on nuclear weapons, either for retaliatory purposes or even for destroying incoming enemy missiles.

Opponents of President Reagan's Strategic Defense Initiative have made several important arguments:

1. U.S. efforts to defend itself against ICBMs may prompt the Soviets to build more and better ICBMs. SDI may simply stimulate an arms race. Even supporters of SDI acknowledge that missile

defenses must be developed that can defend themselves, or else the Soviets will simply attack the defenses before launching their ICBMs. Supporters of SDI also acknowledge that defenses must be cheaper to build than ICBMs, or else the Soviets will simply build more ICBMs than we can build defenses.

2. The SDI might be interpreted by the Soviets as an effort by the United States to gain a first-strike capability— the ability to launch a nuclear attack against the U.S.S.R. and then defend ourselves against their weakened retaliatory response. This is the official line taken by the Soviets in objecting to "Star Wars." They claim we are seeking to "militarize space" in an effort to gain advantage over them.

3. SDI might destabilize the balance of terror currently existing between the United States and the U.S.S.R. If the United States could defend itself against ICBMs and the Soviet Union could not, the United States would gain a strategic advantage.

4. SDI is technologically infeasible; efforts to build missile defenses will waste tens of billions of dollars. A complete protective "super dome" over the United States and its allies is impossible. Even a few nuclear weapons can cause millions of deaths.

5. SDI threatens to violate the SALT I treaty prohibiting antiballistic missiles. Moreover, the SDI program may stand in the way of future agreements with the Soviet Union for promoting or reducing nuclear weapons. The Soviets have stated repeatedly that the United States must give up its SDI before any agreement on nuclear arms can be reached.

In contrast, supporters of the Strategic Defense Initiative make these points:

1. Technological advances offer the promise of maintaining peace by means of space defense rather than by the threat of nuclear retaliation. SDI is only a research program. Decisions about actually deploying ballistic missile defenses are many years in the future.

2. A ballistic missile defense is preferable to threats of retaliation for maintaining peace. What if deterrence fails someday? What if an irrational leader ignores our threat of retaliation and proceeds to attack the United States regardless of the consequences? A ballistic missile defense would provide the president and the nation with a means of defending ourselves in an actual attack.

3. Ballistic missile defenses do not threaten millions of lives, in the fashion of our current deterrent strategy. Defensive weapons would be nonnuclear; they would be targeted on missiles and warheads, not cities. A defensive strategy is morally preferable to threatening millions of lives.

4. Ballistic missile defense can offset the Soviets' superiority in numbers and size of missiles. An effective missile defense may someday convince them that continuing increases in numbers of ICBMs are pointless. Indeed, the Soviets may be pressured to make reductions in their ICBMs in exchange for limiting the U.S. "Star Wars" program.

5. A ballistic missile defense, when employed in conjunction with our retaliating forces, would improve deterrence. Any Soviet plans for a first strike against our retaliating forces would be frustrated by the uncertainties created by our new defenses. Soviet generals could not guarantee that all of our retaliating forces would be destroyed in a surprise attack.

Notes

1. Hans Morgenthau, *Politics among Nations* (New York: Knopf, 1960), p. 27.
2. Quincy Wright, *A Study of War* (Chicago: University of Chicago Press, 1942), pp. 641–646.
3. Frederick H. Hartman, *The Relations of Nations,* 4th ed. (New York: Macmillan, 1973), p. 12.
4. Terms used in Article X of the Covenant of the League of Nations.
5. These moves included (1) the establishment of communist governments in Eastern European nations in violation of wartime agreements at Yalta and Potsdam to support "democratic" governments "broadly representative" of all factions; (2) military support of the communist takeover of Czechoslovakia in 1948; (3) the breakup of a four-power control commission that was to govern the occupation of Germany and the sealing off of the Soviet sector of East Germany; (4) a military blockade of Berlin in 1948 designed to oust American, British, and French occupation authorities; (5) Soviet military support for armed communist troops in Greece and Turkey; (6) the continued maintenance of a large Soviet army in Eastern Europe threatening the security of Western European nations.
6. President Ronald Reagan, *The President's Strategic Defense Initiative,* White House, January 3, 1985.

Discussion questions

1. Define *sovereignty* and discuss the role it plays in international politics. Describe the nature of international law.
2. Describe various systems of international order, giving specific examples of each type of system. Compare and evaluate the relative effectiveness of a balance-of-power system, collective security, and regional security. Include in your discussion a description of the organization of the United Nations.
3. Discuss the current United States policy of assured-destruction deterrence. What is meant by the "triad" of strategic forces?
4. Describe the balance of terror ("MAD") and identify the factors that pose a threat to the stability of this balance, as well as those that act as stabilizing elements.
5. Discuss the SALT I ABM treaty and offensive arms agreement. What did each side gain from the SALT I agreement? What role does satellite reconnaissance play in the SALT agreement? Describe the current status of the SALT II agreement.
6. Describe the topics under discussion in the Geneva talks between the United States and the Soviet Union.
7. Describe the characteristics of the NATO alliance. Why is Western Europe important to the United States?

8. In the context of either the Vietnam War or the Middle East crises of 1956 (Suez Canal), 1967 (Six-Day War), and 1973 (Yom Kippur War), discuss the concept of "minibalances of power." What is the danger of superpower intervention in local wars?
9. Describe the Strategic Defense Initiative (SDI). How does the SDI promise to change U.S. strategy in maintaining peace?
10. Discuss the pros and cons of the Strategic Defense Initiative. What is your own view?

INDEX

PHOTO CREDITS

Part Opening Photos
2, Rose Skytta, Jeroboam, Inc. **34,** Kent Reno, Jeroboam, Inc. **224,** Robert Eckert Jr., EKM-Nepenthe.

Chapter 1
8, David Seymour, Magnum Photos, Inc. **9,** United Nations. **16,** Cary Wolinsky, Stock Boston, Inc.

Chapter 2
20, Alan Carey, The Image Works. **30,** UPI/Bettmann Newsphotos.

Chapter 3
44, Cathy Cheney, EKM-Nepenthe. **46,** Ms. Magazine, March 1978. Photo by Carl Fischer. Courtesy the Ms. Foundation for Education and Communication. **51,** UPI/Bettmann Newsphotos. **55,** The Fine Arts Museums of San Francisco, Achenbach Foundation For Graphic Arts, Gift of Mr. and Mrs. John D. Rockefeller, 3rd. **57,** UPI/Bettmann Newsphotos.

Chapter 4
76 and **77,** Alan Carey, The Image Works. **82,** AP/Wide World Photos.

Chapter 5
94, Mark Antman, The Image Works, Inc. **95,** AP/Wide World Photos. **100** and **103,** UPI/Bettmann Newsphotos. **109,** Karl Schumacher, The White House. **120,** Judy Blamer, Brooks/Cole Publishing.

Chapter 6
131, John Wilde, Wedding Portrait, 1943. Collection of Whitney Museum of American Art, New York. Gift of the artist in memory of Helen Wilde. **135,** The National Library of Medicine. **147,** B.F. Skinner. **149,** George Tooker: Government Bureau, 1956. All rights reserved. The Metropolitan Museum of Art George A. Hearn fund, 1956.

Chapter 7
167, John Trumbull: The Declaration of Independence, 1786. Copyright Yale University Art Gallery. **173,** UPI/Bettmann Newsphotos. **180,** Pete Souza, The White House. **185,** AP/Wide World Photos. **186,** Terry Arthur, The White House. **189,** AP/Wide World Photos. **197,** Pete Souza, The White House.

Chapter 8
202, Culver Pictures, Inc. **211,** UPI/Bettmann Newsphotos. **213,** Brown Brothers. **215,** FDR Library. **217,** UPI/Bettmann Newsphotos.

Chapter 9
229, Ciao Carruba, Camera Press/Photo Trends. **233,** Jan Lukas. **236,** UPI/Bettmann Newsphotos.

Chapter 10
253, Matt Heron, Black Star. **254,** UPI/Bettmann Newsphotos. **259,** Robert A. Sengstacke. **271,** Mark Antman, The Image Works.

Chapter 11
284, Michael O'Brien, Archive Pictures, Inc. **293,** Newsweek, April 5, 1982. Copyright 1982, by Newsweek, Inc. All rights reserved. Photo by Burk Uzzle/ Magnum Photos, Inc. **295,** Alan Carey, The Image Works.

Chapter 12
302, Alan Carey, The Image Works. **308,** John Mahar, EKM-Nepenthe. **315,** UPI/Bettmann Newsphotos. **318,** Peter Southwick, Stock Boston, Inc.

Chapter 13
331, UPI/Bettmann Newsphotos. **344,** Elliott Erwitt, Magnum Photos, Inc.

Chapter 14
354, Pete Souza, The White House. **362,** United States Air Force.

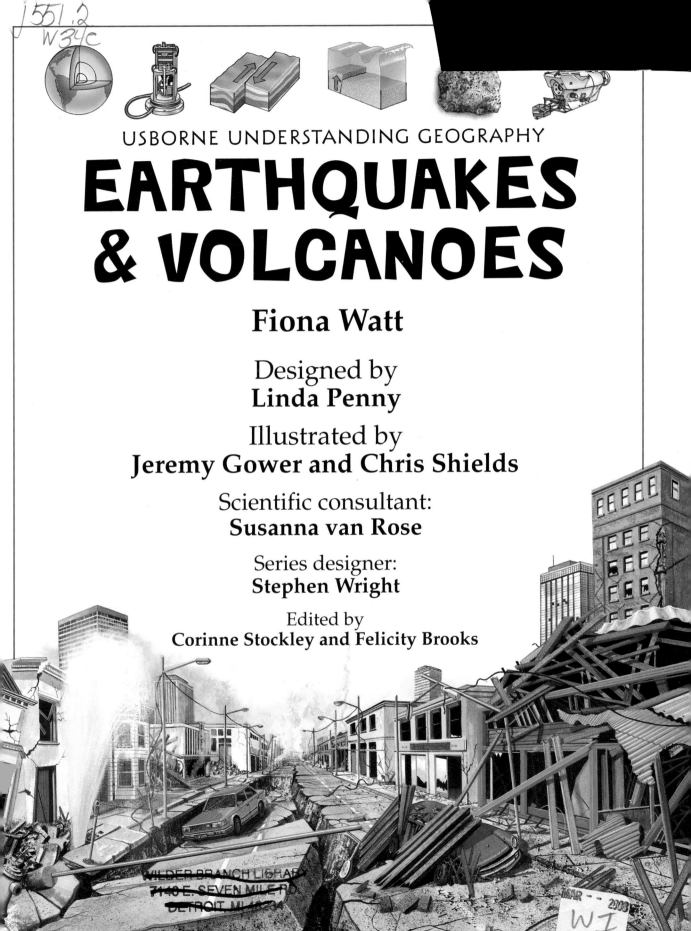

USBORNE UNDERSTANDING GEOGRAPHY

EARTHQUAKES & VOLCANOES

Fiona Watt

Designed by
Linda Penny

Illustrated by
Jeremy Gower and Chris Shields

Scientific consultant:
Susanna van Rose

Series designer:
Stephen Wright

Edited by
Corinne Stockley and Felicity Brooks

Scientists believe that thousands of millions of years ago, the Earth's surface may have been covered by volcanoes.